To Lia,
Thanks for
your support of
Liberty!

GAMING the GOVERNMENT for POWER and PRIVATE PROFIT

BOTTLENECKERS

WILLIAM MELLOR and DICK M. CARPENTER II, PhD

Encounter Books
New York • London

First American edition published in 2016 by Encounter Books, an activity of Encounter for Culture and Education, Inc., a nonprofit, tax exempt corporation.
Encounter Books website address: www.encounterbooks.com

Manufactured in the United States and printed on acid-free paper. The paper used in this publication meets the minimum requirements of ANSI/NISO Z39.48–1992 (R 1997) (*Permanence of Paper*).

FIRST AMERICAN EDITION

LIBRARY OF CONGRESS CATALOGING-IN-PUBLICATION DATA

Names: Mellor, William H., author. | Carpenter, Dick M. (Dick Michael), author.
Title: Bottleneckers : gaming the government for power and private profit / by William Mellor and Dick M. Carpenter II, PhD.
Description: New York : Encounter Books, 2016. | Includes bibliographical references and index.
Identifiers: LCCN 2016020839 (print) | LCCN 2016033220 (ebook) | ISBN 9781594039072 (hardcover : alk. paper) | ISBN 9781594039089 (Ebook)
Subjects: LCSH: Licenses—United States—History. | Trade regulation—United States—History. | Trade associations—United States—History.
Classification: LCC HD3630.U6 M45 2016 (print) | LCC HD3630.U6 (ebook) | DDC 381.30973—dc23
LC record available at https://lccn.loc.gov/2016020839

Interior page design and composition: BooksByBruce.com

Dedication

We dedicate this book to Institute for Justice clients who have courageously and successfully stood up to bottleneckers and, in doing so, paved the way for countless others to pursue an honest living.

Bottlenecker *(n)*: a person who advocates for the creation or perpetuation of government regulation, particularly an occupational license, to restrict entry into his or her occupation, thereby accruing an economic advantage without providing a benefit to consumers.

Table of Contents

Introduction

Some criminals begin at a young age.

Matt Molinari and Eric Schnepf of Bound Brook, New Jersey, tangled with the law at the age of eighteen.[1]

Nathan Duszynski of Holland, Michigan, was thirteen.[2]

Madison Root of Portland, Oregon, was only eleven.[3]

They are not unique. All across the country in recent years, teens, preteens, and children have had run-ins with police, health inspectors, security guards, and even zoning officials, all for the same crime. The circumstances have sometimes been so disgraceful that the stories made national news. In certain cases, community leaders have expressed outrage and even shame, while in other instances officials have noted the young ages of the offenders but concluded that the law had to be applied without prejudice.

The young criminals were all guilty of... conducting business without a license.

Amid record snowfalls on the East Coast in early 2015, Matt and Eric canvased neighborhoods and shoveled snow for money, until they were stopped by police. Nathan set up a hotdog stand to raise money to help his disabled parents—his mom has epilepsy and his dad has multiple sclerosis. Within ten minutes of opening his stand, a zoning official closed him down because he was competing with nearby restaurants.

Madison sought to sell Christmas mistletoe in a local park to pay for her braces. She was told that while she could not sell her wares without a license, she was free to beg for money.

"I don't want to beg!" Madison exclaimed. "I would rather work for something than beg."[4] "People should be able to work for a living," she argued.[5] "The city laws are supporting begging and are against working."[6]

Madison didn't know how right she was. In that one statement, the eleven-year-old described one of the most significant labor economics problems in the United States today. In cities, counties, and states across the country, codebooks are stuffed with laws prohibiting people from working—many laws, like those that shut down Matt, Eric, Nathan, Madison, and countless young lemonade stand entrepreneurs each year, doing so for no rational reason.[7]

It's called occupational licensure. Simply put, an occupational license is a government-issued permission slip allowing a person to work. Although some occupational and professional licenses are familiar, such as those for physicians or attorneys, others are less well known, such as those for interior designers, locksmiths, auctioneers, sign language interpreters, music therapists, florists, and many other occupations.[8]

States (and sometimes cities or counties) require that people wishing to work in such occupations go through often-arbitrary anticompetitive hurdles, like completing mandatory education and training, passing examinations, paying fees, and reaching a prescribed age. Those who cannot clear the required hurdles are prohibited from working in the occupation. Because these hurdles are often purposefully high, occupational licensing is a rare public policy that accomplishes precisely what it sets out to do—keep people out of the occupation.

States that license interior designers, for example, require six years of education and experience, successful passage of a costly national examination, and payment of several hundred dollars in fees to the state.[9] One nationwide study looking at the burdens associated with earning a license to work in more than one hundred low- and middle-income occupations estimated that on average would-be workers spend about nine months in education and training, pay more than $200 in fees, and must pass at least one examination.[10] The result is fewer economic opportunities for workers and entrepreneurs, fewer choices and higher prices for consumers, and artificially inflated wages and profits for those already in the industry.

Historically, the interruption of the flow of workers into occupations effected by licensing successfully preserved the advantages of those already at work in those occupations. And the economic advantages of licensing—for the licensed—have not gone unnoticed. In 1776, the economist Adam Smith observed that trades conspire to reduce the availability of skilled craftspeople in order to raise wages.[11] At that time, the mechanism for accomplishing this was a guild system[12] in which a group of craftspeople who were engaged in the same occupation would create—in association with town councils and other civic structures—an exclusive regimented organization to maintain a monopoly on a particular craft, by shutting out anyone who was not a guild member.[13]

After 240 years, it seems that little has changed. By the 1940s, some observers were already comparing occupational licensing in the United States to the medieval guild system,[14] and that was even before the explosion of new licenses in the latter half of the twentieth century. Indeed, in the 1950s one in twenty workers in the United States needed a government-issued license to work, and some estimates put that number at almost one in three today.[15]

And like the medieval guild system, new licenses are created by governments at the request of those already working within an industry, typically through professional associations. Currently, those already working in an occupation (the modern equivalent of craftspeople) often band together and work in association with legislators (the equivalent of town councils and other civic structures) to create a regimented license to shut out those who have not completed the designated requirements (i.e., nonguild members) in order to maintain a monopoly over their occupation. Representatives of those associations often warn of hyperbolic threats to public health and safety from the specter of unregulated practice—illustrating the need for licensing with a few doomsday anecdotes and no empirical evidence—and conveniently provide sample licensing legislation written by the association. Since occupational licensing is primarily handed out at the state level, it is a process repeated in one state capitol after another, usually as part of a deliberate campaign to regulate the industry.

In just one example, the American Music Therapy Association (AMTA) and its sister organization, the Certification Board for Music Therapists (CBMT), have mounted a nationwide campaign to license the practice of music therapy in order to "[protect] clients or patients from potential harm or misrepresentation from individuals that are not board certified music therapists and are not practicing under the CBMT Scope of Practice."[16]

A music therapist, according to the *Dictionary of Occupational Titles*, "directs and participates in instrumental and vocal music activities designed to meet patients' physical or psychological needs, such as solo or group singing, rhythmic and other creative music activities, music listening, or attending concerts."[17] Regardless of what one thinks of the value of this work, the unregulated practice of music therapy hardly poses a threat to public health and safety. Although it had been practiced freely and safely for years, licenses have recently been adopted in the field, not at the request of harmed or concerned consumers but rather as an exclusive result of the actions of professional associations.

Through the advocacy efforts of a "regulatory affairs" team, the AMTA and the CBMT coordinated state-based task forces to introduce legislation for the creation of music therapy licenses.[18] To date, three states have passed such regulation—Nevada, North Dakota, and, most recently, Georgia. Georgia's adoption of this legislation neatly illustrates the previously described process wherein industry representatives run to the legislature for protection.

Upon its introduction, Georgia Senate Bill 414 was sent to the Senate Health and Human Services committee, which heard testimony from the AMTA in favor of the bill and received a packet containing several letters of support from music therapists, parents of children who were receiving music therapy, and a professor of music therapy at Georgia College.[19] No one testified against the bill; no empirical evidence was presented demonstrating a genuine threat to public health and safety from the unregulated practice of music therapy; and no one asked about the potential economic consequences to consumers in the form of higher prices. As a result, working as a music therapist in Georgia now requires:

- obtaining a bachelor's degree in music therapy or higher from a program approved by the AMTA, the very entity that lobbied for the bill;

- successfully completing 1,200 hours of clinical training, with at least 180 hours of preinternship experiences and at least 900 hours of internship experiences;
- passing the examination for board certification offered by the CBMT, which costs $325 to take;[20]
- paying various fees;
- being at least eighteen years of age; and
- passing a criminal background check.[21]

Consumers in Georgia, North Dakota, Nevada, and any other state that adopts this law could pay as much as 15 percent more for the services of a music therapist,[22] with no evidence that the cost will be offset by increased protection for the public. Should a legislature attempt to repeal the license at some later date, the same association leaders who advocated for the law in the first place will most assuredly mount an aggressive campaign to protect their interests, and now they will be joined by representatives from the state licensing board, populated by licensed music therapists intent on maintaining their bottleneck on new entrants into the occupation.

The *Merriam-Webster* dictionary defines a *bottleneck* as "someone or something that retards or halts free movement and progress."[23] In requiring occupational licensing, industry insiders and government officials embody that definition. Licensing schemes—with their education, training, and experience requirements; examinations; fees; age minimums; various other hurdles; and draconian enforcement—enable bottleneckers to effectively restrict the free flow of workers into occupations, all the while enjoying economic benefits without regard for the unfulfilled promises of the public benefit. And when those schemes are threatened by reform-minded governors who seek to open the marketplace and expand competition and opportunity, by legislators who understand economics, or by determined would-be entrepreneurs who see such licensing schemes for the anticompetitive barriers they are, industry bottleneckers almost always mount a tenacious fight for survival involving legislation and litigation.

The pages that follow tell the story of how bottleneckers of all vintages—from casket sellers to taxi drivers—co-opt the power of government to their own advantage; how government officials themselves become bottleneckers; and how it is that only through the persistent efforts of individuals like those introduced in this book are bottlenecks able to be broken open and people freed to earn an honest living in the ways most fitting to their gifts, talents, and interests, unburdened of onerous government regulation.

The term *bottleneck* originated not as a way to describe obstructions or obstructionists but as a metaphor for something narrow—a bottleneck harbor, for example—drawn from the physical properties of, well, the neck of a bottle. Applied to economic markets, the metaphor and its origin are particularly apt, for, as chapter 1 illustrates, the quintessential bottleneckers dominate an industry whose stock-in-trade is captured in bottles.[24]

CHAPTER 1

How Bottleneckers Got Their Name

Sitting atop her tractor, Juanita Swedenburg bounced along a dirt path, seething with anger.[1] Earlier, the sixty-something-year-old Virginia farmer had been flipping through a new issue of a magazine delivered to her house when she stumbled upon an article that started her slow burn. According to the article, she—a card-carrying Daughter of the American Revolution—was allegedly a criminal, a felon.

In 1976, Juanita and her husband, Wayne, had retired from careers in the US foreign service and bought a 120-acre farm in bucolic Middleburg, Virginia. Both were raised on farms, and they drew on their experience to raise cattle on their new property.[2] Although they never entirely abandoned this pursuit, they soon shifted their efforts to a crop that was ideal, though then sparsely grown, in their slice of Loudon County: grapes. Prompting this course of action was Juanita learning that Thomas Jefferson thought that Virginia's soil was like that of France, known, of course, for its wines.[3]

With experience only as wine consumers, Juanita and Wayne set out to start a winery specializing in the type of wine they had enjoyed while serving in Saigon in the foreign service. "In those days, it was the Paris of the East, and I was so much a wine novice," Juanita recalled. "We drank really good 1948 and 1949 Bordeaux and cabernets. It taught me a lot about good wine."[4] Juanita and Wayne immersed themselves in learning the craft of wine making. After copious reading, workshops, trial and error, sharing of notes with neighbors, and years of physical labor,[5] they planted their first grapes in 1982 and opened the Swedenburg Estates Winery in 1988.[6]

Their chardonnay, cabernet, and fruity Riesling began drawing a following, and they shipped cases to customers all over the country who wanted something different from what was available in their neighborhood stores.[7] In any given year, mail-order sales amounted to somewhere between 10 and 20 percent of the two thousand cases they sold[8]—that is, until that fateful day when Juanita was alerted of her criminal ways.

Always looking to grow her skills as a winemaker, improve the business, and stay abreast of the industry, Juanita read wine publications religiously. It was in one of these magazines that she discovered her crime[9]—the laws of twenty-four states made it illegal for Juanita to ship wine from her farm in Virginia directly to consumers in the respective states.[10] At first she ignored her new realization and continued shipping out wine,[11] but her conscience—pricked by a pocket copy of the US Constitution she carried with her everywhere—got the better of her. When out-of-state customers visited her tasting room and asked for cases of alcohol to be shipped to their homes, Juanita's reply became, "Sorry, I can't."

Three thousand miles away, the owner of another small family winery was also coming to the realization that he had been breaking the law for years. Only, in his case, he had learned of his criminality from threats of prosecution rather than a magazine. David Lucas had also started in the wine business later in life, after years spent serving the United States abroad. Raised in an agricultural family in California, as a young man David served in the peace corps, first growing rice in remote parts of India and then serving as a peace corps director in Iran. After leaving the peace corps, he worked in the fruit-and-vegetable canning industry, saving his money to buy some land and build his dream business—a winery.

He began his wine making as a sideline while still in the canning industry. His first wines tasted much like other popular wines in the United States—sweet and fruity with plenty of alcohol. A few years into his part-time wine-making pursuit, he landed a position with a company that would alter his wines and the course of his life—the Robert Mondavi Winery. As head of global research and joint ventures, David worked closely with Mondavi for sixteen years, learning the business and traveling around the world. Along the way, he tasted some of the world's great wines and made a painful observation: his own wines were embarrassingly bad.

Making full use of his position at Mondavi, David became a student of wine making, paying close attention to how the world's great wineries crafted their products. He abandoned his earlier efforts and began making wines that were food friendly, refined, and restrained and whose taste reflected the vineyards from which they came.

By the time David left Mondavi, his business was small but thriving; so much so that his tasting room was regularly full of out-of-state customers asking for his wines to be shipped to their homes. Although such shipments would never represent a large percentage of his business, they were nevertheless important to it. David only sold his wines directly, not through supermarkets, big-box stores, or other retailers. He was, therefore, all too happy to fulfill individual customer requests for shipment.

A concern, however, nagged him. He knew other wineries in his area shipped to out-of-state customers—it was common practice, in fact—but he wondered occasionally if there were restrictions on interstate alcohol shipping. All doubt was laid to rest when he received the first in a series of cease-and-desist letters from state liquor commissions. Like Juanita Swedenburg, David Lucas, a small-business owner and veteran public servant, was a felon. Or so said the laws of various states—laws intended not to protect the public from harmful perpetrators but to guard a powerful private interest from competition using government power. The origins of such laws can be traced to one of history's leading industrialists—John D. Rockefeller Jr.

THE ORIGINS OF PROTECTIONISM

At the turn of the twentieth century, Rockefeller, and other industrialists like him, believed America had a problem—a "liquor problem."[12] It was a belief that had been building around them for decades in the form of the temperance movement.[13] In the early nineteenth century, physicians, ministers, and employers had grown increasingly concerned about the drunkenness of workers and servants. Throughout the first half of the century, this concern mushroomed into a mass movement, encompassing more than a million people across a broad spectrum of the middle class who committed themselves to complete abstinence from alcohol.[14] The 1840s saw the first state attempts at prohibition, followed in the 1880s by a second wave of attempts. Although most of these laws were overturned, a few survived into the early twentieth century as a new prohibitionist organization—the Anti-Saloon League—came to dominate the movement.[15]

The league operated with a level of sophistication not known before. It hired lawyers to write model laws, built up a war chest of funds, and collected political favors subsequently used to expand the number of elected officials beholden to it.[16] First working state by state, the movement wielded those resources to achieve prohibition of alcohol in twenty-three states by 1916 and seven more by 1919.[17] It also came out for a federal constitutional prohibition in 1913, working to achieve it in Congress in 1917, and then achieved a final ratification in Nebraska in 1919. The Eighteenth Amendment—commonly called Prohibition—went into effect a year later.[18]

Throughout this period, the league's efforts were bankrolled by Rockefeller—a lifelong teetotaler—and fellow industrialists. Like early temperance adherents, they believed alcohol undermined the morals of their workers and hampered productivity.[19] Moreover, the league thought that by enacting Prohibition, saloons would become unavailable as meeting and recruiting places for unions and socialist organizations, and social blight in the form of crime, poverty, insanity, disease, and urban disorder would come under control.[20]

At first, Prohibition seemed to work. In the early years, alcohol consumption appeared to decline, and police, social workers, ministers, and journalists reported reductions in problems associated with alcohol abuse.[21] But these effects—to the extent that they actually resulted from the Eighteenth Amendment—were fleeting and never entirely successful. The drinking of alcohol continued, especially in large cities, and, as the 1920s progressed, additional negative effects of Prohibition materialized and metastasized—alcohol was illegally produced and distributed, organized crime flourished, bribery and corruption of public officials prevailed, cases of alcohol poisoning arose, and there was a widespread violation of the law. It was particularly this last problem that prompted Rockefeller and others to begin rethinking their support of Prohibition.

Although the "lawlessness" associated with Prohibition is sometimes thought to describe organized crime, it actually refers to the disrespect for all law, and the law's loss of legitimacy, resulting from the mass disobedience of Prohibition. This lawlessness was aggravated by the looting, rioting, and mass demonstrations that grew out of the Great Depression.[22] By 1932, such lawlessness had sealed the fate of Prohibition: John D. Rockefeller Jr. announced his support for repeal, the momentum for which had been building for some time, and other industrialists followed suit. As Rockefeller explained,

> In the attempt to bring about total abstinence through prohibition, an evil even greater than intemperance resulted—namely, a nation-wide disrespect for law, with all the attendant abuses that followed in its train. That this intolerable situation should be done away with has seemed to me even more important for the moment than the promotion of temperance.[23]

On November 16, 1932, the US Senate submitted the Twenty-First Amendment, repealing the Eighteenth Amendment, to state constitutional conventions for ratification. On December 5 of the following year, Utah became the thirty-sixth and deciding state to ratify the amendment, putting repeal into immediate effect.[24]

In the minds of Rockefeller and others, however, repeal was no solution to the root problem. Rockefeller warned, "As Senator Capper has aptly said, 'We may repeal Prohibition, but we cannot repeal the Liquor Problem.' If carefully laid plans of control are not made, the old evils against which prohibition was invoked can easily return."[25] Among other things, the Twenty-First Amendment left such control to the states, but legislators—most of whom had little personal expertise in the complexities of liquor regulation—were ill equipped to navigate the difficult policy and political choices that accompanied it.[26] Into this vacuum stepped Rockefeller; this time with a highly influential study that produced model legislation for the states.

Toward Liquor Control,[27] a book bankrolled by Rockefeller and written by two of his close and trusted advisors, Raymond Fosdick and Albert Scott, outlined the details of two post-Prohibition systems of regulatory policy: one that the authors greatly preferred and another that they included for pragmatic purposes. The first, which they strongly recommended, was a monopoly approach, in which states would allow individual sales of alcoholic beverages in restaurants and hotels while maintaining a public monopoly on the sale of packaged goods. The second was a licensing system under the auspices of a state board that would ideally be as far removed from politics as possible. Critical to the success of the latter scheme was the control of the number of businesses allowed to sell liquor and the complete elimination of the "tied-house system."

Tied houses were taverns owned by or under exclusive contracts with alcohol manufacturers.[28] Prior to Prohibition, alcohol was not transported across the country as it is today. Instead, there were many breweries and other producers operating in cities and counties that were engaged in aggressive competition to exclusively sell products. They did so through a combination of manufacturer-owned taverns and independent establishments that agreed to sell only a certain brand of beverage. To compel such loyalty, producers sold to taverns on generous credit terms, provided them with equipment and supplies, and paid rebates. This tied-house system was widely believed to be a principal cause of excessive alcohol consumption and related social ills.[29] The licensing system described in *Toward Liquor Control* called for the decoupling and separation of the producer and retailer "tiers" to avoid control or coercion. Newspapers, magazines, and prominent leaders hailed the book, and elected officials turned to it and the model legislation that stemmed from it to create new state alcohol laws. In the months that followed the ratification of the Twenty-First Amendment, states in quick succession adopted alcohol-control policies patterned after those recommended in *Toward Liquor Control*.[30] Today, those same policies largely govern the alcohol industry: seventeen states operate under monopoly control and thirty-three states plus DC operate with licensing systems.[31]

As part of their licensing systems, states interposed a required third tier—the distributor (or wholesaler)—to place a separation between the manufacturer and retailer tiers. At the outset of the three-tier system, producers could only sell to and retailers could only buy from distributors. Firms in one tier could not hold ownership in companies in another. Nothing of value could be given to induce sales. All businesses across the levels were licensed by the state to operate only in their specific tier.[32] In other words, lawmakers created a bottleneck. All alcohol sales flowed through, and only through, distributors—the quintessential "bottleneckers."

It is these licensing systems that sixty years after their creation ensnared Juanita and David. If manufacturers like them wanted to sell their products to consumers in a given state, they had to find a distributor willing to carry their product. Yet the bottleneck created by the three-tier system provided little incentive for distributors to deal in specialty products from small manufacturers like Juanita and David, particularly if they were out of state and essentially unknown. Instead, the distributors' preference was, and remains today, for well-known brands that sell easily and in greater volume.[33]

The effects of the bottleneck were predictable, and, in fact, predicted. The authors of *Toward Liquor Control* warned,

> Any licensing system tends to project the whole question into politics and to keep it there. Indeed, it compels the traffic to be in politics of self-protection. The licensing body becomes a powerful political engine. Every licensee ... begins to marshal his own political strength to serve his own ends.[34]

It did not take long for the political process to begin. When Utah voted for the Twenty-First Amendment in December 1933, Congress was in recess, which meant the federal government had no statutory means by which to manage the instantly legal alcohol industry. As an interim measure, President Franklin D. Roosevelt, by executive order, established the Federal Alcohol Control Administration (FACA) to guide the transition from Prohibition to regulation.[35] Roosevelt chose Joseph H. Choate Jr., an East Coast upper-class attorney, to head the FACA. Choate worked in the interest of repeal and assisted in the reestablishment and growth of the liquor industry. He helped the industry, especially the trade associations, to design the market structure most amenable to alcohol businesses and also to the collection of taxes.[36] The latter was of particular concern for state and federal governments, the representatives of which met with leaders from the liquor industry to set standards and policies and to develop procedures for efficiently collecting taxes.[37] And so it happened that in the months following the end of Prohibition, as states considered various options for liquor control, alcohol businesses came to play a central role in crafting policies.

MAINTAINING THE BOTTLENECK

In the years that followed, distributors (also known as wholesalers) used favorable state policies—specifically three-tier laws—to build a powerful position and protect their government-manufactured slice of the market.[38] Whenever attempts to reform or alter the three-tier system have surfaced, distributors have lobbied aggressively to protect their privilege.[39] But their activities are not purely reactive. According to David Rehr, the former president of the National Beer Wholesalers Association, today the association is one of the most influential lobbies in America, boasting operations in every state and congressional district.[40] It has a presence in every community and state legislature, and distributors visit every member of Congress as part of the association's annual meeting in Washington, DC, with the stated intent of "shoring up the three-tier system."[41] In its annual reports from 2013 to 2015, the NBWA boasted that its members conducted more than 450 meetings on Capitol Hill during its 2014 legislative conference[42] and more than 400 meetings in 2015.[43]

Such influence earned the NBWA the title of "heavy hitter" from a campaign-finance watchdog organization.[44] Additionally, through its political action committee, the NBWA has consistently been one of the largest contributors to state and federal political candidates. From 1990 to 2014, its PAC contributed more than $32 million to candidates and spent more than $11 million in lobbying, including expenses associated with more than twenty lobbyists just at the federal level.[45] The primary focus of this lobbying has been to protect the distributors' interests in the three-tier system. For example, as Anheuser-Busch InBev worked to finalize its acquisition of Grupo Modelo, the maker of Corona beer, and to clear a review by the US Department of Justice in 2013, the NBWA lobbied to ensure that the beer conglomerate would not encroach upon the distributors' turf.[46]

The NBWA's annual legislative conferences in Washington, DC, routinely include a who's who of elected officials and members of the media.

The 2014 conference, for example, featured addresses by former House speaker John Boehner and former House majority leader Steny Hoyer. The conference also included a lunch with former representatives Aaron Schock and Tulsi Gabbard. Journalists from *Politico*, the *Washington Post*, and *ABC News* were panelists. Legislative issues on the conference agenda included state-based alcohol regulation, and conferees attended sessions like the "Perfect Pitch: Selling the Value of Alcohol Laws."[47]

The Wine and Spirits Wholesalers of America (WSWA) works alongside the NBWA, having contributed more than $11 million to candidates between 1990 and 2014, more than $18 million through lobbying activity, and more than thirty federal lobbyists.[48] Although not as prolific as the NBWA, the WSWA has nevertheless "made a concerted effort to aggressively build [its] industry grass roots and develop a broad base of political engagement across the country," as President and CEO Craig Wolf boasted in a 2012 press release.[49] The WSWA's government affairs are managed by a senior vice president, four vice presidents, and a coordinator, all of whom keep members apprised of state and federal issues, provide resources for members' political activity,[50] and coordinate efforts with thirty-two state affiliates.[51] The WSWA's Web site includes a feature that enables members to identify a specific congressional or state legislative district and then produce custom reports with industry information for use in lobbying.[52] The site also offers information on such topics as the economic impact of distributors, jobs created, and taxes paid. The NBWA offers a similar feature on its Web site.[53]

At the state level, alcohol bottleneckers likewise protect their interests through lobbying and contributions. For example, from 2009 to 2012, legislators in Juanita Swedenburg's home state of Virginia considered a series of bills—none of which saw any action beyond committee hearings—to privatize state-owned alcohol retail stores. While the bills were being considered, legislators sitting on the respective committees received a total of more than $200,000 in campaign contributions from the Virginia Wine Wholesalers Association and the Virginia Beer Wholesalers Association.[54]

For both organizations, prolific spending and lobbying is the cost of ensuring that the government allows them to maintain their grip on a significant industry. Today, an estimated 6,690 distributor facilities serve more than four thousand breweries nationwide, up from fewer than fifty breweries in the late 1970s and early 1980s.[55] Similarly, wine wholesalers total 5,900 across the United States.[56] Together, distributors report an annual revenue of $135 billion.[57]

BATTLING THE BOTTLENECKERS

Because of the influence bottleneckers have held on state and federal legislatures, Juanita and David had only one viable recourse if they wanted to serve out-of-state customers—the courts. On February 3, 2000, they sued in federal district court in New York—a state with one of the biggest wine markets in the country but one that prohibited those that didn't operate within its bounds from shipping wine directly to consumers in the jurisdiction—thereby bypassing distributors.[58] Although Juanita and David were challenging New York's laws, it quickly became apparent that it wasn't the state's interests that were really at stake.

No sooner had they filed their lawsuit than the state's four largest liquor distributors, whose combined revenues exceeded $1 billion annually, intervened to help defend the bottleneck,[59] with additional help coming from the WSWA and the NBWA.[60] In the first hearing, Juanita and David's two attorneys from the Institute for Justice were taken on by eighteen attorneys mostly representing industry insiders.[61] Throughout the trial, the state attorney said nothing while the liquor distributors' lawyers litigated the case with a degree of bombast and hyperbole that demonstrated that the real purpose, and result, of the laws was to protect liquor distributors, not public health and safety, as the distributors' attorneys claimed.[82]

The health and safety assertions were particularly important because courts are sympathetic to regulations that purport to protect public health and safety but are skeptical about laws designed to economically favor a special interest group—like those laws protecting the favored position of alcohol distributors. With such a concern in mind, the lawyers fighting for the distributors relied heavily on the underage access issue, asserting that the direct shipment of wine would facilitate increased alcohol consumption by minors.[63]

Attorneys for Juanita and David responded by presenting data showing how sixteen thousand minors had acquired alcohol through the three-tier system over a five-year period, whereas none had managed to obtain wine by means of direct shipment, such as would happen if they purchased it over the Internet.[64] Moreover, they presented evidence from the Federal Trade Commission indicating that protecting against underage drinking could be facilitated through regulatory actions short of discriminatory prohibitions against direct shipping.[65]

Casting doubt on the opposition's public health and safety rationale was not enough, though, so Juanita and David's attorneys demonstrated how the original three-tier system was adopted and protected at the behest of liquor distributors. One of the examples they cited was the New York legislature's overwhelming passage of legislation allowing direct shipping in the 1990s; something that the liquor distributors urged Governor George Pataki to veto, and he did.[66]

For years, certain scholars had argued that post-Prohibition alcohol regulations had little to do with public health and safety but were instead about economic protection.[67] In candid moments, even the distributors acknowledged what was truly at the heart of their fight. Bob Archer, a distributor in Virginia, admitted, "People we represent all over the world might just decide they want to sell directly to big retailers—Wal-Mart, Sam's Club, and Costco—without us."[68] And when then chief executive of the WSWA Juanita Duggan criticized Juanita and David for their lawsuit, her accusations revealed that her primary concern was not public safety—it was that Juanita and David allegedly wanted to "legitimize the growing black market in illegal alcohol sales, sell direct to consumers, pocket outrageous profits and avoid state taxes."[69]

The public health and safety assertions of the distributors were further undermined by the alcohol regulations themselves. As small wineries began to bloom in the 1970s, more states began to create exceptions to the three-tier system, allowing wineries to market and sell their wines directly to consumers. Direct sales further exploded with the expansion of the Internet in the 1990s.[70] At this point, exceptions were granted to microbreweries to sell directly to consumers, reciprocity arrangements were set up between states that allowed the direct shipment of wine to consumers, and, as usual, not all fifty states prohibited direct inter- or intrastate shipment of alcohol or required a physical presence in the state.[71] If alcohol distribution not involving distributors truly posed a threat to public health and safety, these exceptions would have been seen as too dangerous to allow.

More than two years after Juanita and David filed their lawsuit, Judge Richard Berman declared New York's law unconstitutional. Simply put, Berman did not accept the distributors' arguments, finding that "the direct shipping ban was designed to protect New York State businesses from out-of-state competition."[72] He also reasoned that the state had "not established that its goals [could not] be accomplished in a nondiscriminatory manner."[73]

Not surprisingly, the bottleneckers quickly appealed, and on February 12, 2004, the Second US Circuit Court of Appeals sided with the distributors, on the basis that "all wineries, whether in-state or out-of-state, are permitted to obtain a license as long as the winery establishes a physical presence in the state."[74] Although this was consistent with the text of the law, the actual effect of upholding the direct sales ban was to discriminate against out-of-state businesses—particularly smaller ones—in favor of in-state distributors. Juanita and David would have had to open and fully staff a warehouse just to sell a small number of cases of wine in New York—an economic impossibility.[75] Their next step was the US Supreme Court.

As attorneys for both sides prepared their briefs for the hearing, the bottleneckers and their allies continued their drumbeat about protecting public safety, particularly the dangers of underage drinking that would take place if the three-tier system were to be disrupted. John Fitzpatrick, a spokesman for the WSWA, warned, "As a society we need to be thinking about ways to make it harder for children to get alcohol, not easier."[76] His organization called Juanita an "elite" member of a "special interest" trying to facilitate underage drinking for financial gain.[77] The attorneys general of some states even launched high-profile sting operations, ostensibly designed to demonstrate how easy it was for underage buyers to access alcohol. Revealingly, the sting artists never successfully ordered from wineries; they did, however, manage to order from retailers, which were licensed by the three-tier system.[78]

In the end, the bottleneckers' efforts were for naught. On May 16, 2005, the Supreme Court decided 5–4 to strike down the laws on grounds of discrimination. Justice Anthony Kennedy, writing for the majority, held that the laws' effect was to "allow in-state wineries to sell wine directly to consumers in that state but to prohibit out-of-state wineries from doing so, or, at the least, to make direct sales impractical from an economic standpoint."[79] The court ruled that laws such as New York's "depriv[ed] citizens of their right to have access to the markets of other States on equal terms."[80] The court also dismissed the assertions about underage access to alcohol, finding that less onerous alternatives were available to serve legitimate state interests. Indeed, a state official in Georgia, which at the time already allowed shipments from out-of-state wineries, added that the Peach State had regulations in place to discourage purchases by minors.[81]

A key element in the court's decision was the fact that the bottleneckers were unable to demonstrate compelling reasons for the law to stay in place, even after they had been asked to give specific examples of such reasons. Moreover, Justice Antonin Scalia pointed out that the fact that twenty-six states currently allowed direct shipment from out-of-state wineries "certainly suggests that what [the state] is arguing is not essential to the state's enforcement of its alcohol laws."[82]

THE BOTTLENECKERS STRIKE BACK

The Supreme Court's decision was called "landmark"[83] and a "pivotal moment in the long history of alcohol."[84] Although the court did not speak directly to the efficacy of the three-tier system, the ruling had a significant-enough effect on bottleneckers that they initiated efforts in state legislatures and the US Congress to nullify the high court's decision and protect their position.

One approach taken by the bottleneckers was to lobby states to limit *all* direct shipping, from both in-state and out-of-state producers.[85] This would apply in cases such as that of Michigan, whose variation on a total ban had been to prohibit commercial carriers such as FedEx and UPS from shipping wine. This meant that wine retailers must use their own vehicles to deliver product to Michigan residents, effectively closing Michigan to out-of-state retailers.[86] Another approach of the bottleneckers was to seek onerous permitting systems with expensive fees to ship into the state in order to discourage out-of-state producers, particularly small ones, from shipping directly to consumers.[87]

At the federal level, distributors' lobbyists responded to the 2005 Supreme Court decision by turning to Congress for a ban on direct shipping of wine and other forms of alcohol. Their effort was embodied in a bill put forth by Utah representative Jason Chaffetz titled the Community Alcohol Regulatory Effectiveness Act of 2011, or CARE, which was similar to legislation previously proposed by Massachusetts representative William Delahunt.[88] Support for the act came primarily from alcohol distributors, which, through their PACs, had donated generously to those assisting their cause.[89] In the decade since the Supreme Court decision, CARE's nine sponsors have accepted more than $312,500 from the NBWA and $181,735 from the WSWA.[90] And those nine lawmakers are not alone. According to an analysis by the National Association of Wine Retailers, wholesalers spent more than $80 million in contributions to state and federal legislators and on federal lobbying between 2005 and 2010.[91]

The bottleneckers also continue to defend their economic advantage against possible threats. In 2006, Costco sued Washington State for the right to stock its shelves with alcohol without going through distributors. As in similar cases throughout the country,[92] distributors intervened in support of the law, and the court ultimately rejected Costco's claims. Rather than appealing to the Supreme Court, Costco took its battle to the people with two ballot initiatives in 2010.[93] Voters rejected both initiatives after being bombarded by advertising campaigns funded mostly by distributors. Whereas the campaign supporting the ballot initiatives collected donations from Costco, supermarkets, and others, amounting to a total of $2.28 million, opponents of the initiatives outspent supporters by almost a three-to-one margin, collecting a total of $6.1 million. Of this amount, $1.1 million came from the Washington Beer & Wine Distributors Association (WBWDA), $2 million came from the NBWA, and $2 million came from the Beer Institute, and there were contributions from distributor organizations in other states as well.[94] Undeterred, supporters of the ballot initiatives returned in 2011 with another initiative, eventually achieving voter approval after substantial spending by Costco.[95]

In 2011, another example took place in North Carolina, where the grocery store chain Harris Teeter partnered with a large wine producer to offer an online service allowing customers to view past purchases and receive recommendations, which would have required a three-tier exemption. Distributors vigorously opposed the exemption, and the store eventually withdrew its application.[96]

Down the road from North Carolina, a 2014 Florida Senate bill created a "beer war."[97] In April of that year, lawmakers had adopted a bill to legalize half-gallon "growlers."[98] In the days before the bottling, canning, and wide distribution of alcohol, local establishments sold fresh beer to consumers, who transported the product to their homes in small galvanized pails called growlers, allegedly named on the basis of the sound they made as carbon dioxide escaped through the lid.[99] With the advent of bottling and canning, growlers fell out of fashion, but they have seen a resurgence in recent years with the explosion of craft breweries and home brewing.[100] Ever vigilant, distributors saw growlers' popularity as a threat. If consumers could buy directly from producers, they estimated, the distributors would be cut out. To appease distributors, the Florida Senate bill contained a compromise: Breweries that produced more than two thousand kegs of beer per year had to sell all bottled or canned beer to a distributor—and then buy it back at a markup—before serving it in their own tasting rooms. As the owner of one brewery saw it, the bill would accomplish nothing beyond transferring $175,000 from his bank account to the bank account of a local distributor.[101]

The Senate bill, and a companion measure in the House,[102] created a tidal wave of efforts to influence legislators' votes. Senator Jack Latvala, a Republican from western Florida, said he received more feedback about the bill than he had about any other piece of legislation in the session.[103] And when the House introduced its companion bill, one representative observed, "I have never seen this amount of lobbying on anything as much as this issue since I have been here."[104] Both bills eventually died in House committees.

Bottleneckers don't merely play defense, however. They also go on the offensive to strengthen their already-substantial positions. For example, the Wholesale Distributors of Texas decided its privileged place within the three-tier system was not enough and successfully pushed for a law to pad profits in 2013. The new law made it illegal for producers like craft breweries to charge distributors money for territorial distribution rights. For years, Texas producers and distributors had entered into agreements under which the distributor bought the right to sell the producer's product in a particular geographic territory. Although producers were, and are, required under the three-tier system to distribute their products through a distributor, they could choose the distributor they wanted to do business with and enter into contracts granting it exclusive territorial rights. For example, if a craft brewer based in Austin wanted to sell beer in Dallas, it could enter into an agreement with a Dallas-based distributor. The brewer would then receive a supply chain (warehouses, trucks, and staff), and the distributor would receive exclusive geographic rights to distribute that particular beer in the Dallas area.

In such a scheme, if the product is popular with consumers, gaining the exclusive rights to distribute it is valuable. The distributor enjoys the exclusive right to sell the product within a territory and can move enormous volumes of an in-demand commodity free from competition. Not surprisingly, then, distributors would traditionally pay anywhere from a few hundred thousand to a few million dollars in exchange for the exclusive right to distribute in a territory. The distributor would then own the rights to the product in that territory and could resell them to another distributor in the future.

The 2013 law made it illegal for producers to charge money for territorial rights; instead forcing them to give these valuable rights to distributors for free.[105] Even worse, even though distributors would be able to acquire those rights at no cost, they could sell them to other distributors for a profit. In a state with a booming craft-brew industry, the economic advantage to distributors was therefore considerable. The Texas bottleneckers worked hard to achieve this provision, partnering with state senator John Carona, who introduced the language at the end of a long and hectic session.[106] The distributors testified in favor of the provision in legislative hearings and relied on already-cultivated relationships with legislators to overcome strong resistance.[107] Like their bottlenecker brethren nationally and in other states, Texas distributors have invested heavily in state politics. From 2009 to 2012, distributors in the Lone Star State gave $7 million to legislators, dwarfing the $17,924 given to them by craft brewers. Carona alone received $135,000 from alcohol distributors during that period, the second-highest payment received by any Texas lawmaker.[108]

Meanwhile, in the same year, more than 1,700 miles away, some New York distributors were on the verge of realizing their own beneficial scheme, even sacrificing some fellow bottleneckers in order to strengthen their position. In February 2013, New York legislators introduced similar bills in the Assembly[109] and Senate[110] to require that all alcoholic beverages sold by distributors in New York remain "at rest" in warehouses in the state for twenty-four hours prior to delivery to retailers. The target of the bill was at least 150 New York distributors that had warehouses in New Jersey, where space was vastly cheaper than in New York, and that delivered directly to New York City restaurants and retailers.[111] The main beneficiaries of the legislation were New York's two largest distributors, Southern Wine and Spirits and Empire Merchants. Because the law would have required those distributors with warehouses in New Jersey to spend enormous sums of money to rent or build climate-controlled warehouses in property located among some of the most expensive real estate in the world, as many as one hundred of these distributors might have been forced to close.[112]

If these bills had passed, they would have left more of the field open for Southern Wine and Spirits and Empire Merchants, both of which made significant contributions to New York politicians. Southern contributed almost $30,000 to New York lawmakers during the 2012 election year, while Empire contributed more than $330,000 to New York politicians during the same time.[113] The bill's Senate sponsor, Jeff Klein, received $53,000 in campaign contributions between 2009 and 2014 from Empire Merchants and some of its senior leadership.[114]

THE REAL EFFECTS OF BOTTLENECKING

In their efforts at self-protection, the distributors in the alcohol industry—like bottleneckers of all industries—have defended their government-enforced monopoly interests, and continue to do so, by using claims that they are protecting the public and serving a civic good. On the heels of the 2005 Supreme Court decision to overturn the direct sales ban, for example, Nida Samona, chairwoman of the Michigan Liquor Control Commission, said the decision was a setback for efforts to battle underage drinking. Her commission successfully urged lawmakers to ban direct shipments for both local and out-of-state wineries. "[This] protects the class we are fighting for—to make sure minors cannot purchase and consume alcohol before they are of age," she said.[115] Moreover, according to Craig Purser, president of the NBWA, the three-tier system aids in tax collection, maintains an orderly marketplace, and prevents overconsumption and related problems, such as underage drinking and drunk driving.[116]

Evidence of such benefits, however, simply does not exist. In fact, when pressed to substantiate their claims, three-tier proponents are forced to concede the truth. In legislative testimony, John Peirce, chief counsel for California's Department of Alcoholic Beverage Control, admitted,

> I haven't specifically studied or have any data to back me up.... [I]s there a cause and effect relationship here? I don't know.... You know, we are happy with what we see out there by and large.[117]

Even when stakes were at their highest, three-tier advocates could not cobble together enough convincing evidence to support the benefits. In Juanita and David's case before the US Supreme Court, attorneys for the states asserted the aforementioned benefits of regulatory systems but could not substantiate their claims in any way that proved compelling to the court.[118]

On the other hand, there is plenty of evidence for the negative economic effects of alcohol bottlenecking. For consumers, the three-tier system restricts the diversity of available products and forces them to pay more.[119] Conservative estimates put the distributor markup on alcohol at somewhere between 15 and 25 percent,[120] with some appraising it as high as 30 percent, earning wholesalers the title of "fat cats" from small alcohol producers.[121] As Deb Carey of Wisconsin's New Glarus Brewing put it, "This debate boils down to the fact that the wholesalers do not want a drop of beer going to market...without them making their 30 percent profit from it. That's it."[122]

In fact, as analysts cited by the Federal Trade Commission concluded, the alcoholic beverage industry in the United States has "the most expensive distribution system of any packaged-goods industry by far, with margins more than twice those in the food business."[123] Additionally, by limiting the number of businesses that are issued permits at each tier and prohibiting out-of-state producers like Juanita and David from selling within their borders, states can control the types and amounts of alcohol sold. Bottleneckers assert that these burdens to the market are outweighed by the benefits to public health and safety, but, as discussed, little evidence exists to suggest that the three-tier system promotes such benefits.[124]

Small family producers like Juanita and David feel the harm caused by the bottleneckers. Despite the increased demand for a greater diversity of products, small producers struggle to place their products on the shelves.[125] Burdensome state laws continue to make interstate commerce difficult, and distributors have little incentive to expend efforts and resources to distribute products with comparatively small returns on investment. Although Internet wine sales and microbreweries have expanded options for some consumers, these products represent a tiny fraction of the alcohol market and pose little threat to the dominant position of distributors, which continue to wield their considerable clout to maintain that dominance.[126]

BOTTLENECKERS OF A DIFFERENT BRAND

As will be demonstrated in the chapters that follow, distributors are not alone in their use of government levers for personal gain. Although our use of the term *bottleneckers* originates from the actions and effects of alcohol distributors, it is an appellation that aptly describes many interest groups that enlist the power of the government to establish an economic advantage through occupational licensing.

When describing a licensing system for the alcohol industry, the authors of *Toward Liquor Control* warned:

> Under the license system, the will to survive permeates every department of the trade, and the means to press a tenacious fight for survival are abundant. As proposals to dismember any part of the liquor selling business become more threatening, the entire trade combines more solidly to protect itself. In brief, a licensed liquor trade, once established, cannot easily be dislodged.[127]

The following chapters show that Fosdick and Scott might as well have been describing occupational licensing across almost all occupations. Some of the licenses we chronicle—such as those in interior design—are new enough that we can see how the genesis of the law was entirely a product of creative and intensive lobbying by industry representatives, rather than consumers asking for protection and relief from harm. Other licenses—such as those in cosmetology—have existed for decades, their precise origins often lost to the passage of time. Yet the bottleneckers' efforts to preserve their licenses at the present time illustrates all too well how a bottleneck, in any occupation, "once established, cannot easily be dislodged." In chapter 2, we see both how a license for selling a product to dispose of the dead is brought to life and how bottleneckers fight for the license's survival when someone attempts to kill it.

CHAPTER 2

Casket Cartels

Robbery without a Pistol

Death is big business in the United States. Each year, Americans arrange more than two million funerals for family members and friends.[1] Almost twenty thousand funeral homes handle most of those funerals, resulting in a $16 billion industry.[2] On average, families spend between $8,000 and $10,000 for funeral and cemetery costs.[3] Of all the elements of a funeral—flowers, music, burial clothes, transportation, the grave plot, and so forth—the single-most-expensive item is typically the casket.[4] Average casket costs hover around $2,000 but can easily extend up to $10,000, and sometimes twice that, for ornate hardwood caskets equipped with inner-spring mattresses, satin linings, and hermetic seals. Such prices yield big profits for funeral businesses.[5] Funeral home customers pay markups of anywhere from 250 to 600 percent.[6]

In 1998, Pastor Nathaniel Craigmiles of Chattanooga, Tennessee, was one of those customers. For his mother-in-law's funeral, Pastor Craigmiles and his family paid $3,200 for a canary-yellow casket that they purchased from a local Chattanooga funeral home. A few months later, while traveling in New York, he was stunned to find an identical casket for sale at a casket retailer for $800.[7] Like most consumers, the pastor knew little about the economics of the death-care industry, even though he had ministered to many parishioners as they grieved the loss of loved ones. His own experience compelled him to research the industry; what he found was bottleneckers of what he called "criminal proportions."

BUILDING MONOPOLIES IN DEATH CARE

Up until the past hundred years or so, American funerals were fairly simple affairs.[8] Embalmings and viewings took place in people's homes, and parlor doorways were purposely built wide enough to allow a coffin to pass through.[9] Furniture makers manufactured coffins as a side business, and some of them soon began serving as undertakers, or those who would "undertake" to prepare a body for burial.[10] Near the end of the nineteenth century, as funerals started becoming more elaborate and the people who worked at them more specialized, companies sprang up to make coffins.[11]

With the funeral home emerging as the primary service provider for the preparation and disposition of the dead, undertakers organized their trade so that they could control funeral prices.[12] They did so, in the words of the National Funeral Directors Association, to "protect themselves from excessive and therefore harmful competition from within their own ranks... [and to] bring a sense of professionalism to what had formerly been for many a mere trade or sideline."[13] The first formal organization of undertakers was the Undertakers Mutual Protective Association of Philadelphia, founded in 1864.[14] In most of the major American cities during the period from 1865 to 1880, undertakers formed associations for the purposes of mutual protection.[15]

State-level undertakers' organizations formed soon thereafter; the first of them in Michigan.[16] From the beginning, associations in states, like those in the cities, were formed to advance the economic interests of their members by protecting them from competition.[17] The founding documents of Michigan's Association of Funeral Directors, for example, stated its purpose as "mutually disseminating the most correct principles of business management, the best methods of protecting our own interests in professional practice, and the general good of all recognized legitimate undertakers."[18] The various city and state undertakers' associations eventually coalesced into the National Funeral Directors Association (NFDA), which was founded in 1882.[19]

Even in those early years, there was a protective motivation focused on casket sales. Shortly after its formation, the NFDA adopted a resolution to keep prices as high as possible, stating: "We, as funeral directors, condemn the manufacture of covered caskets at a price less than fifteen dollars for an adult size."[20] Throughout the late-nineteenth and early-twentieth centuries, the association successfully lobbied state legislators to pass laws licensing funeral directors and embalmers.[21] In 1894, Virginia became the first state to pass a law regulating embalming. The next year, Alabama, Missouri, and Pennsylvania adopted similar laws; five years later so did twenty-four other states.[22] Eventually, all fifty states and the District of Columbia would adopt licensing laws of some sort for funeral directors or embalmers, although Colorado abolished its law in 2009, converting its mandatory license into a voluntary state-certification program.

Under voluntary certification, an occupational practitioner can complete certain requirements associated with education, training, and testing and thereby describe him or herself as a "certified funeral director," or whatever the position may be. Those who do not complete the requirements and register with the state can still do the work of a funeral director, but they are not permitted to use the title of certified funeral director. Such an arrangement provides greater diversity of options for consumers. Some may value using the services of expensively certified funeral directors and be willing to pay the generally higher costs associated with doing so, while other consumers may see little value in credentials and instead desire the lower-cost services offered by noncertified providers.

In jurisdictions other than Colorado, these options do not exist. Practitioners must have a government-issued license to work. By requiring practitioners to achieve a minimum amount of schooling (often one year), complete an apprenticeship, and pass a licensing examination, state laws created a bottleneck restricting competition within the occupation, insulating it from competition. Consequently, funeral directors grew emboldened to significantly inflate prices of goods and services and institute practices so venal as to capture the attention of the Federal Trade Commission (FTC).

THE FUNERAL RULE TARGETS BOTTLENECKERS

In 1972, the FTC began investigations[23] that in 1984 resulted in the adoption of a set of rules governing the funeral industry generally. In its investigations, the FTC found that funeral directors often pressured families to buy unnecessary merchandise, such as caskets for cremation, when no laws required them; inaccurately represented legal, cemetery, and crematory requirements; only discussed prices in person, so that they could apply high-pressure sales tactics; and performed services without permission.[24]

Because the casket represented the greatest opportunity for profit, funeral directors engaged in unscrupulous techniques—often learned as part of their required schooling[25]—to persuade people to buy high-priced ones.[26] Lavishly decorated display rooms were organized to make the most expensive caskets easily seen. Inexpensive caskets—if they were displayed at all—were often stored out of sight or presented in an unappealing manner. Funeral directors manipulated mourners with comments such as: "This is the last act you can perform for your mother"; "He deserves something better than that"; and "Consider what the neighbors will think when they see the casket."[27] Worst of all, funeral establishments made the purchase of a casket the precondition of providing body handling and other services that they alone could offer, a practice known as "bundling." If a customer tried to purchase a casket elsewhere, funeral directors would refuse to provide these services.

Known as the Funeral Rule, the regulations adopted by the FTC attempted to restrict such practices. The rule states that: (a) consumers have the right to choose only the funeral goods and services they want; (b) funeral homes must provide a general price list (GPL) of goods, services, and prices; and (c) funeral providers must state the right of consumer choice in writing on the GPL. The regulations further prohibit: (a) misrepresenting embalming as being legally required or necessary (it is not), (b) misrepresenting a casket as being required for direct cremation, (c) misrepresenting any funeral goods or services as having protective or preservative abilities (this is not the case), (d) charging for embalming without permission to perform the service, and (e) subjecting consumers to bundling arrangements.[28]

The economic advantage bundling and other practices provided to funeral directors was evident in their reaction to the rule. From its conception, the rule was met with strenuous resistance by funeral directors and their trade associations, state funeral boards (usually composed of funeral directors), and members of peripheral industries that served the funeral industry.[29] These groups inundated the FTC with written comments while the rule was being considered,[30] and upon its adoption, they challenged it in court on evidentiary, policy, procedural, statutory, and constitutional bases.[31]

Funeral directors also vigorously lobbied members of Congress against any regulation by the FTC,[32] finding a champion in Representative Marty Russo, who sponsored legislation prohibiting the FTC from implementing the rule.[33] The eventual result was the FTC Improvements Act of 1980,[34] which forced the commission, when regulating, to comply with elaborate rule-making procedures and submit them for public comment before final rules could be promulgated. The effect was to directly limit the FTC's power over the industry. The delay tactics produced yet more opposition commentary by the funeral industry, but in 1984 the Funeral Industry Practices Rule, or Funeral Rule, was finally put into full effect.[35]

The response was predictable and swift—a separate marketplace for funeral goods sprang up in which independent casket retailers began offering caskets at prices much lower than those offered by funeral homes.[36] In typical bottlenecker fashion, however, funeral directors struck back by charging fees for "handling" caskets that were purchased through third-party vendors.[37] As one funeral director wrote in a trade magazine, "the selection room," referring to the room where caskets are displayed for consumer purchase, is after all "the *only* room in the entire funeral home where we make our money" (emphasis in original).[38] The handling fees came to the attention of the FTC during a rule-making review, and the commission began a process to amend the rule to prohibit the practice. Again, the funeral directors organized to fight the amendment, but their efforts were rejected in the courts.[39]

In many—but not all—states, the Funeral Rule resulted in additional entrepreneurs offering more choices for consumers. Over the years, legislators in a dozen states specified in their laws that only licensed funeral directors could sell funeral merchandise, such as caskets. Bottleneckers' fingerprints were often all over such laws. Georgia's law, for example, came about after a cemetery owner began infringing on what the funeral directors considered their turf by selling caskets. Funeral directors responded by pressing for a law limiting the ability to sell to licensed funeral directors, and the legislature quietly obliged in 1992.[40] The legislation's two sponsors—Senator Wayne Garner and Representative Jimmy Lord—happened to be funeral directors themselves. They successfully created the casket bottleneck, which went almost completely unnoticed.[41]

When Lord first introduced the legislation, it was a minor bill that dealt only with funeral home apprentices. It breezed through the House on a vote of 106–2 and then moved to the Senate. It was assigned to the Governmental Operations Committee, an odd placement, except that the committee chair—Senator Culver Kidd—shared some of his Senate district constituents with Lord's House district. The bill was allowed to lie dormant in committee for two months. Then, as one observant funeral-industry lobbyist noticed, the committee altered it in a way that he cryptically described as "a substitute [that] was presented to the committee."[42] Included in the substitute legislation was the casket restriction. The bill passed the committee, the Senate, and the House, all without dissent. Indeed, it is likely no one else in the legislature even realized a monopoly was being created. As the editorial page editor of the *Atlanta Journal-Constitution* wrote, "A monopoly was created and probably not more than four people knew it was happening—three legislators and a lobbyist."[43]

"ROBBERY WITHOUT A PISTOL"

In Pastor Craigmiles's home state of Tennessee, the restriction on casket sales likewise owed its genesis to a state legislator who was a longtime funeral director—Senator Fred O. Berry. In 1972, Berry—a second-generation funeral director—led a successful push to amend the Funeral Directors and Embalmers Act (FDEA), which Tennessee had passed in 1951, and to restrict the selling of funeral merchandise to licensed funeral directors. He was joined by other state senators and representatives who were also licensed funeral directors.[44] Typical of bottleneckers, Berry supported his bill by appealing to the need to protect the public from "very unscrupulous people." A funeral director colleague in the House,

Representative Perry Coffey, was more candid about the bill, objecting to anyone being able to sell funeral merchandise, suggesting that "they are infringing on funeral directors, we think."[45]

By the time Pastor Craigmiles began looking into the funeral industry, the anticompetitive measures like those advocated by Berry and his colleagues were already having their intended effects. One analysis estimated that funeral homes under a regime of licensure charged approximately 11 percent more than retailers not burdened by licensure.[46] Another study found an even-greater disparity—68 percent—when comparing the prices of caskets sold in funeral homes to those available through Internet casket sellers.[47]

For Pastor Craigmiles, it was "robbery without a pistol,"[48] especially for the modest-income parishioners he served. When he began pastoring in 1988, his congregation comprised just fourteen people. By the time he retired, his church had grown to more than four hundred members. The core of its membership included many poor and uneducated members of the community who came to the church off the street. In Pastor Craigmiles, the parishioners of Marble Top Missionary Baptist Church found not a man of inaccessible piety but one of their own who had turned away from his own life on the street in order to care for his family and heed a call to ministry, which might have surprised those who knew him before he settled down in Tennessee.

Although Craigmiles was born and raised in Chattanooga, he eventually left his hometown to serve in the military in Vietnam and then settled in Boston, where his life took a dark turn. He began associating with a criminal element in the city and over time began laundering money for the mafia. Making matters worse, a recreational drug habit turned into a gripping heroin addiction, and he tumbled out of control, finally landing in both state and federal prison. The man who emerged from prison was not the same as the one who entered it. Unlike many who grow hardened and embittered, Craigmiles gave his life over to God, resulting in a radically changed life and, unlike so many who leave incarceration, a successful transition back into society.

After his father died in 1983 and his mother became ill, he returned to Chattanooga to care for her. She died just a few years later, but by then he had decided to remain in Tennessee. There, he married, raised a family, and began pastoring a growing-yet-needy flock, caring for church members at the beginning of their lives and at the end. For a decade, he presided over the funerals of church members, unaware of what funeral directors were doing to their loved ones.

The course of his life changed again when it came time to help his wife bury her mother. Outraged by what he learned from this experience, he invested his life savings, took out a loan, and opened a business in May 1999 to help the people of his church by providing caskets at a much-less-expensive price than was offered at Chattanooga's funeral homes.[49] "I couldn't stand any longer to see people having to mortgage their homes to pay for a decent burial," he said.[50] The caskets he sold in his store were priced anywhere from half to a quarter of what local funeral homes were charging.[51] His caskets typically sold for $800. The exact-same caskets—bought from the exact-same manufacturers—sold for $2,000 in local funeral homes.

Although Pastor Craigmiles had secured city and county business licenses, no one had told him casket sellers required a funeral director's license.[52] For the pastor, getting one was simply not an option. Securing such a license would have required him to either enroll in a school approved by the state funeral board and participate in a one-year apprenticeship or to complete a two-year apprenticeship and assist with twenty-five funerals. At the time, the only Tennessee school approved by the funeral board was Gupton College, more than 130 miles away from his home, in Nashville. The most popular program took sixteen months to complete and cost between $10,000 and $12,000 in tuition and other expenses. Applicants also had to pass a funeral board exam.[53]

Even if he had had the time and resources to complete all those requirements, Pastor Craigmiles saw no point in doing it. Nothing about the selling of a casket—essentially an empty box—necessitated such requirements from his perspective. "You don't have to buy a car from a mechanic," he protested. "Why should you have to buy a casket from a funeral home?"[54] Moreover, he rationalized that he would never be handling any human remains; he merely sought to sell a casket at a discount and then deliver it to a funeral home for the customer's use.

On July 7, 1999, just months after Pastor Craigmiles opened for business, the state funeral board forced him to close.[55] A cease-and-desist order was, in fact, delivered to him personally by the funeral board's president. The pastor told the president to take his order back to where it came from and vowed to continue operating, but the next morning he found the store sealed by the sheriff "with the biggest padlock I'd ever seen."[56] Had he cut off the lock and opened the store, he would have been arrested.

His outrage over artificially inflated casket prices intensified following the funeral board's actions, and on September 16, 1999, he and three other plaintiffs sued the board and the attorney general's office, calling the licensing law an unconstitutional deprivation of their right to earn an honest living.[57]

Publicly, the funeral board—made up of six funeral directors and an attorney[58]—defended its actions by pointing to the law's bureaucratic function: "Our responsibility is to enforce the law as passed by the legislature. We're doing what we're supposed to do," said Arthur Giles, the board's executive director.[59] Reasons given by other funeral-industry representatives in support of the law ranged from the routine to the ridiculous. Citations of concern for public health and safety, such as safe disposal of bodies and consumer protection, were the most common,[60] and the potential for the inaccuracy of death statistics unless only licensed funeral directors sold caskets was asserted by other industry insiders.[61] Funeral-industry leaders stuck to such claims, even though residents could buy discount caskets over the Internet without the help of a representative or from other out-of-state third-party sellers, and funeral homes were required by law to accept them. Moreover, residents of Tennessee were legally permitted to use homemade caskets, and families or church groups could dispose of bodies without an undertaker or a funeral director.[62]

Months after filing the lawsuit, as the case was underway, the judge lifted the cease-and-desist order, and Pastor Craigmiles reopened his business. As attention to his case increased, he began receiving threatening calls and notes. Although he did not know their precise source, he suspected they were from funeral home competitors: "They said unless we shut down something was going to happen. This is big money, and we are just little people. I consider it a threat, and we're taking this seriously and are thinking about repercussions."[63]

As the legal proceedings wore on, the hooliganism continued. Caskets Pastor Craigmiles delivered to funeral homes in mint condition were intentionally scratched and damaged by funeral personnel to sully his reputation. His store windows were regularly smashed, and funeral-industry thugs threatened him with bodily harm.[64] Unbowed, he continued to sell caskets to his clientele, who had grown to include not only poor members of the community in need of moderately priced caskets but also middle- and upper-income buyers who were becoming increasingly aware of the rapaciousness of the funeral-home bottleneckers. Even after getting his store burned to the ground—the perpetrators never identified—Pastor Craigmiles persevered, replacing his lost store with two others in strip malls in different parts of the city.

The funeral bottleneckers were not content, however, with merely defending their license. In 1999, two state legislators associated with the funeral industry sponsored a successful bill to give funeral directors even-greater advantages in selling funeral merchandise. With the support of the Tennessee Funeral Directors Association, Representative Tim Garrett and Senator John Ford, the latter eventually caught in and convicted as a result of an FBI bribery sting,[65] pushed through a bill to require a twenty-four-hour waiting period before cremation.[66] The law was criticized for the burdens imposed on the bereaved, forcing them to pay for embalming in places where refrigeration for the interim period was not an option and giving funeral directors time to convince families to select more expensive funeral options.[67] It was also suggested that the law was put on the legislature's consent calendar, where bills that are not expected to cause controversy are placed, without discussion.[68] It turns out the law *was* controversial; it provoked a "public outcry," according to legislators, when people realized what it said.[69] The *Knoxville News Sentinel* called the law "an insult to consumers and a clear favor to special interests."[70] The following year, the law was repealed,[71] but an even-bigger blow to the bottleneckers was still to come.

In August 2000, the US District Court for the Eastern District of Tennessee ruled in favor of Pastor Craigmiles. In his decision, Judge R. Allan Edgar held that

> there is no reason to require someone who sells what is essentially a box (a casket) to undergo the time and expense of training and testing that has nothing to do with the State's asserted goals of consumer protection and health and safety.[72]

On August 29, the board convened a special meeting via teleconference to discuss whether to appeal its district court loss, but it was not just members of the state board who attended. Also on the call and participating in the deliberation were the executive director of the Tennessee Funeral Directors Association and three funeral directors. Upon their urging, the board voted unanimously to appeal.[73]

The following month, the state officially appealed the decision, clinging to its assertion that there were threats to public health and safety posed by unlicensed casket sellers. The Sixth US Circuit Court of Appeals would have none of it, however.[74] On December 6, 2002, the court produced the following ruling:

> Dedicating two years and thousands of dollars to the education and training required for licensure is undoubtedly a significant barrier to entering the Tennessee casket market. The question before the court is whether requiring those who sell funeral merchandise to be licensed funeral directors bears a rational relationship to any legitimate purpose other than protecting the economic interests of licensed funeral home directors. The weakness of Tennessee's proffered explanation indicates that the 1972 amendment adding retail sales of funeral merchandise to the definition of funeral direction was nothing more than an attempt to prevent economic competition. Indeed, Tennessee's justifications for the 1972 amendment come close to striking us with "the force of a five-week old, unrefrigerated dead fish," a level of pungence almost required to invalidate a statute under rational basis review.[75]

The court further noted that "even if casket selection has an effect on public health and safety, restricting the retailing of caskets to licensed funeral directors bears no rational relationship to managing that effect."[76] The court concluded that the Tennessee legislature's "measure to privilege certain businessmen over others at the expense of consumers is not animated by a legitimate governmental purpose."[77] In the face of two strong court rejections, the state board chose not to appeal to the US Supreme Court this time.[78]

BOARDS OF BOTTLENECKERS

The case of Pastor Craigmiles illustrates how bottleneckers don't just consist of trade associations looking to maintain the fence around their occupation. They are also made up of government licensing boards ostensibly charged with protecting public welfare but actually functioning as state agents acting on behalf of license holders. This is the result of membership on such boards being dominated by practitioners of the regulated trade, which happens through a process known as "regulatory capture."[79] Having control on these boards not only allows industry representatives to restrict entry into their own occupation by setting up licensing schemes but also gives them state-granted power to punish those operating without a license with fines and jail time, including entrepreneurs like Pastor Craigmiles who merely sell caskets.

Through enforcement, licensing boards police the fences around their occupations so strictly that even nonprofits whose efforts are aligned with their fundraising activities sometimes receive punitive action. In Louisiana, for example, Catholic monks from the Saint Joseph Abbey faced the possibility of a jail term for daring to sell handmade caskets to fund their religious mission. On March 30, 2010, the Louisiana State Board of Embalmers and Funeral Directors subpoenaed Abbot Justin Brown and Deacon Mark Coudrain of the Saint Joseph Abbey, commanding them to appear before the board and answer allegations under oath about caskets the Abbey had been selling to fund its day-to-day expenses. If found guilty, they would have faced fines of between $500 and $2,500 for each casket sold and up to 180 days in jail. The subpoena was the culmination of a three-year crusade by the funeral board against the Abbey, which sought only to support itself through the sale of simple handmade wooden caskets, the type Abbey monks had made for their own burials for years.

Saint Joseph Abbey dates back to the late nineteenth century, when it was established by Benedictine monks for the pursuit of a monastic life that included liturgical prayer, the singing of psalms, simple labor, education, and hospitality toward those seeking a contemplative respite from the world. Consistent with the teachings of their namesake, Benedictine monks have for centuries supported themselves through trades including brewing beer, making wine, and farming. At Saint Joseph Abbey, operational funds come from a seminary the monks direct, a retreat center, timber farming, and small enterprises such as a gift shop that features Abbey-made "Monk Soap."[80]

In the 1990s, it became clear to Abbey leaders that these income sources were not enough and a new means to support themselves financially was needed. However, any new undertaking had to be in keeping with the monks' quiet and simple life. In the meantime, attention was increasingly being paid to the caskets that the monks made for themselves and friends of the Abbey. People attending the funerals of prominent Louisiana Catholics buried in Abbey-made caskets began to inquire about buying similar caskets for their loved ones. And so the monks sold a small number of caskets beyond the Abbey. That all changed in 2005, when Hurricane Katrina destroyed the part of the Abbey's pine timberlands whose harvest had been so profitable.[81]

With the loss of 60 percent of its adult pine trees, the leaders at the Abbey knew that they would not be able sell timber for twenty years, making critical the need to find alternate sources of funding.[82] It was then that Deacon Coudrain approached Abbot Brown with an inspired idea—to make and sell caskets to meet a growing demand. It represented the perfect opportunity: Casket making was a simple occupation that could be performed at the monastery, and selling caskets would enable the monks to share their view of the simplicity and unity of life and death.

The monks prayed, voted on the plan, and eventually expanded their casket-making capacity by investing $200,000 to convert an old cafeteria building on their property into a well-equipped woodshop.[83] On November 1, 2007, the monks officially unveiled Saint Joseph Woodworks, which would produce two models of honey-colored caskets, one for $1,500 and another for $2,000, both priced at the lower end of caskets offered at funeral homes[84] and each blessed and marked with a medal of Saint Benedict.[85]

The Clarion Herald, the official newspaper of the Archdiocese of New Orleans, ran an article about the proposed new venture that caught the eye of the Louisiana State Board of Embalmers and Funeral Directors. On December 11, 2007—before the Abbey had sold even one casket—the state board sent the Abbey a letter stating that selling caskets violated the law and would subject the monks to crippling fines, jail time, and a possible lawsuit by the state. Unbeknownst to the monks, Louisiana law made it a crime to sell funeral merchandise, including caskets, without a funeral director's license. To sell caskets legally, the monks would have to apprentice at a licensed funeral home for one year and take a funeral-industry test. They would also have to convert their monastery into a "funeral establishment" by, among other things, installing equipment for embalming human remains.

The monks were flummoxed: Why would a funeral director's license be required to sell an empty wooden box? There were no health and safety concerns, and a casket is not even a requirement for burial in Louisiana. A human body is allowed be placed directly in the ground, buried in a shroud, or entombed in a cardboard casket.

In fact, from its origins, Louisiana's casket law had nothing to do with protecting the public; it served only to protect the interests of the bottleneckers. The Louisiana Board of Embalmers and Funeral Directors was created in 1914, ostensibly to protect against infectious or communicable diseases. But, in yet another example of regulatory capture, the board quickly came under the control of the industry it was charged to oversee. Today, all but one of its ten members are funeral directors. One of the board's most important achievements came in the 1960s, when Louisiana—like Tennessee would do the following decade—made it a crime to sell funeral merchandise without a funeral director's license.[86] With this law in place, the funeral-director bottleneckers possessed the necessary power to punish anyone who posed even the smallest competitive threat to their sheltered market, including a small band of modest monks producing simple wooden caskets.

In the face of the cease-and-desist order, the monks continued selling their caskets. Following the December 2007 letter, the funeral board swiftly launched an investigation—spurred on by an official complaint lodged by a funeral home director. The board obtained sworn statements from funeral homes that had received the Abbey's caskets and from the board's investigator, Jude Daigle, who spotted the Abbey's truck at a funeral home and helped Deacon Coudrain unload a casket. On January 30, 2008, the board questioned Abbot Brown, concluded the Abbey was violating the law by selling its caskets, and once again threatened him with penalties of between $500 and $2,500 per violation—the monks had only sold sixty caskets at that point—and 180 days in jail.[87]

The Abbey disagreed with the board's legal conclusions and stated that it intended to try to change the law. Nonconfrontational by nature, the monks assumed the board's conclusion was essentially a misunderstanding that could be cleared up through negotiation or, if the board was simply enforcing a legal technicality, with a simple revision of the law. Made up of mostly licensed funeral directors, the board had no incentive to compromise and remained completely intractable. So, in what amounted to an act of civil disobedience, in the face of what they believed to be an injustice, the monks continued to sell their caskets—though without advertising and only to those who requested them—while pursuing change through the legislature.[88] It was not an easy decision. As Abbot Brown, a soft-spoken man in his midfifties, explained,

> I was concerned that it would disturb the peace of the monastery by getting involved in something somewhat controversial, adversarial, but it hasn't.... If you study monastic history, there were often conflicts between monks and civil authorities.[89]

To seek justice, the monks first went to their local state representative Scott Simon, who agreed in May 2008 to introduce a bill amending the law through the Commerce Committee. Deacon Coudrain and Abbot Brown attended the committee hearing in favor of the bill, while the funeral-industry lobbyists opposed it, with eleven funeral directors there to speak against it. In rambling testimony, funeral directors asserted that their casket monopoly was necessitated by their supposedly unique and specialized knowledge about the complexities of preparing bodies for burial and burying them in Louisiana. But when a committee member asked a different question, about whether someone could buy a casket anywhere and have it shipped to a funeral home in Louisiana for use in a burial, a representative of the Louisiana Funeral Directors Association admitted that this was indeed the case, completely undermining the bottleneckers' other arguments about burials. Nevertheless, the bill was killed in committee. "I learned that funeral directors have the last word in life, and in the legislature," Representative Simon said.[90]

The Abbey pursued legislative reform again in spring 2010. This time, state senator Francis Thompson drafted a bill to exempt the Abbey and other nonprofit casket sellers from needing a funeral director's license to sell caskets. But, once again, the funeral industry opposed the bill and it never emerged from committee. Along the way, the Louisiana Funeral Directors Association attempted to placate the monks by offering to house Abbey caskets in various funeral homes free of charge. But having their caskets displayed in funeral homes alongside other manufacturers' products would not allow the monks to interact directly with their customers, so they declined the offer, citing their belief that contact with customers was an integral part of their service.[91] Moreover, as Abbot Brown observed, "It became clear that we were fighting not only for ourselves but for other people like us who encounter these kinds of regulations and keep them from going into business or to make an honest living."[92]

Unable to achieve a legislative remedy due to the power of the funeral bottleneckers, Saint Joseph Abbey filed a federal lawsuit against the funeral board on August 12, 2010. To protect its monopoly, the board increased its legal budget[93] and hired an expensive private attorney to work with the board's attorney to represent it in court.[94] In the trial, the monks argued that they should not be punished for doing something that should not be considered a crime—thereby exercising their right to earn an honest living—particularly when they were being punished for no other purpose than to protect the private financial interests of the funeral-industry cartel. The board responded by asserting a need to maintain a standard of quality in the industry by protecting the public from aggressive sales tactics—by monks!—at a time when consumers were vulnerable. The board further claimed that in some parts of the state many burials are above ground, which it said requires "knowledgeable decisions" about casket sales given Louisiana's unique situation.

In response, the Abbey's attorneys from the Institute for Justice reminded the court that the state did not require anyone to be buried in a casket and that under the Funeral Rule funeral directors must accept a casket purchased elsewhere. They pointed out that Louisiana consumers were free to purchase a casket from online retailers or out-of-state casket sellers but not from in-state casket makers.[95] In short, Louisiana's ban on the activities of unlicensed, in-state casket sellers did nothing to protect consumers but did insulate the state's funeral directors from competition.

In July 2011, the monks won a huge victory when US district judge Stanwood Duval ruled the state law unconstitutional, saying, "The sole reason for these laws is the economic protection of the funeral industry," and adding "there is nothing in the licensing procedures that bestows any benefit to the public in the context of the retail sale of caskets."[96] The funeral board pressed its case with the federal appeals court in New Orleans the following year. The result, however, was the same: The Fifth US Circuit Court of Appeals rejected the state's claims, concluding that "neither precedent nor broader principles suggest that mere economic protection of a particular industry is a legitimate governmental purpose" and that "the great deference due state economic regulation does not demand judicial blindness to the history of a challenged rule or the context of its adoption nor does it require courts to accept nonsensical explanations for regulation."[97]

Still, the funeral board bottleneckers battled on, requesting a review by the US Supreme Court. On October 15, 2013, the justices denied the board's petition, thus leaving in place the lower court's ruling and confirming what Abbot Brown had known all along: the monks of Saint Joseph Abbey had committed no sin in creating plain wooden caskets and selling them to their Louisiana neighbors.[98]

WHEN COURTS IGNORE THE BOTTLENECKING REALITY

At the most obvious level, the courts' decisions meant that Pastor Craigmiles, the monks, and anyone else in their states were finally free to enter the casket market. But the fact that the courts gave the arguments of Pastor Craigmiles and the monks any consideration at all was itself virtually unprecedented in the legal arena.

Since the late nineteenth century, courts have paid scant attention to the economic rights of petitioners, instead deferring to the supposed will of the people in the form of legislatures. But what really occurs in state capitols across the country is not lawmakers proactively seeking ways to protect citizens from dangerous occupational practitioners or responding to harmed consumers demanding increased regulation of an industry. It is trade associations wielding influence over legislators who are all too willing to comply with their demands in order to secure votes and favors from an identifiable, energized voting bloc.[99]

What the courts have essentially done for many decades is to allow the co-option of government power by small interest groups for their own benefit to go unchecked. These groups deny the right of others to practice their occupation free from onerous and unnecessary government intrusion[100]—the type of intrusion that requires someone who merely wants to sell a wooden box to be required to apprentice at a licensed funeral home for one year, take a funeral industry test, and maintain a funeral establishment complete with embalming equipment. More often than not over the last hundred-some-odd years, the result has been stories like that of Kim Powers Bridges.

In the early 1980s, Kim was on the executive fast track. Raised in a family of hardworking Oklahoma entrepreneurs, she began work after college in the Texas office of a real estate management firm, where she quickly became the youngest regional manager in the company. In 1991, she returned to her hometown of Ponca City, Oklahoma, joined a financial services company, and grew to become one of the top producers in the state.[101]

Despite her success, Kim was restless. The economic rewards of her accomplishments failed to satisfy a long-simmering desire to combine her sense of determination with a call to serve others, but she could find no clear direction on where or how to do so. The answer came from her children's babysitter,[102] whose husband was a funeral home director looking for someone to run his business's "preneed" services—for those who choose to make funeral arrangements before their deaths.

At the babysitter's urging, Kim reluctantly agreed to meet her babysitter's husband and discuss the position, but she harbored deep skepticism about such a move. She had established herself successfully in the financial services field in Ponca City and doubted that this industry about which she knew essentially nothing could hold any promise for her. Her attitude, indeed her whole life, changed when she learned more about the work.[103] "I realized this job would put me in a position to help someone on the worst day of his or her life, or to prepare a person for that day," Kim explained. "I knew this was something I would do for the rest of my life."[104]

In 1993, Kim joined one of the largest funeral home operators in North America, and, as before, her hard work resulted in numerous promotions—area sales manager, regional sales manager, and beyond. But the promotions came at a price. Each move took her further away from serving clients and deeper into the morass of corporate bureaucracy and office politics. After five years, she sensed it was time to take what she had learned and return to her entrepreneurial roots.

Kim was a third-generation female entrepreneur. Her mother and grandmother had both been entrepreneurs, running a series of successful businesses by discerning a need in the market, shaping the business to meet demand, and growing it to sustainability and profitability. Growing up and working in such an environment conditioned her well. During her time in the funeral business, Kim came to recognize an area of significant consumer need—reasonably priced funeral merchandise.[105] She formed a partnership with Dennis Bridges, who had recently left the same funeral corporation as she had with the goal of opening a business. Together they spent a year developing an online store that would operate in Oklahoma. "It's not been something that we just dreamed up [one] morning and then said, 'Hey, let's go sell a casket,'" she said.[106] Although an online store could operate from any location, Kim elected to remain in her native state to maintain relationships with family and friends and raise her children in her hometown.

The store, Memorial Concepts Online, would offer caskets, among other things, at deeply discounted prices to better serve customers who had few options beyond funeral homes that charged markups of as much as 600 percent.[107] As other online funeral merchandise retailers had already demonstrated, even with such discounts the business stood a good chance of turning a profit.[108] At the time, critics of online casket sales, like the NFDA, advised against the practice, asserting that visits to funeral homes by the bereaved were therapeutic. But as the popularity of online retailers grew, even the NFDA recognized the change in consumer practices: "More and more, instead of going to the funeral home, people are saying, 'I don't need that—I'll e-mail you,'" admitted Robert M. Fells, general counsel for the NFDA.[109] According to Jay Kravetz, the editor of a funeral trade publication, the reason for the shift was simple: "When you visit casket dealers online, you can look at something over and over again.... You're not pressured—you have time to look with relatives and friends. It's really easier online."[110]

Although Kim and Dennis believed they had a winning business plan, they faced a significant problem. Like Louisiana and eight other states at the time,[111] Oklahoma required casket sellers to be licensed funeral directors. And similar to other states' licensing schemes, Oklahoma's licensing required two years of full-time college coursework, involving a one-year apprenticeship during which the student would have to embalm at least twenty-five human bodies and maintenance of a funeral establishment that included a "preparation room," a "selection room" with inventory on hand, and "adequate areas for the viewing of human remains."[112]

As if it were not irrational enough to require all of that simply to sell an empty box, the law also applied only to Oklahoma companies selling caskets to consumers within the state. Any casket seller located anywhere other than Oklahoma could sell to the state's citizens without having to be an Oklahoma-licensed funeral director. And Oklahoma-based casket retailers without a funeral director's license could sell to anyone in any other state.[113] Simply put, Memorial Concepts Online, planning to operate as an Oklahoma-based company, would be able to sell to anyone except people in Oklahoma. As Kim noted, "We could just have moved the [Internet] servers 40 miles north" into Kansas and been allowed to sell caskets to fellow Sooners.[114]

Instead, Kim elected to keep the business in her home state and fight a law she believed to be not only wrong but injurious. As she put it, "The restriction was unfair, and ultimately, harmful to the families our industry serves."[115] Because of the inflated prices it created, the law imposed an unnecessary hardship on grieving families, something that offended Kim in her belief that it is the industry's obligation to serve these families in their hour of need.[116]

Kim was not alone in viewing the law as harmful. Beginning in 1999, state legislators repeatedly attempted to eliminate the restriction on casket sales. The first attempt came in a House of Representatives bill introduced by Carolyn Coleman, but the bill never received a committee hearing.[117] So, Representative Coleman tried again to pass the measure by appending it to another House bill focused on licensing counselors and therapists.[118]

During the debate on the amendment, Coleman supported her position with facts about severe casket markups, citing research indicating that a casket that sold for $5,000 could be found at a price as little as $2,000 if purchased directly from a manufacturer. The bill, if adopted, was estimated to save the state's consumers up to $20 million per year.[119] Opponents responded to Coleman's facts with scare tactics—citing poor casket quality, delayed casket deliveries, and grandma's dead body propped in a corner while awaiting the arrival of a casket ordered over the Internet. They ignored that online retailers could deliver merchandise anywhere in the country within twenty-four hours of purchase[120] and that third-party merchandise sales from unlicensed providers were already legal, as long as they came from outside of Oklahoma.

The absurdity of the bottleneckers' arguments only highlighted the weakness of their position, an observation not lost even on members of the funeral-director cartel. One lawmaker with a background in the funeral industry admitted:

> I would be hard pressed to argue that you necessarily have to have a license to sell a casket. We don't license automobile dealers to sell you an automobile, and they're certainly selling you a product that's much more expensive and much more complicated than a casket... [I]s there some mystical something about the structural components of a casket that forces someone to be licensed? No, not necessarily.[121]

Coleman's amendment failed 31–64.

The following year, Coleman tried again to pass the amendment, but the bill met the same fate as its predecessor, never even receiving a hearing in the House Public Health Committee. Undeterred, Coleman was back at it in 2002, and again in 2003, finally receiving a committee hearing, only to see the bill defeated 5–4.[122]

According to Coleman, the various defeats could be traced to one source—the state's funeral directors.[123] With lawmakers, paid lobbyists, and several former funeral directors having a strong presence in the ranks of the capitol, Oklahoma funeral directors wielded significant influence. "The power of the funeral industry in this state is such that they were able to prevent this bill or one like it from even being heard for several years," observed Edwin Kessler from Common Cause, a citizens' advocacy organization.[124] Even with support from Common Cause, the AARP, the Oklahoma Conference of Churches, and the Farm Bureau, Coleman could not overcome the bottlenecker juggernaut.[125]

Kim and Dennis could not place their business on hold in order to wait for a legislative fix might never materialize. The state's funeral board had already shut down at least one other unlicensed casket retailer,[126] and Kim and Dennis were not rule breakers by nature. There was also the matter of the stiff fines and possible jail sentences they would face if they proceeded on their path. On March 14, 2001, they sued the State Board of Embalmers and Funeral Directors, seeking to have Oklahoma's anticompetitive casket-sales laws struck down as unconstitutional. The lawsuit drew the private ire of funeral-industry insiders. "While in my office, I would receive phone calls from funeral homes. I could tell who they were because of caller-ID," Kim recalled. "They would tell me to drop the suit, that I was hurting the industry." She also received letters from incensed funeral directors. "I received a scathing letter from a young man telling me I was unprofessional and ruining the industry. He told me drop the whole thing."[127]

While still supporting the law, industry leaders were more measured in their response. Scott Smith, then president of the Oklahoma Funeral Directors Association, told *NBC Nightly News*: "The law is good. I see it as protecting the consumer." On the same broadcast, Joseph McCormick IV of the Oklahoma attorney general's office added, "There's just no evidence in the record to support an argument that this law is anti-competitive."[128] McCormick's statement put him at direct odds with none other than the FTC, which had by then been studying and overseeing the funeral industry for decades. As part of the trial court proceedings, the FTC filed a brief on behalf of Kim and Dennis. Noting the intent of its then-almost-twenty-year-old Funeral Rule, the FTC argued that competition and choices are good for consumers and that being forced to do business with a state-mandated cartel is not. "Rather than promote consumer choice, the FSLA [Oklahoma's Funeral Services Licensing Act] forces consumers to purchase caskets from funeral directors," the FTC's brief said. "Whatever ends the FSLA can be said to be advancing, it is not advancing the ends of the FTC's Funeral Rule."[129]

Regardless, on December 12, 2002, Judge Stephen P. Friot ruled against Kim and Dennis. He acknowledged that "less than 5 percent of the education and training requirements necessary for licensure in Oklahoma pertain directly to any knowledge or skills necessary to sell caskets" and that those who wish to sell caskets "are required to spend years of their lives equipping themselves with knowledge and training that is not directly relevant to selling caskets."[130] Nevertheless, he placed deference to the bottlenecker-controlled legislature above the right to earn an honest living, writing,

> The Legislature may determine...that protection of the consumer lies in creation of a cartel-like scheme for protection of an industry....The choice of whether to be paternalistic, and, given that choice, as to how best to be paternalistic, was one for the Oklahoma Legislature to make.[131]

Kim and Dennis appealed the case to the Tenth US Circuit Court of Appeals, but the appellate court upheld the lower-court ruling on August 23, 2004. Like Friot, the appellate court was fully aware of both the inefficacy of the law and the private interests it served. One tenth-circuit judge even noted that the law's "limitations on the free market of casket sales have outlived whatever usefulness they may have had."[132] The court also acknowledged that by the time it ruled, three attempts to change the law had failed, and in a now-(in)famous quote, it cast its judicial eye on the reason for those failures: "While baseball may be the national pastime of the citizenry, dishing out special economic benefits to certain in-state industries remains the favored pastime of state and local governments."[133] Nevertheless, the appellate court, too, deferred to the legislature.

But Kim remained undeterred. Upon the release of the court's decision, she noted, "This is wrong. All we want to do is give consumers a choice to buy their caskets at reasonable prices and where they won't be exploited or subjected to high-pressure sales practices that are often found in funeral homes."[134] On November 22, 2004, Kim and Dennis appealed their case to the US Supreme Court, but on March 21, 2005, almost four years to the day after they had filed their first lawsuit, the high court declined to review the appellate decision. In so doing, it let stand the demonstrably unrealistic ruling that Kim and Dennis should seek relief through the legislature.

When the 10th Circuit pointed to the legislature, Kim was exasperated. "We've tried through the Legislature," she said. "The Legislature has chosen not to cooperate, and the consumer loses."[135] Upon the

Supreme Court's 2005 decision, the citizens of Oklahoma lost even more as Kim and Dennis moved Memorial Concepts Online to Tennessee, where they eventually, and given Kim's background not surprisingly, expanded their operations to work with thirty-two funeral homes and cemeteries in nine states, eventually employing more than 130 people.[136]

As Kim departed Oklahoma, the illusory nature of the legislative remedy recommended by the courts was further illustrated when an attempt to change the state's law was once again turned back by the bottleneckers. After Representative Coleman left the legislature, Representative Paul Wesselhoft picked up the flag in 2005, introducing a bill to free casket sales from the monopoly held by the state's funeral directors.[137]

As before, the powerful funeral-home cartel was instrumental in killing his bill. "My colleagues were receiving phone calls from their funeral homes in their district. They were all against this law," Wesselhoft recalled, and went on to say,

> The funeral industry has a cartel on caskets being purchased in the state of Oklahoma, and that's unfortunate.... [T]hey will definitely contact their representatives if they see a bill that threatens their dominance, and that happened during that time that I ran that bill, and so my bill died.[138]

In a sort of postscript to the years-long battle, in 2010 Wesselhoft proposed to introduce competition in the state's casket market by allowing sales by Native American tribes in addition to funeral directors.[139]

To date, Oklahoma's bottlenecker status quo remains.

CHAPTER 3

When Licenses Creep

Jestina Clayton nervously approached the armed guard standing outside the US Embassy in Conakry, Guinea. The soldier's hard gaze and automatic rifle were having their intended effect. Desperate for a visa to escape her war-ravaged home country of Sierra Leone, she, along with many others, had been sitting outside the embassy for three days. Absent the visa, she would be forced to return to a home devastated by civil war and, perhaps, to a terrible fate she had seen befall family members and friends. "Young girls, young women my age were being taken," Jestina recalled.[1] As a child, she narrowly escaped the same happening to her. "We were hiding in a building. My mother dressed me like an old person and then stood in front of me to hide me while the rebels took my best friend."[2]

At the age when girls in the United States are just beginning fourth grade, Jestina was worried about whether she would live to see the next day: "I was nine when the civil war started, and for a long time it was just survival, making sure that ... I'm alive the next day, that my family is alive, and that my friends are."[3] Jestina's life of survival lasted for nine of the eleven years of Sierra Leone's civil war.

The war in Sierra Leone began in 1991, forming the bloody climax of a postcolonial history marked by frequent coups, juntas, contested elections, and rampant corruption.[4] By the time Jestina was born in

1982, the country had already suffered decades of political upheaval, economic turmoil, social distress, and the pauperization of its people.[5] As she grew, her mother provided her as stable a life as possible and passed on elements of a cultural heritage she had learned as a girl, one of which was hair braiding. She learned to braid hair at the age of five, first braiding her mother's hair and then spending her youth braiding for other girls and women.[6] As a young girl and then as a teenager, braiding was more than a way to style hair for Jestina; it was also part of her identity. Little did she know what role it would play in her life in the years to come.

When the civil war erupted in Sierra Leone, her family spent the next nine years struggling to survive in and out of displacement camps, fleeing in the face of rebel soldiers. Constantly aware of the fate of other young girls, her mother insisted that Jestina find a way to escape. Reluctantly, Jestina tracked down the phone number of an aunt living in the United States and used funds her aunt provided her to travel to Conakry in neighboring Guinea—a trip of more than 160 miles—to secure a visa to escape to the United States.

And so it came to pass that this young woman of eighteen approached a US soldier at the embassy in Guinea, not as a naïve teenager seeking a cosmopolitan life in the United States but as a war-weary survivor leaving her family to avoid what had befallen so many females of her age. Through a stroke of luck, Jestina's request to the embassy guard resulted in an interview, then a visa, and then, in relatively short order, a trip to the United States. On August 10, 2000, Jestina arrived in New York, where she lived with family for three years. She quickly set about seeking to provide for herself. She completed her GED in 2001 and began taking a course in computer literacy. All the while, she applied the knowledge she had gained through her cultural roots by braiding the hair of members of her family.

In 2003, Jestina got married and shortly thereafter moved to Utah, where her husband's family lived. A year later, she enrolled at Weber State University to earn a degree in political science. Her husband, Paul, was also in college, and they began a family. Paying tuition for two, regular bills, and the expenses that go with having children added up quickly. Jestina and Paul were getting by, but just barely.

Paul worked at the local hospital, and Jestina tutored on her college campus and worked at the student newspaper. She secured scholarships for her studies, and members of her family helped when they could, but the couple had no money for even the simplest of luxuries such as eating at a restaurant. They considered applying for government support but ultimately rejected it. "It's my responsibility," Jestina explained, adding:

> When you think about how I was raised, we did not get anything from the government. I felt like I needed to handle my own affairs. It was important that we do our best to take care of ourselves. We did not even take financial aid, no student loans. This was about ourselves, not getting handouts. There were times we wanted to give up. It was hard, and after we had our second child, it was pretty tough.[7]

Jestina and Paul lived a frugal existence, cutting every conceivable corner to provide for their family and pay for the schooling they knew would afford them a better life in the future, but despite their best efforts, more money was going out than was coming in. Jestina cast about for a way to earn extra money. It had to be something with enough flexibility that she could care for her family and continue her education. She also needed to be able to generate income immediately, without significant upfront training. It was then that a confluence of circumstances provided the answer. She would do the thing she had done her entire life—indeed, something African women have done for thousands of years—she would braid hair.[8]

THE ART OF HAIR BRAIDING

The highly specialized and intricate crafts of twisting, braiding, weaving, and locking natural hair into different styles are types of hair braiding mostly used by African Americans. Today, these distinct techniques are generally grouped together under the rubric of "natural haircare," because they do not use any chemicals or artificial hairstyling techniques. The history of this type of hair braiding is thousands of years old.[9]

In African cultures, the grooming and styling of hair has long been an important social ritual. Elaborate hair designs reflecting tribal affiliation, status, sex, age, occupation, and the like are common, and the cutting, shaving, wrapping, and braiding of hair are centuries-old arts.[10] Anthropologists have identified the symbolism associated with hair as particularly powerful and important in individual and group identity in numerous world cultures.[11]

When African captives were brought to America to serve as slaves, the symbolism of and emphasis on their hair was preserved,[12] but by the nineteenth century the physical attributes of African Americans—their skin color, facial structure, and hair characteristics—had become freighted with negative connotations. Whites frequently referred to black hair as "wool" in order to differentiate it from the "superior" texture of white hair.[13] Blacks were taught to view straight, light-colored hair as the paramount expression of female beauty, which led to racial self-hatred, shame, and pervasive hair straightening in the African American community, typically accomplished through chemical means.[14]

It was not until the 1950s and 1960s that natural African hairstyles began to reemerge. As the civil rights movement gained momentum, Afros; dreadlocks; cornrows; and braids decorated with chevrons, beads, and mirrors became the symbols of black pride and a rejection of the white aesthetic that had for so long dominated the black sense of self.[15] The effect of such symbolism was profound. As Roberta Matthews, an African American woman, now in her early seventies, recalled, "When I first saw a woman with an Afro, I was shocked. I could barely look at her. I almost fainted." That was 1958. Yet, moved by the symbolism of natural hair, Roberta, too, began wearing her hair in an Afro two years after that encounter. The disapproval among her relatives was immediate and severe. "'Why do you want to mess yourself up like that?' they asked me. They thought I was awful."[16]

Ever so slowly, the negative view of natural hair changed. Today, although still viewed with some skepticism both inside and outside of the African American community,[17] natural hairstyles for African Americans have become so popular that natural haircare has grown into a multimillion-dollar industry, with specialized products and training. Braiding salons operate in cities large and small all over the country, and the number of women (and some men) who braid for money out of their houses may comprise even more people.

HAIR-BRAIDING BOTTLENECKERS

In 2005, Jestina was one of those women.[18] When she fled Sierra Leone, she had already been braiding hair regularly for more than a decade.

So, when she began looking for ways to make some extra money for her family, circumstances in her small Utah town provided the answer. Her community of about fifteen thousand people had no professional braiding salons, and there was demand for braiding services. Some families in her town had adopted African or Haitian children and had no idea how to style their hair.[19] Jestina quickly picked up twelve to fifteen clients and made, in a good year, about $4,800.[20] She braided in her home, mostly on Saturdays, while Paul cared for their children. "It's not like it was bringing me millions, but it was covering groceries," she explained.[21]

After earning her degree, she considered taking a job in an office but instead decided to open her own hair-braiding business.[22] As Jestina recalled,

> I did apply for jobs and had interviews, and I could make 12 to 16 dollars an hour, but the costs of childcare would have meant making about two dollars an hour, plus all of the family responsibilities and added stress, it was just not worth it. But if I could continue to braid, even though it's not a lot of money, I could do it from home and I could care for my children and not add things in my life I didn't need.[23]

So Jestina advertised her hair-braiding services on a local Web site and slowly began growing her business—until the day she received a fateful message.[24] While checking her business e-mail account, she came across a chilling anonymous note: "It is illegal in the state of Utah to do any form of extensions without a valid cosmetology license. Please delete your ad, or you will be reported."[25]

Jestina was stunned. When she first began braiding for money, she had checked the required credentials and was told by a state regulator that she did not need a cosmetology license as long as she did not cut or use chemicals to style hair.[26] Additionally, she had been braiding for years without a single complaint. Her modest income certainly posed no serious threat to established cosmetologists in town. And besides, she wasn't even doing cosmetology. She thought, "I'm not using chemicals. I'm not doing cosmetology stuff"[27]—the practices the regulator had told her required a license.

To confirm what the regulator had said, she contacted the state cosmetology board, and this time the answer she got differed. To her disbelief, she was told she had to get a government-issued license requiring two thousand hours of training and the successful completion of a licensing test.[28] That disbelief turned into dismay when she began calling cosmetology schools in her area: "I called about six schools along the Wasatch Front and they told me that they don't teach braiding and that . . . if I want to specialize in braiding[,] I would have to get independent help with that."[29]

Like Kim Powers Bridges, the monks of Saint Joseph Abbey, and Pastor Craigmiles, Jestina was caught in a bottleneck. To get the license and continue working, she would have to spend two thousand hours in classes that would cost her up to $18,000[30] and teach her nothing about braiding but only about skills completely irrelevant to her work.

The cosmetology laws were not specifically designed to block hair braiders; indeed, they typically contain no explicit language about hair braiding. In this way, they are very different from casket laws, which were created for the express purpose of limiting sales of caskets to funeral directors. In hair braiding, the requirement to get a license is the result of the initial adoption of cosmetology laws in the early twentieth century, at which time African hair braiding as a specialization, let alone an occupation, was unheard of. As the demand for and supply of professional hair braiding increased in the latter half of the century, cosmetology bottleneckers did not bother to change laws in their own favor. They simply used the power of licensing boards, through the vehicle of license creep, to achieve their ends.

LICENSE CREEP

License creep is a phenomenon in which regulators expand the scope of an existing licensing regime to cover a different occupation—one that presents new competition to the established trade.[31] In the case of hair braiding, license creep was the result of expanding cosmetology licenses to cover those who offer only hair-braiding services. Because regulatory boards that are established to oversee a licensing process are typically made up of current practitioners in a field and funded by licensees' dues, the boards have tremendous incentives to adopt and enforce a broad interpretation of a license's scope. The boards fight to preserve their power and the status quo rather than allowing seemingly complicated innovations that could disrupt the status of current service providers and force them to adapt or work harder. All too often, the result is that new business models or techniques are choked off as the would-be innovators are forced to undergo costly and irrelevant training or testing, or are effectively shut down with threats of fines, injunctions, or even criminal prosecution.

Hair braiding has not been the only target of license creep by cosmetologists and their regulatory boards. Also targeted has been the all-natural grooming practice of South Asian and Middle Eastern eyebrow threading, in which practitioners remove unwanted facial hair by forming a loop with cotton thread and then quickly brushing it along the face of a client to remove hair. Like hair braiding, this increasingly popular service has existed for centuries and requires no heat, chemicals, or sharp objects; it merely uses thread that it glides along the surface of the skin. Yet cosmetology boards in several states require that eyebrow threaders obtain expensive and irrelevant Western-style cosmetology licenses.[32]

Dentists, too, have joined the trend of license creep. In a number of states, dental boards and dental associations have pressed for laws that require entrepreneurs who sell, provide guidance, and host the application of over-the-counter teeth-whitening kits to be fully licensed dentists. Yet it is perfectly legal for someone to take the very same products home and use them without supervision. On average, a dentist can earn $25,000 annually by performing teeth whitening, and in states where nondental entrepreneurs can still whiten teeth, dentists routinely charge two to six times more than nondentists.[33]

Elsewhere, veterinary boards have tried to sweep the traditional practice of horse-teeth floating into their domain. Because horses' teeth grow throughout their lifetimes, it is necessary to file them. Floating is a safe, proven, and painless procedure for doing this, and the trade has often been passed down in families through the generations. Although floating has been practiced for centuries without requiring a government-issued license, state veterinary boards in Minnesota and Texas blocked their less expensive—and often far-better-qualified—nonveterinarian competitors from offering the service. This bottleneck is imposed even though few veterinary schools provide significant instruction in dentistry, let alone teeth floating.

In yet another example, Texas regulators, at the behest of politically powerful private investigators, defined the practice of private investigation so broadly that it even included a variety of computer repair services, forcing computer technicians in the state to obtain a costly private investigator's license before servicing computers—or else face steep penalties. Thanks to the fallout from a legal challenge, that bottleneck was cracked open and is no longer imposed.

BEATING BACK THE CREEP

A defining characteristic of license creep is the tenuous-at-best relationship between the targeted occupation—like hair braiding—and the requirements of complying with the licensing scheme imposed upon it. Indeed, in Jestina's case, she found the incongruity so stark that she thought an appeal to the state board would be sufficient to resolve the matter. Armed with a detailed PowerPoint presentation, she displayed illustrations of the discrepancy for the state licensing board for cosmetology/barbering, esthetics, electrology, and nail technology. The board, made up almost entirely of licensed barbers and cosmetologists, remained unmoved.[34] So, Jestina had two choices: to get a license or to stop braiding.

Jestina resolved to do neither. Marshalling what she had learned to get her newly acquired degree in political science, she allied with Utah state representative Holly Richardson, who had adopted several children from Africa,[35] to introduce a bill in 2011 to exempt natural hair braiding from the cosmetology license. In support of the bill, Richardson noted braiding's importance to several ethnic communities for which it is traditional. But the representative and Jestina were no match for the cosmetologists, who mounted an aggressive lobbying campaign against the bill, flooding Richardson with e-mails and letters and turning out in full force at the legislature.[36]

When Jestina arrived at the capitol to testify in support of the bill, she found the hearing room overflowing with cosmetologists and cosmetology students. The latter had been told to log their required hours for the day by attending the hearing rather than going to class, and their behavior soon grew unruly. "The chairperson told the people that if they did not calm down they would have to leave," Jestina recalled. "It was very intimidating. We had a few supporters, but it was pretty intense."[37]

The message of the cosmetologists was clear: "We encourage regulation," said Brad Masterson, a spokesman for the Professional Beauty Association (PBA). "Why should everyone else who's doing hair have to conform to requirements and not her?"[38] The PBA is the nation's largest cosmetology trade association, boasting more than seven thousand licensed professionals and 1,900 companies as members.[39] Its thirty-one-member staff includes an office dedicated to "government affairs and industry relations,"[40] and the association funds the work of a nine-member government-affairs committee primarily composed of salon owners.[41]

Like the Utah cosmetology board, the PBA saw and continues to see any activity involving the styling of hair as being in need of regulation. Any threat to its monopoly produces a swift and coordinated response. Through a legislative tracking system, the PBA watches bills in every state and issues advocacy alerts to engage members in the respective areas.[42] Members can then use the system to lobby legislators through a letter campaign. In 2012, for example, approximately twenty-one thousand letters were sent to state officials through the system in response to legislation.[43] In addition to the legislative tracking system, the PBA hosts an advocacy blog to draw attention to threatening legislation or even a whiff of deregulation. For example, when former US House majority leader Eric Cantor singled out cosmetology licenses as examples of employment regulation in need of reform,[44] the PBA responded with an open letter about the importance of licensing and provided "information" about deregulation to Cantor's office.[45]

For in-person lobbying, the PBA organizes and provides resources to state-level coalitions. On its Web site, the association provides a list of "state captains" who lead advocacy efforts in their respective areas and serve as the PBA's "eyes and ears on the ground when it comes to legislative matters."[46] As a state captain in Louisiana explained, "If [deregulation] comes to Louisiana, we will need to drop our shears and drop our combs, because we will need to go down to the state capitol and fight this."[47]

In Indiana, that is precisely what happened. In 2011, state representative Dave Wolkins introduced House Bill 1006, which sought to eliminate the cosmetology board. In response, the PBA produced a captain-led effort in the state to storm the capitol, amassing one thousand cosmetologists to attend the committee hearing and protest the bill, thereby prompting thirty thousand phone calls, letters, and e-mails to legislative committee members.[48] In response, Wolkins pulled the bill from consideration, noting, "I knew it was going to be a difficult day when all the cosmetologists were downstairs and started cheering: 'We've got scissors, yes we do, we've got scissors, how 'bout you?'"[49]

A longtime staple in cosmetologists' repertoire of bottlenecking activities is, similar to that of funeral directors, the threatening description of the "parade of horribles" that will befall consumers in the absence of licensing. In the late 1990s, for example, Gordon Miller of the National Cosmetology Association, which is now part of the PBA,[50] defended California's cosmetology requirement for hair braiders by raising the specter of disease. "They're working in an environment where diseases and where head lice can be transmitted from person to person," he cautioned.[51]

More than a decade later, the parade of horribles continued to march on. For example, in an advocacy document titled "Beware the 'D' Word," Myra Irizarry, the PBA's director of government affairs, warned:

> If deregulation of cosmetology were to become a reality, any person without any formal education would be able to practice cosmetology, putting consumers at risk of injuries, burns, infections, and the spread of diseases, such as hepatitis and Methicillin-Resistant Staphylococcus (MRSA), due to unsanitary practices.[52]

Indeed, in the frenzy surrounding Richardson's bill to exempt braiders from Utah's cosmetology license, cosmetologists warned state legislators of just such scourges. Brenda Scharman, a representative of a cosmetology school, chairperson for government relations of a Utah beauty school association, and PBA state captain, described how braiding could "cause dangers to the scalp, to the skin, [and] allergic reactions."[53] Tamu Smith, a salon owner in Provo, Utah, testified that braiding was dangerous due to its potential to "create permanent hair loss if it is not done correctly."[54] And Brandy Pierson, a licensed Utah cosmetologist, drew applause from the hearing's audience when she cautioned the committee, "When you do hair braiding, if the hair is not properly done right or taken care of, mold can grow in the hair, considering the hair is a keratin and protein-based product."[55] Lost in all the hyperbole was the fact that braiders don't use chemicals that can burn consumers' skin or engage in practices that can lead to injury. Moreover, as is often the case, the Utah bottleneckers did not advance their assertions with evidence that licensing could or would protect against such dangers.

Had the state board simply required minimal training on sanitation practices commensurate with the negligible risks associated with hair braiding, Jestina would have willingly complied. But, for Jestina, the fight to unshackle hair braiders from the cosmetology license was no longer just about her. With her degree in hand, she could have easily found a job making significantly more money than braiding could provide and let the status quo prevail. But after witnessing the cosmetology board's arrogance and watching helplessly as the bottleneckers wielded exaggeration and influence to manipulate the legislature for their own benefit—and ultimately killing Richardson's bill—she could not walk away.

On April 26, 2011, Jestina filed a lawsuit with the US District Court for the District of Utah to challenge the state's hair-braiding regulations. In it, she argued that the state's requirements for obtaining a license had nothing to do with her job and infringed upon her constitutional right to earn a living.[56] She hoped that the state would move to change the law under pressure of a lawsuit, but the board held firm. In characteristic bottlenecker fashion, lawyers for the state asserted that the regulations were designed to protect public safety, health, and welfare.[57] In this case, the judge was unimpressed.

On August 8, 2012, US district judge David Sam wrote:

> Utah's cosmetology/barbering licensing scheme is so disconnected from the practice of African hair braiding, much less from whatever minimal threats to public health and safety are connected to braiding, that to premise Jestina's right to earn a living by braiding hair on that scheme is wholly irrational and a violation of her constitutionally protected rights.[58]

In a similar message to the one Jestina had conveyed in her plea before the cosmetology board, Judge Sam pointed out that there was no good reason to require a person wishing to braid hair to complete hours of classes unrelated to hair braiding. As evidence, the judge noted that hair braiding of any kind was mentioned in only 38 of the 1,700 pages of texts commonly used in Utah's cosmetology schools. "Most of the cosmetology curriculum is irrelevant to hair braiding. Even the relevant parts are at best, minimally relevant," he wrote.[59] In response to this issue, the state's attorneys could not answer "which, if any, schools teach hair braiding."[60]

Finally, although he did not use the term as such, Sam highlighted the role of license creep in the board's actions. He noted that it was "undisputed" that the legislature never considered African hair braiding when it enacted the cosmetology act, which meant the board was "irrationally squeeze[ing] 'two professions into a single, identical mold' by treating hair braiders—who perform a very distinct set of services—as if they were cosmetologists."[61]

It did not take a multiday hearing to discern the irrationality of the board's position. Just days after news of the judge's decision broke, a letter to the editor appeared in one of Salt Lake City's newspapers that illustrated how plain to see the bottleneckers' motivation was:

> Let me see if I have this straight. After a ground school and approximately 50 hours of instruction and flight experience, a person can be licensed to take himself or herself and any other trusting soul into the air in a private plane. And after a short school, a few hours of instruction and a few more of supervised driving, a 16-year-old can be licensed to take his or her friends and hurtle them down a highway at a murderous rate of speed. But to get a license to touch another person's hair requires 2,000 hours of supervised experience and school tuition approaching $16,000. And the Utah barber/cosmetology licensing board wanted to require that Jestina Clayton of Centerville obtain such a permit before being allowed to braid a friend's hair! Makes sense to me. I cannot imagine why the court sided with Clayton instead of the licensing board. If public safety is indeed the issue, we have it all backwards.[62]

Perhaps sensing a lost cause, the state declined to appeal the decision.[63]

A QUARTER CENTURY OF BOTTLENECKING

From the time of the appearance of that threatening e-mail to the time of the release of Judge Sam's opinion, Jestina endured three years of occupational uncertainty, lost wages, and emotional turmoil. Had she been the first braider to battle the bottleneckers, resistance by the board and inaction by the legislature might have been explainable on the basis of low levels of awareness and misunderstandings about hair braiding.

But in 2009, Jestina's dustup with Utah's truculent cosmetology board was just the latest in a series of battles against cosmetology bottleneckers going back at least a quarter century to when Taalib din Uqdah began his fight against the District of Columbia's cosmetology board.

Taalib's battle began in 1989 when he received a series of sharp knocks at his salon door.[64] It had been a particularly busy day, and the persistent knocking was an unwelcome interruption. When he answered the door, Taalib found himself face to face with an enforcement officer from the DC Board of Cosmetology who demanded to see his cosmetology license. He replied that he had not realized that he needed one and promised to apply promptly. It was a promise he intended to keep—until he learned what the process required.

In order to continue braiding hair in the District of Columbia legally, Taalib would have to complete at least 1,500 hours of prescribed training in one of a handful of licensed cosmetology schools, which, at that time, charged between $3,500 and $5,000. He would be required to master chemical and heat treatments of hair—irrelevant to braiding—and spend 125 hours practicing shampooing techniques. Each of the ten people employed by Taalib would also have to get licensed in this way, and as a manager he would be required to undergo further training.

Seeing the training as nonsensical and unable to afford such time and expense, Taalib and his wife decided to stay open without a license. Soon the cosmetology police returned; this time with a cease-and-desist order and a $1,000 fine. He faced a choice: to close his business for months while he went to school or to continue to operate without a license and confront the prospect of more hefty fines and up to ninety days in jail.

By the time Taalib was informed of the licensure requirement, his business was already quite successful. In 1980, he and his wife, Pamela Farrell, had opened Cornrows & Co. with $500 in cash and three clients.[65] It was the first hair-braiding salon in Washington, DC. Through hard work and excellent service, they developed a booming business in an urban area desperately in need of successful businesses. They built a clientele of thousands of customers, employed almost a dozen people, and enjoyed a revenue stream of half a million dollars a year. Some customers came from as far afield as Connecticut, six hours away, to receive hair styling.[66] Then came those knocks at the door.

The laws that the cosmetology board used to approach Taalib were first enacted by Congress in 1938. The legislation was proposed by the Washington chapter of the national cosmetology trade association and was backed strongly by "an organization composed of most of the so-called exclusive, higher priced shops, and whose total membership today does not represent one-tenth of the beauty shops in Washington."[67]

Among those opposed to the bill was a representative of small beauty salons who charged that those in favor were motivated by protectionist impulses:

> This bill . . . is sponsored by the owners of the remaining number of exclusive and once high-priced beauty shops that remember the tremendous prices they once received from their fashionable patrons—and I fear that these same persons hope to get control of the situation in the legislation as proposed, limit or control competition, and perhaps somehow get back into the rich green pastures of yesterday.[68]

The District of Columbia's health officer was equally skeptical: "In the title of the bill . . . where the language 'for the protection of the public health' occurs," he testified, "I believe that this should be eliminated, to make it quite clear that this is a bill that means to protect primarily the guild interests."[69] Representative Martin Dies closed the debate by proclaiming:

> In the guise of sanitation and health, the bill gives the board dictatorial powers which are not needed to accomplish the avowed purposes of the bill, but which may be used to narrow the field of competition so that competent and worthy people will be denied an opportunity to make a living.[70]

More than fifty years later, Dies's proclamation sounded like prophesy. Rather than shutter his business, complete the irrelevant licensure requirements, and impose the same on his employees, Taalib petitioned the board to create an exemption for natural braiding.[71] Using the same logic that Jestina Clayton would employ almost twenty years later, he argued that since his shop only braided hair, its work had nothing to do with cosmetology.[72] He went so far as to hire a lawyer to draft proposed exemptions for African hairstyling, but the DC Board of Cosmetology—at the time made up entirely of licensed cosmetologists[73]—was recalcitrant. Taalib then lobbied the DC City Council, again asking that an exception be made for braiders. The result was the same. Finally, in September 1991, the DC Board of Appeals decided to uphold the $1,000 fines.[74]

Unbowed, Taalib sued the DC Board of Cosmetology on November 1, 1991, seeking an exemption from the licensing laws and the cessation of the board's enforcement efforts, including its attempt to shut down his business.[75] By that time, his plight had attracted national attention, so much so that a member of the cosmetology board appeared on ABC's *20/20* program to defend the board's attempts to close Cornrows & Co.

The appearance backfired. As the late William Raspberry wrote in his nationally syndicated column following the broadcast:

> A member of the District of Columbia's Cosmetology Board was on ABC's "20/20" program the other night, looking hidebound and ridiculous. Small wonder. She was defending the city's attempt to close down Cornrows & Co., a beauty salon that specializes in African-style hair braiding, all because the operators are not school-trained and certified in pin-curling, chemical treatments and a host of other techniques the shop never uses.... It looked for all the world as though the members of the Cosmetology Board, almost all of them beauty shop and/or beauty school operators, were more interested in protecting their own interests than in reaching a sensible resolution of the licensing case.[76]

On February 2, 1992, US district judge Stanley Sporkin reluctantly ruled against Taalib, citing an old Supreme Court precedent,[77] but he nevertheless chided the DC City Council for its actions.[78] Stating that he was "very disturbed" by the council's failure to change its regulations, Sporkin wrote, "It is difficult to understand why the District of Columbia wants to put a legitimate business out of operation."[79] He thus urged the district to reconsider the issue:

> Certainly the D.C. Council can exercise sound judgment and common sense to accommodate Plaintiffs' needs... the Court would certainly

> urge the District to consider the plight of Plaintiffs and the good citizens they have faithfully served for over twelve years.[80]

Taalib appealed the decision, but the suit was eventually dropped when, in December 1992, the city council amended the cosmetology law, creating a less onerous and more sensible specialty license just for natural haircare.[81] Although this represented a victory for Taalib and other braiders who would later open shops of their own, it did not come cheap. "I think about all the things I could have done... if I hadn't been so consumed by my struggle just to earn an honest buck," Taalib said ruefully.[82]

Although the issue was settled in DC, in the years after his battle, Taalib's story would play out again and again with the bottleneckers in states across the country, only with different actors and slight variations in circumstance. On October 1, 1997, Cheryll Hosey sued the state of Ohio because it required that hair braiders earn a cosmetology license in order to braid hair for a living. The cosmetology license required about nine months of training at a cost of between $3,000 and $5,000 (at that time) and passing a state test.[83] By the time Cheryll opened her salon in 1996, she had already been braiding for eighteen years, having first learned the skill as a young child. As the years went on, she realized the potential to make braiding a career. "I've had so many family members and friends who said 'braid my hair, braid my hair' that I said, 'I can make this my business.'"[84] And so she did; by the one-year anniversary of her business, she was serving more than two hundred regular customers who kept coming back because she offered a service traditional salons had neither the time nor the skills to offer.[85]

All of this, however, was irrelevant to the Ohio State Board of Cosmetology. The board slapped Cheryll's salon with several legal notices of violation and prevented it from receiving a much-needed small-business loan by telling the lender the salon would not be able to continue operating without a cosmetology license. According to Dave Williamson, then executive director of the board, getting the license was necessary to learn about public health and safety,[86] but that weak justification did not enjoy much support among legislators.

As the lawsuit made its way through federal court, a bill was introduced in the state House and an amendment offered in the Senate to exempt braiding from the cosmetology law. Senator Eric Fingerhut had learned of the plight of braiders trying to make a living and was appalled and sponsored the Senate amendment. “Then in comes the State of Ohio, the same state that just told single women to get off public assistance, to put them out of business,” he said. “I’m outraged by it. I think it’s terrible public policy.”[87] He was not alone. In 1999, the state legislature reformed the cosmetology laws, creating a natural haircare license, thereby making Cheryll’s lawsuit moot.[88]

While Cheryll faced the real possibility of losing her business, braiders in other states were experiencing even-worse trials.[89] In places like Texas and California, investigators, often accompanied by police, threatened to lock braiders up and put them out of business.[90] In October 1997, Dallas police arrested Dana “Isis” Brantley, a single mother of five children, who was running a salon as a way to transition from welfare to work.[91]

As Isis stood in her salon consulting briefly with a prospective client—who turned out to be an undercover officer with the Dallas County Sheriff’s Department—seven more officers rushed in, accompanied by a Texas State Cosmetology Commission inspector, who happened to be a former employee of a nearby cosmetology school. “I was placed in the back of the police car while my clients watched,” Isis recalled. “I have never been so humiliated in all my life.” Things only got worse from there. “I was strip searched, fingerprinted, photographed, and then placed in a holding cell with some really bad people. I just couldn’t believe I was being handcuffed and taken to jail like a common criminal for hair braiding.”[92]

In another crackdown, three undercover investigators from California’s Department of Consumer Affairs, posing as state police officers, staged a sting operation at a popular braiding salon in West Los Angeles on July 1, 1998. Investigator Ayn Lauderdale spent five hours having her hair braided by shop owner Sabrina Reece, then slipped into the bathroom and reappeared in a police jacket, soon to be joined by two more investigators. The three carried guns and rifled through the shop without a warrant, threatening to arrest Reece. After taking photographs and the Social Security numbers of everyone present, the investigators left with the so-called evidence—styling gel, a pair of scissors, a page torn from an appointment book, and a single hair clip—sealed in a plastic baggie. It wasn't Sabrina's first run-in with the state's cosmetology board. The thirty-two-year-old mother of two had been fined the previous year for operating without a license.[93]

The motivation for such-aggressive police action was captured in a statement given to the *Los Angeles Times* by a licensed cosmetologist saying that Sabrina was "a threat to those of us who are licensed and went through the normal channels" and that unlicensed braiders could undercut cosmetologists' earnings.[94] Sabrina herself dismissed any notion of public health and safety concerns in the actions of the police and the state board, observing, "They had to pass a mountain of drug activity at the corner of West Adams to get to me."[95] Instead, she said, the actions were designed to stifle competition.[96]

But observers at the time identified a second reason for the raid on Reece's salon: During the prior year, Dr. JoAnne Cornwell had sued the state of California over the requirement that braiders obtain a cosmetology license to practice. Cornwell, an associate professor of French and Africana studies at San Diego State University, is also a third-generation hairstylist and entrepreneur. Both her mother and grandmother owned hair salons in Detroit, and these businesses allowed them to gain a level of independence unheard of for most black women during that time. Cornwell first learned to braid as a young girl and then in the early 1990s created a new braiding technique called "sisterlocks," using small, finely manicured locks. After trademarking the technique, she designed training materials and led workshops all over the country to teach it to others.

Cornwell then sought to expand her training program by opening her own salon in California, but she chose not to do so since it was illegal for someone who was not a licensed cosmetologist. Expanding her training program would not only have been personally profitable for her; it would also be a way of creating opportunities for black women to pursue entrepreneurship using their cultural heritage of braiding. On January 28, 1997, she sued the California Board of Barbering and Cosmetology, arguing that the cosmetology licensing requirement for African hair braiders violated her rights and the rights of others to pursue their profession free of onerous and unnecessary government regulation.

By July 1998, when the undercover investigators from California's Department of Consumer Affairs raided Sabrina Reece's braiding salon, Cornwell's lawsuit was still ongoing. "That the sting was authorized while the lawsuit filed on behalf of California braiders [was] still pending was a heavy-handed show of authority, rather than a case of pressing public concern," wrote a commentator for the *Village Voice*.[97]

The *Village Voice* was not alone in its skepticism about the need to impose—and enforce—a cosmetology license on hair braiders for the purpose of public safety. On August 19, 1999, US district judge Rudi Brewster struck down California's requirement that African American hairstylists secure a cosmetology license. In a twenty-six-page decision, Brewster wrote, "There are limits to what the State may require before its dictates are deemed arbitrary and irrational."[98] On the basis that only 7 percent of the required training was even "possibly relevant" to hair braiding, the judge ruled that the licensure requirements were "wholly irrelevant to the achievement of the state's objectives," namely protecting public safety.[99] The 1999 ruling confirmed an earlier decision in which the judge concluded that the regulations placed "an almost insurmountable barrier in front of anyone who seeks to practice African hair styling," suggesting that the effect was "to force African hair stylists out of business in favor of mainstream hair stylists and barbers."[100]

BOTTLENECKING INTO THE TWENTY-FIRST CENTURY

Despite such positive decisions and legislative changes, braiders continued, at the dawn of the new century, to find themselves caught in the cosmetology bottleneck. Essence Farmer, an Arizona native, sought to open a hair-braiding salon in her hometown of Glendale. To do so, Essence was required by the state of Arizona to complete a 1,600-hour training program, at an approximate cost of $10,000, to earn a cosmetology license.[101] The skills she needed to run her business, however, she had learned at the age of ten. As a teenager, she began braiding out of her parents' home for money, serving five to six clients a week, some traveling forty miles or more for her services.

As Essence recalled about her early years,

> There were not a lot of braiders at the time, and my client-base grew by word of mouth. Some of my clients were going to California or other long distances to have their hair done, so even though I was a teenager, I had a talent for braiding and clients liked going to someone local.[102]

Essence moved to Maryland in 2000 to attend Prince George's Community College. Because Maryland exempts hair braiders from cosmetology licensing laws, she was able to braid many clients' hair at Blowouts Salon and a barbershop called Hairstons.[103] When she moved back to Arizona in 2003, she began braiding out of her house but soon learned she was doing so illegally. "I was reading an article in a magazine about someone who was arrested for braiding in California," she explained, "and thought, 'That's crazy, why would she be arrested for braiding hair?' But it made me cognizant of the idea that there might be a license in Arizona." In a call to the state cosmetology board, her suspicion was confirmed. Moreover, she was informed that her years of professional experience were not sufficient: "They told me anything that involved touching hair was considered cosmetology and required the full license."[104]

Essence was caught in the bottleneck, but she refused to remain stuck there. "I was discouraged, but I knew something had to be done about this. So I began looking for representation to sue the state board." Her search led her to the Institute for Justice, which had represented Taalib and other braiders before her. In December 2003, Essence sued the state cosmetology board over her right to pursue the occupation of her passion. Her suit never made it to trial.

During the 2004 legislative session, Arizona lawmakers—in direct response to Essence's lawsuit—did what the state board wouldn't: it allowed people to practice the art of hair braiding without a cosmetology license. Representative Deb Gullett took up the cause, tacking the exemption onto a broader measure dealing with mobile cosmetology salons.[105] "It just seemed to me that [forcing braiders to train as cosmetologists] was the stupidest thing that I had ever heard of," recalled Gullett. "And thankfully people agreed with me."[106] On April 12, 2004, the provision passed Arizona's legislature, opening the door for Essence and others to braid freely.

Four months after Arizona's bottleneck was dislodged, Melony Armstrong, a hair braider in Tupelo, Mississippi, sued her state cosmetology board to achieve the same end. Similar to what happened in Arizona, the Mississippi legislature eventually changed the law to allow hair braiders to practice without a cosmetology license, but not before a fierce months-long battle, the roots of which can be traced back to a 1995 hair appointment for Melony.

The $75 appointment lasted about an hour. Melony had never had her hair braided professionally before, but she decided to try something new. One the day of her appointment, she and her husband, Kevin, drove about ninety minutes north into Memphis, the closest braiding salon to their home. While she was getting her hair done, Melony faced away from the mirror and chatted with the friendly stylist as she glanced curiously around the room at the styles other braiders were creating. Upon completion of the relatively simple style, the braider slowly turned her chair to face the mirror. As she did, Melony made a life-changing decision.[107]

"After having my hair braided and looking in the mirror, it immediately clicked—this hair thing, these braids, is what I want to do," Melony remembered. "Even during the process, seeing this is a real live business. On the drive back—and that drive is one-and-a-half hours—it's all I talked about to my husband. I'm going to be a professional hairbraider."[108]

"She's crazy," Kevin thought to himself. They had a toddler at home. Besides Melony's formal education was in psychology; she had worked at a battered women's shelter, a boys' home, and a state hospital. She knew nothing of braiding. Unlike many black women, she had never learned how to braid hair as a child. But she longed to create a business of her own.[109]

"I've always had that entrepreneurial spirit flowing in me," she said. "My mind was clicking, ticking. It was just itching, gnawing at me, to do something else."[110] Melony saw the opportunity braiding presented for the Tupelo area. On the ride home from Memphis, Kevin couldn't get a word in edgewise. Melony was suddenly on a mission that, unbeknownst to either of them at the time, would make headlines.

After a series of workshops, classes, and endless hours of practicing braiding, Melony began working on clients in her home in late 1995—first for free to gain experience and then for a fee. Because she was the only professional braider in the area, clients were drawn to her, especially those once forced to travel for their hairstyling. Melony knew she was on to something. The next step was moving her business outside of her home.[111]

To work as a hair braider in a salon, Melony needed to earn a license. Regulations required 1,200 hours of classes to obtain a cosmetology license. She had neither the time nor the resources to complete so many hours, but she soon discovered that Mississippi also had a largely moribund "wigology" license that required only three hundred hours of training. None of the training covered braiding, but for Melony it was a less costly means to an end.[112] Melony obtained her wigology license and, to prepare herself for her own venture, began working at someone else's salon on Mondays, when she didn't conduct her own cosmetology services. This enabled her to work in a salon setting, which otherwise would not have been possible for her. But she soon tired of walking into someone else's postweekend mess and, with her husband's expertise in construction, started her own salon at a small shop where she also sold natural hair products. She named her business Naturally Speaking and steadily built up a clientele.[113]

Opening her own business was an important first step, but Melony wanted to do more. She felt she had a calling to teach other women not only about the hair-braiding trade but also about how to run a business, so that they could take what they learned from her and go out and support themselves. But, as she quickly realized, to fulfill that calling would require a battle with the bottleneckers.[114] Before allowing her to teach others how to braid hair, the state cosmetology board required that Melony obtain a cosmetology license, then a cosmetology instructor's license (another two thousand hours of class), and finally a school license—none of which would actually teach her anything about braiding. Paradoxically, the state awarded cosmetology instructors who had no experience in braiding licenses to teach braiding, even as it forbade experienced braiders from teaching their craft—unless they were willing to sacrifice three years and thousands of dollars to take a class teaching unrelated skills to earn the license. The result was that students of braiding had no skilled and legal instructors from whom to learn.[115]

For Melony, the injustice was too much. On August 5, 2004, she sued the state of Mississippi to free hair braiding from the cosmetology stranglehold. To protect its bottleneck, the state board introduced a bill in the 2005 legislative session designed to encompass hair braiding under the cosmetology law. Melony responded quickly, finding a sponsor for a bill of her own to exempt braiders from cosmetology regulations. The fight was on.

Throughout the first months of 2005, Melony made weekly seven-hour round-trips to the state capital of Jackson to convince legislators to change the law. She also organized potential braiders to contact lawmakers, responded to opposition from traditional cosmetologists, and engaged in other grassroots efforts, all of which meant spending countless hours away from her family and her business.[116]

In response, the bottleneckers flooded the capitol building, lobbying legislators aggressively for their cause. "The cosmetology industry is very powerful in this state, and they dictated the policy when it came to that industry," explained Senator Hillman Frazier.[117]

"Literally for, I'm going to say, at least a week, maybe 10 days of that 90-day session, the Capitol was consumed by cosmetologists," recalled Representative Steve Holland.[118]

And it was not just fully licensed cosmetologists; cosmetology students, too, were among the crowd, sent there by their schools. "Cosmetology students... were actually told, 'In order to receive your hours for today, be at the Capitol.' Some of them had no idea why they were even there," Melony reported.[119]

The showdown finally occurred in a hearing before the House Public Health and Human Services Committee, chaired by Representative Holland, in which the cosmetologists' bill to regulate hair braiders was considered. "I bet a thousand cosmetologists showed up, and they were not nice, let's just leave it at that," said Holland.[120] Committee members heard all interested parties throughout the contentious meeting, but it became clear that the need to regulate hair braiders as cosmetologists was illusory. Instead, the bottleneckers were working to maintain their monopoly on hair care. Nevertheless, pressure on Holland to pass the bill out of committee continued.

"In the end, the Senate chairman even came down pretty hard on me," remembered Holland, who then said,

> Look, it's just real simple, I do not give a damn whether there is a cosmetology law in the state of Mississippi or not, so don't you come back to my office. It is over, do you understand? I will not put braiding in the law.[121]

And that was the end of it.

Meanwhile, Melony's bill made it through the House but ran into trouble in the Senate, where the Public Health Committee voted almost along racial lines to maintain the licensing requirement for braiding. Most of the committee's white senators voted to sustain the license.[122] The only crossover was one white senator, Hob Bryan, who voted with the five black senators to deregulate braiding. The bill was eventually sent to a conference committee, and on April 19, 2005, all of Melony's efforts paid off: Mississippi governor Haley Barbour signed legislation enabling hair braiders to practice their occupation without being required to take 1,200 hours of class to get a cosmetology license or 300 hours of class to get a wigology license. Currently, the only requirements are that hair braiders pay a small fee to register with the state and abide by all relevant health and hygiene codes.[123]

It is the latter requirement, in fact, that represents the one thing all parties have agreed on—at least rhetorically—during the decades-long hair wars. When Taalib's story made national news on ABC's *20/20*, William Raspberry asked, "Why couldn't [the cosmetology board] just make sure the place was kept safe, clean and sanitary for its customers?"[124] In response, Taalib agreed: "I don't have any problem with government wanting to protect public health and safety."[125] And when Dr. Cornwell sued the state of California, she argued from the beginning that braiding salons should be subject to applicable health standards,[126] something even many braiders believe might be justified to include in mandatory training.[127]

Courts have come to the same conclusion. In April 2005, Lillian Anderson, an immigrant from Cameroon, sued the state of Minnesota over its requirement that braiders earn a cosmetology license to practice. Lillian first learned to braid in a local school in Buea, Cameroon. When she was a teenager, Lillian and her two sisters would sit in a circle and braid one another's hair to practice their skills.[128] After arriving in the United States in 1993, Lillian began braiding to support herself. By 1998, she was operating her own salon that served a loyal clientele of men and women of all races.[129] But in doing so without a license, she was subject to up to $1,000 in fines and ninety days in jail, not to mention the stigma associated with breaking the law.[130]

It was the latter she found most vexing. She wanted to make an honest living, but she simply could not agree to complete irrelevant training. "Why should I have to pay when they don't even teach this craft?" asked Lillian. "I learned everything I know as a little girl, sitting with my sisters, braiding in a circle."[131] In a judgment made on June 6, 2005, Judge Isabel Gomez vindicated her. In the thirty-two-page decree, the judge described in detail the content of cosmetology schooling and noted that none of it included training related to hair braiding. She also noted that if at some point in the future the state board were to enact genuine health and safety standards relevant to braiders, the court would deem these appropriate.[132]

Although leaders in the cosmetology industry similarly point to a need for training to protect public health and safety, they do so for strategic reasons. As Judge Brewster's ruling illustrates, courts evaluate laws such as these based, in part, on intention and effect. Laws that are intended to protect public health and safety, and that are successful in doing so, are often upheld. On the other hand, laws whose primary purpose is or appears to be using state power for the purpose of giving one group an economic advantage are more likely to be struck down.

To fulfill the court's criteria, industry leaders justify training requirements by rolling out the aforementioned parade of horribles. Where cosmetology bottleneckers diverge from others in this regard is in the amount of training time they believe is required to protect against disease and injury stemming from poor sanitation. As a house editorial in the *Las Vegas Review-Journal* asked,

> Some states require up to 2,100 hours of study... at considerable expense... to acquire a cosmetology license. And even if it were true that a cosmetology school diploma guarantees the holder will never engage in unsanitary practices—it doesn't—does anyone really need 2,100 hours, or even the "compromise" 300 hours now required to become a licensed "natural hair stylist" in Tennessee, to learn the importance of basic hygiene?[133]

Indeed, from the perspective of many observers, the only regulatory requirement that is necessary for braiders is spending enough hours in training to learn proper sanitation, and nothing else.[134]

But for all of the industry leaders' talk, it is cosmetologists themselves who most aptly describe the motivation behind their licensing schemes. "If we have to take a minimum of 1,200 curriculum hours and pay up to $10,000 to learn our trade, why shouldn't braiders?" one licensed cosmetologist asked.[135] When Essence Farmer sued the state of Arizona, cosmetologists there reacted similarly. "We have to pay for our licenses to be trained to do things and just because [hair braiding is] the only thing she wants to do [doesn't mean she should be exempt]," said Arizona Academy of Beauty instructor Elaine Rucker. "We have to undergo training and we pay for our licenses. If people start getting exemptions, what's left for the rest of us?"[136]

Another reason that cosmetology schools are reluctant to support exemptions for hair braiders is because the licensing requirements mean big business for them. At the time, JoAnne Cornwell was suing the California state board, for example, total cosmetology classroom revenues and test admission fees came to $544 million in California.[137] Practicing cosmetologists and the state boards that represent their interests perceive an economic threat from braiders.[138] As Taalib explained, "Traditional cosmetologists are feeling the financial pinch of a rising and popular hairstyle.... In the effort to recover lost income, they are pressuring states to act as police agents for their cartels."[139] Indeed, some estimates put the size of the cosmetology industry at more than $20 billion in annual sales, generated by the more than seventy-five thousand salons and approximately half-a-million workers.[140]

Thus, bottleneckers defend their economic interests to the point of legal threats, fines, and armed police raids. "Regulations are more likely to be broadened by those who administer them than to be removed when they cease to serve a useful purpose," observed the *Orange County Register*.[141] Such broadening can occur stealthily through license creep, as when cosmetology has swallowed hair braiding, or it can be pursued more openly, such as by requiring licensure in an industry where the relationship between regulation and public health and safety is tenuous. Such an industry is the one focused on in the next chapter on interior design.

CHAPTER 4

Designed to Exclude

The Interior Design Cartel's House of Lies

In 2006, Sherry Franzoy owned and operated an interior design firm in Las Cruces, New Mexico. The trouble was, by state law, she couldn't tell anyone.

At the time, New Mexico enforced a "titling" law, which allowed anyone in the state to provide interior design services but restricted the use of the title "interior designer" and the words "interior design" to those with a government-issued license. To earn the license, would-be interior designers were required to complete a minimum of two years of post-high school education, possess a combination of six years of education and experience in interior design, and pass an exam. Because she lacked some of the necessary credentials, Sherry could not tell anyone of her interior design work through advertising, business cards, or even casual conversation.

Her lack of credentials did not mean Sherry had entered the business completely untrained, however. As a young girl, she'd dreamed of working as an interior designer.[1] But when she married, began raising children, and started managing the business operations of a family farm in New Mexico, her dreams of being a designer faded—until life circumstances intervened. When she and her husband divorced, Sherry needed to find a way to support herself. She worked as a produce broker for a year to make ends meet, but her childhood dream remained in the back of her mind. When she explored the idea further, she came across a business franchise opportunity called Decorating Den Interiors.[2] It was a prospect tailor-made for Sherry.

Founded in 1969, Decorating Den Interiors employs interior design professionals throughout the United States and Canada.[3] Its work has been featured in *Good Housekeeping*, *Better Homes and Gardens*, *Woman's Day*, *House Beautiful*, and *House and Garden*. In addition, the company has been featured in a variety of design segments on HGTV and the Discovery Channel.[4]

Decorating Den Interiors franchises are full-service businesses that specialize in complimentary, "we come to you" interior design consultations and sell everything needed to make a room over from floor to ceiling. Important to Sherry, purchasing a franchise came with intensive, condensed schooling on the intricacies of both managing a business and practicing interior design. Before being allowed to start her franchise, the company required Sherry to pass five rigorous tests covering the spectrum of operating an interior design business, including tests on interior design work, people skills, finance, entrepreneurship, and business math. Sherry passed the tests and opened her franchise in 2000. By 2006, she was managing a thriving business with a stable of subcontractors and clients from all over the country. Many of her clients have been East or West Coast transplants who lack the know-how of designing their homes in the Southwestern style that characterizes New Mexico. Sherry has provided these clients with design services ranging from window treatments to kitchen and bath remodels in homes valued from the mid-$200,000s to more than $1,000,000.

Despite her success, in 2006, if she had told anyone that she worked as an interior designer, she would have been violating state law. And New Mexico was not alone in restricting people's right to talk about their profession. Six other states also restricted the use of the title interior designer, and the requirements for gaining use of it were almost identical across the states. To that were added sixteen other states that prohibited the use of other similar titles such as "certified interior designer" or "registered interior designer," all on the basis of education and examination requirements similar to New Mexico's. The presence of titling laws with similar requirements across the states was no coincidence. It was the result of a scheme of national regulation traceable back to yet another group of bottleneckers—the American Society of Interior Designers.[5]

The roots of the American Society of Interior Designers (ASID) reach back to the early 1930s, when it was known as the Association of Interior Designers (AID), and previously to the Association of Interior Decorators,[6] which operated as a professional association for the emerging interior design industry. Even then, some in the trade pushed for regulation, but the industry rejected it as unnecessary.[7] With the building boom after World War II, the 1950s saw rapid growth in the interior design industry,[8] and with it the formation of a second influential association, the National Society of Interior Designers (NSID), and the beginning of a serious push for regulation of the industry.[9]

The movement for regulation accelerated in the 1960s, culminating in the 1968 introduction of licensing bills in California, New York, Massachusetts, and Texas.[10] Although they were rival organizations, AID and NSID worked in concert to advance licensing.[11] Relying on a key bottlenecker trope, industry leaders asserted that "there ha[s]to be a set of standards to protect the public,"[12] but their economic motivation was plain to see. As the *Boston Globe* put it at the time, Massachusetts's bill was designed to stop "amateurs" from "undercut[ting] the professional by selling at a lower margin of profit."[13]

Support for regulation was not, however, unanimous within the industry. Many working designers believed accreditation would be adequate to protect consumers.[14] Others portrayed licensure as "professionally unnecessary" and best left to occupations that required science and mathematical skills, like architecture, as a former chairman of NSID later wrote to the *New York Times*.[15] With the industry divided on regulation, none of the bills passed into law.

Upon the legislative failure, AID and NSID regrouped to better organize their efforts. They began by merging in 1975 to form ASID, becoming, with thirteen thousand members, the world's largest interior design association.[16] According to one commentator, the new organization "consider[ed] itself an exclusive group" in which "membership to frustrated housewives and exiled princesses [was] not available on demand."[17]

The core of ASID's efforts was the development of model legislation—funded by a $13,000 grant from the National Endowment for the

Arts[18]—and a detailed plan for a state-by-state campaign to regulate interior designers.[19] The plan called for the "establishment and maintenance of a state-wide interior design society in each state where none now exists. The state society should be the vehicle for conducting the legislative program and public dialogue on the licensing issue."[20] The guidelines also stressed the importance of determining how to raise and distribute funds, producing "educational" (i.e., lobbying) materials for use by legislators, conducting personal lobbying, establishing priority states, and coordinating the effort nationally.[21]

ASID wasted no time in implementing the recommendations. In 1976, in an attempt to coordinate efforts, it adopted a policy that required state chapters to seek permission from the national organization to pursue regulation in their respective states. That same year, the Florida chapter was granted permission to do so.[22] Four years later, ASID established a state legislative network to equip state chapters in licensing efforts.[23] The creation of the state network coincided with plans for a national campaign, kicked off in 1985, to support state-by-state regulation of interior designers. ASID announced the start of the campaign at a well-attended press conference, with its then president, Gail Hayes Adams, declaring, "In our role as the leader of the design profession, ASID has declared title registration its top priority in 1986."[24] The campaign included training and resources provided to state chapters by the national organization and the commitment of $275,000 in the first year alone to fund the efforts.[25] By then, ASID could count twenty-eight thousand of the nation's two hundred thousand interior designers among its membership.[26]

The campaign's launch was aided by the fact that three states had already adopted titling laws, one in each of the three preceding years—Alabama in 1982, Connecticut in 1983, and Louisiana in 1984.[27] The experience of working with the state chapters, which had in each case been instrumental in the adoption of legislation, was invaluable for the national ASID organization, as it worked to craft and implement the national campaign.

The first state to adopt a titling law as a result of the national campaign—and after years of lobbying on the part of its ASID chapter—was Florida in 1988.[28] New Mexico followed a year later, also as a result of intensive campaigning by the national and state divisions of the ASID.[29]

Apart from Florida the other states that adopted titling laws throughout the 1980s were small, but 1990 saw three of the nation's largest states take up such regulations—California, Illinois, and New York.[30] New York's passage of the bill was particularly noteworthy, given New York City's status as the fashion-and-design capital and the onerous certification requirements—a minimum of seven years of education and training and two examinations.[31] This victory for the bottleneckers came as a result of a vigorous five-year campaign by a coalition of four design associations led by the state ASID chapter with support from New York City's Office of Business Development.[32]

Whereas most of ASID's efforts were focused on title acts, 1987 saw Washington, DC, pass the nation's first practice act under the influence of ASID.[33] Practice acts go a step further than titling laws, legally restricting interior design work to those who have earned a license, the requirements of which are often the same as those of title acts. As with the title acts in New York and other states, the practice act in Washington, DC, came about after years of intense pressure from the interior design community.

In 1983, an interior design coalition had formed in DC with the initial goal of achieving a titling law.[34] The coalition included members of ASID and other design organizations,[35] nonaffiliated designers, and educators and students from area colleges and universities with interior design programs.[36] It hired an attorney to craft a bill and focused its lobbying efforts on the mayor and nine members of the city council.[37] The lobbying effort required the coalition to remain active in DC's political process and to donate to individual council members' election campaigns.[38] Even the manner in which the coalition donated to political campaigns was strategic: it maximized the number of people donating and presented them in such a way as to suggest a greater constituency. As one leader of the coalition explained, "It demonstrated the breadth of the support, so it was better to have a list of 100 donors rather than two big contributors."[39]

Similarly, when the proposed bill entered a phase for review by a council committee, numerous coalition members testified at a contentious public hearing about the need to protect public health and safety by regulating interior designers.[40] Their assertions were refuted by city officials, among others. Deputy Mayor Carol Thompson, then director of the Department of Consumer and Regulatory Affairs, told the council that licensing designers was unnecessary and redundant: "This industry does not provide services... essential to the well-being of the residents of the District of Columbia."[41] Likewise, Valerie Barry, head of the Occupational and Professional Licensure Administration, opposed the measure, calling it an "unnecessary government intervention."[42]

Nevertheless, after the hearing, council member John Wilson changed the bill from a titling law to a practice act, citing the need to better protect the public. Based on the committee's approval, council members approved the bill on the first vote in October 1987. The congressional review approved the bill, and the mayor signed it into law.[43] Upon the law's adoption, a five-member board was created, composed almost entirely of bottleneckers. The membership included three interior designers, one interior design educator, and one consumer, all appointed by the mayor.[44]

The payoff for the bottleneckers was immediate. One of the first appointees to the board was Martha Cathcart, the president of a local interior design firm and an active member of the coalition that had lobbied for the bill's creation.[45] Designers also saw the new Washington, DC, practice act as a momentum builder. At the time of its passage, almost two dozen other states were considering interior design regulation,[46] and design activists were hopeful about the DC bill's effect. As one regulation proponent said, "It's a long, uphill battle.... Hopefully, this will have a domino effect."[47]

Whether DC's law actually set a domino effect in motion is unknown, but the rapid pace with which states began to adopt interior design regulations suggests that it may indeed have done so. Between 1991 and 2002, eleven states passed titling laws, and three instituted practice acts. Although design regulation enthusiasts chalked the new legislation up to an increased awareness among consumers and legislators "about interior designers' responsibilities for the public's health, safety, and welfare,"[48] the true impetus was relentless lobbying by the bottleneckers. This can be seen in the example of Alabama converting its titling law into a practice act in 2001, upon which a leader in the state's design coalition acknowledged the efforts by state activists in support of the transition and also noted that "it was ASID that provided the constant focus for us and kept us steady in our efforts until we were successful."[49] And when New Jersey created its titling law in 2002, a coalition leader said,

> I am not sure we would have achieved passage of the [bill] without the help of ASID. Through training sessions, lobbying templates, financial support and links to a nationwide network of politically knowledgeable designers who helped establish legislation in their respective states, ASID buoyed a committed group of New Jersey volunteers during a 10-year voyage to certification.[50]

Multiyear efforts like New Jersey's were common. Virginia's 1990 titling law, for example, came about after an eight-year campaign.[51] A coalition had formed in Virginia in the early 1980s to begin lobbying for a bill sponsoring certification of interior designers.[52] It hired attorney and lobbyist Mark Rubin, who had recently succeeded in achieving licensure for landscape architects.[53] The interior design coalition worked with Rubin to draft legislation, identify bill sponsors, and monitor the timing of bills.[54]

Simultaneously, the coalition organized a grassroots lobbying effort. Lacking substantial funds to donate to legislators' campaigns, it instead relied on its wide support base of interior designers to engage in grassroots lobbying, which Rubin had trained it to do.[55] After the national ASID organization began its campaign in 1985, the Virginia coalition benefitted from its substantive legislative materials and resources for lawmakers. One coalition member recalled that the new resources enabled the group to go to their first legislative hearing "loaded for bear."[56]

Nonetheless, Rubin paid close attention to legislators' support and had to pull the bill from consideration in 1986 and again in 1988, when it lacked the requisite number of votes to pass.[57] The bill was brought back in 1990, at which point the coalition took advantage of three nursing home fires that had happened in Virginia that year to generate support for the legislation, with one coalition leader saying, "Nobody wants a disaster, [but] if it happens, grab-a-hold of it."[58]

In addition to exploiting nursing home fires for their benefit, state and national members of ASID poured resources into the 1990 licensing push. Financial aid from the national organization paid for Rubin's lobbying, representatives from ASID provided guidance and training to the state coalition, and the national office monitored all the bills in the legislature to alert the committee of other proposed legislation that might threaten the Virginia licensing act.[59] After almost a decade of relentless petitioning, the designers received their titling law in 1990.

One of the primary reasons it took so long for design coalitions like those in Virginia, Washington, DC, and other places to win the law was that the need for regulation was far from self-evident. Although proponents of regulation euphemistically cite the requirement of having to "educate" legislators about the law's importance as a reason for the repeated attempts to pass it,[60] the intensive lobbying, political campaign contributions, and politicking tell a different story. In fact, when the costs and benefits of interior design regulation have undergone genuine scrutiny, results indicate that it carries significant costs for consumers with benefits accruing for only one group—licensed interior designers.

A 2009 analysis at the University of Minnesota examined insurance premiums and fire death rates as indications of the need for regulation of the interior design industry on public health and safety grounds. The researchers found no evidence that licensing would provide any measurable benefit in these respects.[61] They did, however, find that interior designers' wages were consistently greater in states with more restrictive regulation of the occupation. For consumers, this translates to greater costs, as the regulation enables practitioners to charge more for their services—as reflected in higher wages—in the face of less competition.

A separate analysis completed in the same year by two economists at Kenyon College found similar results.[62] Drawing upon national census data, the authors found that in states where the interior design profession is regulated, consumers pay higher prices for design services; fewer entrepreneurs are able to enter the market; and blacks, Hispanics, and those wishing to switch careers later in life are disproportionately excluded from the field.

These two studies are only the latest in a series of examinations of the interior design occupation. An earlier study done in 2008 compared the complaint data for interior designers in states with stringent regulation of interior design to the data for states with lighter or no regulation.[63] Complaint data here acted as a measure of the quality of service, with regulation proponents frequently asserting that licensing would result in higher quality among regulated practitioners. Results from the study found that states with no or less-stringent licensing regulations did not have more complaints than those with stricter regulations.

State agencies, too, have examined the need for interior design licensing and consistently found it lacking. Throughout the 1990s and 2000s, as ASID fomented its wave of title and practice acts, several states completed "sunrise" reviews—legislatively mandated processes designed to ensure that proposed regulations are really necessary for the protection of the public interest. It is common for state agencies to complete the reviews and present the results to the legislature in sunrise reports. The reviewers typically look for threats to the public from the unregulated practice of an occupation, weigh the costs of regulations, invite input from interested parties, explore regulatory alternatives, analyze the findings, and make recommendations—the first and foremost of which is on whether regulation is even necessary and, if so, what shape it should take. A related document is the "sunset" review, which examines an existing license or regulation to determine if its continuation is necessary. The review processes are often similar, with the primary difference being their timing.

These reports can be—or at least should be—particularly helpful to part-time legislators elected to office from widely divergent backgrounds. Few of them are likely to arrive at their legislative posts with expertise or experience in general occupational regulation or with detailed knowledge of particular occupations. Term limits also mean that legislators who do develop such expertise do not remain in the legislature longer than a few terms, after which they are typically replaced by novice lawmakers. These dynamics, joined by the near-constant campaigning required of many state legislators, whose terms span only two years per election cycle, and the intensely local nature of state politics, also make legislators comparatively more vulnerable to interest groups like ASID and other professional associations. They also increase the role of state agencies and legislative staff in informing regulatory decisions, such as through sunrise or sunset reports.

In the case of interior design, five states—Colorado, Georgia, South Carolina, Virginia, and Washington—have produced sunrise reports.[64] Without exception, none of these reports found sufficient and reliable evidence to suggest that harm occurs as a result of unregulated interior designers. Moreover, when given the chance to provide such evidence for the reports, interior design associations either could not produce any[65] or else could only produce complaints pertaining to the practice of unlicensed interior design in which no actual harm was alleged.[66] The reports further found that means were already in place to ensure the quality of interior designers' work and failed to identify any economic benefit to the public from such regulations. All of the reports ultimately recommended against titling laws in their respective states. Added to these sunrise reports were sunset reviews in three states—California, Maryland, and Texas—that came to the same conclusions, recommending the elimination of existing interior design regulations.[67]

And, on a few occasions, even governors have seen through the bottleneckers' public health and safety rhetoric, vetoing bills to regulate the occupation. In Ohio, for example, former governor George Voinovich vetoed enabling legislation in 1992, saying:

> After carefully reviewing Senate Bill 75, it does not appear to me that it addresses a significant health and safety issue.... Rather, it would appear that the registration requirements... follow the traditional model of professional licensing standards which often have anti-competitive affects [sic] and ultimately, lead to increased cost to consumers.... Senate Bill 75 furthers an already bad precedent of continuing to expand the well over 400 separate Boards and Commissions in Ohio.[68]

Six years later, when ASID tried again to pass the bill, the governor's administration signaled its continued opposition. "Our primary concern is that this is needless regulation, and that supporters have not demonstrated adequate health and safety concerns exist," said Bill Teets, then public affairs officer for the Department of Commerce.[69]

And, in Indiana in 2007, then governor Mitch Daniels vetoed a bill that was multiple years in the making by the Indiana Interior Design Legislative Task Force, led by the state ASID chapter. After several bills had died in committee over the years,[70] the coalition finally saw its legislation adopted by the legislature, only for it to be vetoed by Daniels in a strongly worded text:

> I can find no compelling public interest that is served by the establishment of new registration requirements for interior designers...nor in the bill's effective "criminalization" of violations of such registration requirements. Indeed, it seems to me that the principal effect of [the bill] will be to restrain competition and limit new entrants into the occupation by requiring that they meet new educational and experience qualifications previously not necessary to practice their trade.... [This bill] is an example of government intrusion into the private marketplace, unnecessarily expanding the power and reach of a professional regulatory board (of which we have for too many already), and protecting the "ins" at the expense of would-be competitors. The marketplace already serves as an effective check on poor performance; designers doing inadequate work are more likely to be penalized by negative customer reaction than by a government agency trying to enforce arbitrary and subjective qualification standards.[71]

That same year, Colorado governor Bill Ritter vetoed a voluntary registration scheme for interior designers, concluding: "This regulation does not have a public safety element....I believe that it is inappropriate to use powers of the state to provide the type of additional recognition provided for in [this bill]."[72]

As the veto messages and sunrise reports demonstrate, a common concern among policy makers is the relationship between licensing interior designers and protecting public health and safety. Like hair braiders, funeral directors, and every other brand of bottlenecker, interior designers portray their desired regulation as being in the interest of the public. When the Texas Association for Interior Design lobbied for its titling law, for example, the group's president insisted that the regulation was a safety issue.[73] And New York's titling law was hailed as an official demonstration that the effects of the work of designers extended beyond aesthetics into public health and safety.[74]

But just as rank-and-file cosmetologists let slip the true motivations behind their desire to see hair braiding covered by cosmetology licensure, interior designers have revealed that the real reason behind the push for licensure of their industry is their desire for legitimacy and professional recognition.[75] "There's been a lack of credibility," said a Manhattan interior designer who supported New York's licensing bill. "A segment of the population still thinks of us as glorified shoppers."[76] Another New York designer said, "I think [regulation is] a very good thing. This will divide the real workers from the 'social' workers."[77] Similarly, after Washington, DC, adopted its practice act, a locally based designer concluded, "The impact of the practice act has been major for interior design in DC. It raised the level of acceptance and level of authority."[78]

In 2006, the scope of that professional authority reached the high watermark of twenty-six states when Oklahoma adopted a titling law after twenty years of lobbying efforts.[79] The official line was, again, that licensure was necessary to protect public health and safety,[80] but, as in other campaigns, designers in this campaign revealed their true motivations. Kim Paddleford, who was then the president elect of the Oklahoma ASID chapter, noted the actual motivation behind titling, in her description of the desired result of the state's universities enrolling seven hundred students in interior design programs: "We're trying to keep our students that we educate in our state. We wanted legal recognition for the profession to encourage our students to stay."[81]

Oklahoma's law rewarded two decades of efforts by the interior design bottleneckers to fence off an ever-larger territory. By the early 2000s, ASID was dedicating significant resources to that quest. Its legislative activities were led by a full-time government and public affairs staff that included three lobbyists registered with the US House of Representatives and US Senate.[82] At the federal level, ASID legislative staff campaigned aggressively before numerous agencies, pushing for additional legislation and advocating for professional legitimacy, but because licensing is chiefly a state issue, the society's primary efforts were dedicated to spearheading the fight for new state laws.[83]

ASID's legislative staff primed the pump for new state laws by actively educating members on legislation and encouraging participation in legislative efforts. The education included legislative strategies, legislative training sessions, quarterly newsletters and updates, and tools to lobby legislators.[84] Staff members also wrote model legislation and provided day-to-day support for interior design legislative coalitions working in the states.[85] And, like the bottleneckers of every industry, ASID spent millions of dollars to erect legislative fences around the occupation. By 2007, the society had donated more than $5 million to legislative efforts,[86] and from 2010 to 2012, it added more than $650,000 to that total, all of which was dedicated to lobbying and legislative expenses and grants to state-level affiliates for the same.[87]

The effect was severe. In the early 1990s, only 36 percent of interior designers were subject to state regulations of one type or another. By 2007, that number stood at more than 60 percent.[88] It was right about then that New Mexico interior designer Sherry Franzoy began to push back against the rising tide.

In 2006, Sherry was five years into her growing business, and New Mexico's seventeen-year-old titling law was having its intended effect. She could advertise her work but not with the term "interior designer." She was forced to find other words or phrases, such as "interior decorator." Although the difference may seem one of mere semantics, the consequences were quite real. "Interior designer" was and remains the more common vernacular, helped along by popular design magazines and entire television networks. And if potential clients went to the phone book looking for interior designers, they would not, by law, find Sherry there.

So in September 2006, Sherry sued the state of New Mexico, arguing that the titling law violated her First Amendment right to tell others truthfully what she did for a living. The approach was unique, particularly compared to other lawsuits concerning licensing laws. In the context of economic liberty, courts frequently prove overly deferential to other branches of government and the regulations they create, resulting in, among other nonsensical rules, the requirement to earn a funeral director's license to sell caskets. But this is not so in the context of freedom of speech. In cases where the latter is alleged to be infringed upon, courts scrutinize laws much more closely, requiring governments to provide sufficient justification and evidence of the need for a law before regulating citizens' speech. Because New Mexico regulated what interior designers could say rather than what they could do—that is, it had a titling law, not a practice act—Sherry could sue the state under the First Amendment, thereby triggering greater scrutiny by the court.

The distinction was not lost on the state's interior design board or legislators. Facing a real possibility that their regulation would be thrown out entirely by the court, state leaders moved quickly to reduce their law's restrictiveness in order to preserve its existence. In January 2007, a bill was introduced in the state legislature to change the titling law so that it restricted the use of the title "licensed interior designer" to those who completed the mandatory requirements and allowed anyone to use the broader term "interior designer."

On the heels of the bill's introduction came a fiscal note. In many state legislatures, representatives or senators can request an analysis of the estimated fiscal effect of proposed legislation. The resulting report is called a fiscal note, the results of which often proves decisive in a bill's fate.[89] Although such analyses focus primarily on budgetary matters, they can sometimes include nonfiscal issues. This was precisely the case with Sherry's case in New Mexico.

After identifying no fiscal impact from the bill, the fiscal note observed that "the Interior Design Act is open for constitutional challenge and could ultimately be determined unconstitutional and therefore invalid." It consequently recommended that "to avoid litigation on the constitutionality of the Interior Design Act, the term Interior Designer needs to be defined as a 'licensed interior designer.'"[90] The bill subsequently sailed through the legislature, with unanimous votes in four separate committees, approval by both chambers, and Governor Richardson's signature on April 3, 2007. Although not a complete repeal of the regulation, the change significantly reduced the interior design bottleneckers' power to fence off their competitors in New Mexico.

Sherry quickly capitalized on the change and began advertising—accurately—as an interior designer, and her renown grew. She was cited in local newspapers as an expert on interior design[91] and featured in home-and-garden shows in New Mexico.[92] In 2009, she won an international design award in a room makeover competition.[93] Four years later, she received an award for being among the top forty sales producers at the Interiors by Decorating Den company.[94] This success led to Sherry receiving appointments to top leadership positions within the company a year later.[95] Such was the result of the freedom provided to her and others throughout New Mexico.

Next door in Texas, however, that same freedom came only after a long-fought battle that almost resulted in the regulation of not only the title but also the practice of interior design. Signed into law by Governor

Ann Richards on June 15, 1991, following a seven-year campaign, Texas's titling law was part of the wave of such laws that ASID pushed across the country.[96] Just like in New Mexico and other states, only those who completed the education, training, and examination requirements were allowed to use the title interior designer. Breaking the law was punishable by as much as $5,000.[97]

Not content with regulating just the interior designer title, in the early 2000s the Texas chapter of ASID began working to elevate the titling law into a practice act.[98] Over three successive legislative sessions, beginning in 2003, a practice act bill was introduced. In 2003 and 2005—the Texas legislature meets every other year—the bills failed to advance beyond committee hearings,[99] but on April 18, 2007, the Texas House Licensing and Regulation Committee passed House Bill 1985 to regulate the practice of interior design. Simultaneously, a companion bill was making its way through the Texas Senate.[100]

Resistance to the bill was fierce. An estimated ten thousand people practicing interior design—although not calling themselves interior designers—stood to lose their livelihoods. In addition, the interior design wholesalers who provided products to those thousands of practitioners were threatened. The hundred design showrooms in Dallas, fifty in Houston, ten in Austin, and others scattered around the state saw approximately 80 percent of their business come from unregulated designers.[101] As then president of the Interior Decorators of Texas, Donna Stockton-Hicks, said at the time,

> This would severely hurt the wholesale business in Texas.... With the wording "criminal penalties," it will scare many smaller decorating businesses to close. With the number of bills being pushed through this session, it could easily be passed and put thousands of decorators, wholesalers, workrooms that make draperies and bedding, installers, wallpaperers, faux painters, etc., at a huge risk to lose much of their business. This will also eliminate a lower-cost alternative to those seeking design help.[102]

Many of those threatened by the bill jumped into action to protest, and Stockton-Hicks hired government affairs firms and lobbyists to stop the bill.[103]

Meanwhile, Vickee Byrum was opening a second front in Texas's interior design range war. When the war erupted in 2007, Vickee was operating her own interior design firm in Austin. However, without the required license, lest she run afoul of the titling law, she couldn't tell anyone about it. Despite this limitation, she was running a successful firm that she, like Sherry Franzoy, had built from the ground up after a midlife career change.

Vickee's first exposure to the design world—and her realization that she had a flair for interior design—came when she bought her first house. At the time, Vickee worked in sales for FedEx, and she was good at it. During her final year with FedEx, she was number one in sales nationwide. Then came the purchase of her first house and an accidental discovery of her hidden talent. "I hired someone to help me design my house, and in working with her I discovered I had a real knack for this. And more than that, I had a burning passion to do more of it," she explained.[104] So, Vickee dedicated herself to learning more about interior design—reading about it, attending design shows, and spending time with designers.

Coupled with that exploration, Vickee started her family and began thinking about what type of mother she wanted to be: "I wanted to be a hands-on mother. But because I traveled so much, I needed to make a change."[105] Not coincidentally, that change found her working first as a bookkeeper for an interior design firm, then as an assistant to the firm's owner. This job provided her hands-on experience and an opportunity to hone both her newfound talent and her passion for design.

After a few years, Vickee started her own interior design business, eventually building a clientele in Texas, Colorado, Utah, and Massachusetts. The quality of her work speaks for itself: 80 percent of her customer base is long-term clients. For Vickee, interior design is not just her job; it's her passion. She effused, "I absolutely love it. I never grow tired of it. I love the change, the color, the design, and most of all I enjoy creating a nest for someone or for families. That's what I do."[106] In 2007, although she could do her job, she could not tell people what it was, as a result of the state's titling laws.

Fed up with the restriction on her right to speak truthfully about what she did for a living, and to engage in as basic a business need as advertising, she sued the state on May 9, 2007, arguing that Texas's titling law violated her freedom of speech. Just hours after she filed her lawsuit, the Texas State House of Representatives killed ASID's practice act, after heavy lobbying by bill proponents and opponents.[107] Still stinging from the defeat, state ASID leaders and their allies in the Texas State Board of Architectural Examiners, which oversaw the interior design titling law, shifted their efforts to defending against Vickee's challenge to the regulation.

Over the course of the next two years, the board and the state attorney general's office tried to justify a scheme that would restrict people who lawfully performed interior design work from calling themselves "interior designers." For their part, ASID representatives spoke frequently in public about the need for the law, essentially parroting the position the state was taking in its defense. As Donna Vining, executive director of Texas ASID, described it, "The citizens of Texas know that when they hire an 'interior designer' in Texas, that person meets the professional standards of education, examination and experience."[108] The problem was, that wasn't true.

Like other states that created interior design regulations, Texas's titling law included a grandfathering provision. When the titling law was adopted, the provision exempted anyone already practicing interior design from the new law. This enabled such individuals to continue using the appellation "interior designer," even though they may have failed to meet the newly imposed education and training requirements. Practically speaking, this meant Vining's statement was false.

Nevertheless, the state continued to defend its law by saying the inherent definition of an interior designer is a person who has completed six years of education and experience and passed an examination. Yet research findings presented by experts in Vickee's court case proved that the public thought otherwise. First, a researcher had asked a sample of 1,400 respondents in regulated Texas and unregulated Ohio a series of questions designed to determine how they defined the term interior designer.[109] If the estimations of the state and ASID were correct, study participants would consistently identify education, experience, and examination as the defining characteristics of an interior designer, as compared to, say, the nature of work one does as a designer. Second, a study had been conducted examining a sample of prominent interior design trade publications to determine the extent to which they paid any attention to state-mandated requirements when identifying practitioners as interior designers.

The results completely undermined the state's and ASID's assertions. The survey of 1,400 participants indicated that the public does not associate the term interior designer with someone who has the qualifications of completing a specialized education, apprenticeship, and exam. Instead, the public thinks that interior designers, first and foremost, design interiors. Moreover, leading interior design publications pay no attention to state-mandated qualifications when they refer to people as interior designers.

To provide "ammunition" to the state in defending the bottleneckers' law, Marilyn Roberts, the president of the Texas Association for Interior Design (TAID), an ASID affiliate, sent an urgent e-mail to members on June 6, 2007:

> We must get cases of harm in Texas!!!!!!! Any jobs you have had that you have corrected something potentially or proven harmful to your clients (harmful physically or emotionally). Any contacts you have with building plan reviewers, Registered Accessibility Specialists, inspectors, fire marshalls [sic], inspectors of any kind that would have found violations that hopefully a registered interior designer corrected. Would help to have cases from residential, commercial-large or small projects, medical facilities, nursing homes, etc. Remember, not just fire code related issues, but using materials that are not antimicrobial where needed, not having areas accessible, anything..........[110]

Her plea proved futile. In 2009, as the bottleneckers tried again for a practice act, a local news reporter asked Roberts for examples of harm, forcing her to admit, "Actually there are not things that I can document right now."[111]

Undeterred, hundreds of interior designers and design students descended on the capitol to lobby for the new bill.[112] Yet, despite TAID's $26,500 in campaign donations to thirty-seven legislators after the end of the 2007 session—including $5,500 to members of the House Licensing and Administrative Procedures Committee, at which its practice act had been heard for three consecutive sessions—the bill failed to find a sponsor.[113]

Instead, several days after TAID's visit, legislators introduced a bill killing the titling law—explicitly in response to constitutional concerns raised in Vickee's lawsuit.[114] House Bill 1484, passed the House 147–0[115] and the Senate 30–1,[116] and Governor Rick Perry signed it on May 12, 2009—weeks after a federal appeals court had ordered the state board to stop enforcing the titling law.[117]

ASID's regulatory high water continued to recede when, in 2008, Susan Roberts, a resident of Lyme, Connecticut, sued her state over its twenty-five-year-old titling law.[118] For two decades, Susan had complied with the law, calling herself a "freelance designer" or a "design specialist," rather than an "interior designer," because she lacked the background required by law to call herself the latter. She had attended the Connecticut Institute of Art and Design for a year and a half but left when managing school and her responsibilities as a single mother proved too challenging. She later worked for and with other interior designers, before eventually striking out on her own. However, she had neither the time nor the money or inclination to jump the ASID-induced hurdles required to use the title.

Instead, Susan focused her efforts on building a successful business. Over the course of two decades, she provided interior design services to hospitals, medical offices, commercial sites, and residences, but as the years passed, the prohibition against her using the interior designer title increasingly interfered with Susan's ability to find work.[119] She also came to see the state's law as an infringement of her First Amendment rights. So in July of 2008, Susan filed suit.

At first, the state appeared committed to preserving the regulation. The legislature considered a change to the interior design law that would have preserved the titling provision by creating a new alternate category of "interior residential decorators," but the bill died with others the governor identified as fiscal poison during the height of the recession.[120] Connecticut's attorney general also said he would defend the lawsuit, as long as the state's consumer protection department supported the titling law, which it did.

The following year, a similar bill failed in the legislature. Although it passed the Senate unanimously, the House failed to act on it, prompting a federal district court judge to give Susan her day in court. Had the bill passed, Susan and others like her would have their own title—"interior residential decorator"—which would have made a lawsuit against the titling law nonviable. But because the bill failed, the way was clear for Susan to sue the state. The result was another blow to the bottleneckers. On June 30, 2009, Judge Mark Kravitz declared the titling law unconstitutional, writing, "Neither common sense, history or even consensus supports this restriction."[121]

In addition to losing ground, ASID's efforts to elevate its long-standing titling law in Minnesota into a practice act continually failed. In 1992, as part of its initial success in facilitating the adoption of regulations, the North Star State adopted a titling law to restrict the use of the term "certified interior designer." Subsequent efforts to convert the titling law into a practice act, however, were fruitless. The legislature considered a series of bills, first in 2003 and then every biennium through 2009,[122] that would have made the state's protections of the bottleneckers' interests complete.

The bottleneckers' efforts to erect the licensure fence around their occupation were led by the legislative action committee of ASID Minnesota. Joining the groups were individual interior designers and professors from the University of Minnesota interior design school.[123] Like practitioners, there is also a significant benefit for universities, colleges, and trade schools from licensure schemes created by legislatures. Although aspiring workers often voluntarily complete training at postsecondary institutions before entering their chosen field, the educational requirements associated with licensure force all who wish to work in a licensed occupation to complete a minimum amount of schooling, artificially inflating demand for college courses at the institution and providing a reliable source of income for schools.[124]

Representatives from these schools would never say as much, of course. Instead, they recite the bottlenecker motto—"Licensure, and all of the training that goes with it, is necessary to protect public health and safety." Proponents in Minnesota said exactly that, but unlike in prior years and states in which such claims typically went unchallenged, in the Minnesota committee hearings licensure opponents testified about and drew legislators' attention to the utter lack of evidence to support the proposed threats to public health and safety. For example, a representative of the National Kitchen and Bath Association, which represents the interests of small businesses, agreed with the idea of requiring licensure in the event of threats to public health and safety but testified that in the case of interior design "there [was] absolutely no evidence of that."[125]

ASID's extensive and multiyear efforts to establish full licensure in Minnesota were ultimately futile, but its biggest and ultimately most successful challenge came more than 1,700 miles away, in Florida, where the decades-old practice act for interior designers was threatened by the state's most powerful elected official and a small-business owner from the town of Gulf Stream.

In 1988, Florida adopted a titling law,[126] but ASID was not content with regulating just the terms with which Florida designers were allowed to describe themselves. In 1994, the interior design bottleneckers lobbied successfully for a full-blown practice act for interior design work in commercial settings, making Florida the first state to regulate both the speech and the work of interior designers. The licensing requirements have been severe—six years of education and experience, involving graduation from a state-approved interior design program and completion of an apprenticeship under a state-licensed interior designer, passage of the ASID-approved national interior design examination, and state fees.

The state's Board of Architecture and Interior Design also took the extraordinary step of policing its interior design fence by farming out investigation and enforcement services to a private law firm in Tallahassee called Smith, Thompson, Shaw, Minacci & Colon.[127] Every year, the firm initiates proceedings against hundreds of citizens and businesses both in Florida and outside the state, in most cases for nothing more than simply using the terms "interior design," "interior designer," or even "space planning" without the board's permission. The consequences for violating the titling and practice act are harsh—thousands of dollars in fines and up to a year in jail.[128]

Florida's interior design bottleneckers therefore enjoy significant economic benefits thanks to their anticompetitive efforts, an effect not lost on Eva Locke. Like many Americans, Eva sought to begin a new career in midlife. Her family came to the United States from Cuba when she was just three years old. They left behind everything they owned in their country to start a new life in America, which Eva had always considered the land of opportunity—a place where those who work hard to achieve their goals can not only survive but flourish, as her family eventually would.

After completing a Spanish degree at Tulane University and raising a family, Eva followed her passion for design by enrolling in a two-year interior design program at Palm Beach Community College. While there, she joined ASID as a student member, eventually rising to the rank of vice president of the student chapter. She attended and volunteered at all of the ASID events available to her, learning as much as she could and acculturating herself to the design community.

Upon graduation in 2007, Eva apprenticed for a licensed interior designer for eighteen months, elevated her ASID membership status to "allied"—only those who successfully pass the design exam can be full ASID members—and planned to take the state-mandated exam once she completed her apprenticeship. As she understood the state's requirements, her combination of education and experience was all she needed to sit for the exam and earn the license.

Her apprenticeship was a frustrating experience, however, making her feel like an "indentured servant" and offering virtually no useful design training in return: "I worked as a design assistant in a high-end business with a portfolio of multi-million dollar homes, but mostly all I did was office work, ordering, and pricing. Rarely was I involved in the actual design process."[129]

When she completed her internship in December 2008, she sought to take the required exam but was dismayed to discover that the state interior design board did not honor her degree from Tulane. As she explained, "My degree had to be in design. Without that, I would need to do another internship lasting at least two-and-a-half years."[130]

Even if she had wanted to, landing another internship at that time was essentially impossible. Florida was in the throes of the recession, with a national real estate market that had collapsed and family incomes that were at 1992 levels, with the median net worth of families having plummeted from $126,400 in 2007 to $77,300 by 2010, according to a survey of consumer finance produced by the Federal Reserve.[131] "People I went to school with could not find interior design internships," Eva remembered. "But schools were still turning out students by the thousands, and the state still required the internships to qualify for a license."[132]

Even during the recession, Eva had enough personal connections to do design work and start building a business. However, all of the opportunities were in the commercial sector, where she could not work without a license. Making matters worse, the state's titling law prevented her from advertising as an interior designer, crippling her ability to engage in one of the most essential functions of building and sustaining a business: telling others what she did.

As a student, Eva had joined and participated enthusiastically in ASID, believing what ASID leaders, her instructors, and licensed practitioners told her: licensure is essential to being a professional interior designer. But her own experience and what she observed around her soured her on the state's licensure scheme, causing her to question its entire purpose. "When I was a student, I had no clue what was going on, what ASID was doing to maintain its hold on the industry," she said. In the early months of 2009, she realized that, as she put it, "The real reason for this law is that the licensed designers want to keep out new competition,"[133] and she proceeded to resign her ASID membership in protest.

But her resignation was just the beginning. On May 27, 2009, Eva sued the state, arguing that the law censored her speech and unreasonably interfered with her ability to earn an honest living. Nine months later, on February 4, 2010, US district court judge Robert Hinkle decided in Eva's favor on one part of the lawsuit: He ruled the titling provision in Florida's law unconstitutional but upheld Florida's practice act.[134] Although pleased that she could now honestly describe her work, Eva was nonetheless dissatisfied with the continued restriction on the practice of interior design in commercial settings. Practically speaking, the practice act meant that she could provide interior design services in someone's home but had to decline an invitation to provide the same type of services in that person's office.

The prohibition seemed to Eva to be absurd and unnecessary, so she appealed Hinkle's decision to the Eleventh US Circuit Court of Appeals.[135] On March 1, 2011, the appeals court rejected her case, in yet another example of judicial deference to a state legislature. The court said it would not "second guess the legislature's judgment as to the relative importance of the safety justifications,"[136] despite an utter lack of evidence for the alleged threats of unlicensed interior design to public safety. The following year, the US Supreme Court declined to hear the case, thereby leaving in place the appellate court decision.

The irrationality of the appellate court's deference to the "wisdom" of the legislature was highlighted by a subsequent attempt on the part of Florida governor Rick Scott to eliminate the interior design regulations. As Eva's lawsuit approached its final disposition in 2011 before the court of appeals, Scott challenged the Florida legislature to identify and repeal "job-killing regulations."[137] House members returned with a bill listing thirty occupations it suggested should be deregulated,[138] including auctioneers, travel agents, telemarketers, and yacht brokers.[139] Prominent on the list was eliminating the state's interior design regulations.

Given the age of its law, the strictness of its enforcement, and the cumulative economic benefit licensed designers enjoy from it, Florida became the primary battleground in the interior design bottleneckers' fight to maintain the fence around their occupation. Representatives from the national ASID organization descended on the state's capitol, and the state ASID chapter hired Ron Book, one of the state's most influential lobbyists, to fight the bill.[140] In classic bottlenecker fashion, interior designers crowded into legislative hearings, warning of the chaos that would follow should the bill be adopted. Among the scenarios they conjured were flammable carpets sparking infernos, porous countertops spreading bacteria, and mischosen jail furnishings being used as weapons.[141]

"The hearing room was packed with militant ASID members," Eva recalled. She and a few others had driven to Tallahassee to testify in favor of the legislation, but they were severely outnumbered. "I was as nervous as could be, because I never liked public speaking. And then there were all these militant people from ASID, just lying their butts off, saying just insane stuff, and nobody challenged them."[142]

One licensed designer, for example, testified that use of the wrong fabrics in hospitals could spread infection. Citing a study on deaths from hospital-acquired infections authored by the Centers for Disease Control and Prevention (CDC), she told lawmakers that in deregulating, "what you're basically doing is contributing to 88,000 deaths every year."[143] The problem was, however, the CDC study never mentioned interior design as a cause of such infections. The battle raged for weeks, with a series of emotional hearings[144] that pushed the final decision into the last few hours of the legislative session.[145] When the final gavel fell, the bottleneckers' anticompetitive fence remained standing.

It stayed standing not because of any self-evident need to protect public safety but rather because of a massive national and statewide lobbying effort by the interior design industry. Similar to the legislative battle over caskets in Oklahoma, the Florida fight demonstrates the truth of bottlenecking that judges seem content to ignore. When the Eleventh US Circuit Court of Appeals said it would not "second guess the [Florida] legislature's judgment as to the relative safety justifications" for interior design regulation,[146] the court displayed either complete obliviousness to or willful ignorance of the chimera of safety justifications and the actual way licenses are created and maintained—indeed, to the phenomenon of special interest legislation in general.

From the country's founders to modern political observers, there has been wide recognition of the problem of legislatures doling out favors to certain groups at the expense of others, particularly in the regulation of economic affairs. Because governments hold authority over things that many people would like to see controlled for their own benefit, the potential for abuse is practically self-evident.[147] As James Madison put it in a letter to Thomas Jefferson, "Wherever there is an interest and power to do wrong, wrong will generally be done."[148] Madison was particularly wary of such potential in the legislature, writing in the *Federalist Papers* that "the legislative department is everywhere extending the sphere of its activity, and drawing all power into its impetuous vortex."[149]

More than a hundred years later, the Michigan Supreme Court noted:

> It is quite common in these later days for certain classes of citizens—those engaged in this or that business—to appeal to the government—national, state, or municipal—to aid them by legislation against another class of citizens engaged in the same business, but in some other way. This class legislation, when indulged in, seldom benefits the general public, but nearly always aids the few for whose benefit it is enacted, not only at the expense of the few against whom it is ostensibly directed, but also at the expense and to the detriment of the many, for whose benefit all legislation should be, in a republican form

> of government, framed and devised. This kind of legislation should receive no encouragement at the hands of the courts.[150]

And, on the cusp of the twenty-first century, one political pundit observed that people pursue government favors for the same reason as Willie Sutton robbed banks: That's "where the money is."[151] In short, give government a great deal of power to control the means of accumulating wealth, and people will soon seek to capture and harness it to their personal benefit,[152] even if such benefits wrongfully limit the rights of others. It's a reality of human behavior that bottleneckers exemplify.

Yet, for decades, many courts have discounted this reality in deference to bottleneckers' flimsy, unsubstantiated, and self-serving assertions of threats to public health and safety resulting from unlicensed practice—assertions that go largely unchallenged and unexamined by legislators, who have their own interests in acquiescing to bottleneckers' demands. Consequently, the relationship between licensure requirements—or the need for licensure at all—and public safety has grown more tenuous. So tenuous, in fact, that the justification is now applied to occupations, like the one we will discuss in chapter 5, that are as simple and as harmless as telling a story.

CHAPTER 5

To Speak Freely, Pee in This Cup

On December 22, 1864, in the waning months of the Civil War, General William T. Sherman sent a message to President Abraham Lincoln, saying: "I beg to present you as a Christmas gift the city of Savannah."[1] The taking of Savannah had been the climax of Sherman's monthlong, three-hundred-mile march from Atlanta, during which he promised to "make Georgia howl."[2] After three years of bitter fighting between armies, Sherman pursued a new strategy of "total war," in which psychological and economic warfare would be meted out against the civilian population of the South.[3]

The "destroyer," as Margaret Mitchell called Sherman in *Gone with the Wind*, began his assault after witnessing a third of Atlanta burn to the ground. In order to break the South's will to fight and demonstrate that it could not protect its homes or families, Sherman ordered his sixty-five thousand men to forage liberally and destroy anything of military value as they advanced through the heart of Georgia toward Savannah. The army responded by tearing up railroads, burning factories, raiding farms, plundering plantations, and confiscating livestock and other items of value. By his own estimates,[4] Sherman destroyed approximately $100 million in property (almost $1.5 billion in 2014 dollars).

Upon entering Savannah on December 21, however, Sherman's orders changed. Eager to demonstrate to the people of the South that surrender would mean peace and security, he ensured that no plundering, violence, or burning was inflicted on the city. By both his own and others' descriptions, Savannah during Sherman's monthlong occupation was quiet and orderly.[5] Consequently, while other cities were devastated by the fires of Sherman's army, Savannah remained, and remains to this day, an unmolested example of antebellum architecture, a sort of city-sized museum of pre–Civil War life that includes the largest historic district in the nation.[6] Moreover, thanks to preservation efforts, it has escaped the ravages of inner-city decay typical of many American cities.[7]

The city's culture also remains seemingly untouched by time. Its population has grown slowly, only increasing from 118,000 in 1970[8] to 144,352 in 2013.[9] While many of Georgia cities have urbanized, Savannah's city leaders have taken a decidedly conservative posture, refusing to "take yes for an answer" with regard to development.[10] Consequently, the city has historically remained insular and in the process developed a unique local culture.[11]

Indeed, when author John Berendt—a longtime New Yorker—first arrived in Savannah in the early 1980s, he described it as "sealed off from a world that suddenly seemed a thousand miles away.... I had stumbled on a rare vestige of the Old South."[12] What had begun for Berendt as a side trip in search of authentic Southern food turned into one of the bestselling books of all time, *Midnight in the Garden of Good and Evil*, which was set in Savannah.

The writer spent eight years living off and on in Savannah, immersing himself in "an adventure peopled by an unusual assortment of characters and enlivened by a series of strange events, up to and including murder."[13] The result was this true crime book that spent four years on the *New York Times* bestseller list and jumped to the screen in Clint Eastwood's 1997 movie of the same title.

The story centers on a murder at Mercer House, one of the city's pre–Civil War mansions spared by General Sherman and once owned by a progenitor of the songwriter Johnny Mercer, although never by the songwriter himself. The narrative explores the murder of a young escort named Danny Hansford and his accused murderer—the antiques dealer Jim Williams—a closeted gay man with whom Hansford had had a relationship. Surrounding the central protagonists is a Greek chorus of odd and colorful characters, like African American transsexual nightlife entertainer the Lady Chablis, intermittently named Frank; the Voodoo priestess Minerva; an inventor named Luther Driggers who possesses a vial of poison strong enough to kill the whole city were it to infiltrate the water supply; and Sonny Seiler, whose bulldogs—all named Uga—are the University of Georgia mascots. But the most important character, and the one who is omnipresent throughout the book, is the city of Savannah itself. Through luxurious descriptions and female personification, the city takes on a life of its own, seeming to participate in the events of the story.[14]

The book—Berendt's first—vaulted the author to fame and turned Savannah into a popular tourist destination, which it remains today. Just months after the book's 1994 release, tourism in Savannah increased by 46 percent. That year, convention bookings grew by 40 percent, and in 1995 they grew by another 30 percent; new businesses opened in Savannah's main shopping thoroughfare previously littered by empty storefronts;[15] bed-and-breakfasts began operating in the historic district; and gift shops and tours of book and film locales sprang up to serve the many tourists.[16] In 1996, Berendt received a special award from the Savannah Economic Development Authority, and April 26 of that year was declared "John Berendt Day" by the city's mayor.[17]

The momentum for Savannah's tourism continued to increase as even-more movies were filmed there following *Midnight in the Garden of Good and Evil* and celebrity chef Paula Deen rose to prominence. More than eighty-five other films were made in Savannah, such as *Forrest Gump* and *Something to Talk About*, including ten Academy Award winners.[18] When Paula Deen became a sensation on the Food Network, her Savannah restaurant, along with her brother's, drew tourists by the thousands. Tours capitalized on the movies, and "Paula mania" filled buses to Savannah at more than $50 per ticket to visit movie locations and restaurants.[19] By 2011, tourism in the city had generated a staggering $1.95 billion in annual revenue, with more than twelve million people visiting the city per year.[20]

On the front lines of the crush of tourism have been tour guides, for which there has been a huge swelling of demand. Normally, this would result in a commensurate increase in the supply of tour guide workers and entrepreneurs, but growth was bottlenecked by the city's licensure requirement for tour guides, adopted in 1978.[21] According to the Bureau of Labor Statistics, 210 people were employed as guides in Savannah in 2000;[22] by 2013, the number had only grown to 290.[23] For almost forty years, the Old South city that welcomed scores of Tinsel Town storytellers required a license to tell the stories behind the stories.

STORYTELLING IN SAVANNAH

In order to speak about the city for a living, tour guides had to pay $100 to take a hundred-question multiple choice exam on "obscure history," and they had to pass with a grade of 80 percent or better, submit to a background check and a biennial physical, and pay an annual licensing fee.[24] Penalties for unlicensed storytelling included a $1,000 fine or spending thirty days in jail or on a municipal work gang.[25] The city provided a 111-page test preparation guide with sample test questions like: "Tomochichi was the chief of: a) Oconee Indians [,] b) Yamacraw Indians[,] c) Seminole Indians[,] d) none of the above."[26] Other questions focused on the ethnic and national background of the Telfair family, the historical significance of Alfred E. Beach, and the location of the "graves of the Yellow Fever victims of 1820."[27] The college professor who authored the city's study guide estimated that aspiring guides had to devote three months of full-time study to prepare for the test.[28]

Unlike bottleneckers in other occupations who claim a need to protect public health and safety, the bottleneckers for Savannah's tour guide industry justified the need for a license with an even-more-tenuous purpose. According to Bridget Lidy, the city's tourism administrator, licensure was a way to ensure quality tours.[29] James Caskey, a member of the city's Tourism Advisory Committee and owner of a tour company, agreed, calling the license "a selling point for the city of Savannah."[30]

In order to prove he could give a quality tour of Savannah and promote the city, Dan Leger had to provide blood and urine samples, chronicle his sexual history, and submit to a "cough test."[31] And after he first applied for a license in 2008, he had to do the same every two years, with a criminal background check required every year.

But after six years in business, Dan knew the licensing scheme had nothing to do with providing a quality tour. "If you can't tell a good story, you won't be in business long," he observed.[32] And Dan knows how to tell a good story. He has a five-star rating on the travel Web site

TripAdvisor, which has earned him a certificate of excellence and more than six hundred reviews gushing with superlatives such as: "History teacher loves the tour,"[33] "Don't miss Savannah Dan,"[34] and "One of the highlights of our Savannah stay."[35] A search of the online review site Yelp yields a similar result—glittering reviews and a perfect five-star rating, neither of which owes to Dan's holding a license.

"Nobody cares if you are licensed," Dan stated plainly. "Customers don't care if your history is right. They want to be entertained. They are not here to get a degree in history. They are here for entertainment, and I am an entertainer."[36]

He wasn't always an entertainer, however. Dan left his native Omaha, Nebraska, at the age of seventeen to join the army. He was stationed in Georgia and worked as a military police officer, later leaving the service to continue his career in law enforcement as a sheriff's deputy and then as a police officer in Savannah. Dan left law enforcement to pursue other interests, first working as a wine buyer for a local café and eventually opening his own photography business, a deceptively difficult business made even more difficult in the first decade of the twenty-first century by the explosion of digital photography. "The invention of the digital point-and-shoot meant a monkey could be a wedding photographer," he noted.[37] By the time the Great Recession rolled over Savannah, the city was swamped with photography outfits offering cut-rate services. Dan's business dried up, and, like so many other people at the time, he faced the real possibility of losing his house. "I was at the end of my rope," he recalled.[38]

While mulling over his options, he was struck by a clear but random thought—the work of divine intervention, as he called it. He could give walking tours at 10 a.m. and 2 p.m. every day. The idea came from out of nowhere. Dan had never led a tour. He had only been on tours of the city when friends or family visited. Nevertheless, he followed the inspiration by donning a seersucker suit, bow tie, and hat; brushing up on his local history; and marshalling his mellifluous voice—he once worked as a radio disc jockey—and love of storytelling to create the persona of "Savannah Dan."

Now, six days a week, Savannah Dan leads two ninety-minute walking tours that cover the city's colonial history all the way up to its star turn in movies and current events. Although the heat forces him to cut back to one tour a day during the summer, the city's climate is otherwise so agreeable that serving as a tour guide is Dan's full-time, year-round occupation. In this respect, he is rather unusual compared to tour guides in other cities. During peak seasons, guides can work as many as fourteen hours a day, six days a week,[39] but few make their livings conducting tours all year round,[40] mainly because of the seasonal cycle of tourists and high competition. As a result, most tour guides juggle other jobs or lead tours as a way to stay busy and supplement their incomes during retirement.[41]

As an occupation, the role of tour guide has evolved little[42] since it first appeared in the United States and perhaps even before then. It goes back to at least to the Greek and Roman Empires, when guides proliferated to serve an enormous tourism industry,[43] and has persisted through the millennia and into the modern age. One of the longest-running fee-based tour guide services in the United States is probably that serving the Gettysburg battleground.[44] These guides emerged after the battle to escort the deluge of friends and relatives of the soldiers, who would go to the battleground to see or identify the wounded and dead.[45]

Throughout the rest of the nineteenth century, tour guides spread to other venues. The 1876 Centennial Exhibition in Philadelphia featured costumed ladies who led visitors through a reconstructed New England farmer's home. At Mount Vernon, the resident director led tours of the home. The Essex Institute in Salem, Massachusetts, now the Peabody Essex Museum, employed women dressed in homespun period costumes to show an historic home to visitors. The number of tour guides continued to grow into the twentieth century, as the proliferation of the automobile and mass transit made it possible for greater numbers of people to visit sites and destinations outside their immediate regions.[46]

By the early years of the twenty-first century, more than thirty-five thousand people worked as tour guides in the United States,[47] serving a local tourism industry worth a staggering $800 billion.[48] Because tourism has become such big business and because tour guides work on the front lines, some cities themselves have become bottleneckers.

Governments have always played a central role in bottlenecking, of course, but the licensing schemes they create typically come at the request of industry leaders seeking to protect their interests. Once a system is created, industry representatives populate boards and other oversight authorities, using the power of the state to their advantage. And in the case of tour guide licensing, although some industry insiders—usually established tour companies—do benefit, the primary group leading the way for such regulatory schemes has been city leaders. With reputational interests at stake, and tourism dollars tied to them, city officials and the industry leaders who support them believe that controlling the tour guides' occupation—and, to whatever extent possible, their messages—can safeguard the city's image and economy.

Guides are frequently seen as unofficial ambassadors or representatives of a city, leading city officials to seek ways to ensure that the "true" or "most appropriate" stories are told. The result has been an increasing number of regulatory mechanisms, chiefly licensure, being put in place by authorities—often working in concert with existing tour companies—under the official cause of "quality assurance" but often less overtly serving as a way to monitor and manage the city's image (i.e., as a means of "impression management").[49]

As Bridget Lidy explained it, in Savannah, with its $2 billion tourism industry, "we feel as though there needs to be some kind of standard in place that protects the integrity of our community."[50] Ironically, even the very book that transformed Savannah's tour industry into a multibillion-dollar juggernaut is itself not entirely true in its depictions of the city.[51] As Berendt acknowledged in an author's note at the end of the book, *Midnight in the Garden of Good and Evil* contains fabricated dialogue and fictional scenes. Berendt's "story-telling liberties" led the Pulitzer Prize committee to exclude the book from consideration for an award, though it had been selected as a finalist.[52]

The irony of claiming that a license would ensure that guides told the true stories of the places, people, and events of a book in which the author "round[ed] the corners" of truth[53] was apparently lost on Savannah's bottleneckers. Indeed, picking up the city's line, Phil Sellers, the owner of a Savannah tour company and the Tour Guide Institute, presumed to speak as a representative of Savannah's citizens in a newspaper interview about the license: "The residents of the city want better tour guides, not to open up the floodgate of incompetent tour guides."[54] Incidentally, the push for quality also benefited Sellers directly: his Tour Guide Institute counted among its services test preparation for the city's exam.

Savannah's bottlenecking may have been a city initiative, but tour operators also did their part to prop up the system for their own benefit. The city council appointed the Tourism Advisory Committee to oversee the tourism industry, including tour guides. Of the committee's thirteen members, four worked for or owned tour companies, and the spouse of a fifth member owned a tour company.[55]

While those in the industry profited from the licensing scheme, there was no evidence that it produced higher-quality tour guides for the city. And there is little reason to expect a different result. As Phil Sellers himself acknowledged, "Having a tour guide license does not make you a tour guide."[56] For decades, economists have studied whether licensing produces greater quality of service, and the answer has almost always been that it does not.[57] Nobel-laureate economist Milton Friedman was the first to cast doubt on the supposed relationship between licensing and quality of service in the early 1960s,[58] but it was not until about a decade later that the first empirical studies offering systematic evidence began to appear.[59] These early results largely confirmed Friedman's conclusions that licensing accomplished little in the way of improving quality of service, and some findings even suggested that it might do the opposite.[60]

One of the first such studies compared the proficiency of clinical laboratory personnel in states with restrictive licensing to the proficiency of personnel in states without it. The results indicated no improvement in quality of service as a result of licensing.[61] A steady stream of related studies soon followed, with examinations of television repair people,[62] dentists,[63] plumbers,[64] optometrists,[65] sanitarians,[66] real estate agents,[67] health paraprofessionals,[68] veterinarians,[69] physicians,[70] teachers,[71] and electricians.[72] All the studies found the same thing—that there was no improvement in quality from licensure. The study of electricians even suggested that licensing, by design, artificially reduced the number of electricians per capita, thereby contributing to more deaths by electrocution from do-it-yourself accidents.

Twenty years later, analyses with better data and more sophisticated analytical techniques confirmed the early studies. Studies of teachers,[73] dentists,[74] mortgage brokers,[75] and construction contractors[76] consistently found little relationship between licensing and quality. In the latter study, for example, economist David Skarbek of King's College in London conducted an experiment looking at the aftermath of hurricanes Frances and Katrina in Florida, during which the state relaxed its licensing restrictions for contractors. In an analysis of the period, Skarbek concluded, "I find little evidence of significant detrimental effects from the policy change" and recommended the policy change be made permanent.[77]

For Michelle Freenor, it didn't take a PhD in economics to know that licensing had little to do with serving as a quality tour guide. As she put it, "Just because you pass that test, it won't make you a great tour guide. Tour guiding is about interpretation and entertainment."[78] A tour guide in Savannah since 2009, Michelle has shared her love of history and of Georgia with vistitors through rich storytelling, trivia, and a sense of fun. "I want people to think differently about Georgia," she noted. "They think they are going to see a bunch of plantations, but Georgia is more than that."[79]

Although she was born and raised in central Florida, Michelle spent much of her youth with family in central Georgia, combing battlefields, visiting historic sites, and searching for Indian artifacts. "Everybody is good at something, especially things they love," she said. "I love history. I grew up loving it in school. If there's a book about Savannah I read it."[80]

Like Savannah Dan, Michelle began working as a tour guide later in life. A career in nursing, which she loved, was cut short when she was diagnosed with lupus, an autoimmune disease that causes fatigue, joint pain and swelling, and headaches, among other symptoms.[81] The condition—which involves a constant cycle of flare-ups and remissions—made the physical demands of nursing too great for Michelle to continue doing the job full time, so she looked for other options that would provide her the flexibility to do the nursing work she loved so much only when she was able. Working as a tour guide would enable her to return to her first love of history, but first she had to clear the hurdle of the city's licensing scheme.

After studying for three months, Michelle passed the test on her first attempt and promptly began working under the name "Savannah Belle Tours." Her tours were "mostly fact based," focusing on the colonial period, the civil war, monuments, churches, pop culture, and movie locations—the content that fills most tours in Savannah. "Because there are 74 companies in 2.2 square miles all talking about the same thing, you need to be original, special, or good, or you won't last," she observed. "Most tour companies around here fold in a matter of months. They think it's so easy."[82]

With her skill at storytelling, well-rounded knowledge, and fun approach, Michelle built a successful reputation as a tour guide and was soon working as much as she was physically able, but the unnecessary restrictions of the licensing system gnawed at her. "The city talks about 'protecting its brand,' but it's not really about that. People here are afraid of free markets. Businesses that are struggling don't want more competition."[83] Unwilling to simply go along with the system, Michelle began meeting with city officials in an attempt to abolish the license. The meetings led to an invitation to sit on the city's Tourism Advisory Committee, where she spent two years advocating for change. The effort proved futile. "When city officials began telling me how to vote, that's when I left," she recalled.[84]

She wasn't alone. Dan Leger also met with city officials, lobbying for change in the city's licensing laws. "I always got the same answer: 'Your idea is really interesting. You should put that on paper, and we will look into moving that forward,' except nothing ever happened," he remembered. "But it's not too surprising. We have a $2.3 billion tour industry regulated by a branch of the parking services, the same people who specialize in handing out parking tickets. They are regulators; this is what they do."[85]

Jean Soderlind, a longtime owner of a Savannah tour guide company specializing in ghost tours, Ghost Talk Ghost Walk,[86] also agitated for the elimination of the city's licensing system. "For 17 years, I tried to get the city to change this law, but they wouldn't listen," she remembered. Her efforts included regularly attending city council meetings, at which she asked probing questions about the purpose of the licensing system and how the money generated from the city's preservation fees was being used.[87] "I asked questions so often they began preparing responses ahead of time just to shut me up," she said. "They think I am a crazy old woman."[88]

Crazy like a fox. Jean stumbled into the business in the late 1990s, when a friend asked her to take care of his tour business for a few weeks while he attended to out-of-state matters. Weeks turned into months, and Jean continued to maintain the business, eventually buying the company in 2000, when the owner decided not to return to Savannah. Although she had no experience as a tour guide, she recognized an opportunity when she saw one. At the time, the company was almost the only ghost-tour outfit in the city, and it was very profitable as a result. "With fifty-four ghost companies in town now we are not making money like we did, but we still do OK," she recently said.[89]

Over the years, Jean's company has provided part-time work for those close to her, helped some of them work their way through college, and provided "pick-up money" for the local school teachers who make up almost all of the company's guides. Because all tours are given at night—one at 7:30 p.m. and a second at 9:30 p.m.—teachers can guide after school and during summers. Her family members lead tours when they're not engaged in other pursuits, including working as costumers and set designers in theater and film, a vocation they picked up from Jean herself.

While studying political science and history at the University of Minnesota, Jean took a theater class to satisfy an elective requirement. A few weeks into the class, the professor offered her a deal—if she worked in the department's costume shop as a seamstress for course credit, she wouldn't have to attend the class. She accepted the offer, and after working on her first production she was hooked. She finished her political science degree—which included an internship in one of Lyndon B. Johnson's "Model Cities"[90]—but continued working as a costumer thereafter, eventually working her way into movies. By the time she bought the ghost tour business, she had already amassed screen credits for working on *Forrest Gump*, *Something to Talk About*, and a long list of other movies and stage productions all over the country.

Although Jean continues to work as a costumer now and then, the popularity of her tour business now consumes most of her time. From 7:30 a.m. to when the last tour heads off, she works the phones, taking requests from customers that include school groups, families, travelers looking for something to do in the evening, and Girl Scout troops. As the home city of the Girl Scouts, Savannah draws scores of scout groups, many of which take Jean's ghost tours. "We're very family friendly," Jean explained. "We don't do zombies or hatchet murders. We tell traditional ghost stories of haunted houses and throw in a little history along the way." The bargain-basement price of $10 for a ninety-minute tour also helps draw business. "The price has not changed in the entire 27 years of the business," she noted.[91]

What Jean misses in unit price she makes up for in volume. The company keeps six to seven regular guides busy every day, with two or three backups standing by. Jean herself used to lead tours after she earned her license in 2004, but she let her license lapse in 2009 out of disgust with the entire system. "I just got mad at all of the hoops that were required, so I decided at 70 years old I wasn't going to jump through them anymore," she recalled. But she continued to pester city officials, who remained not only unmoved by her protests but practically tyrannical. "City officials would say in these meetings, 'Right or wrong, you will do this because that is what we require,'" Jean described.[92]

Dismayed by the city's intransigence, she and some other owners of tour guide companies even went to a local attorney in 2009 to talk about suing the city in order to dismantle the licensing system. The attorney declined to take the case but offered to do research and provide other services if they chose to bring a suit, all for a hefty fee of about $20,000. "He said we would probably lose, which made $20,000 look ridiculous."[93]

Then, one morning, Jean opened the morning paper to find an article about a couple from Washington, DC, who had successfully sued their city over its tour guide licensing system. "There it was in black and white," she said. "Finally, confirmation that I was not so crazy after all. Other people thought tour guide licensing was wrong, too."[94] She quickly called Michelle, a friend and sometime tour guide for her company, and told her to read the article. For days, the two of them talked about how they could do the same thing in Savannah, eventually calling the law firm that had represented the DC couple, which the firm had done at no cost. Although Michelle and Jean did not know it at the time, their budding effort to tear down the fence around Savannah's tour guide industry would also contribute to striking down a law that had inspired other cities to engage in their own bottlenecking.

PHILADELPHIA'S LOVE FOR LICENSING

Although it is a small, insular city removed from the development of neighboring communities, Savannah and its tour guide license nonetheless proved inspirational to a much-larger and more-prominent city more than seven hundred miles away—Philadelphia.

In April 2008, in the city that gave the nation the First Amendment and its protection of free speech, Mayor Michael Nutter had signed a law making it illegal for individuals to give tours without first passing a 150-question test and obtaining a government license. Like their counterparts in Savannah, proponents in Philadelphia—who included those already working in the tour guide industry—had cited a need to improve the quality of tour guides.

The licensing push had begun in 2007, when a local tour guide, Ron Avery, sent a letter to Councilwoman Blondell Reynolds-Brown and other city council members advocating for a tour guide licensing system.[95] Reynolds-Brown took up the cause, introducing a bill on March 29, 2007.[96] Two hearings followed in which Ron and others—those in the tour guide industry and city officials—testified in support. Identical to Savannah, the prevailing justification was the need to protect the tourism interests of the city. As Reynolds-Brown described, "We want well-informed, knowledgeable tour guides. If cities like Williamsburg, Virginia, or Savannah, Georgia, have this measure, clearly Philadelphia must consider implementation."[97] Ron made the link between tourism dollars and licensure even more explicit: "Philadelphia's economy depends on its tourism and convention business. . . . It would be great if those guides were real experts on the city—its historic past and its interesting present."[98]

When the bill was under consideration, tourism statistics indicated that the Philadelphia region annually attracted 27.5 million visitors, who spent a combined $10 billion.[99] To protect and take advantage of those interests, Ron and the councilwoman first hatched a scheme that required mandatory training, testing, and fees and penalties of $300 for acting as a tour guide without a license.[100] Throughout testimony provided during both public hearings,[101] bill supporters referred to extensive training regimes required in other countries.[102] Although training requirements were dropped from the final version of the bill, the exam, fee, and proof-of-insurance qualifications were kept in place.[103]

As is almost always the case at the hearings for the genesis of licenses, Philadelphia's tour guide session saw a flow of industry bottleneckers supporting Reynolds-Brown's bill in attendance, with almost no one there to oppose it. Joining them in support was Greg

DeShields from Philadelphia-based Temple University's School of Tourism and Hospitality and Management. His interest, however, was not purely in civic improvement. As in other occupations where postsecondary institutions enjoy an economic benefit from licensure requirements, Greg saw the potential for his institution to get in the game early, offering to create curriculum, training, and testing procedures for the license.[104]

Greg also provided a rare moment of honesty when asked by a councilman if requiring guides to be licensed would increase their earnings. His answer was seconded by the CEO of the Independence Visitor Center—the official visitor center for the greater Philadelphia region—who called licensing "a great PR benefit, which will help drive business that will help these [licensed] companies increase their business."[105] Entirely absent was any discussion of how the increase in profits and earnings would mean greater costs to consumers. Indeed, any shortcomings of the bill were given only cursory attention.

One of the most important of these shortcomings was raised by one of the few people to testify in opposition to the bill: Mark Beyerle. The spokesperson for the Tour Operators of Philadelphia, a group of eight tour companies, said:

> We don't necessarily believe that an application and test is going to make a better guide. . . . [A] guide has the right to say whatever they want and will continue to say whatever they want or remember whatever facts they do or don't long after a test is over. So we don't necessarily believe that taking a test and wearing a badge will now make you a better guide.[106]

It was a point Ron himself acknowledged: "You can't arrest somebody for saying something wrong. You can't fine them. Guides will say whatever they want to say. You're not going to put an inspector with every guide, are you?"[107]

As it turns out, the city had given little thought to enforcement of the bill, other than the imposition of the $300 fine, and just months after adoption of the ordinance, it was this very shortcoming that resulted in the law's downfall, when Mike Tait sued the city. Born and raised in Philadelphia, Mike began giving tours in 2006 when he was laid off from his job at Blue Cross/Blue Shield. For a decade after he finished college, he had been tied to a desk for eight hours a day, working a series of office jobs that paid the bills but generated little enthusiasm. Being laid off is seldom welcome, but in Mike's case the result was a positive life change that he never would have anticipated, let alone pursued.

After working at odd jobs for a short period of time, Mike noticed an advertisement in a local paper for guides with a local tour company that operated trolleys. At the interview, he was shocked to discover that individuals could actually make a living working as tour guides. His only exposure to the occupation until then had been friends who practiced it part time as a way to pay for college or make extra money.

Upon taking the job, Mike discovered that he enjoyed the work. It was an outlet for his lifelong interest in history, and he found he had a knack for giving an engaging performance. Added to that was the variety inherent in the job and the ability for him to work in an environment free of the drudgery and pettiness of office confines. By giving amphibious tours—"duck boats," as they are commonly called—on a regular basis and giving walking tours focused on either traditional history or "haunted history" as an independent contractor, Mike now pieces together a respectable living, something the licensing system would have prohibited.

"After paying the licensing fees and the insurance premiums, it just would not have worked out financially," Mike said, referring to Philadelphia's licensing scheme. But that was not even his primary objection. "The way it had been handled left a bad taste in my mouth," he remembered. "We were being railroaded. The bill sponsors made it sound as though all tour guides were making up information. I felt angry about that mischaracterization." In addition, guides had little say in the creation of the licensing scheme. "When they had hearings, very few guides and companies were there," he described. "The industry was not represented very well."[108] When Mike heard that some people were recommending that the tours emphasize certain elements of the city's history over others, he knew he could not stand by and do nothing.

On July 2, 2008, Mike sued the city of Philadelphia, arguing that the bill was violating his freedom of speech in requiring him to gain the city's permission to talk for a living.[109] In an attempt to preserve a law, cities will sometimes alter or eliminate certain provisions that are considered offensive if they are secondary to its intent, and retain other primary elements that fulfill the law's purpose.

Philadelphia's approach differed, however. It used its inability to enforce the law as a way to preserve it. City attorneys argued that because Philadelphia could not and would not enforce the law, Mike's lawsuit was moot, meaning that the judge need not decide on the merits of the case—that is, specifically, whether the city was infringing upon the First Amendment with its licensing scheme. If accepted as moot, the law would remain on the books, but guides could continue to work without licensing, which would be technically illegal but without consequence.

On August 5, 2009, Judge Jan DuBois decided just that: "Plaintiffs' requests for a declaratory judgment and for injunctive relief are not presently ripe for review," she said. "Plaintiffs' Complaint—and the action in its entirety—are dismissed for lack of subject matter jurisdiction. All pending motions are denied as moot."[110]

The problem with such a ruling is, of course, that at some future date the city could choose to begin enforcing the for-now-dormant law, a possibility to which Mike remains vigilant. "Some recent noises were being made about a tour guide who was spreading false information, so I watched closely to see how the city would respond," he said. "But nothing came of it, perhaps because they know if they do something, I will jump on it immediately."[111]

The city may also be mollified by a voluntary certification system that began operating during the lawsuit. By taking a test through the Association of Philadelphia Tour Guides, individuals can earn certification and a badge indicating their status. Mike estimated that more than a hundred people have completed the certification, "despite the city's claim that such a system would never work because nobody would do it," he laughed. "I see a lot of people with those badges, and I hear city leaders saying the certification system works well, particularly since it accomplishes the same thing as the license but costs taxpayers nothing."[112]

"TELLING THE SAME HISTORY"

Although the certification may accomplish the signal-sending function of licensing for consumers, it does not necessarily satisfy what bottleneckers really want out of tour guide licensing, control over what tour guides say, which effectively allows the city to protect its "brand." Throughout the process of creating the license in Philadelphia, for example, bill supporters continually asserted that the license would keep guides from perpetuating "inane information"[113] and ensure consistency in the message and quality of guides in order to protect the city's tourism economy. As Amy Needle, president and CEO of Historic Philadelphia, described, "If we are to be America's next great city, everyone needs to be telling the same history."[114]

The idea of telling the same history assumes everyone is giving essentially the same tour, but, as it turns out, tours in Philadelphia, like those in other cities, include a diverse offering of subject matter, not just that which is associated with traditional history. As travel surges in popularity, travelers increasingly seek out unconventional tours.[115] Although "heritage tourism"[116] draws many people to cities rich in history like Philadelphia, Savannah, and others, the past several decades have seen a significant expansion of different types of tours, such as alternate history tours, disaster tours, dark tours, and—the specialty of Mike Tait and Jean Soderlind—ghost tours.

When it comes to ghost tours, the precise structure varies, but generally tour guides take groups to various locations while spinning out tales of hauntings and apparitions, or perhaps the grisly accounts associated with them.[117] The tours tell participants that the stories they hear along the way are true and that they might actually encounter ghosts on the tour stops.[118] And unlike traditional historical tours, ghost tours are not purely scripted recountings of places, people, and events. Instead, the group encounters guides, participants, and even locals along the way who share stories that the guides weave into the tour narrative.[119] Basically, ghost tours are not interested in "telling the same history" as other tours. Rather, they challenge the preferred, often idealized, images of cities put forward by the heritage tourism industry,[120] which, once dominant, now has serious competition.

As tourist attractions proliferate, there is an increased need to produce a more titillating experience in order to compete successfully for customers.[121] Ghost tours have been very successful in this competition, finding great popularity with tourists. For example, in Savannah, where walking tours are a year-round business, more than half of tourists opt for a ghost tour out of all the tours.[122] Likewise, in Charleston, South Carolina, which has been ranked as one of the nation's most popular tourist destinations, brochure racks are full of advertisements for ghost tours, rather than for the traditional plantation tours that once dominated the local industry.[123] Other cities with burgeoning ghost tour industries include Philadelphia, Atlanta, New Orleans, and Salem, Massachusetts.[124]

Ghost tours are not alone in their unconventional offering. Dark tours satisfy participants' interests in locations linked to suffering, death, and other macabre themes.[125] These tours differ from ghost tours, which focus more on the paranormal or supernatural and have a lighthearted touch and emphasis on entertainment.[126] Dark tourism is not a new concept. Crime scenes such as the Jack the Ripper murders in London in the late nineteenth century attracted legions of tourists, and the places and events of the incident remain famous to this day. Although the events are now more than a hundred years past, Jack the Ripper–themed tours still operate in London's Whitechapel district.[127]

Although popular with tourists, dark tours do not always enjoy the support of cities interested in conveying a particular, more positive, even sanitized, image or story of what they are. In the tiny town of Amityville, New York, for example, the book *The Amityville Horror* and the related movies produced a flood of visitors eager to see the site of the DeFeo family murders and subsequent alleged paranormal activity.[128] In 2005, former Amityville mayor Peter Imbert complained: "[*The Amityville Horror*] constantly brings a bunch of freaks to the neighborhood."[129] Freaks to some, dark tourists to others, Mayor Imbert's comment sheds light on the viewpoint of city leaders and residents who would rather that the tours focused on something else than a portion of the town's dark past.[130]

There are also grief tours, which take tourists to sites of smaller-scale tragedies and focus on the motivations and emotions of those involved;[131] ecotours, which use rhetorical tactics to advocate for environmental justice;[132] poorism, or slum tours, which visit impoverished areas, usually under the guidance of a local resident discussing issues of social justice;[133] and food tours, which enable tourists to see different culinary establishments, taste products, and even try their hands at making things[134]—just to name a few.

The sheer diversity of tours offered in cities demonstrates how a license built primarily on a test can never improve the quality of tours, despite bottleneckers' claims to the contrary. It would be a fool's errand to try to compile a list of testable facts that are important and relevant to the array of tours available, some of which do not even operate on the basis of facts in the traditional sense—or in the sense that cities would prefer. Indeed, not only do many tours focus on content outside traditional facts but some guides *intentionally* convey stories contrary to the idea of "telling the same history."[135]

Since the 1970s, such "alternate tour guides" have increased in number. These practitioners differ from guides who work for major tour operations in that instead of offering the stories and images conveyed in standard tours, they present a more naturalistic view of the lives and places that city leaders might prefer remain hidden. On these tours, the "negative" places and aspects of a city are not avoided but are, in fact, actively sought out.[136] Instead of a litany of facts, alternate guides use anecdotes or provocative statements designed to facilitate discussion, change the way tourists view cities, and lead them to think beyond the traditional stories and histories.[137] City leaders often do not appreciate having alternate guides lay bare the "bruises of the city" or share their less-than-flattering opinions about the city's past or present. In the midst of hearings on Philadelphia's tour guide license, for example, Councilman Frank Rizzo complained about guides who criticized the city's public art, saying the comments "didn't particularly sell well with me."[138]

Alternate guides also focus on places, people, and stories ignored by conventional tours. Chicago Neighborhood Tours, for example, is an urban tourism project in which tourists experience the culture and history of racial and ethnic minority groups living in segregated neighborhoods.[139] Guides select sites and craft narratives to bring attention to social problems, tell a different history, and lead tourists to consider the real effects of policies on communities of color—policies concerning such factors as tax increment financing, urban renewal, health care, public transportation, education, and gentrification.[140]

Similarly, African American guides in New Orleans have developed their own tours to create counternarratives that oppose the city's mainstream histories, which they see as "racialized mythology." In these tours, guides integrate alternative histories of such subjects as civil rights achievements, black business success, and significant African American institutions.[141]

Not that visitors to New Orleans interested in such tours have a long list from which to choose. Quite the opposite, in fact. According to Dr. Mary LaCoste, a retired college professor and longtime guide in the city, "We urgently need more African-American and foreign language guides who are less apt to become new guides because of cost and the hassle of licensing."[142]

In a city where anything goes,[143] unlicensed storytelling is one thing that doesn't.

LICENSING SPEECH IN THE BIG EASY

In the 1970s, the city of New Orleans responded to a request by a group of tour guides—the Friends of the Cabildo (FOC)—to create a license. As in Philadelphia and Savannah, the reason they claimed this needed to be done was to ensure that tour guides possessed the "requisite" knowledge to represent the city to tourists.[144] The means of accomplishing this was a history exam written by city officials and the FOC.[145]

Not content with simply requiring this exam to earn the license, the city added additional requirements—a drug test, a federal (rather than city or state) background check, various fees, and fingerprinting. Because all of these hoops only had to be jumped through once, except for the recurring renewal fee, tour guides went along with licensure for a time. For more than thirty years, the bottlenecking proceeded with few complaints.

That all changed in 2011, when Mayor Mitch Landrieu hired Malachi Hull as the new head of the city's transportation bureau, which oversees the tour guide license. Hull had previously served in Atlanta's city government and left under a cloud.[146] Upon arriving in New Orleans, he abruptly changed the decades-old regulations governing the licensing of tour guides by adding mandatory background checks and drug tests that had to be passed every two years. This meant that any tour guide—even a volunteer—was required to go to the Louis Armstrong Airport every other year to give fingerprints, urinate in a cup, and pay as much as $100 in fees.[147]

Tour guides, led by the Tour Guides Association of Greater New Orleans (TGAGNO) and the FOC, cried foul, pointing out that the background check requirement exceeded that for even police and public safety officials. The mayor's office remained unmoved, asserting that the requirements were necessary because "visitors taking tours must be assured that no tour guide has been convicted of a felony in the past five years,"[148] despite thirty years of incident-free work by tour guides under the previous licensing regime.

To be sure, TGAGNO and FOC didn't object to the license or the test, only to the biannual background checks and drug tests. So when mayoral spokesman Ryan Berni responded to their criticisms by arguing that the change ensured "tour guides, who are important ambassadors for New Orleans, provide a consistent standard of information"[149]—a non sequitur—Robert Freeland, president of the TGAGNO, appeared unfazed. Indeed, Freeland voiced enthusiasm for the test: "It obliges you to study up. We think tour guides should be telling visitors the truth, and they should know as much history as possible."[150] Not only do the statements of Berni, Freeland, and other bottleneckers assume, wrongly, that all New Orleans tour guides lead heritage or history tours—the city's tour industry is replete with ghost tours, dark tours, food tours, and all the rest—but they also demonstrate a failure to reckon with a question inherent to the licensing scheme: whose truth and whose history are tour guides meant to transmit?

Cities are a collage of overlapping meaning, histories, symbols, interactions, practices, and stories.[151] And guides, who are almost always city residents, do more than regurgitate rote facts; they tell stories that to one degree or another provide interpretations of cities. These interpretations are inevitably influenced by their own backgrounds and experiences—their own stories.[152] Nowhere is this more evident than in the disaster tours available in New Orleans.

Hurricane Katrina made landfall in New Orleans on August 29, 2005. The rising waters breached the surrounding levees, flooding 80 percent of the city with up to twenty feet of water.[153] The floodwaters, coupled with inept government responses, meant that those who had not evacuated, whether by choice or by circumstance—predominantly the sick, elderly, poor, or black residents—were stranded for days. Within a month, another hurricane and two tornados compounded the disaster, which caused $108 billion in damages in New Orleans and elsewhere and cost approximately 1,800 people their lives.[154]

Shortly thereafter, companies began offering disaster tours of New Orleans.[155] As the name implies, disaster tours provide participants the opportunity to view areas devastated by natural or human-made catastrophes. Although the first disaster tours in New Orleans drew sharp criticism, they were nonetheless enormously popular. And given the collapse of the city's once-robust tourism industry in the aftermath of the storm, disaster tours were the only thing keeping the companies that offered both the new and old tours in business.[156]

In the year just prior to Katrina, the tourism industry provided more than eighty thousand jobs and generated $4.9 billion in revenue by hosting 10.1 million visitors. The industry represented 17 percent of the city's jobs and 30 percent of its operating budget.[157] After the storm, tour companies barely functioned. For example, Gray Line, which had been running tours in New Orleans since 1924, reduced its staff in the city from sixty-five before Katrina to six immediately after, and the company now only offered disaster tours, since that was all customers wanted.[158] By 2007, tour companies of all types offered tours related to Katrina.[159]

Some early tourists were international visitors, but others were people from the area trying to see parts of the city they could not access any other way. In subsequent months, many tours were populated by former residents or frequent visitors to the city wanting to see what was left of the city they knew.[160]

Each tour ran on a prescribed course, focusing on areas frequently featured in the crush of media stories about Katrina. Tour guides provided a history of the city, a timeline of the hurricane and its destruction, and facts about the city's rebuilding.[161] To these scripts, tour guides added stories based on their insider knowledge, personal opinions, and individual memories.[162]

On one tour, for example, the guide reminisced,

> Soul food's only good if it's cooked with pots that are burned on the bottom. Miss Jordon had the most famous restaurant in the 9th Ward, used pots that were burned on the bottom. Now that restaurant is totally gone.[163]

Thus the narratives that tour guides share do not present a unified picture of a city. In fact, in any given locale the diversity of stories told by guides on all types of tours, not just on disaster tours, is enormous.[164] Some guides tell romanticized stories about their city, stressing the good and the beautiful, while others prefer to tell stories about life as it is or was, including the blemishes.[165] Some guides punctuate a city's history with stories of their own lives, while others spice up their narratives with unique tales they pick up from books, friends, families, media, or their own studies.[166]

The rich texture of stories told and retold through a diverse menu of tours makes New Orleans's licensing test particularly irrelevant, although proponents claim otherwise. "It's a pretty comprehensive test. It talks about the rules and regulations of being a tour guide, the history of the city, the culture of the city, physical landmarks of the city," said Tom Nagelin, president of TGAGNO. "Just about anything people in the city would ask about is on the test."[167]

However, the notion that a seventy-question test can actually comprehensively cover a city founded in 1718 by the French on land previously occupied by the Chitimacha Indians[168] is laughable. Compounding this absurdity, the exam draws heavily from a book written in 1983,[169] meaning that it utterly ignores any new discoveries about the city's history, to say nothing of anything that has happened in the past thirty years.

The most obvious shortcoming of the test is that it does not and cannot possibly cover "just about anything people in the city would ask about," as Nagelin suggested it does. And although ghost tours might dabble in the history covered on the test, culinary tours rarely touch on it. Further, bottleneckers cannot possibly anticipate the locations to which untapped consumer demand will lead entrepreneurs to take future tours. Take the Americana Music Triangle (AMT), for example.[170]

Conceived in 2015, AMT is an initiative to celebrate nine different American musical styles birthed in a geographical region between New Orleans, Memphis, and Nashville, including blues, jazz, country, rock 'n' roll, R&B/soul, gospel, Southern gospel, Cajun/zydeco, and bluegrass. The heart of the experience is traveling the "golden record road" and visiting historic locations, music events and festivals, museums, and other iconic sites. Although many tour stops are located in the three major cities defining the Triangle, others can be found in smaller communities along the way, such as Natchez, Mississippi; Ferriday, Louisiana; and Leipers Fork, Tennessee.

Those following the prescribed 1,500-mile route can use cell and wi-fi technology to follow and learn about the music landmarks along the way.[171] Alternatively, travelers can sign up for a guided bus tour. Such tours have created a new market for the area's tour guides, like Candace "Candy" Kagan, who are now taking their expertise on the road.

A New Orleans tour guide since 2011, Candy recently began guiding tours for the AMT. "I had to spend some time researching the musical history in order to prepare"—something New Orleans's licensing test and sourcebook failed to cover—"but I was able to step in and provide much of the rest of the tour content based on my experience," she explained.[172]

That experience includes leading bus tours throughout the city of New Orleans and walking tours of cemeteries and the French Quarter. The New Orleans native works as an independent contractor for various tour companies to supplement her retirement income but also to share the city with others. "I have a love for the City. I became a tour guide so I could share this love and this information that I have on the city of New Orleans with those that come to visit," Candy described.[173]

Guiding tours is not her first experience working in the city's hospitality industry. Before her many years working in the city's juvenile court system, Candy spent seventeen years providing hospitality services in the French Quarter and grew up in a family who worked in the city's hospitality sector. After retiring from employment for the city, working as a tour guide provided an opportunity to combine her loves of New Orleans, people, and history.

When not on a two-week trip with the AMT, Candy's workdays vary from two to three hours providing walking tours to eight hours leading a bus tour. She also spends some days preparing for upcoming tours, usually reading up on points of interest she knows forthcoming tour groups will want to see or gathering information to share with customers. "Group tours require research to know about the groups and tailor the tour to their interests," she noted.[174]

The unanticipated choices of group tours is yet another example of the irrelevancy of the city's test, a fact not lost on Candy. "It's such a joke, it's unbelievable," she said, adding, "It's the most poorly constructed test I have ever seen," an observation informed by her bachelor's degree in education and master's degree in guidance and counseling. She explained: "Part of the test requires reading out loud. All of us [test-takers] sat in a big u-shape in the room and read out a recipe for pralines. The recipe was not long enough, so people reread things already read by others." Then she wryly noted, "And doing all of this will keep the city safe. I can read a praline recipe, and that's a great protection for visitors to the city."[175]

Making matters worse is the inconsistency of the licensing requirements. Mule-driven buggy operators who might inadvertently let slip some tidbit about the city must earn the license, but those who provide materials for self-guided tours do not need to. Candy observed, "By the city's logic, the [self-guided tour] recording could be full of misinformation, and that would be OK. Guide books have misinformation, and that is OK."[176]

But for Candy, the poor quality of the test and irrelevancy of the requirements were secondary to the violation of her right to speak freely. She suggested that by requiring people to obtain a license before they could describe the city's points of interest, New Orleans placed a content-based restriction on the speech of tour guides. Guides were free to walk around and talk about the weather, politics, or the history of New York City, but they were not free to talk about the history of New Orleans. Candy took her concerns to the head of head of taxi cab bureau, which oversees tour guide licensing, but that resulted in no change. So she talked to members of the city council, who responded that they were merely enforcing city code.

The issue came to a head when Candy tried to renew her license but was rejected after she was unwilling to hand over her Social Security number—which is required for the background check—for fear of identity theft.[177] Facing up to $300 in fines or imprisonment if she continued working without the license,[178] Candy filed a lawsuit on December 13, 2011, in the US District Court for the Eastern District of Louisiana.

In the September 2012 hearing, Candy's attorneys argued that although the licensing requirements did not ban speech outright, they were nevertheless unconstitutional because they placed conditions on tour guides' right to speak freely to earn a living. But the judge was unconvinced. In her ruling, US district judge Susie Morgan held that the requirements were "content neutral" and that the city's concerns "related to the quality of the consumer's experience, which a city dependent on tourism has a substantial interest in protecting."[179]

Candy quickly moved to appeal, and, in April 2014, her attorneys argued that the city's license scheme was not in fact content neutral, since the requirements were triggered by what guides talked about,[180] pointing out that reciting a recipe for pralines required no license, while recounting the history of a cemetery did. They further countered the city's claims about the necessity of the license to protect public health and safety, by noting how the city—in typical bottlenecker fashion—had provided no evidence of harm.

The three-judge panel of the Fifth US Circuit Court of Appeals didn't see it that way, affirming the lower court's ruling and agreeing with the city that tour guide licenses amount to a regulation of business—not speech—and have "no effect whatsoever on the content of what tour guides say."[181] The panel also agreed that the license protects the city's tourism interests by identifying reliable and knowledgeable tour guides,[182] a position the bottleneckers parroted endlessly through the trial court and appellate court process.[183]

The final setback came when in February 2015 the US Supreme Court declined to review an appeal. And so, to date, the law stands, although with slight modifications to streamline the application process. "It now only takes 15–20 minutes at city hall, but we still have to renew every two years, do our fingerprints—even though those don't change between each visit—and make two trips to get it all done," Candy explained.[184] The test is still required for first-time applicants. The personnel overseeing the licensing system also changed. Bureau chief Malachi Hull was fired after one of his department's inspectors manhandled a tour guide, slamming her onto the hood of a car in front of her customers. Although Hull witnessed the incident, he failed to intervene.[185] The inspector was later found guilty of assault.[186]

What makes the Supreme Court's denial so curious is the fact that the year prior, a nearly identical tour guide law in Washington, DC, was struck down by the US Court of Appeals for the DC Circuit. The decision was the culmination of a four-year battle initiated by two immigrants leading tours around landmarks of freedom in the nation's capital.

"LITERALLY SPEECHLESS"

In 2003, the husband-and-wife team of Bill Main and Tonia Edwards opened an Internet café and bicycle rental shop in Annapolis, Maryland. Bill was born in Scotland and raised in Australia, where he met and married Tonia, an Australian native. The pair immigrated to the United States in 1993. Here, Bill worked as a mobile telecom consultant and Tonia completed the years-long process of becoming a US citizen. After retiring, the couple sailed throughout the Caribbean for a few years, but their entrepreneurial fervor eventually won out over the island life, and they settled in Maryland to open the first of several successful businesses.[187]

A year after their 2003 launch, someone riding a Segway rolled into their bike-rental store in Annapolis, suggesting the new conveyance might make for an attractive addition to their business.[188] Prior to its December 2001 release to the public, the Segway was rumored to be transformative. Tech leaders like Jeff Bezos of Amazon and Steve Jobs of Apple talked up the battery-powered vehicle, with Jobs declaring that cities would be designed around it. Some even speculated that Segway inventor Dean Kamen was working on an antigravity hoverboard or some kind of teleportation device.[189] Kamen himself said the project would "be to the car what the car was to the horse and buggy."[190] In the end, the Segway fell far short of the hype,[191] relegated largely to the purview of mall cops,[192] parking patrols, and, thanks to Bill and Tonia, tour groups.

At first, Bill and Tonia simply offered Segway rides around their store for $5 a whirl, but they soon struck upon the idea of leading Segway tours of Annapolis's historic district. The idea proved to be so popular that a few weeks into their venture they shipped a vanload of the machines twenty-five miles west to Washington, DC, where they began what they believe was the capital's, if not the nation's, first guided Segway tour—Segs in the City.[193] The business soon succeeded beyond their wildest expectations, supporting up to five tours a day, seven days a week, and ten thousand riders a year.[194] Unable to lead all of the tours themselves, they began hiring part-time employees, mostly college students on break, eventually numbering a dozen or more.[195]

In Washington, DC, a city that already has a tourism industry attracting fifteen million visitors every year and generating more than sixty-six thousand jobs,[196] achieving success with a new tour business is a significant accomplishment. But as Bill and Tonia discovered early on, the popularity of their tours owed less to the sightseeing than to the Segways themselves. While the devices might look a little intimidating at first—the battery-powered scooters are entirely self-propelled—they are remarkably easy to use. It generally takes only a few minutes for guests to get comfortable—and gleeful—rolling on their own. Tours begin outside the Ronald Reagan Building, near the National Archives, with a lesson on how to ride a Segway, followed by a narrated, two-hour circuit of DC landmarks, all for about $70.[197]

When Bill leads a tour, the tan, lanky, white-haired seventy-year-old offers up entertaining stories with references to various city sights. Speeding by the Museum of Natural History, for example, he might tell guests through Bluetooth earpieces, "If you know the Hope Diamond, you know it is a cursed stone." But most tour takers are only partly listening, focusing more on maneuvering up the sidewalk ramps. As Bill explained, "You don't have to tell them who shot James Garfield because they don't particularly care. What they want to know is, 'How do I make this thing go faster?'"[198]

After launching their shops in Annapolis and DC, Bill and Tonia expanded thirty miles north into Baltimore. In those places, too, Segs in the City became a tour fixture. But while they were celebrating their successful expansion into Charm City,[199] Bill and Tonia discovered that the business was in jeopardy in their biggest market. Unlike Annapolis and Baltimore, Washington, DC, required a license to work as a tour guide. Based on a more-than-one-hundred-year-old city code,[200] aspiring guides were required to pay three separate fees—an application fee, a license fee, and an exam fee—totaling $200, and submit a time-consuming application. This was followed by a hundred-question examination, which they had to pass with a score of at least 70 percent. The exam covered fourteen different categories—architecture; dates; government; historical events; landmark buildings; locations; monuments and memorials; museums and art galleries; parks, gardens, zoos, and aquariums; presidents; sculptures and statues; universities; pictures; and regulations[201]—and information drawn from nine separate publications.[202] Guiding without a license exposed an individual to a $300 fine and up to ninety days in jail.[203] And prior to a 2010 change in the law, guides were required to be US citizens—Bill is not; he holds a green card—had to have lived in the area for some time, and had to testify they were not "drunkard[s]."[204]

As guides who persevered through the application process learned firsthand, the requirements on paper vastly underrepresented the difficulty of clearing the licensing hurdles. In 2007, the International Tour Management Institute, a certificate-granting school, interviewed a graduate—Rhonda Briel—about her experience gaining licensure in DC. As she explained it:

> It was long and arduous. It was confusing. It was frustrating.... [G]etting through the paperwork and dealing with DCRA [Department of Consumer and Regulatory Affairs] was a nightmare.... You must be persistent when it comes to calling DCRA. Don't send emails and don't leave messages.... [Y]ou absolutely have to keep dialing the phone. I think I dialed their number 20 times one afternoon just trying to get a live voice to answer. And that's the only way to get anything accomplished.... I also thought that it would be a short process—that I could get the paperwork done in a month, and study in a month, and, you know, maybe take the exam in a month. No. That's not going to happen.... I'm still waiting for my license. I passed the test in November. This is late January.[205]

To prepare, Rhonda studied the nine publications recommended for test takers, only to discover that "there is misinformation in the blue guide, the Michelin green guide, Mary Carter's book, and everything else I read. So everybody's got misinformation, so you really have to do your research to figure out what's right."[206]

And, as Rhonda described it, the application process included more than an application form:

> You need a health certificate. You need a criminal background [check]. You need fingerprints. You need a driver's license verification. You need six letters from your best friends. And... they want you to give them a letter that says this tour company is going to hire you, and

> they're going to support you.... Good luck [with the licensing process]. You'll need it.[207]

When Bill and Tonia discovered the licensure requirement and all that it entailed, they were flabbergasted. They didn't object to routine business licenses or even to the regulation of their business for health or safety reasons—for example, in the District, people must be at least sixteen years old to ride a Segway.[208] What they did object to, however, was having to obtain a license just to describe things. Although city leaders would deny this was the case, Bill and Tonia saw the license as a burden on their speech triggered by the content of their communication—a clear violation of the Constitution. An example would be that if someone rode a Segway down the street behind Tonia as she, sans license, chatted about the prospects of the Washington Redskins, no law would be broken. But if, during that same ride, Tonia said, "Hey, that's the Washington Monument," she would face a fine of $300 or three months in jail.

Realizing the futility of trying to foment legislative change in the District, on September 16, 2010, Bill and Tonia instead sued the city in the US District Court for the District of Columbia to vindicate their right to earn an honest living by speaking and to establish the principle that the Constitution does not allow the government to decide who is—and who is not—allowed to speak about various topics.

The first stop in their legal fight resulted in a loss. In February 2011, US district court judge Paul L. Friedman accepted the bottleneckers' defense, finding that "the licensing scheme is aimed at conduct and does not unconstitutionally burden speech."[209] He also upheld the licensing law on the grounds that administering a hundred-question exam to prospective tour guides represented a "substantial government interest."[210]

Undeterred, Bill and Tonia appealed the decision in a hearing before a three-judge panel on May 5, 2014. As it had done at the trial court, the DC attorney general's office defended the licensure policy as "content neutral," asserting, "Licensing of tour guides is not based on what they say. It does not affect the content of any tour and neither requires nor prohibits any speech of any kind.... The District has an interest in assuring visitors will be properly cared for and guided."[211]

For good measure, and like bottleneckers in other industries, the city also marched out a parade of horribles that the license allegedly protected against. These included "unscrupulous businesses," "unethical or uninformed guides" who might victimize vulnerable visitors, unfair or unsafe treatment of tourists, swindling or harassment, and "guides who might abandon tourists in some far-flung spot or charge them additional amounts to take them back."[212]

The appellate court, however, found such arguments unpersuasive. In a unanimous June 2014 ruling, the judges reversed the trial court's decision, finding that the exam and licensing fees violated Bill and Tonia's right to free speech and conduct. "This case is about speech and whether the government's regulations actually accomplish their intended purpose," Judge Janice Rogers Brown wrote for the court. "The District failed to present any evidence the problems it sought to thwart actually exist."[213]

In fact, the city's legal counsel was "literally speechless" when asked how the speech-regulating measure accomplished its goals.[214] The appeals court said the city "rehearses a plethora of harms it claims to forestall with the exam requirement," but despite the city's "seemingly talismanic reliance on these asserted problems," the record contains no evidence that ill-informed guides were actually harming the city's tourism industry.[215]

In particular, the judges took direct issue with the trial court's pronouncement that the test represented a substantial government interest. In an opinion that dismantled the bottleneckers' arguments, Judge Brown wrote,

> What, pray tell, does passing the exam have to do with regulating unscrupulous tour businesses and unethical guides? How does memorization of addresses and other, pettifogging data about the District's points of interest protect tourists from being swindled or harassed by charlatans?[216]

Things went from bad to worse for the city when several inconsistencies in the law surfaced during the appellate hearing. The regulations did not apply to guides fixed in one spot rather than those who moved with customers from one site to another, and audio guides were exempt.[217]

When asked by the court whether the regulations would permit a tour bus company to recruit a drunk off the street to prerecord the audio narration, the city's attorney unequivocally answered, "Yes." Finally, the city had, at one point, told Bill and Tonia that they could give unlicensed tours if they used a recording, but it later advised them that they could only conduct tours if they handed out pamphlets. As Judge Brown noted, "The District's failure to provide any justification—let alone a persuasive one—for the glaring inconsistency, effectively eviscerated what was left of the regulations' waning credibility."[218]

The appellate court ended its withering rejection of the city's defense by noting that "there is no evidence in the record the District's interests would be achieved less effectively absent the exam requirement."[219] Like other tourism businesses not burdened with a special license, tour guides have a large interest in maintaining a high level of quality, absent government regulation. In fact, market regulation effectively polices the industry on consumer-review sites like Yelp and TripAdvisor. "One need only peruse such websites to sample the expressed outrage and contempt that would likely befall a less than scrupulous tour guide," the court wrote.[220]

Remarkably, despite the court's stinging decision, the city clung to its license by interpreting the ruling as applying to the test but not to the licensing scheme as a whole. As of this writing, guides in the nation's capital no longer have to pass a test to speak, but they do still have to complete an application.[221]

MEANWHILE, BACK IN SAVANNAH

Just as the legal battle in Savannah, Georgia, inspired city leaders in Philadelphia to adopt a tour guide license, Bill and Tonia's fight against the DC bottleneckers inspired Savannah Dan, Michelle, and Jean to launch a battle against the Hostess City of the South.[222] Bill and Tonia were, in fact, the couple from Washington, DC, whose story inspired Jean to call Michelle with the idea of taking down the city's licensing system.

As Michelle recalled, "I kind of floated the idea of a lawsuit with a city official once by saying to her, 'You know, I wouldn't be surprised if someone sued the city over this license.' Her response was telling. 'Go ahead; maybe *you* should,' she said, 'Other people have tried to sue us, and we never lose.'"[223]

In November 2014, Dan Leger, Michelle Freenor, and Jean Soderlind[224] did just that. They sued the city, arguing that the license violated their First Amendment right to speak freely in the course of earning a living. In a by-now-familiar response, the city defended the license by claiming that the requirements "serve an important governmental purpose and are a proper exercise of the city's police power."[225] In particular, city officials asserted the license protected tourists from harm and ensured minimum competence among guides.[226]

A month after the lawsuit was filed, however, the Savannah City Council moved to moot the lawsuit, at least in part, by amending its tour guide regulations to eliminate the requirement to get a physical examination.[227] Dan and the others remained unmollified. "Until they quit licensing my free speech, I won't be satisfied," Dan said. "While in the army and in law enforcement, I swore to defend the Constitution against all enemies foreign and domestic, and that includes the city of Savannah."[228]

Three months later, attorneys from both sides met after being ordered to discuss settling out of court. But in a status report that the lawyers for the tour guides and City Hall wrote for the judge on March 12, 2015, they agreed that they were so divided that "settlement negotiations are unlikely to continue," leaving it to the judge to decide.[229] Dan, Michelle, and Jean dug in for a long fight. "There will nothing better than sitting in the Supreme Court argument and hearing the justices ask the city why it thinks it's a sovereign," Jean said.[230]

Although city leaders continued to claim that the license was a proper application of their police power, not everyone who supported licensing was certain of the lawsuit's outcome. "My position at this point is, how do we prepare to lose?" said Bill Durrence, a Savannah native and member of the Downtown Neighborhood Association who had long supported the licensing standards. "This isn't a political argument we can make; this is going to happen in a court of law. We can protest and we can write letters to the editor, but it's going to have no impact on the court."[231]

In case the licensing scheme was toppled, Durrence suggested creating alternatives for conveying the credibility of guides, such as programs for voluntary certification.[232] Tour companies were already required to acquire a business license, which could be revoked if guides or other company personnel engaged in illegal activities or practices that threatened public safety. Implementing a voluntary certification program—coordinated by the city or third-party organizations—would enable guides to distinguish themselves from competitors and provide a way for the city to designate "city-approved" or "industry-approved" guides for the benefit of visitors who value such appellations,[233] all without limiting the free speech and practice of aspiring tour guides.

This is precisely what the DC appeals court suggested when striking down the district's law,[234] and, indeed, the tourism industry has been moving in this direction for more than a decade, emphasizing accreditation and professional certification.[235] Organizations like the National Association for Interpretation,[236] city-specific associations, and even some tour companies now offer certification and training programs.[237] Many of these programs rival training programs offered by colleges and universities and have become so well regarded that they serve as tacit regulation, as many companies—without a city compelling them to do so—require aspiring workers to complete the programs before being hired.[238]

The benefits of such systems include allowing companies to give themselves a competitive edge by distinguishing themselves from others—"All of our guides are certified"—and providing consumers with a menu of companies from which to choose.[239] Such certification programs—particularly those conferred by national organizations—also give tour guides portable and widely recognized industry qualifications with which to market themselves and to offer interested companies in the hiring process.[240]

The experience of other cities strongly suggests that Savannah did not need to wait for a time- and resource-intensive lawsuit to enjoy the benefits of such a system. By the time of Dan, Jean, and Michelle's lawsuit, the state of Florida,[241] as well as at least ten other large cities in the United States—Chicago,[242] San Antonio,[243] San Diego,[244] San Francisco,[245] St. Louis,[246] Dallas/Ft. Worth,[247] Houston,[248] Las Vegas,[249] Denver,[250] and Philadelphia[251]—did not license tour guides but instead relied on voluntary certification systems.

And after an October 2015 decision by the Savannah City Council to discontinue its licensing regime for tour guides,[252] one more city was added to that list. During the course of the suit, the city attorney of Savannah, W. Brooks Stillwell, obstinately defended the license as essential to ensuring tour guide competence: "We don't want people who don't know what they're doing out there conducting tour services," Stillwell told the Associated Press at the time.[253] But in October 2015, the attorney advised council members to scrap the regulations, not out of a newfound concern over their effects on free speech but to take "some of the issues off the table."[254] This is illustrated in an exchange that took place between Stillwell and a councilwoman at a city council meeting that month:

> COUNCILWOMAN: I move that we do not act on this [licensing repeal] today . . .
> CITY ATTORNEY: Could I suggest that you pass this today. We have some reason. We have a good reason we need to get this done today.
> COUNCILWOMAN: Tell that to me. Because I don't see it. Tell me why—what's the good reason?
> CITY ATTORNEY: We have a pending motion in a lawsuit that we're trying to get rid of.[255]

The city council reluctantly agreed, voting to replace the license with a voluntary certification and examination in Savannah.[256] Stillwell's intention may have been "to get rid of" the lawsuit, but his public statement focused on a new appreciation for the private sector: "We believe the private sector can do a better job of training and certifying tour guides, but without the government having a role in it," he said.[257]

For their part, city council members were less sanguine, and their comments about the change were particularly revealing about the bottleneckers' view of the world. "I'm disappointed," said Councilman Van Johnson, "But I also realize that when you come up against the U.S. Constitution, you lose."[258]

A bottlenecker's loss is freedom's gain.

CHAPTER 6

The Regulatory Stone Age

In 1955, Dr. Martin Luther King Jr. had a problem.

On December 1, Rosa Parks had been arrested in Montgomery, Alabama, for refusing to yield her seat in the "colored" section of a city bus to white passengers. Segregation on the city's buses—overseen by the Montgomery City Lines, a subsidiary of Chicago-based National City Lines[1]—had become a source of frustration and anger among Montgomery's black population. Parks's arrest sparked a one-day protest on December 5, 1955, that saw most of the company's black riders—70 percent of the system's patronage—refuse to use the buses.[2]

Seeking to build on that success, Dr. King—in his first significant leadership role in the civil rights movement—E. D. Nixon, and other civil rights leaders in Montgomery created the Montgomery Improvement Association (MIA) to continue and coordinate the bus boycott. But they faced a practical challenge. For the boycott to work, Montgomery's black residents, many of whom relied on city buses to get to work, would need an alternate mode of transportation.[3]

King turned to black taxi owners and convinced them to transport protestors to and from work and charge the same ten-cent fare busses charged—thirty-five cents less than the taxi owners normally charged their passengers. But within the first few days of the protest, King learned from Montgomery's police commissioner that, by city law, taxis were required to charge a minimum fare. It was only a matter of time before the city would attempt to crush the protest by enforcing the law against the taxi owners who were undercharging black passengers.[4]

On December 9, the city issued an order to taxi owners notifying them that they had to charge the required minimum of forty-five cents per ride, posing King with a problem of enormous proportions if he was to keep the boycott alive—how to provide sustained, affordable daily transportation for tens of thousands of protestors across the city.[5]

Dr. King recalled the bus boycott in Baton Rouge, Louisiana, two years earlier, and how his friend, Theodore Jemison, had organized a private "carpool" in order to provide transportation for protestors. After a hasty call to Jemison to discuss the intricacies of his system, King met with MIA leaders to create a similar plan for Montgomery. The result was a network of volunteer drivers who shuttled between 80 and 90 "stations" throughout the city, providing much-needed transportation for the forty thousand black boycotters.[6] The MIA's transportation system far eclipsed Baton Rouge's in size and sophistication, even earning grudging praise from the White Citizens Council—a civil rights opposition group—for its "military precision."[7]

As days turned into weeks and then into months, the protest continued, seriously harming the bus line. The company was hemorrhaging money, bleeding its way toward bankruptcy.[8] When the boycott started, Montgomery City Lines partnered with the city to protect segregation, but the company's resolve weakened over time as its financial losses increased.[9] It eventually went to court against the city as part of an unsuccessful attempt to discontinue segregation on its buses in order to save itself.[10]

Meanwhile, although the MIA's carpool faced numerous challenges in serving the needs of thousands of protestors over a sustained period, it was able to cover its costs of $5,000 a month (almost $45,000 a month in 2014 dollars) through contributions first from local churches and later from supporters all over the country and even the world.[11] The service grew so successful that over the course of the 382-day boycott, it evolved from a volunteer-based system to a semipermanent one with hired staff and drivers, purchased vehicles, and rented office space.[12]

It was this success, however, that eventually led to the service's ruin. Montgomery, like many cities, required that transportation companies—like taxis—be licensed. In its early existence, the MIA's service was entirely voluntary, both by description and in practice, but as it took on the trappings of a business—with paid dispatchers and drivers and ownership of vehicles—it looked less and less like the voluntary carpool Dr. King insisted on calling it. Had the city enforced its licensing provision against King and the MIA early in the boycott, it would have given them much trouble.[13] Indeed, it was the legal weapon King and his attorneys feared most,[14] since the end of the carpool would likely mean the end of the boycott.

As King himself put it, "How could [the protestors] function at all with the car pool destroyed? Could we ask them to walk back and forth every day to their jobs? And if not, would we then be forced to admit that the protest had failed in the end?"[15]

In January 1956, MIA leaders tried to protect the carpool by applying for a license to operate a transportation system, but city officials rejected their application.[16] For reasons that have never been entirely clear, the city waited until October 30, 1956—a full ten months after the boycott began—to file for a court injunction against the carpool as an unlicensed municipal transportation system.[17] King and the MIA tried to block the move in federal court, but their request was denied; the hearing on the MIA's carpool was set for November 13, 1956.[18]

On the appointed day, Dr. King sat at the defendants' table, listening to attorneys argue over whether the MIA's system was a private enterprise operating without a license or a volunteer carpool provided by local churches to serve city residents. At the end of the hearing, Judge Eugene Carter ruled in favor of the city. The carpool was deemed a business operating without a license and ordered to cease service.[19] But this decision would be largely forgotten; that same day, midway through the carpool hearing, the US Supreme Court declared Alabama's state and local laws requiring segregation on buses unconstitutional.[20]

Throughout Dr. King's yearlong, high-stakes chess match with Montgomery city leaders, the invocation of licensing schemes created years earlier was among the city's more effective legal moves—and one that might have proven decisive. Of all the attempts to suppress the boycott, including police harassment and arrests[21]—not to mention subordination efforts by others that included intimidation and violence[22]—the use of licensing is the tactic that continually gave the city the advantage, almost from day one. Indeed, enforcing Montgomery's minimum-fare regulation—a typical feature of taxi licensing schemes—could have won the match for city leaders had King not hit upon the idea of the volunteer carpool.[23] Much the same can be said for the city's denial of King's application for an operating permit, which left the door open for the city to go after the carpool. And had the Supreme Court decision on Alabama's segregation laws not checkmated the city, Judge Carter's ruling against the carpool as an unlicensed operation would likely have ended the game in a perceived loss for King.

Just as licensing was used during the Montgomery Bus Boycott to defend entrenched segregation interests and deny people's rights, transportation licensing schemes all over the country continue to be used to protect the rapacious interests of taxi and limousine company owners, inefficient city transit systems, and transportation unions, as well as to deny the rights of others to earn an honest living free from unnecessary government intrusion. Although not as historically significant as the Montgomery Bus Boycott, efforts by individuals to bust open government-sanctioned bottlenecks have nonetheless enabled many people, including many people of color, to work freely and legally to the benefit of consumers—including, again, many people of color and others served poorly or not at all by licensed transportation providers.

Indeed, when Hector Ricketts wanted to build a business providing a simple, convenient van service that would charge customers a mere dollar per trip and to help other entrepreneurs to do the same, bottleneckers, in the form of the New York City Taxi and Limousine Commission and its labor union, attempted to choke off this competition. But in Hector they found a man who refused to say die.

HECTOR VERSUS GOLIATH—AND GOLIATH'S LABOR UNION

In 1992, Hector wasn't looking for a fight. He was looking for work.

When Hector was laid off from his hospital health care administrator position, jobs were scarce. The 1990–91 recession, although milder than many of the post–World War II recessions before it,[24] was unique in that economic growth was anemic in the years preceding and following it.[25] The labor market continued to deteriorate long after the official end of the recessionary period,[26] as evidenced by the 7.3 percent unemployment rate a year after the recession ended.[27] Employment declines were widespread across major occupational groups, particularly in the white-collar sector, and, in the years following the recession, a comparatively smaller share of those who lost jobs expected to be rehired.[28]

Hector Ricketts was one of those who had lost their jobs. Despite a decade of experience and a master's degree in community health from Brooklyn College, the Jamaican-born immigrant struggled to find work in the health care field, so, as a way to make some extra money to continue providing for his wife and three children, Hector began working full time in a side business he had first started in 1987—dollar vans.

New York City's dollar-van industry emerged in the 1970s, ferrying commuters from the outer boroughs to Manhattan and other job centers around the Big Apple. When the city's public transit workers went on strike for eleven days in 1980, thousands of new dollar vans took to the streets and remained there after the strike ended.[29]

Although the vans are capable of carrying far-fewer passengers than a bus or subway car, they make up for that by being nimble, changing routes on the fly to meet demand, and providing door-to-door service for a small extra fee. This flexibility allows them to do such things as wait while parents walk their children to the door of a daycare center or drop passengers off at their doorsteps, making sure they get inside safely—a comfort to commuters arriving home after dark. They do all of that while also cutting commute times in half and being much more reliable than the services provided by the Metropolitan Transit Authority (MTA).[30]

Today, New York City's dollar vans perform one million rides per month.[31] If they were counted as their own system, they would rank as the twentieth-largest bus system in the country.[32] Both the drivers and their customers are overwhelmingly immigrants—Caribbean, Asian, Hispanic, and African. The vast majority of customers live in the outer boroughs; without the vans, many of their commutes would entail first taking a bus and then switching to the subway.[33] Thus the dollar vans form a huge informal network that makes life easier and safer for the thousands of commuters it serves.

And yet the service they provide is often deemed to be illegal.

As Hector recalled of the situation in the 1980s, "I would see the vans transporting passengers to and from the neighborhood, and they seemed to be under siege from the police department." At the time, the state, rather than the city, regulated dollar vans, many of which operated without licenses. But even operators who satisfied the state's licensing requirements were, as Hector put it, "so heavily regulated that it was almost impossible for them to do what they were doing with any dignity and freedom."[34]

Indeed, the level of regulation far exceeded any rational explanation. Given the comparably low risk that the vehicle-for-hire industry represents to public health and safety, entering it should be as easy as acquiring a vehicle and passing safety checks. The industry requires comparatively little start-up capital and little formal education, making it ideal for individuals climbing up the economic ladder or entrepreneurs like Hector seeking to start and grow a business, hire others, and contribute to the economic life of their communities.

Yet transportation is one of the most heavily regulated low-skill industries in the country, largely because established companies have long been highly effective bottleneckers. Indeed, bottlenecking in the transportation industry is almost as old as the motor vehicle itself.

The nation's first jitney service—the forerunner to dollar vans—began in Los Angeles in the summer of 1914, when an entrepreneurial Ford Model T owner started driving commuters around for a nickel a ride. By the next summer, an estimated sixty-two thousand jitneys operated across the country daily.[35]

But heavily subsidized private streetcar operators fiercely opposed these upstart competitors—calling them a "menace" and a "malignant growth"—and industry leaders soon convinced politicians to enact burdensome restrictions far above and beyond what concern for public health and safety could justify. Cities began dictating jitneys' routes, schedules, and hours of operation; requiring independent jitneys to form a single company subject to franchise rules; and imposing outsize fees or surety bonds, rendering part-time driving uneconomical.[36]

Drivers tried to fight back, but, as unanimously as if they were following a federal law hindering jitneys, cities and states passed comprehensive laws to regulate them. The laws were so severe that by the early 1920s jitneys had virtually disappeared from the 175 American cities where they had operated. In the end, their demise did not even help the streetcars, which turned out to be money-losing endeavors even with the benefit of municipal largesse.[37]

Although jitneys have reemerged in various times and places, they have never recaptured their former glory. They operate in neighborhoods poorly served by public transit and private accommodations like taxicabs—or where public services are shut down. For instance, in Houston, which effectively banned jitneys in 1924, city leaders temporarily allowed them back on the road during transit strikes in 1949 and 1974.[38] Elsewhere, in cities like New York, Chicago,[39] Miami, and St. Louis, jitneys became cultural fixtures, so much so that in 1982 playwright August Wilson immortalized Pittsburgh's jitney culture in the play *Jitney*. The play is set in a dispatch center soon to be bulldozed, along with the rest of the neighborhood, as part of an urban renewal scheme.[40]

Today, the industry exists in much the same form as it has for decades—illegal in many places but tolerated because the official system serves the community so poorly. The vans still serve mostly poor, African American neighborhoods where taxicabs resolutely refuse to go, despite laws requiring them to do so.[41] Customers prefer jitneys for various reasons, most often because the service is faster, sometimes significantly faster, than public transportation.[42] In St. Louis, for example, because city leaders cut a third of the city's public bus routes in 2009 (until voters approved a new transit tax), average commute times from low-income neighborhoods to business districts soared to three hours. Ride vans slashed such commutes to less than an hour.[43]

Nevertheless, city leaders continue to be hostile to dollar vans, although not out of a supposed concern for public health and safety, as consumers rarely complain about this in regard to the service. In fact, according to a report by New York City's MTA, "Riders prefer vans because they are faster, less costly, and more comfortable" than public buses. Rather, the concerns of city officials are those of bottleneckers everywhere—they see the vans as competitors that "steal" business from the city. In New York, that lost revenue amounted to $30 to $50 million annually.[44]

Hector's entry into the van business began simply: He bought a van, and each day before and after his job at the hospital he ferried commuters from Queens to their jobs. By the time he lost his job in 1992, he knew that the demand for van service was great. So he created a company called Queens Van Plan and completed the necessary licensing requirements to run his business. His timing could not have been better.

The following year, with the support of transportation officials and transit unions, city and state leaders passed new rules for the vans, assigning regulatory oversight to city as well as state officials. Under the thicket of new rules, would-be van drivers had to acquire a state-issued commercial driver's license, take a physical, get added to a company's roster, obtain a hack license from the New York City Taxi and Limousine Commission (TLC), and sign an affidavit saying they owed no child support. If they received a ticket for driving a van without a license, they would be banned from applying for two years.[45] The new rules also gave TLC officials unbridled discretion to deny license applications by implementing the public convenience and necessity (PCN) law, the bottleneck of all bottlenecks.

Also called "certificate of need" and other variants, PCN laws, like occupational licensing, require entrepreneurs to gain government permission to work. However, the process for doing so is different. Moreover, the purpose of PCN laws is purely protectionist. Whereas under occupational licensing, any number of aspiring workers can get permission to work by clearing the necessary hurdles of education, an examination, and the like, under PCN laws, even if an applicant completes all of the necessary requirements, a regulatory agency may still reject the application based on a determination that the public is sufficiently served by other businesses already in the market.[46] Agencies may also reject an application if they believe the aspiring entrepreneur will harm the economic interests of existing businesses by competing with them.[47] And that's not the worst of it: PCN laws allow existing businesses to veto the applications of potential competitors. It's as though McDonald's were given the power to stop Burger King from opening across the street.

Getting certified under the PCN laws involves a lengthy, onerous, and expensive multistep process that begins with an application wherein aspiring business owners are required to describe the service they will provide, their experience and training, the equipment they will use, the insurances they will carry, and any number of other details required by the oversight agency. By signing the application, they also acknowledge the various regulations governing their potential business—including restrictions on what they may charge customers—and agree to comply with them.[48]

On receipt of the application, the regulatory agency notifies existing businesses that a newcomer seeks to enter the market and gives them the opportunity to object.[49] And, as is often the case when bottlenecking is strong, their objections need not be supported by evidence.[50]

When an objection is filed, the agency holds a hearing to decide the application's fate. During the hearing, the entrepreneur is required to prove the need for his or her business. However, what constitutes need is often vague, leaving enormous discretion up to the regulating agency.[51] Applicants must spend significant amounts of money, hire attorneys, and wait a long yet typically undefined time to make it through this maze and get government permission to start their businesses.[52]

The forerunners of modern PCN laws date back to the 1870s and were designed to protect businesses that provided desirable-yet-capital-intensive services to the public—services such as railroads, utilities, moving goods, transportation,[53] and, years later, health care.[54] Companies undertaking to provide such services wanted to be sure of seeing a return on their investments,[55] so they demanded protection from competitors. Governments agreed to provide such protection by limiting new entrants into the market, but they restricted what existing businesses could charge and where they could operate, among other things.[56]

Although jitneys, taxis, and other forms of personal transportation do not fit the description of businesses requiring large capital investments—quite the opposite, in fact—they were nonetheless swept up by the PCN wave of 1913, when New York became the first state to apply its PCN laws to motor carriers.[57] The law was modified in 1915 after the emergence of jitneys, explicitly because of the threat they posed to the profitability of trolleys. Even then, the process was so onerous that one lawyer arguing on behalf of a jitney applicant wondered whether there would be any street railways still in existence if railway companies had been faced with conditions similar to those imposed on the jitneys within their first sixteen months of existence.[58]

Similar to occupational licensing, PCN laws accomplish their primary goal of keeping competitors out of the market to serve existing businesses. And like occupational licensing, PCN laws have, over time, proven not to be in the public's best interests. As far back as 1965, economists were finding evidence that PCN laws in the transportation sector—specifically the trucking industry—resulted in poorer service, operational inefficiencies, and higher costs to consumers, despite price controls.[59] The higher prices were largely a result of the consolidation of firm ownership as a way to increase market power and influence, among other things, and using that influence to lobby agencies for rate increases and other changes.[60]

Later research found similar effects of the laws on prices and service quality, not only in trucking and other surface transportation[61] but also in the airline industry. In 1978, deregulation resulted in more airline carriers entering the market and lower prices for consumers—compared to both what prices were during regulation and what they were projected to be if regulation were to continue.[62] Similar effects have been found in health care, in which PCN laws have been applied to hospitals and other medical facilities and services.[63] Excluding competitors from the market means fewer services,[64] higher costs,[65] and decreased innovation in the medical industry.[66]

For bottleneckers, such negative effects for consumers are irrelevant. The primary purpose of PCN laws, after all, is not to protect public health and safety, or to provide economic or other benefits to the public, but rather to protect current businesses by keeping competitors at bay with the cooperation of such agencies such as New York's TLC. In fact, when the city council voted 41–4 to pass the new rules for jitneys, which city leaders said would promote safety, a councilman who voted against the law rightly said that they were "not regulation, but strangulation."[67]

Even if the TLC did approve a license, the city council served as a pernicious backstop. As Hector described it,

> Nobody could get a license. The city council had the right to approve individual licenses. The Taxi and Limousine Commission and the Department of Transportation would approve putting vans on the street, and the city council—under the influence of the bus drivers' union—simply intended to eliminate vans.[68]

As a result, applicants might spend years and thousands of dollars on legal fees trying to navigate the process, only to be denied a permit. After the regulatory scheme was installed in 1994, 98 percent of the van drivers who sought licenses from the city council were denied.[69] In one instance, 938 businesses, church groups, commuters, and community members submitted statements urging the city to accept the application of one driver—Vincent Cummins. The application had cost Vincent, a native of Barbados, five years and $40,000 to shepherd through the TLC's process before it even reached the city council.[70]

When it finally was received, in November 1996, a city council committee, packed with members of the thirty-three-thousand-strong Transit Workers Union (TWU), voted 8–0 on a preliminary motion to reject the application, prompting the TWU workers to break out in cheers and applause. "I plead guilty to protecting union jobs," said Councilman Archie Spigner, a former transit worker, at the hearing. "The backbone of my community is made up of members of the Transport Workers Union who have good jobs with good wages, and I don't want to see them competing with people who are much worse off."[71]

Cummins arrived at a subsequent hearing before the full city council to find that the TWU's president was seated with the council as a guest of honor—and to learn that no final vote would take place because the TLC had withdrawn its approval for his application. By way of explanation, the TLC would say only that it had reconsidered "the manner of operations of the vans and the effect on mass transit."[72]

The saga did not end there. A few months later, Mayor Rudy Giuliani, a ride-van supporter, vetoed the city council's denial. At the veto ceremony, the TWU turned out in force to oppose the veto, chanting in protest on the steps of City Hall. During the ceremony, Councilman Spigner railed against van operators for threatening the union, inadvertently revealing its true concern: "Given a choice between a van costing a dollar and a city bus costing $1.50, people will take the van."[73] The council overrode the mayor's veto the following month.[74]

The bramble of new rules created in 1993 and 1994 not only choked off entry into the industry but also banned vans from driving routes used by city buses and from picking up street hails—essentially criminalizing the entire business model of Hector and others like him. Even more perverse, the regulations required vans to maintain a manifest of passengers' names and addresses[75]—a requirement that is, as Hector put it, "burdensome and serves no purpose at all" and that "many passengers view as an invasion of privacy."[76]

Not surprisingly, the bottlenecking worked just as intended. "How can you employ a young worker who wants to build a career as a small business owner in these circumstances?" asked van-company owner Lateef Ajala. "You go out tomorrow and get eight summonses.... The union understands. Its leaders are sophisticated and knowledgeable. It has deeper pockets and uses its wealth to effectively kill what it sees as competition."[77]

Also not surprisingly, the bottleneckers portrayed the regulations as a matter of protecting the public, asserting that the vans were not safe and pointing to the many illegal vans operating without licenses, insurance, or inspections. However, as Hector noted, the city's perverse rules only pushed would-be entrepreneurs into the gray market. Further, many of the alleged safety issues could have been addressed by applying a more rational regulatory structure that actually focused on safety—by allowing vans to operate with licenses, insurance, and inspections, rather than by thwarting competition.[78]

Unable to bear the injustice of this bottlenecking, Hector formed a coalition of van drivers and began trying to convince politicians that dollar vans provided a much-needed service to city residents. "We tried to have meetings with elected officials," explained Hector. "We protested. We blocked the streets. We went on strike. We demonstrated." Despite their efforts, officials were, as Hector described,

> not interested in speaking with us most of the time, and when we did get a meeting they would shut us down as outsiders, and there was an immigrant piece to it too you know. Most of us at the time were immigrants. They saw us as outsiders, intruders. At the time, the only voice that was on our side was Una Clark, who was the first Jamaican to be elected to the city council. She was the one who championed [our cause]...with her voice the issue got some press coverage and the issue got louder and louder.

Other than Clark, "the unions had every politician," said Hector.[79] At a city council hearing, for example, a *Wall Street Journal* correspondent noted that the TWU's president summoned a council committee chair for a conference, rather than the other way around.[80]

After years of futile efforts to break open the bottleneck, Hector and other dollar-van operators sued the city in 1997, arguing that the entry restrictions and rules banning drivers from driving on bus routes and accepting street hails were unconstitutional. The city council responded in a move that could only be described as vindictive—it adopted a one-year moratorium on new van licenses.[81] For all practical purposes, the moratorium merely codified what the licensing process was already accomplishing, but the move symbolized the council's hostile commitment to preserving its bottleneck.

It also demonstrated why Hector's lawsuit was so important. A decision came in 1999, two years after Hector filed suit, and brought only partial victory. Justice Louis B. York ordered the city to open entry into the field but left the other rules in place.[82] The decision meant new operators could begin driving but only under conditions that would make business unnecessarily difficult. Dissatisfied with York's half-loaf compromise, Hector appealed the decision, only to see it upheld. In 2002, New York's highest court, the court of appeals, refused to hear his appeal.

And so it is today that licensed vans are barely tolerated and hundreds of drivers choose to operate entirely illegally. From January 2013 to September 2014, TLC enforcers seized more than one thousand vans that lacked the proper permits.[83] And police officers have enforced regulations to the point of harassment. Given the long menu of rules, a van driver can receive anywhere from eight to sixteen tickets in a single stop. Drivers can have most of the citations dismissed by going to court, but each day they spend doing so is a day not spent driving and earning.[84]

Nevertheless, the vans remain omnipresent because of the enormous demand for fast, reliable service.[85] Some researchers have counted as many as forty-five to sixty vans passing a given point in the span of an hour—compared to four city buses over the same period.[86] One van customer described the value and popularity of the service in allowing her to avoid "an extra half hour [a day] with the MTA. I don't want to be stuck on the bus forever. I can get home faster and spend more time with my kids."[87]

BOTTLENECKING TAXIS

In 1993, when Hector was just beginning his fight with bottleneckers in New York City, taxi driver Ani Ebong was doing the same thing

1,800 miles away in Denver, Colorado. Ani, an immigrant from Nigeria with an entrepreneurial streak, had come to the United States in 1973 on a student visa.[88] To support himself while in school, he drove a taxi for Yellow Cab, an ideal job for a student and an immigrant. As Ani explained the job,

> All you have to know is how to drive, which most of us do, and how to get around the city, which is easy enough to learn. And it's flexible; you can set your own hours and fit them around being a student, so that you can take English classes or go to college.[89]

Upon graduating from college with a marketing degree, Ani continued driving a cab, with an eye toward saving money to open his own business. In 1990, he left Yellow Cab, the largest of Denver's three taxi companies, to start his own taxi business. By then, Yellow Cab was in financial trouble, and working conditions for drivers were poor. "There were so many drivers at Yellow Cab who were unhappy," Ani remembered.[90]

Much of the drivers' dissatisfaction grew out of the financial relationship they were forced to maintain with the company and the conditions that grew from it. Across the industry, taxi drivers generally work under one of three arrangements: as an employee-driver, a lessee-driver, or an owner-driver.[91] The lessor-lessee relationship, in which drivers operate as independent contractors, is popular among taxi company owners because it enables them to avoid tax and finance responsibilities that come with having employees.[92] Under this arrangement, drivers lease cars from the taxi companies and keep as profit any money they make after the lease payment—"the payoff" in industry jargon—and paying other expenses, such as gas, maintenance, and other necessities.[93] In Denver, Ani and other drivers were paying up to $400 a week to lease the cabs.[94] To turn a profit, they often had to work up to fourteen-hour shifts.[95]

The conditions in Denver were in no way unusual, and, in many cities, they remain the rule. Cabdrivers regularly work six days a week, twelve hours a day[96]—a routine that can take a serious toll on their health. Numerous studies have documented myriad health problems associated with long hours behind the wheel, including back and leg issues,[97] heart problems,[98] high blood pressure,[99] and even reproductive-health deficiencies.[100] All that for incomes that can often best be described as meager.[101] For example, in 2006, two UCLA professors surveyed Los Angeles cabbies and found that they earned a median income of just $8.39 per hour.[102]

Despite such drawbacks, entrepreneurs like Ani are willing to remain in the industry because they think that through hard work and perseverance they can earn enough money to open businesses of their own. This is precisely what Ani did, although Denver's bottleneckers did everything in their power to stop him.

Upon leaving Yellow Cab, Ani and two friends formed Quick Pick Cabs. As it turned out, that was the easiest part of starting their business. They next had to make it through the bottleneckers' gauntlet—the PCN process.

As New York had done with jitney operators, Colorado imposed a PCN application on aspiring taxi-company owners, requiring them to prove both that their new company would meet a public need and that the company would not harm any existing businesses. The rule amounted to a de facto ban on new competitors by existing companies. At the time that Ani and his friends were striking out on their own, Colorado's Public Utilities Commission (PUC) had not granted a single PCN application to start a new cab company in Denver since 1947. Three companies owned all of the permits needed to put a cab on Denver's streets[103] and had since the 1930s, when taxi regulations first appeared in cities all over the country.

EIGHTY YEARS OF BOTTLENECKING

Denver's bottleneckers weren't Ani's only foe—he was also up against a tide of regulatory history going back decades. Popular lore has it that taxicab regulation emerged during the so-called taxi wars of the 1920s and 1930s,[104] when fierce competition between cab companies sometimes erupted into bloodshed. But closer examination of the record reveals that regulation significantly predates those tumults. In Chicago, for example, taxi regulation can be traced to the 1860s, when cabs were horse drawn.[105] Calls to regulate modern taxis began almost as soon as they hit the road,[106] and already by the 1920s many cities imposed fare restrictions (or required posting of fares), licensed drivers, or required insurance.[107]

As for the taxi wars, there is evidence to suggest that in some jurisdictions they stemmed, in part, from regulation and bottlenecking. Chicago's taxi war, for example, began after a new ordinance requiring licenses for the use of cab stands in the Loop shut out every cab company but one, which had likely bribed corrupt officials for this exclusive privilege.[108] Smaller firms fought back, and the war was on,[109] complete with murder and arson.[110] New York City's taxi war broke out after the city imposed a five-cent tax on fares. Outraged cabbies went on strike and beat up and wrecked the cabs of those cabdrivers who stayed on the road.[111]

The taxi wars also involved fare wars, in which taxi companies competed on price to increase market share. The idea was to drive the other company out of business and crush small competitors,[112] of which there were many, particularly as the Great Depression wore on and the unemployed flocked to the occupation, causing prices to fall even further.[113]

Although the first taxi regulations predate the taxi wars, and may have even helped to foment them, the hypercompetitive market they engendered, exacerbated by the Depression, intensified calls for government intervention. As is so often the case, those demanding action were not consumers enjoying taxi service at cut-rate prices but members of the mass-transit rail industry, which perceived the cars as a threat,[114] and taxi companies seeking to protect their interests and increase their profits.[115] In typical bottlenecker fashion, they did so through professional associations, namely the American Transit Association and the National Association of Taxicab Owners (NATO),[116] the latter having been formed in 1919 by the owners of two of the leading taxi companies—John D. Hertz and Morris Markin.[117]

Hertz, an immigrant from Slovakia, began his career in the automobile industry as a successful car salesman but expanded into the taxi business when he saw a specific need. Hertz noticed that when he sold customers new cars they would trade in their old ones, and that this was a problem for the infant car-sales industry since there was not then a market for used cars. He decided to make money on the used cars by turning them into taxis. He and a partner launched a taxi business in

1907. Hertz was farsighted in his business plans, instituting profit sharing with drivers and providing employee benefits that included health care, savings plans, and legal services. He also created other systems and practices still in use today.

When he first launched his cab company, taxis were a service only for the rich. Hertz changed that by charging half of what his rivals did, eliminating the "deadhead" charge (an extra fee customers had to pay when one leg of their trip was driven without passengers), and promising his cabs could be at anyone's home in ten minutes. After reading a University of Chicago study that found that yellow is the most visible color from far away, Hertz painted all of his cabs this color. He also installed a telephone dispatch system and began manufacturing his own cars in 1915 under the Yellow Cab Company. Yellow Cab eventually became the largest taxi company in the world, and Hertz helped to organize branches in Kansas City, Philadelphia, and New York City. In the 1920s, Hertz bought a rental car company, and sold Yellow Cab to the Parmelee taxi company, which was later purchased by Checker—both of which were owned by Morris Markin.[118]

Markin, an immigrant from Russia, was already a successful clothier when he purchased the Checker Cab Manufacturing Company, which specialized in converting cars for use as cabs, and he also ran a taxi service. The manufacturing business was very competitive, and Markin saw the taxi business as a way to ensure a market for his cars. In 1929, he organized the National Transportation Company in New York City, which would eventually operate 1,500 cabs there. He also bought Yellow and Parmelee in Chicago, Yellow in Pittsburgh, and Yellow in Minneapolis.[119]

Through NATO,[120] Hertz, Markin, and others called for strict regulation of the taxi industry, pushing for five provisions in particular: placing taxicabs under the control of a city- or state-utility commission; ensuring that PCN requirements were met before additional cabs could be licensed; making operators financially responsible for damages to the cars; requiring that taximeters be placed in cabs; and designating minimum and maximum fares. The bottlenecking spread quickly as company owners urged legislatures and city councils across the country to adopt these regulations.[121] By the end of the 1930s, many cities had adopted ordinances creating regulatory bodies, entry restrictions, and minimum fares for the taxi industry and requiring that the PCN process be applied to it.[122]

Limits on the number of cabs that could operate were, and remain, common. In 1930, Boston capped the number of cabs at 1,525, where it remained for more than fifty years.[123] New York City capped the number of its cabs in 1932 and again in 1937, first at 16,900 licenses and later at 11,787, where it remained until 1996.[124] Chicago restricted the number of cabs to 4,108 in 1934 and lowered that number to 3,000 three years later.

PCN laws were another popular tool for restricting entry into the industry: By 1932, 19 percent of cities with populations of twenty-five to a hundred thousand and 39 percent of cities with populations greater than a hundred thousand required PCN processes for approving new cab companies. Eight states also had PCN requirements, and two cities capped the number of permits for cabs. At least fifty-three cities with populations greater than twenty-five thousand required taximeters, and twenty-two cities regulated fares.[125] Mass transit operators particularly appreciated the taximeter requirement because it allowed taxi operators to limit their passengers to those taking exclusive rides. However, because the drivers were unable to provide a shared-ride service, taxis could no longer compete quite so directly with mass transit modes.[126]

Although the drive for regulation was justified as being about public health and safety—the standard bottlenecker trope—the true motive was clearly to drive up profits by forcing competitors out of the market.[127] Indeed, the history of taxi regulation has been one of market concentration, in which taxi company owners gain monopolies or oligopolies over their markets by seizing opportunities created by regulations.

Markin, for example, bought up a number of smaller cab companies to get control of their licenses. Then, to inflate prices, he suspended those companies' operations and abandoned their licenses, fully confident that cities wouldn't issue new ones.[128] By 1930, Markin controlled all of the cab licenses in Pittsburgh through ownership of several companies. He also controlled 125 of Minneapolis's 214 licenses[129] and came close to obtaining a monopoly in New York City after Mayor James Walker recommended granting his company exclusive operating rights for cabs in the city. It later emerged that Walker had accepted stock in Markin's company—otherwise known as a bribe—and the mayor resigned in 1932.[130] Markin's holdings grew so large that in 1946 the federal government sued him for having a monopoly—a case that went all the way to the US Supreme Court, where Markin eventually prevailed.[131] When he died in 1970, Markin controlled 80 percent of Chicago's taxi licenses.[132]

He was able to do so because few changes to the regulatory framework had occurred in the taxi industry before the 1970s,[133] and any attempts to alter the licenses were met with great resistance by the bottleneckers. For example, in New York City, where a shortage of taxis had created a "mess," in the words of the *New York Times*, Mayor John Lindsay created a task force that recommended, among other things, that new licenses be issued. Taxi owners fiercely fought the move, and their political influence eventually won the day.[134]

So, too, did the number of licenses remain static in many other cities, as the entry restrictions adopted in the 1930s continued in force, untouched by city councils or licensing officials.[135] This meant that as demand for taxis grew in line with the population, the supply of licensed taxis held constant.[136] A 1984 study commissioned by the US Department of Transportation found that regulations restricting the entry of new cabs and establishing minimum fares cost consumers hundreds of millions of dollars. The study estimated that removal of these regulations would have created thirty-eight thousand new jobs in the taxi industry.[137]

Entry restrictions also put owning a cab company out of reach for most aspiring taxi entrepreneurs. Cities weren't issuing new licenses, but existing ones were transferrable through private sales. Because of the artificially low supply, licenses originally sold by the city for a few hundred dollars took on a staggering street value.[138] By the mid-1990s, Boston's licenses commanded $95,000 on the open market[139] and New York City's, $140,000.[140] Two decades later, prices in Boston and New York reached $700,000[141] and $1.3 million,[142] respectively.

The value of taxi licenses—also called "medallions" after the badges affixed to taxis—grew so dramatically that a finance company, Medallion Financial, emerged to loan money to aspiring taxi owners. The company has its origins in a New York City cabdriver, Leon Murstein, an immigrant who bought the first license for his own cab in 1937 for $10. By the 1970s, in yet another example of market concentration, Murstein controlled five hundred licenses. In 1979, his son began lending money to cabdrivers so that they could obtain their own licenses.

The company—which finances taxi permits in Miami; Boston; Chicago; Baltimore; Philadelphia; Newark, New Jersey; and, of course, New York City[143]—went public in 1996 and trades on the NASDAQ. "Taxi medallions have been maybe the best investment to own in the United States over the past 70 years," said Andrew Murstein, Leon's grandson and now the president of Medallion Financial. "They've outperformed the Dow Jones, the Nasdaq, real estate, gold, almost every major index you can think of."[144] Indeed, taxi medallions have even been heralded as a better investment than gold as a hedge against inflation because of the artificial scarcity created by bottlenecking.[145]

The decades preceding the 1970s were mostly very good to the taxi bottleneckers, but starting in the 1960s other changes got underway that would later threaten their cartels. The first change occurred in the larger mass transit industry. In 1948, only thirty-six public transit systems in the nation were owned by the government. However, by 1975, government systems carried 90 percent of all public transit. While most mass transit is currently city owned, the money to pay for it comes from the federal government. Beginning in 1961 and expanding in 1964, the federal government gave significant amounts of funding to local governments to build public transportation systems. Taxicabs weren't part of the equation,[146] which meant that, suddenly, cities and taxi owners were competitors.[147]

The second change was widespread transportation deregulation in the 1970s and 1980s, most notably executed in the 1978 Airline Deregulation Act, the 1980 Staggers Rail Act, and the 1980 Motor Carrier Act. Deregulation also occurred in the taxi industry, albeit not nearly as extensively. Almost two dozen cities—mostly in the Sun Belt—deregulated taxis.[148] Some of these cities—particularly those with robust airport markets[149]—would eventually reregulate,[150] but the initial liberalization yielded positive outcomes.

As a result of the liberalization, in Cincinnati 209 new taxis, most of them driven by driver-owners, began providing the city with additional service.[151] In Indianapolis, after only six months of deregulation, the number of cabs on the street at any given time doubled, and average wait times fell by more than half. Of the over forty new companies that entered the market in the city, 75 percent were owned by women or minorities. Fares fell and customer complaints, which used to tally in the hundreds each year, dropped sharply.[152] "Nearly overnight," wrote then mayor Stephen Goldsmith, "the dress code for taxi drivers went from ripped t-shirts to collars and ties. Cabs are noticeably cleaner, cabbies are friendlier, and their vehicles are more visible on our streets."[153]

BOTTLENECKING AT A MILE HIGH

Meanwhile, in Denver, the bottleneck remained firmly lodged in place. Cabdrivers faced restrictions on what they could charge customers, but cab companies were unlimited in what they could charge cabbies for the use of a permit. Consequently, "most drivers appear to be working for between $2.75 and $3.00 an hour, excluding gratuities," wrote a PUC administrative law judge in 1990. "Further, because there are only three certificated taxi companies (an oligopoly) the companies are in a position to extract 'economic rent,' i.e. sums of money greatly in excess of costs from the drivers."[154]

The cab companies' oligopoly was also bad news for consumers. Testifying before Congress, Leroy Jones, one of Ani's compatriots, said that in the Denver downtown neighborhood of Five Points, "like in most inner cities, a cab is the only thing harder to get than a job."[155] The payoff system encouraged drivers to disfavor short trips, more likely to be demanded by senior citizens and the poor, in preference for longer hauls.[156] And without fear of new competition, Yellow Cab—and Denver's two other cab companies, Metro Taxi and Zone Taxi—"[got] so fat and lazy," as Ani put it, that "half the time when you call a cab it doesn't come."[157]

But if the established companies were lazy when dealing with the public, they were on permanent full alert in the legislature. In the decade before Ani and the others formed Quick Pick, no fewer than five bills to deregulate the taxicab industry failed in the General Assembly, thanks to the industry's tireless lobbyists. Like bottleneckers in every other industry, the taxi lobbyists beat the drum of public health and safety with characteristic hyperbole. "The people who want to have this industry deregulated are the ones who don't want health inspectors in restaurants," proclaimed Freda Poundstone, a cab company lobbyist.[158] In 1990, drivers asked the PUC to consider regulating lease rates, but cab companies successfully countered the attempt.[159] And, in 1991, the legislature forbade the PUC from interfering with the payoffs.[160]

Unsuccessful in the legislature and unable to convince Yellow Cab to lower its lease rates, Ani, Leroy, and other drivers applied for the PUC's permission to allow their new company to begin offering service. To set their company apart from the industry incumbents, their business plan called for focusing on underserved areas and instituting lower weekly payoffs for drivers.[161] The next step was to complete Denver's onerous PCN process, which Ani described as follows:

> Oh, man, you should have seen what we had to go through. It was lots of paperwork, tons of paperwork, a blizzard of paperwork. They said we had to prove a "need" for a cab company, so we had to go all over Denver, knocking on doors, asking people to sign statements that they had called a cab but it didn't come. Then we found out we had to get the statements notarized, so we had to go back and ask all these people to drop their work and come with us to the notary.[162]

And those were just the PUC's requirements. All three of Denver's cab companies, as well as ten other transportation companies around the state, intervened in the application process.[163] Although nominally rivals, Yellow Cab and Zone Taxi were represented by the same lawyer. They demanded that Ani and his colleagues produce even-more documentation, including an indication of which of the drivers from Yellow, Metro, and Zone were likely to switch over to Quick Pick.[164]

"They asked us to present our five-year advertising plan for our new company," said Ani. "And they asked us for all the names of the people we would be hiring in the next 10 years. I think even if we were IBM we couldn't have answered that. Does IBM know the name of every person it's going to hire in 1997?"[165]

In November 1992, the PUC rejected Ani's application, just as it had done for all the other applications before his, going back decades. "The regime at Yellow Cab, the PUC—it's exactly like Nigeria.... It's a clique," Ani said. "The whole system is like a nutshell, and you can't break into it. It's just like a poor Third World country."[166]

His application denied, Ani found himself unable to drive a cab at all. Although he and the other applicants all owned their own cabs, they couldn't put them on the streets without paying Yellow or another company for permits—and the companies had blacklisted them.[167] Not content to simply walk away, Ani filed a suit against the PUC in federal court, arguing that while some rules, like insurance requirements and safety inspections, served the public interest, protecting incumbents plainly did not. But in 1993, a district judge, in yet another example of judicial deference to the legislature, upheld the rules, writing: "I need not satisfy myself that the challenged rules will in fact further their articulated purposes; it is sufficient that the Colorado General Assembly could rationally have concluded that the purposes would be achieved."[168]

But that wasn't the end of the story. As Ani's appeal was pending, the Colorado legislature revised the law, *slightly* easing entry requirements.[169] When Ani filed another application, this time for a new company called Freedom Cabs, the PUC granted him fifty permits to do business in 1995. It was the first new cab company in Denver in almost fifty years.[170]

BOTTLENECKING VAMPIRES

Unfortunately, Ani's victory, although important, did not open the market to more competition. The new rules enacted in 1994 were still very restrictive, and well into the first decade of the new century, industry conditions remained much the same as they'd been in 1994.[171]

After some mergers and consolidations—including the sale of Freedom Cabs to new owners—Denver once again had only three taxi companies: Freedom, Yellow, and Metro.[172] Taxi companies and their lobbyists, including the bottleneckers who now owned Freedom Cab, had fought off further attempts to liberalize entry in the General Assembly.[173] And the PUC had denied several applications from drivers wishing to start new companies.[174] Moreover, consistent with the history of taxi regulations, the number of permits had actually *shrunk* from 1,142 in 1995 to 942 in 2008—even though Denver's population had increased by 15 percent over the same period.[175]

And although Freedom's lease rates were far lower than Yellow's or Metro's, cabbies had not for the most part realized much improvement in their working conditions.[176] In 2001, some two hundred cabbies picketed outside the state capitol building, complaining of sixteen-hour days.

"As cabdrivers we're fed up," said a Metro Taxi driver. "These companies are making a killing off us. By the time we pay the companies what we owe them, a lot of us aren't able to make a living wage."[177] According to PUC audits, Metro drivers accrued 175 violations for driving longer shifts than allowed over a thirty-day period, Yellow drivers accrued sixty-two, and Freedom drivers just one.[178] In 2009, a group of Yellow Cab drivers filed suit against the company, claiming that managers had subjected them to verbal and sometimes even physical abuse. An arbitrator awarded the drivers more than $200,000 in 2012.[179]

Nor was the public enjoying better service. "The current state is the worst of both worlds for the public, which is being charged a monopoly price, and the drivers, who are being exploited with a monopoly lease rate," said former PUC chairman Ray Gifford in 2014.[180] State representative Jerry Frangas's elderly and disabled constituents had complained to him that they were having trouble finding cabs for short trips. Concerned, and having himself recently endured a chilly walk with his wife to their hotel after being unable to find a cab on New Year's Eve, Frangas sponsored another deregulation bill. The bill passed in 2007, but it was amended twenty-four times and completely stripped of its deregulatory aspects along the way. In the end, it only authorized the PUC to reexamine lease rates.[181] Unfazed, Frangas cosponsored another bill the following year, this time managing to modestly modify the application process.[182] Specifically, once an applicant had proved to the PUC that the company was responsible and financially fit, it no longer had to prove a need for its services. Rather, the burden was on intervening companies to show that an additional firm was unnecessary.

Several cabbies, fed up with the long hours and low wages, took this change as a positive sign. In September 2008, Mekonnen Gizaw and several other drivers, mostly East African immigrants, applied for 150 new permits to start Mile High Cab. With two young daughters and his wife in nursing school, Mekonnen was single-handedly supporting his family, working as an accountant, and driving a cab on weekends—and paying Yellow Cab $300 per weekend for the privilege.

Like Ani had done more than a decade before them, Mekonnen and his colleagues planned to operate primarily in Denver's underserved areas, particularly the suburbs, where most of the drivers lived.[183] With their application filed, Mekonnen waited.

In August 2009, almost a year after he had filed the application to start Mile High, a PUC administrative law judge finally held an evidentiary hearing, which lasted three weeks. Denver's two largest companies—Yellow and Metro—intervened in the process, arguing that more cabs would result in

> too many cabs chasing too few customers ... [;] drivers working more hours for less revenue; a deterioration in customer service and vehicle maintenance[;] and the resulting market exit of firms with the lowest financial reserves typically, and in this case, the smallest firms and most recent entrants.[184]

The incumbents also brought in experts, one of whom, undoubtedly with a straight face, authored a report concluding that "the correct number of taxi permits in Denver is 942"[185]—the exact-same number of licenses that were active at that moment, due to the bottleneckers' manipulation. When the hearing was over, Mekonnen waited some more.

Finally, in July 2010, almost two years after Mekonnen had filed the application, the presiding administrative law judge released his decision: Mile High was financially and operationally fit, but—parroting the bottleneckers—additional cabs would oversaturate the market. New cabs, the judge wrote, "could very well result in impaired services, higher rates, and ultimately the type of destructive competition this commission is charged with protecting against."[186]

The decision, subsequently upheld by PUC commissioners, appalled the cabbies. Mekonnen explained that although there was no proof that the market was oversaturated, "the PUC believed them. But there is no data; there is no proof for that."[187] Even more perplexing, the very same judge granted 300 new permits—150 of them to Yellow Cab—several months later, in early 2011.[188]

By then, Mekonnen and the other Mile High cabbies had lost their jobs driving for the established companies[189] and were forced to find other work.[190] Unwilling to give up, Mekonnen appealed the ruling and lost in a Colorado trial court. However, in April 2013, the Colorado Supreme Court reversed the lower court's decision, finding that the PUC had disregarded the 2008 legislative change in continuing to presume that new competition is inherently harmful.[191] In December 2013, more than five years after he applied for a permit, the PUC finally allowed Mekonnen to enter the market.[192]

Still, the bottleneckers persisted. Denver's two biggest companies filed motions with the PUC attempting to force Mekonnen and his colleagues to begin the application process anew, but the commission denied the motions in March 2014. In July of that year, Mile High Cabs opened for business.[193]

The new company's presence was felt immediately. Mile High Cabs was the first cab company in Denver to install credit card machines in the backseat, obviating the need to pass one's card to the driver over the seat, a change that proved popular with customers, according to Mekonnen. Drivers also found better working conditions and lower lease rates for cabs at Mile High. The ability for drivers to work less afforded by the savings allowed them "time to spend with the family—good time to spend with the wife, the kids," according to Mekonnen. "So they have spare time. Some of them go to school. That's great for the driver. The driver's life is improved."[194]

Things may improve for many other taxi drivers as well in the future. Despite what the *Denver Post* called a "massive lobbying campaign" by the bottleneckers,[195] the Colorado legislature substantially deregulated the taxi industry in June 2015, removing established companies' ability to oppose new entrants.[196]

BOTTLENECKING IN MINNESOTA IS NOT SO NICE

Denver's tightly controlled cab market was hardly an aberration. Minneapolis officials, for example, had not issued a new taxi permit for years, but then Luis Paucar saw an opportunity to help a significantly underserved segment of the city's population with a safe, reliable taxi service. However, providing that service required a multiyear fight that went all the way to the US Supreme Court.

In 1990, Luis Paucar emigrated from Ecuador to New York City, where he drove a taxi.[197] Over the next decade, he started a family and decided to move to Minneapolis, with its rapidly growing Spanish-speaking population and relatively affordable homes. For the first few years, he operated a small corner grocery store, but with his years of experience in the transportation industry he soon noticed a niche that the city's taxi businesses were ignoring: no cab company was offering Spanish-speaking dispatchers or drivers.[198] So, in 2003, Luis founded A New Star Limousine and Taxi Service in a small basement office near his store.

But, as he discovered, dispatching cars to customers was not that simple. In 2003, the Minneapolis taxi market was closed to new businesses. The city imposed a strict cap on the number of licenses: 343,[199] or only one cab per 1,100 residents.[200] It also had a PCN process on the books. By law, city officials were supposed to hold biennial hearings to consider raising the cap, but no such hearings had been held for more than ten years.

The results of this standstill were as predictable as the outcome of a Russian election. According to letters written by forty-four hotel managers to city staff, their guests frequently experienced bad service when they called a taxi: late cabs and cabs that never came at all.[201] Tourists weren't the only ones who experienced the crummy service. "Trying to get a cab to the North Side is like trying to get to the moon in a Model-T Ford," said the city council president.[202]

This miserable state of affairs had come after years of vigilant bottlenecking on the part of industry insiders. Like in so many cities, Minneapolis had seen almost no change in its taxi regulations for decades. In 1984, the Federal Trade Commission (FTC) sued Minneapolis, arguing that the city's decades-old cap on licenses—then set at 248—along with its prohibition on cabs licensed in St. Paul or the suburbs from picking up passengers within the Minneapolis city limits, violated antitrust law and hurt the poor, who, after businesspeople, were the most likely to rely on cabs.[203] The taxi industry fought back, enlisting the help of US representative Martin Sabo from Minnesota. Within weeks of the filing of the FTC suit, Sabo slipped an amendment into an appropriations bill prohibiting federal money from being used in antitrust actions against local governments.[204] The gambit passed the House but failed in the Senate.[205]

For its part, the city successfully staved off further FTC action by agreeing to issue new licenses in 1985 and to consider releasing up to twenty-five new licenses per year thereafter.[206] The FTC dismissed its suit after the city adopted the ordinance, but the Minneapolis Taxicab Owners Association (MTOA), a group of 117 Yellow Cab drivers, immediately challenged the ordinance in state court.[207] The city quietly repealed the decree, purportedly to settle with the taxicab owners. But, in May 1988, the MTOA's suit was dismissed with prejudice, meaning it could not be appealed or refiled. Under a court order to resolve the FTC's suit, the city subsequently issued a one-off batch of twenty-five permits to a single new company. Otherwise, the cap remained in place, albeit slightly elevated.[208]

In 1988, Minneapolis received 221 complaints from passengers about the city's cabs—nearly one complaint per cab. Most of the complaints were about rude drivers, unsafe driving, dirty cabs, and cabs that were late or did not show up at all.[209] "When you call for a cab and you're told it'll be five minutes and you wait 45 minutes you have a lot of time to sit and think about ways that maybe it might work better," said a visually impaired Minneapolis resident, who started a new company with the licenses the city issued pursuant to the court order.[210]

In the 1990s, the complaints began to have their effect. In 1993, a city councilor attempted to issue fifty new licenses, but the bill failed by a 7–6 vote.[211] A year later, two first-year council members authored a bill that would have ended the cap in 1999.[212] The bill narrowly passed on a 7–6 vote, after being amended to simply raise the cap and to commit the city to holding biennial PCN hearings to consider adding more licenses. The mayor vetoed the bill after an intense lobbying campaign by the bottleneckers.[213]

Under ordinary circumstances, a mayor's veto would have meant a victory for the bottleneckers, but public criticism was severe. "No other industry regulated by the city generates the magnitude of public complaint, controversy, criticism, and scrutiny as taxicabs," said Councilman Steve Minn, who coauthored the deregulation bill.[214]

The city council consequently overrode the veto in 1995 and increased the number of licenses to 343—it was the first time since the city's streetcar days that officials had voluntarily issued new licenses.[215] Again the bottleneckers, now calling themselves the Minneapolis Taxi Federation, sued.[216] "There's been no evidence that there's a need for more taxis in this city," claimed Larry Williams[217] of Rainbow Taxi.[218] The court was unconvinced, however, and again the bottleneckers lost.[219]

But even as they lost in court, the bottleneckers maintained their grip on the city's cab market. By law, the city was required to hold hearings every other year to consider whether new licenses were necessary,[220] but no such hearing had been held by 2003, when Luis Paucar wanted to start his company. Moreover, of the seventy new licenses issued as a result of the 1995 ordinance, half were given by lottery to existing license holders. The other thirty-five went to a new company that had hired a former mayor to lobby on its behalf.[221]

Doing something like hiring a former mayor wasn't in Luis's purview. Even to operate a cab, he would have had to purchase an existing license on the secondary market at a cost of $25,000—this for a license with a $500 face value. The law also required that Luis join a cab association, cooperative, or company—a group of license holders that coordinated dispatching services. But nothing in the law required that associations accept new members. Alternatively, Luis could buy the number of licenses necessary to start his own association—fifteen—all at once. In other words, he could scrape up $400,000 and hope to find a potential competitor willing to relinquish significant market share[222]—a tall order, to say the least.

Locked out of the existing associations and without $400,000 to spare, Luis obtained licenses to operate A New Star in nearby St. Paul and Richfield. Doing so enabled him to serve Minneapolis, though only in part: he was allowed to drop passengers off there, but he was prohibited from picking anyone up on his way back. This meant his taxis had to deadhead back to their staging areas without passengers, severely limiting their earning potential. Luis also tried to serve Minneapolis with a limousine service, but city regulations also made this endeavor unnecessarily difficult. By law, all pickups had to be scheduled in advance, an impractical requirement for all but Luis's most regular customers—and yet another regulation designed to protect the taxi bottleneckers. And a limousine service was also simply more expensive to offer, putting it out of the price range of his clients.

In June 2005, Luis's frustration with the rigged system boiled over. That month, a Minneapolis police officer observed one of A New Star's drivers picking up a customer and impounded the vehicle, leaving the passenger—Blanca Prescott, a visually impaired single mother—stranded on the side of the road.[223] A New Star had been a godsend for Blanca. She felt insecure on city buses, so she relied on cabs to get around town. After years of bad experiences with other taxi companies, she had found

A New Star and become a regular customer. Blanca liked that A New Star's employees spoke Spanish, that its cabs arrived at the time promised, and that its drivers, unlike those of other cab services, would walk her to the door when she arrived at her destination.

Fed up with the unnecessary hurdles to offering an honest service to people who desperately needed it, Luis applied for eight licenses from the city, even though he had not joined an association. City staff rejected Luis's application that very same day. But after hearing about the debacle involving Blanca Prescott, city council members decided, at long last, to hold PCN hearings—and to put Luis's application on the agenda. Also on the agenda: repeal of the cap.[224]

Councilman Gary Schiff supported the repeal, saying that more competition would be "a shot of tonic for customer service problems," which he noted were legion among Minneapolis's cabs.[225] Councilman Paul Ostrow, too, said more cabs would mean better service. He explained, "Whether you're in town or a visitor, you'd know that you can easily hail a cab and if you do, you'll get first-class service."[226]

Ever vigilant, the bottleneckers showed up in force to the May and June 2006 city council committee hearings. In total, twenty-seven of them testified against raising the cap. A license holder argued that owners were counting on the inflated value of their licenses to subsidize their retirement and that there were already too many cabs. Zack Williams of Rainbow Taxi—who, along with his father, Larry, had spearheaded the suit against the 1995 ordinance—testified that allowing more cabs would jeopardize driver income.[227]

But the proponents of deregulation also showed up in force. The Hispanic community attended, as did drivers who had emigrated from Egypt, Laos, and various East African countries, including Somalia—all drivers eager to serve Minneapolis. In total, twenty-two proponents of deregulation testified. "The reality is that once the cap is lifted, many immigrants can easily own taxicabs with no strings attached," said Abdisalam Hashim, a manager at Bloomington City Taxi, which, like Luis's company, was barred from picking up customers in Minneapolis.[228]

Also testifying was a transportation expert from the University of Minnesota, who debunked the bottleneckers' assertion that the cap should remain unchanged because the demand for cabs was fixed: "The improved service due to shorter waiting times and increased availability of cabs will increase total demand for cabs." By contrast, forcing taxi drivers to rent an artificially scarce permit turned drivers into "modern urban sharecroppers."[229]

After the hearings, city staff returned to the committee with a report stating that the city's taxicab service was, indeed, insufficient—especially during peak hours and for disabled passengers. The committee consequently recommended that the city add forty-five new cabs per year and then repeal the cap entirely after several years.[230] The editorial board of Minneapolis's *Star Tribune*, the city's most influential newspaper, also came out in favor of liberalization, arguing that if city leaders wanted to create a twenty-four-hour city, as municipal boosters had long envisioned, more taxis were necessary "to fill an increasingly obvious void in the city's transportation system."[231]

In October 2006, the city council voted 8–4 to add forty-five new cabs per year until 2011, when the cap would be lifted entirely, allowing anyone who was fit and willing to obtain a license. Luis was elated and immediately set to work expanding into underserved South Minneapolis with the licenses he received for seven new cabs. "All I ever wanted was to have the chance to enter the market and compete," he said.[232] In 2007, three new companies, including A New Star, opened for business in Minneapolis, bringing the total number of cab companies serving the city to fourteen.[233]

As with previous reform efforts, the bottleneckers were ready to fight—all the way to the US Supreme Court, as it turned out. Their concern was pure economic protectionism: "Are you telling me that some people are getting in a single stroke what I worked for years and spent thousands on?" asked Zack Williams, owner of Rainbow Taxi. "That's just not fair."[234]

In March 2007, the bottleneckers, now called the Minneapolis Taxi Owners Coalition, sued again, arguing that since the ordinance would reduce the value of their permits from $25,000 to zero, the city had deprived them of property without just compensation. If the law were to be struck down, as the bottleneckers wanted, Luis would be forced out of Minneapolis, a fact that gave him standing to intervene in the suit—a tidy irony given bottleneckers' frequent abuse of the PCN process to intervene against new entrants.[235]

In December 2007, a federal district court judge granted Luis's motion to dismiss the bottleneckers' lawsuit, accepting a magistrate judge's earlier finding that "the license allows its holders to drive a taxi in the City. It does not guarantee that the City would indefinitely limit the number of taxi licenses issued."[236] The bottleneckers appealed—to the same result. In July 2009, the US Eighth Circuit Court of Appeals ruled that the licenses do not "provide an unalterable monopoly over the Minneapolis taxicab market."[237]

In February 2010, the US Supreme Court declined to hear the appeal, making Luis's victory final. As Luis put it, "Now that this legal cloud has finally been removed I can carry on my business without fear."[238] And carry on he has. A New Star has grown from seven cabs in 2006 to forty-five today. His wife and son help Luis with the business, and his daughter is now in medical school at the University of Minnesota.

Nor has he been the only entrepreneur to carry on. Today, 950 cabs representing thirty-six taxi companies serve Minneapolis.[239] "To the delight of the Convention Center and the government downtown, it's pretty easy to grab a cab in Minneapolis," fumed Zack Williams, owner of Rainbow Taxi.[240] The effect of removing a bottleneck was undeniably obvious—even to the bottleneckers.

BEER CITY BOTTLENECKERS

A year after Luis's victory, neighboring Wisconsin got a taxi bottlenecker battle of its own when Jatinder Cheema, an Indian immigrant, sued the city of Milwaukee to open up a taxi market that had not seen the issuance of new permits since 1991.[241]

Jatinder came to America in 1981 looking for a better life. After working in a New York City garment warehouse, he began driving limousines in 1986. Eventually, he bought a gas station in Racine, Wisconsin, but the venture failed. So, in 2002, Jatinder started driving a taxicab in Milwaukee, renting the rights from a permit holder. He wanted to go into business for himself, he said, but the city's "laws ma[de] it impossible."[242]

For decades, Milwaukee had had a PCN law like those of Denver and other cities, but obtaining a license there was not the insurmountable goal it was in other places. Throughout the 1980s, the city held annual hearings to renew permits and issue new ones. The process was chaotic, and in some years no new permits were granted, but entry into the taxicab market was relatively open.[243]

That changed in the early 1990s, when officials changed the law in such a way as to enable the bottleneckers to create a cartel.[244] In 1990, a group of taxi company owners hired a law firm to lobby the city council to impose a cap on the number of taxi permits in the city and to make the permits transferrable.[245] Prior to the change, which went into effect in 1991, permit holders were not allowed to transfer the licenses, meaning if they sold their businesses (i.e., the cars, physical location, business name, etc.), potential buyers could have no assurance of receiving the necessary permits. This problem could have been remedied simply by altering the law to allow permits to be transferred as part of an ownership change. By instead making the permits transferable only within a capped market, the bottleneckers' permits suddenly took on an artificially inflated value, since the only way to obtain one was to buy it from a permit holder.[246]

Alderman Thomas Nardelli, who proposed the cap, gave but one reason—administrative convenience. "We want to get out of the permit business," said Nardelli. "We want to let taxicabs self-regulate. We don't want to have to have these hearings once a year."[247] Tellingly, the alderman did not mention anything about promoting public safety during the public hearings leading up to the vote.[248]

Four other aldermen did unsuccessfully oppose the ordinance. They argued presciently that the cap would dramatically escalate the price of a permit, though they grossly underestimated the magnitude of the increase. "I don't want to see the cost of a license go up to $10,000," one said and voted nay.[249] By 1996, permits, which had a face value of just $85, were actually selling for $30,000 on the open market.[250] By 2012, the price had skyrocketed to $150,000—more than the median house price in Milwaukee. Lease rates for drivers jumped as well—from $150 per twelve-hour shift in 1991 to somewhere between $375 and $400.[251] Making matters even worse, permit holders took a cut of drivers' credit card sales, reducing their take-home pay by even more.[252]

Speaking at the time of the 2011 lawsuit, Ghaleb Ibrahim, one of Jatinder's coplaintiffs, described the situation as such: "The rental rates are so high and the gas is so expensive, it's really hard to make a living.

It's only after you pay the company that you make any money. Often, there is no extra."[253] And this was not just carping by drivers. As County Supervisor John Weishan observed, "It's basically a system of indentured servants."[254]

Drivers weren't the only ones suffering from the bottlenecking. So, too, were consumers. As Jatinder observed at the time of the suit, "There is a lot of service Downtown, but people on the North Side have a difficult time getting a cab. When the weather is bad, there are no taxis at the airport."[255]

By standards of the typical American city, cabs in Milwaukee were extraordinarily scarce. By 2007, there was but one cab per 1,850 residents in the city. Denver, by comparison, had one cab per 480 residents. "For many," quipped a *Milwaukee Journal Sentinel* columnist, "the fact that this city has taxicabs at all may go unnoticed."[256] "It's difficult to find a metropolitan area with fewer taxis than Milwaukee," wrote another journalist.[257] "If visitors want a cab, they've got to call one—and wait," editorialized the journal.[258]

The limited service was complemented by lousy service. In a representative customer review, one passenger found American United, Milwaukee's largest taxi service, to be "extremely unreliable and a number of the operators at the dispatch center seem to be reasonably without a care for what constitutes even mediocre customer service."[259] At Yellow Cab, taxis "take forever to come," read one common complaint. "If you are paying with a credit card forget it; no one will come to pick you up. The cabbies and the receptionists are rude at best and the cabs are mostly if not always dirty."[260]

But if cabdrivers and customers were unhappy, the cap suited permit holders just fine. By the time of Jatinder's suit, Michael Sanfelippo, the owner of American United and several other companies, had amassed 168 of the city's 354 permits. Another 33 permits were owned by people who worked for American United,[261] effectively giving Sanfelippo control over greater than half of Milwaukee's taxi market—yet another example of how caps in taxi markets can give rise to concentrated ownership.

At that time, Sanfelippo was spending much of his time in Florida, so he trusted his brother Joe, then a Milwaukee County supervisor, to handle American United's day-to-day operations. According to cabbies, this primarily involved sitting at a desk a few days a week and collecting cash.[262] Now a state representative,[263] Joe Sanfelippo is the registered agent for his brother's companies, which their father started.[264] In addition to the cab company, the Sanfelippo family ran a sod and Christmas tree farm, plus a store in which they sold topsoil, sod, fruits, and vegetables.[265] The sod farm was eventually turned into a private airport thirty minutes from downtown Milwaukee, of which Michael is reported to be the manager.[266]

The family holdings had proven lucrative for the Sanfelippos but not so much for the company's drivers. Cabbies at the largest company, American United, complained of paying more than $1,000 a week to lease a cab and be provided insurance, gas, and dispatching services. In addition, they were also forced to fill up at Sanfelippo's gas station, which, according to the cabbies, often charged 10 cents more per gallon than the going rate.[267] But despite his successful bottlenecking, Michael Sanfelippo once declared, apparently without irony, "This is not a cab town."[268]

Based on how hard he fought to maintain his bottleneck, Sanfelippo gave a good impression that he was someone who believed in quite the opposite approach. When Jatinder and Ghaleb sued in September 2011 to open up Milwaukee's taxi market, Sanfelippo joined with nominal rival Yellow Cab to hire a former Wisconsin governor turned lobbyist, Martin Schreiber, to push the state legislature to impose a taxi licensing system in all "first-class" Wisconsin cities with populations greater than 150,000. Only Milwaukee fit the bill.[269]

The Milwaukee City Council lobbied for the legislation, which would have allowed the city to collect a transfer fee each time a permit changed hands.[270] Eleven individuals, including then Milwaukee County supervisor Joe Sanfelippo, testified on behalf of the bill, and more than two hundred people registered in favor of it. Due to the short notice given for the meeting—just three days—no one appeared to testify against the bill and only one person registered in opposition.[271] The proposal cleared the Wisconsin State Assembly within weeks of its introduction.[272]

Although the assembly hearing was stacked with unrebutted bottleneckers, the Senate hearing was a drink of a different flavor. With time to organize, Jatinder, Ghaleb, and more than two hundred other taxi drivers drove to Madison, the capital, to attend the hearing. A dozen bottleneckers testified for the bill, supported by more than 130 registered in support, while ten taxi drivers testified against the bill, with more than 230 registered in opposition. At the end of the hearing, the committee chairwoman didn't call for a vote on the bill, and it ultimately failed.[273]

Things would grow even worse for the bottleneckers in the following years. In April 2013, a state trial court ruled that the city's two justifications for maintaining the bottleneck—administrative convenience and protecting the bottleneckers' profits to encourage investment—held no water. "The desire of the City to create a valuable asset for the current permit holders so that they could sell them and, as one taxi driver indicated, retire comfortably to Florida," remarked Milwaukee Circuit Court judge Jane Carroll, "that's simply not a legitimate government purpose."[274]

To comply with the ruling, city officials held a lottery in March 2014 to hand out a hundred more permits. More than 1,700 applicants threw their hats in the ring.[275] Unfortunately, neither Jatinder nor Ghaleb was selected, but in July 2014 the city council voted unanimously to repeal the taxi cap altogether, allowing anyone to drive a cab so long as insurance and other health and safety standards were met.[276]

Unwilling to go out quietly, permit holders sued the city—twice. First, the Sanfelippo brothers and other owners filed suit in February 2014 to block the lottery coming up in March,[277] but they voluntarily withdrew the case after failing to win an injunction to do so.[278] Then, in August 2014, after the city had lifted the cap entirely, five companies, all registered to Michael Sanfelippo,[279] sued the city, arguing that they had a property right in the inflated value of the permit and that officials were therefore seizing their property without just compensation, in violation of the Fifth Amendment to the US Constitution. Accordingly, Sanfelippo argued, the city should either reinstate the cap or pay compensation to permit holders.[280]

By then, the city's officials had come a long way from when they'd gone to Madison to urge legislators to impose a state licensing system. They saw the repeal as "a direct response to constituents' calls for increased and improved taxicab service, as well as a judge's order," according to Alderman Bob Bauman. "If existing cab companies feel their monopoly is threatened, perhaps they should focus more on improving their customers' satisfaction instead of trying to throw up judicial roadblocks to progress."[281]

In September 2014, a federal district court denied the Sanfelippos a preliminary injunction that would have stopped the city from opening the market, thereby allowing the repeal of the city's cap to go forward.[282] That month, a crowd of people lined up at City Hall to apply for new permits. In total, 183 people filled out applications on the spot and just as many picked up applications that they would return later, as estimated by a city clerk.[283]

By the next year, there were 1,048 licensed cabs in the city—only 128 of which were registered to Joe Sanfelippo Cabs or another Sanfelippo-controlled company.[284] Later that year, the district court dismissed the bottleneckers' suit, ruling that the 1991 ordinance did not amount to "an irrevocable promise that the City would never issue another taxicab permit or amend its transportation regulations so as to devalue taxicab permits," as they claimed.[285] Unsatisfied, Michael Sanfelippo took his case to the US Seventh Circuit Court of Appeals, where, as of this writing, it remains active.[286]

In the meantime, the end of the cap has ushered in big changes in Milwaukee's cab industry, according to Saad Malik, another driver who, along with Jatinder, intervened in the bottleneckers' suit in order to oppose it. Very few drivers now rent a cab, he said. And compared to a few years ago, "drivers are stress free since they don't have to pay rent," even as competition has stiffened. "Customers are happy because of the good service and nice, neat, and clean vehicles. Since [the drivers] are all owners, we would like to provide the best service possible."[287]

A BOTTLENECKING "FEEDING FRENZY"

Compared to jitneys and taxicabs, the limousine business—which includes stretch limos, luxury sedans, and SUVs, is a free-market utopia.[288] In all but a handful of jurisdictions, entry is open, allowing in anyone who is fit and willing to do an honest day's work.[289] And only a few states and localities limit entry for the express purpose of protecting incumbents using decades-old PCN laws.[290] But bottleneckers have more recently sought to impose new restraints in the form of minimum-fare requirements, which forbid low-cost limousine operators from undercutting higher-priced competitors.[291]

Given the small size of the industry, it's no surprise that this would be the case. The chauffeured vehicle business enjoyed gross estimated revenues of only about $3 billion in 2012 across its 8,339 limousine, sedan, and SUV operators and its several thousand charter bus operators.[292] Those operators have some 115,600 chauffeured vehicles in service, including nearly forty thousand black-car sedans, twenty thousand SUVs, and seven thousand stretch limousines. Many operators are small businesspeople; the median fleet in 2014 was made up of just ten vehicles. In fact, fleets of more than fifty-one vehicles make up only 4 percent of the industry.[293] According to US Census data, the average chauffeured vehicle firm employs fewer than ten employees.[294]

In Las Vegas, one large fleet, Bell Trans, has dominated the limousine market—one of the nation's largest—for decades.[295] When Edward Wheeler arrived in Las Vegas in the mid-1990s, all he saw was possibilities—not from casinos, tourism, or development but from limousines. The stagnating effects of Bell Trans's near monopoly on limousine service were plain to see, and Ed had big ideas.

The son of a 3M executive, Ed grew up in Minneapolis and at the age of twenty-one he headed to Las Vegas on a lark, and something about the place drew him in. "I'm really to this day not sure what," he recalled. "I kind of went out there for a little bit of fun and ended up staying out here for 25 years now." After working briefly for a small limousine outfit, Ed felt "that I could do something better than what at that time was being provided to the public," much of it by Bell Trans.[296]

Bell Trans was founded in the 1960s and was operating more than three hundred limousines in Las Vegas by the 1990s, making it the country's largest limousine company. Its nearest competitor had around a dozen cars in service.[297] With only a few limousine companies operating legally in the market at that time, Bell Trans and the other established operators did not feel much pressure to provide good service, as compared to circumstances in which numerous competitors compel companies to maintain high quality and pursue innovation in order to compete. "They were running very old fleets," said Ed. "Basically oversized cabs is what they were running."[298] Ed knew he could do better and build a successful company in the process, but, thanks to the bottleneckers, just breaking into the limo business would prove to be the most difficult part.

Bell Trans's stranglehold on the market did not come about by accident. Nevada had a PCN process for limousines, much as many jurisdictions did for taxis, and required new entrants to satisfy not only the guidelines of the state's Public Service Commission (PSC), which administered the process, but also those of any existing limousine companies—Bell Trans, in other words. Just as in the taxi industry, the PCN process for limousines gave incumbents the power to intercede in the applications of potential competitors, effectively killing competition. It was a power Bell Trans used with brutal effectiveness.

"A Great White feeding frenzy is prettier than watching Bell Trans's attorneys intervene in a license application," wrote a *Las Vegas Review-Journal* columnist. "The legal blood-letting is costly, but it serves as a deterrent to those who look upon Southern Nevada as an open market."[299] Even Bell Trans leaders were not shy in describing their use of the PCN process. "If an applicant can demonstrate a need that is not being filled by us," said a Bell Trans general manager, "then they'll have no problem from us. But if they're taking business from us, then there is a problem."[300]

It didn't take much for Bell to decide that an applicant was posing such a problem, and the climate was corrosive by the time Ed arrived in Las Vegas. Operators both big and small ran afoul of Bell Trans's bottlenecking. For example, Louis Nimmo, a sixty-eight-year-old former Southern Baptist pastor, applied for a limousine license to run a shuttle from Sun City, his age-restricted retirement community, about twenty minutes away from the Strip—the heart of Las Vegas and the location of the city's major casinos and resorts—to the airport. Louis thought the service would be a lifeline for many of his neighbors who liked to travel but preferred not to drive, especially at night. Cabs in the city were unreliable and prohibitively expensive. "I wanted the license to simply help these people out here," he said. "It's an emotional issue with them."[301]

Six limousine, taxicab, and bus services, including Bell Trans, intervened in Louis's application process, claiming "granting the proposed authority would be a severe adverse economic impact upon these

Petitioners.... [S]uch impact would diminish the transportation service in the quality and availability of transportation services to the public and tend to create detrimental competition."[302] Imagine all of these ruinous effects coming from a single car running between Sun City and the airport!

Louis spent eighteen months complying with document requests from the PSC and the bottleneckers. He even had to spend $2,500 to hire a court reporter for his hearing. "It makes you feel like a criminal," he said. "They make the impression that I've committed a crime because I've made an application."[303] Louis received a limited license after agreeing to stay off the Strip and only shuttle Sun City residents to and from the airport.[304]

Bell Trans once even opposed a quadriplegic entrepreneur's application to operate a single limousine specially modified to accommodate people in wheelchairs on the basis that it already provided such services. Bell was eventually forced to concede this was not the case.[305]

Just as being a small operator didn't escape the bottleneckers' notice, having deep pockets often didn't either. When Music Express, a well-established outfit that operated in Los Angeles, San Francisco, Washington, DC, and New York City, applied for permission to run ten limousines and three vans in Las Vegas, it received similar treatment. Bottleneckers immediately intervened in the process, and the PSC held a nine-day hearing to allow the intervenors to scrutinize their would-be competitor's business plans. "The hearing was a long, drawn-out process," said Music Express's attorney, "in which the interveners oppose every possible point raised by Music Express."[306] After spending more than $500,000 in legal fees and other expenses, the company was denied a certificate. According to PSC officials, it had "failed to demonstrate the need for service in the area."[307]

But the rise of the independent limousine market in Las Vegas proved that there was in fact a need for more service in the area. Knowing that they would never be awarded a license, some limousine operators didn't even bother trying. Instead, they relied on federal transportation licenses that enabled them to run on interstate routes. With these licenses, and the significant insurance required to accompany them, an increasing number of independent operators began operating in Las Vegas, seeing in the city a market with growing unmet demand.

Indeed, in 1997 and 1998, Sin City hosted thirty million visitors each year[308] but had a mere seven licensed limousine companies. Los Angeles, which welcomed a similar number of visitors, had 274 limousine companies. Mathematically, this means each operator in Los Angeles served 109,000 visitors, while each one in Las Vegas served 5.3 million.[309]

In such an enormous market, independent limousine companies discovered that as long as they did not advertise they were able to operate without much fear of getting cited.[310] "For years the independents were kind of left alone," Ed remembered. PSC officials "really weren't out on the road enforcing. They were pretty much just doing vehicle inspections and those kind of things. What happened was some independents started getting pretty good sized fleets."[311]

Sensing a threat to their dominant position, the bottleneckers pushed for draconian enforcement measures. To facilitate these efforts, Bell Trans in 1997 retained Harvey Whittemore[312]—perhaps the most powerful lobbyist in the state and widely known as the unofficial sixty-fourth legislator[313] in the sixty-three-member Nevada legislature—to convince lawmakers to split the PSC in two: one body to regulate utilities and one to oversee transportation companies.[314] Hiring Whittemore paid off in spades.

When Assembly Bill 366 passed the Nevada Assembly in 1997, it was a fourteen-page document designed to make Nevada's electricity markets more competitive. But when it later emerged from a Senate committee, it was lengthened by some five hundred pages of amendments, which legislators had mere hours to consider before voting. Most of them simply followed party leaders, thinking they were approving a deregulation bill. But when the governor signed it in July, it was everything Bell Trans and the other bottleneckers could have hoped for.[315]

The law created the Transportation Services Authority (TSA) and authorized it to impose criminal liabilities on unlicensed limo drivers, further stipulating that any limousines caught without a license "*must* be impounded by the authority if a certificate of public convenience and necessity has not been issued authorizing its operation"[316] (emphasis added).

In addition to giving the TSA the power to prosecute independent limos criminally, the law permitted it to impose $10,000 in civil fines and, separately, up to $10,000 in impoundment fees on them. Even worse, the law established no funding source for the agency other than the fees it collected.[317] Prior to the change, the PSC had only been authorized to issue small fines and misdemeanors to violators.[318]

Dependent on fees for its survival, the TSA immediately began to crack down on independent operators, running weekly stings. "They're a bunch of honest people, who want to make a dishonest living," said one TSA enforcer.[319] The crackdown quite literally turned honest businesspeople into unemployed criminals overnight. For example, William Clutter, a longtime independent operator, held a federal transportation license, repeatedly passed safety inspections, and carried a $1 million insurance policy, but TSA agents seized his car in December 1997.[320]

"We aren't against regulation which insures that operators have a valid driver's license, insurance, vehicle inspection, and a criminal background check," said William Clutter, a thirty-seven-year-old college graduate. "But the government should have no right to tell honest citizens what their economic choices are."[321]

As William fought the case against him, the agency even sold his impounded vehicle at auction. (It was compelled to repurchase the limo after his lawyer intervened.) The episode pushed William to the brink of bankruptcy. And although he was unable to work, he still had to cover insurance costs and continue to repay the loan he'd taken out to buy the vehicle.[322]

Faced with extinction, many independent operators joined together to form the Independent Limousine Owners/Operators Association (ILOA). In an act of both civil disobedience and economic survival, its sixty-three members put one hundred limousines on the streets without certificates. By May 1998, less than a year after the creation of the TSA, sixty of those hundred vehicles had been impounded.[323] At least one driver was jailed.[324] No longer able to run their businesses under the radar, many ILOA members attempted to navigate the PCN process. But when they applied for certificates, the bottleneckers were there waiting.

When Ed applied for a certificate after the TSA's creation, he had to hire a lawyer and an accountant to handle the intervening companies' demands for documentation.[325] As he explained, "They wanted a list of clients. They wanted to see who our potential customers and accounts were... who was going to service the vehicles... what my business plans were, where I planned on advertising, all those kinds of things."[326] After nine months caught in the "paper mill," Ed withdrew his application.[327]

One after another, the bottleneckers buried their potential competitors in paperwork. John West, for example, another ILOA member who applied for a certificate, was required to respond to the intervening companies' demands to know who his mechanic was, how many miles he planned to drive, and how much gas he planned to purchase and at what price.[328]

Twenty-five years old when he applied for a certificate to run his company, AAA Limousine, John saw his new business venture as a great way to provide for his wife and two young children. The bottleneckers thought otherwise. He described himself as "shocked and angry" when he discovered how abusive the process was: "TSA forced me to turn over my client list allowing my competitors to go after my business. In what other profession does someone have to sacrifice his business in order to go into business?"[329]

Seeing that the PCN application process was clearly intended to sap applicants' will and bleed them of money, in 1998 Ed, William, John, and the ILOA sued Nevada in federal court seeking to overturn the rules.

With characteristic bottlenecker hyperbole, state lawyers defended the law by arguing that the suit attacked the state's right to regulate its highways[330] and would jeopardize the state's economic well-being. Three incumbents also filed briefs defending the system: Bell Trans (the largest fleet), Star Limousine (whose sister company, Yellow-Checker-Star, was then the largest taxi fleet), and Ambassador Limousine.[331]

Knowing the litigation process could take years, Ed and other ILOA members approached the legislature for help in 1999. At first, they were encouraged by the results. Their work with bill sponsors produced legislation that would have eased the application process. After weeks of meetings with Senate Transportation committee staff, it seemed the bill had the support of key legislators. At a hearing, the committee chairman, according to ILOA president Richard Lowre, testified that while the committee didn't want to open the "floodgate[s]," the state needed to "to make it a little easier for people to get in in, and we need to do something about the intervention process. We can't have competing companies challenging the licenses." Each member of the panel nodded solemnly in apparent agreement.[332]

But then, Bell Trans's lobbyist Harvey Whittemore arrived. "It was very surprising," said Ed. "Ten minutes before the vote [Whittemore] comes in and says, 'We don't like this. Refer it to Finance.'"[333] And with that, the bill died in committee.[334] After the initial proposal was spiked, the committee chairman proposed a more modest change—the same one that had prompted Mile High Cab to seek a license from the Colorado PUC—the burden from applicants to those in opposition in proving a new license would harm existing businesses. The proposal was withdrawn when Whittemore objected.[335] With the bottleneckers firmly in control of the legislature, Ed and the others were forced to wait for a court decision, a decision that would not come until two years after their thwarted attempt at legislative reform.

In May 2001, Clark County District Court judge Ron Parraguirre ruled that the PCN paper mill violated the rights of Ed and the others. He came down particularly hard on the way the TSA allowed incumbents to abuse the process to frustrate potential new competitors:

> The intervention process amounted to an onerous and unduly burdensome process by which the applicants were forced to either withdraw their applications, agree to limit the operational scope of their proposed CPCNs, or incur increasing litigation fees and costs in order to comply with the numerous financial information and disclosure demands made by the TSA as well as the intervening carriers.[336]

Parraguirre went even further when he declared: "The right to earn a living in one's chosen profession is a liberty interest protected by the due process clauses of both the U.S. and Nevada constitutions."[337]

Within hours of the decision, the bottleneckers, including the TSA,[338] rushed to the legislature, desperate to save the cartel. What happened is a testament to the PCN process's very real ability to create and preserve an oligopoly. The bottleneckers sought to replace their lost veto power with the next best thing: a legislative cap on the number of limousine licenses allowed. Specifically, they proposed an "allocation system" with a fixed number of licenses determined by existing market share. So, instead of celebrating their court victory, Ed and other ILOA members traveled to Carson City to testify, futilely, against Senate Bill 576. The bill eventually passed both the Senate and the Assembly, dying only after the two houses could not reconcile various amendments.[339]

The years-long fight took its toll on those who led the way against the bottleneckers. Rather than start his own firm, William began driving for another limousine company.[340] Nearly bankrupt after the expensive application process, John left Las Vegas in 2000 and took a job as a mechanic in Albuquerque, New Mexico. His application had been denied, with the TSA commissioners asserting he no longer possessed the financial wherewithal to support a company—a direct result of the expensive application process.[341] Richard Lowre delivered newspapers to stay afloat before departing for a teaching job in Vermont.[342]

As for Ed, he refiled his application in 2001. Although he had won the previous case in court, the bottleneckers were still able to intervene because Judge Parraguirre's decision had only deemed unconstitutional the manner in which the TSA allowed the intervention process to be used against Ed and his coplaintiffs, not the process itself. This time, however, the TSA had the good sense to refuse to allow the interveners to harass Ed with endless interrogatories. In November, four years after Ed first lodged his application, the TSA approved it, granting him a restricted license allowing him to put a limited number of vehicles on the road.[343] A year later, he launched Omni Limousines.

But Ed's victory was far from complete. He could not expand his fleet without the TSA's permission, and, without a larger fleet, he struggled to compete. As Ed described his situation:

> They wanted people to start out with fleets of two to three vehicles but at the same time have an office location where your phones are being answered 24 hours a day, which you can't generate enough revenue from two vehicles to pay those expenses.... We couldn't chase after big corporate accounts because we didn't have the fleet to do it. We couldn't go after the hotel accounts because they knew we didn't have the fleets to do it.... If you knew a hotel wanted to use your service and you'd need 15 cars to service them and you only had permission for two, it was impossible.[344]

The limit on vehicles wasn't the only thing holding small operators back. As Ed recalled,

> They also had tariff regulations. You had to get your rates approved from the state, and here again nobody had lower rates than the big guys. Bell Trans has the lowest rates in the industry, so to go out and get an account—couldn't get it because Bell Tran has a lower rate, and we can't charge lower rates than they do.[345]

Refusing to concede defeat, the bottleneckers returned to the legislature in the 2003 session, this time asking for a moratorium on new licenses. Brent Bell, the president of Bell Trans's parent company, testified, as did cab company lobbyists, who complained limousines were poaching their customers. "Sometimes it's less expensive to get a limousine than a cab," shuddered a Yellow-Checker-Star representative.[346]

State senator Maggie Carlton, for one, was unimpressed. She had recently driven her daughter and five other teens to their prom after she couldn't find a limousine company willing to come to her house. "They don't like to leave the Strip," she said.[347] Although a full-fledged moratorium failed to pass, the bottleneckers did see some success. As adopted, Assembly Bill 518 forbade existing companies from expanding for a year and permitted first-time applicants to apply for only two vehicles.[348]

In 2004, bottleneckers were back at the legislature again with another attempt to impose an allocation system, complaining of competition between taxis and limos. They also pushed a proposal that would have allowed vehicles to operate only at certain times and within certain geographic boundaries. The TSA also proposed increasing annual license fees from $100 to $600 to pay for the increased regulation, which Bell Trans was all for. "Our company is willing to pay for good regulation and that means good allocations," said Brent Bell. "I don't think $700 is unreasonable."[349] But a twelve-member legislative commission killed the proposal.[350]

In 2008, frustrated with all the restrictions on his business, Ed sold Omni. Although the result was not what he and the others had hoped for, consumers have ultimately benefitted from a market that, while still restricted, is more open than it was before. In the two decades prior to Ed's lawsuit, the state only granted permission for three new companies to enter the Las Vegas limousine market.[351] Today, forty-three companies possess the required certificates. Of those companies, only five have unrestricted licenses—three of which are owned by the Bell family.[352] A sixth unrestricted company, CLS Transportation, which had been in Las Vegas since 1994 and intervened against Ed, lost its licenses in 2014 after its owner pled guilty to running a multimillion-dollar credit card fraud, prostitution operation, and narcotics ring from his limousines.[353]

Restrictions on the other thirty-eight companies include bans on accepting street hails or providing airport service. Often, companies may drive passengers into or out of Vegas—but not around town. Among the restricted companies, twenty are limited to having eight or fewer vehicles.[354]

Although such regulations might seem minor compared to licensing, caps, PCN laws, and other similar mechanisms, restrictions on businesses' operations can often be designed and manipulated to achieve many of the same effects as the more draconian regulations. Nashville bottleneckers demonstrated this process in 2010 when they tried to push Ali Bokhari and his wildly successful black-car service out of Music City.

INNOVATION (STUCK) IN THE BOTTLENECK

Ali had arrived in the United States from Pakistan in 2000 on a skilled-worker visa. After earning a master's degree in journalism from the University of California, Berkeley, he moved to Nashville, where his brother was in medical residency at Vanderbilt University. Although Ali received several job offers from newspapers outside Nashville, he decided to stay in the city and drive a cab so that he could meet people and learn the culture. As he explained, by driving a cab, "you have freedom. You can study and talk to people. You make your own schedule."[355]

But Nashville's taxi industry was stifling. "In Nashville, you cannot own your own company," Ali remembered. "You have to affiliate with one of the existing cab companies and follow their rules." One of the ways this is accomplished is by companies demanding that their drivers rely on central dispatchers rather than solicit their own customers. And cabbies aren't treated particularly well. "They can fire you for no reason, and they're all friends with each other. One company fires you, nobody hires you, so you are out of a living. So there was no opportunity."[356]

Ali also yearned to start his own business. As he recalled,

> I wanted to own my own taxi service because I have better ideas, and I wanted it to be a better way. I was sick of working for somebody. And there should be a lot of improvements that could be done in taxi business model because everybody—there were like seven taxi companies in Nashville—and everybody was doing the same business model—just a different color.[357]

But when Ali spoke to city officials, he was told applying for permission to start a taxi company would just be a waste of the $900 application fee. He applied anyway. "But I got refused," he said.[358] Nashville, like many other cities, imposed tight entry restrictions on the taxi market, requiring applicants to obtain a PCN certificate.[359]

After a 2005 trip to New York City, where he saw numerous for-hire black sedans cruising the streets, Ali, in true entrepreneurial fashion, hit on a new idea: to bring black sedans, not regulated by the city at the time,[360] to Nashville and charge taxi-like rates. He knew right away the model could work. Black-car services, sometimes called "execu-cars" or "chauffeured cars," typically fill a niche between taxis and stretch limousines. They offer the efficiency of a taxi while providing the customer service of a limousine, without its trappings, such as food, alcohol, electronic media, a bed, or space for fifteen people. Black sedans generally serve busy business travelers who need a vehicle waiting for them and a driver with expert knowledge of a city, so that they can travel between meetings and destinations on a tight schedule and get quickly through busy traffic.

The reason for Nashville's light regulation of black cars was that there were so few of them. Taxi and limousine bottleneckers therefore did not see them as threats. In 2005, all that changed. That was the year Ali started Metro Livery with just one vehicle. By the end of just his first year in business, he was dispatching ten vehicles. And by the end of year two, he was up to thirty-five, serving neighborhoods and niches that established taxi services and high-end limousine services were neglecting—as well as competing directly with them on their turf.[361]

Ali's model was simple: He charged taxi-like prices and offered high-end service for rides in his black sedans. To take passengers from downtown to the airport, Ali charged $25—the same as cabs charged.[362] Grand Avenue, another livery service, charged $57 for the same trip. Indeed, that was Grand Avenue's minimum fare: The company required customers to reserve a car for at least an hour at a rate of $57 an hour.[363] Other companies also required customers to reserve a limo for at least two hours—at a rate of $65 or more per hour.[364]

Ali could charge such low prices because he introduced several efficiencies: The cars did not return to a dispatch center after every trip, meaning fewer miles traveled without passengers, and the company used older-model vehicles—Lincoln Town Cars that were five to ten years old but scrupulously maintained and spotlessly clean. Beyond this, the drivers all wore suits and ties, conveying a professional image. Fees for late cancellations were also eliminated, which customers appreciated.[365]

These amenities were especially welcome in Nashville, where other cabs were not so pleasant. According to a transportation consultant's survey of hotel managers, the city's cabs ranked poorly relative to those of other cities on things like vehicle appearance, promptness, and driver appearance.[366] Secret shoppers also experienced a variety of problems, including rude drivers, some refusing to accept credit cards, and telephone operators who put customers on hold endlessly. One driver was even "a little frightening to a female passenger."[367]

Unsurprisingly, Metro Livery was unpopular among Nashville's five taxi companies, which didn't like the competition and called for the city to create "a level playing field."[368] Nor was Metro popular with Nashville's established limousine services, even though they began adding new black sedans to their fleets after seeing Ali's success.

So, in 2009, when the city's Metropolitan Transportation Licensing Commission (MTLC) put together a proposed ordinance to regulate limousines and sedans—which were overseen primarily by the state at the time—the established limousine companies took advantage of the situation and quickly got to bottlenecking.[369] On seeing the draft ordinance, Ali's limousine competitors joined ranks, forming the Tennessee Livery Association (TLA). The group lobbied for language in the ordinance that would drive low-cost operators like Ali out of business. Specifically, TLA proposed a $45 minimum fare, nearly doubling what Ali and other small operators charged for most trips. According to the TLA's president, the organization spent "hundreds of hours" with MTLC staff rewriting the proposed law. "Not many organizations get an opportunity to contribute and steer the actual content and wording of pending legislation," he bragged.[370]

Ali attempted to weigh in as well: "I contacted my council member and I called him, left so many messages and I got no response from him."[371] Shut out of the backroom negotiations, he attended numerous public hearings on the proposed ordinance. And when it came up for first and second readings at the city council, the minimum-fare requirement was curiously absent. But, according to testimony from the TLA's vice president, the association sent language with a $45 minimum fare to Councilman Bo Mitchell, who added it back to the bill before the third reading the following day[372]—too late for public comment.

The ordinance passed in June 2010. In addition to the minimum fare, it ultimately required that sedan companies use vehicles no more than five years old when put into service[373] and send cars from a central location for each trip—effectively outlawing 70 percent of Ali's fleet,[374] along with his entire business model.[375] "It was nothing to do with the safety," said Ali. "It was just protectionism for industry insiders."[376] The new law specifically exempted large hotels that operated their own shuttle services.[377] And the restrictions did not affect TLA members, who had tailored the law's language to fit their existing practices. In other words, rather than compete with Metro Livery by matching or improving upon its business model, TLA members attempted to snuff out Ali's innovations by using government power to force everyone to adopt their own inefficiencies.

In characteristic bottlenecker fashion, city leaders declared their intentions noble. "Public safety was at issue," said Councilman Mitchell.[378] The TLA also claimed it was chiefly concerned with safety: "We are in support of this," said the TLA's president, "mainly for public safety on the consumer side of things."[379]

But Ali knew better. He also knew that if the law went into full effect, his business might not survive. Knowing that any attempts to plead his case to a city council already in the pocket of the TLA were doomed to fail, Ali sued the city in April 2011. He argued that while he did not oppose genuine public-safety regulations, the minimum fare, the dispatch requirement, and the prohibition of older-model vehicles represented straightforward economic protectionism. "The only people who benefit from this ordinance are the expensive limo companies who want to put me out of business and the taxi companies who want to take over all the low fares," said Ali.[380] Indeed, the MTLC's director said as much in testimony, admitting that one motivation for the law was to protect the taxi industry.[381]

In court, city attorneys argued that the minimum fare wouldn't be such a problem for Ali if he were to charge customers $45 and then give them vouchers for free rides.[382] In a deposition, a TLA officer even argued that the minimum fare would help low-cost operators: Rewriting the law of supply and demand, he said they'd make more money because they had to charge more.[383] During the lawsuit, the MTLC did not enforce the minimum-fare rule. That changed in January 2012—a week after a federal judge denied the city's motion to dismiss the case—when the commission mounted a sting operation, catching one of Ali's drivers committing the "crime" of offering passengers a better deal than established limo companies.[384]

In response, the MTLC fell back on the rule, the enforcement of which was devastating for Ali, as the vast majority of his company's fares were less than $45. "At one point, we were down to 10 cars when they were doing selective enforcement," he remembered.[385] Other small independent operators also complained of being singled out by MTLC enforcement operations and even of being pulled over in their personal vehicles while off duty.[386] MTLC inspectors wore badges, carried guns, put blue lights on their vehicles, and falsely identified themselves as police officers, eventually drawing the ire of the real police.[387] "All of this," mused a *Tennessean* columnist, "in a city where it is nearly impossible to flag down a cab on the street. It takes 20 to 30 minutes for one to come when you call."[388]

In January 2013, despite the law's unequivocally protectionist intent, a jury upheld the regulations. But the rules were not long for this world. After persistent lobbying from Ali; a change in the MTLC's leadership following the police impersonation scandal; and "a clamoring," as the mayor's spokeswoman put it, "by users for more and better transportation options," the city council lowered the minimum required fare to $9 in January 2014—effectively repealing the rule.[389]

Other heavyweights who had previously supported the ordinance also reversed course. "We know from visitor and in our case personal experience that taxi service is inadequate," said the president of the Nashville Convention Center and Visitors Bureau just prior to the change. "I'll say two things: We need more taxis on the street and we need more readily available black-car service."[390]

The repeal kicked Ali's business—and the sedan business in general—into overdrive. Ali purchased five new vehicles in five weeks to handle all the new customers—and he even got back behind the wheel himself for the first time in years to cope with the demand. Today, Ali employs twenty-three drivers. And former Metro Livery drivers have gone on to start more than ten transportation companies serving Nashville today[391]—a legacy of which Ali is very proud. Says he, business is "wonderful."[392]

CONCLUSION

Meanwhile, back in New York City, Hector continues to drive his 2 p.m.–8 p.m. shift after a long morning working to maintain his business, meeting with coalition colleagues, and continuing his decades-long battle with the bottleneckers. But despite the tangle of regulations and constant police harassment, Hector and other ride-van operators hope their way of earning living will soon become legal.

City officials have long tacitly recognized the vans as an important part of New York City's transit system. For example, after 9/11 and hurricanes Sandy and Irene shut down public transportation, ride vans were brought in to shuttle emergency personnel and regular citizens around the city. "They always had us as a part of their contingency plan," Hector said, "but whenever the crisis is over, it's business as usual and they begin ticketing us again."[393]

But that's beginning to change. According to Hector, city officials are now more open to ride vans. The TLC recently wrapped up a six-month pilot plan that officially recognized the vans, and officials distributed pamphlets commending them to the community. "We've never seen that happen in the history of the business," observed Hector.[394]

Union opposition is also wearing thin. After twenty-five years of van-driver activism, the unions "have now come to accept the fact that we're going to be there for the long haul," Hector noted. "And so the hostility is not there. The rhetoric is not there."[395]

As of this writing, two pro–dollar-van bills are advancing in the city council and another in the New York Assembly, all of them designed to ease rules on would-be ride-van entrepreneurs. Former opponents in the city council are expected to support the bills. Decades of battling the bottleneckers finally seems to be paying off. "In a free society, we believe competition is a healthy thing," averred Hector. "If we compete with transit, that shouldn't be a bad thing in the United States of America."[396]

CHAPTER 7

The Schnitzel King Is No More

Laura Pekarik is not who many people think of when they hear the term "street vendor." She holds an associate's degree in business and enjoyed a successful management career in the marketing industry. And then came a life-changing announcement from her sister—cancer.

Diagnosed in 2010, Kathryn Pekarik, Laura's sister, is one of more than 330,000 Americans with non-Hodgkin lymphoma, a type of blood cancer. Laura and her mother both quit their jobs to take care of her. During a benefit held to help defray the costs of Kathryn's medical care, Laura hosted a bake sale, selling 250 homemade cupcakes. Her confections were so popular that her friends and family requested more.

After Kathryn recovered, Laura thought about returning to her job, but she decided instead to go into business for herself. Like many new entrepreneurs, she lacked the money for a storefront location, so she used all of her savings to open the Cupcakes for Courage food truck in June 2011. At 3:30 a.m. every weekday and many weekends, Laura begins a long workday that includes not only baking and selling two hundred cupcakes from her truck but also overseeing a thriving and growing business, from which she donates 10 percent of sales to cancer charities.[2]

Laura's business has grown to employ a dozen staff members. She has branched out to other baked goods and now offers catering and preordering, requiring her to bake hundreds of cupcakes at a time. She also purchased another truck from which to sell her pastries and doughnuts and opened a brick-and-mortar location in September 2012. Named Courageous Bakery, the store also serves as a new station for the food trucks, which continue to operate throughout Chicago—though not all of Chicago, thanks to Windy City bottleneckers.

VENDING'S LONG HISTORY

For as long as there have been cities in America, there have been street vendors. From the colonial period through the nineteenth century, public markets were a major source of food.[3] Beginning as open-air marketplaces in city centers, public markets were later enclosed so trading could continue during inclement weather. Vendors and customers benefited from the change, but so did city leaders. The innovation allowed city governments to build the units and then rent stalls to individual merchants. Some vendors who could not afford an indoor stall took up spaces lining the market outside. Others set up shop close by without permission, the genesis of a separation between merchants and street vendors.[4] Even then, a bottleneck was beginning to form in the vending industry. One way this played out was that, as early as 1691, New York City prohibited vendors from selling outside the city-established markets until two hours after they opened.[5]

Starting in the late nineteenth century, the popularity of public markets began to decline as private stores increased in number and popularity.[6] Yet street vendors continued to enjoy brisk business among consumers looking for lower-cost goods,[7] particularly in poor and immigrant downtown areas that lacked the retailers common in upscale urban areas or suburban communities.[8] Although vendors in such areas often worked without legal approval, they were typically tolerated.[9] Into the first few decades of the twentieth century, vending was viewed as a legitimate business and one ideal for the poor, who were streaming into American cities during this period of significant urbanization.[10] Vending also provided opportunities for the growing immigrant population[11] to generate income, develop skills, and achieve consistent employment in a labor market marked by discrimination.[12]

But just a few decades into the twentieth century, perspectives on vending—or "peddling" as it was known in the vernacular of the day—began to change. No longer viewing vending as a legitimate business, cities increasingly sought to regulate most vendors out of existence, leaving in place only very narrow exceptions for the desperately poor and disabled.[13] In typical bottlenecker fashion, officials cited the need to alleviate overcrowded streets along with providing other public safety rationales in defense of regulations. However, their true motivation was most often a desire to appease more established constituents—brick-and-mortar merchants and the owners of department stores and real estate interests. Such individuals tended to see vendors as posing unwanted competition to their businesses and threatening their property values.[14] These worries were unfounded.

Technological advances in transportation and refrigeration and the accompanying rise and growth of chain stores led to a decrease in demand for street vendors in many areas.[15] The shrinking pool of vendors was evident in census data. Whereas more than three of every thousand workers were street vendors in 1880, only one in every thousand workers held the occupation in 1940.[16] Although vending remained an active occupation in large cities, it was often severely curtailed through licensing and permitting schemes. These schemes, which further contributed to the occupation's declining numbers, typically had bottlenecking written all over them.

THE CHICAGO WAY

When Laura began selling cupcakes in food trucks in Chicago, she discovered that she and other vendors like her were prohibited from operating within two hundred feet of any fixed business that served food. Because brick-and-mortar restaurants tend to cluster together on streets and blocks, this "proximity restriction" has turned entire swaths of Chicago into no-vending zones. The fines for violating the two-hundred-foot rule are $2,000—ten times larger than those for parking in front of a fire hydrant. To enforce the rule, the city forces food trucks to install GPS tracking devices so that it can monitor their every move. Chicago is not alone.

Research on vending laws in the fifty largest US cities completed in 2011 revealed that eleven cities prohibited vending on public property, thirty-four cities made some areas off limits to vendors, twenty imposed proximity restrictions similar to Chicago's two-hundred-foot rule, nineteen limited the time of day when vendors could operate, and five barred mobile vendors from stopping and waiting for customers.[17]

These were the most common regulations, though by no means the only ones. Some cities banned the sale of specific goods on the street, such as flowers in Chicago or "silly string" in Boston. Other hurdles included a one-year residency requirement in Minneapolis, a prohibition on vending in the same spot more than three times a month in San Francisco, and caps on the numbers of vending licenses and permits in New York City.[18] And those are just examples from the largest US cities. Countless smaller American cities also imposed vending restrictions of their own.

Worcester, Massachusetts, for example, drove many of its food vendors away with a 2008 requirement that they receive written permission from restaurants located within 250 feet of where they planned to vend.[19] Lawrence, Kansas, required vendors to secure permission from business owners located near their desired vending location, but in its case the distance was a mere seventy-five feet. Aspiring vendors in Lawrence also had to "instruct said business owners to submit in writing to the City Clerk all comments regarding [their] statement of intention" and, if approved, restrict their business to prescribed locations not already occupied by another vendor.[20]

Cities claim that imposing such restrictions protects public health and safety. A common concern is food safety,[21] even though food vendors in many cities must already submit to the same health inspections as restaurants, sometimes with greater frequency and scrutiny, before these restrictions come into play.[22] One analysis used data from these inspections in seven major US cities to compare the food safety of vendors to that of brick-and-mortar restaurants. Results revealed that food trucks were every bit as safe—and in some cities safer—than restaurants.[23] Other justifications offered for regulations include the need to address sidewalk congestion and cleanliness.[24] Chicago claimed an interest in both those very things when Laura Pekarik sued the city as a result of the restrictions placed on her food trucks.

Seeing the licensing scheme as unjust, Laura filed a lawsuit against the city of Chicago on November 14, 2012, arguing that the regulations represented an unconstitutional restriction on her right to earn an honest living. She believed that government exists to protect public health and safety, not to pick winners and losers in the marketplace, which is, she contended, the sole purpose of Chicago's two-hundred-foot rule, in protecting retail bottleneckers from their vendor competitors. Further, Laura argued, the city violated the Illinois Constitution by using GPS devices for an anticompetitive purpose and gathering data without limitations on their access or use.[25]

Laura's lawsuit does not represent the first time the city had to defend its vending regulations. In 1984, Chicago—under circumstances that remain mysterious to this day—banned mobile food vendors from the Illinois Medical District,[26] a one-square-mile area on Chicago's near west side that is home to an array of medical institutions. At the time, only a handful eateries served the district, and hungry customers were flocking to mobile vendors, who provided an alternative to the long lines in hospital canteens.[27]

The vending ban blindsided mobile vendors, who had operated in the district for years. According to a city staffer, members of the city council's committee for traffic control and safety (who were ostensibly responsible for studying and analyzing proposed ordinances) considered the ban for "maybe three or four minutes" before passing it, because they were "in a hurry to have cake and coffee" to celebrate the committee chairman's birthday.[28] No experts appeared before the committee to testify about the ban. City transportation planners prepared no reports or studies, and the committee did not review any. The ban never appeared on the committee's public agenda.[29]

But if officials exhibited little diligence in enacting the ordinance, they were fully diligent when the ordinance was challenged in court. After a state appeals court struck down the ban in 1988, citing "undisputed evidence" that the vendors posed no health and safety threats, the city appealed to the Illinois Supreme Court.[30]

Less than a year later, in an opinion that starkly illustrates the phenomenon of judicial abdication, the state's high court reversed the decision of the appeals court, holding that the city did not need to produce "accurate, scientific or harmonious" evidence of harm. Rather, as the trial judge that first heard the case wrote, "It is conceivable that the City Council found to its satisfaction that the mobile food vendors do cause traffic and pedestrian congestion and do cause littering in the District."[31] The ban remains in effect today.[32]

In 1991, city leaders approved a new ban—this time one that impacted the entire city. The law prohibited food trucks from operating within two hundred feet of any fixed business that sells food for immediate consumption. The law also prohibited the preparation of food in a food truck—thereby designating prepackaged foods as the only food that food trucks could sell—and put limits on food trucks' hours of operation.[33]

The bottlenecking behind the law was on ready display. The ordinance was first prompted by complaints from the Illinois Restaurant Association that food trucks would park in front of restaurants and lure away customers.[34] Upon the ordinance's introduction, it spurred sharp debate between food truck owners and restaurant owners and the aldermen who represented them, with the mayor's office siding with the bottleneckers. Avis LaVelle, then Mayor Richard Daley's press secretary, claimed the law was necessary because permanent restaurants deserved protection from the competition posed by mobile vendors.[35] Although the ordinance would be painted as a compromise between the Illinois Restaurant Association and the vending industry,[36] it actually leaned in favor of the bottleneckers. As Alderman Patrick Huels, Mayor Daley's point man on city council matters, said, "It's a matter of keeping the businesses in the Loop flourishing, businesses that pay property taxes, license fees, hire dozens of people who pay taxes."[37]

For other aldermen, the two-hundred-foot proximity restriction simply did not go far enough. "I'm going to give this six months," said Alderman Ted Mazola, suggesting that if it didn't protect brick-and-mortar establishments by then, he would "come back to ban all vendors from the Loop area," adding that downtown business owners had complained to him about mobile food vendors.[38]

Statistics on the number of food vendors in Chicago indicate that restaurant owners got precisely what they wanted. Despite a population of almost three million, Chicago was left with only 127 food trucks in July 2012. By comparison, Travis County, Texas, which boasts the state capital of Austin and a population of just one million, had 1,200 mobile food vendors in July 2012[39]—almost ten times as many trucks, in a city with one-third the population.

The 1991 ordinance remained in effect for two decades, seeing no substantive change until the Great Recession, when the perfect storm of economic hardship and consumer interest in street food compelled city leaders to make small changes to Chicago's vending law—the emphasis here is on *small.*

Although the precise causes of the recession remain the subject of much debate, the effects were plain for all to see:

- By mid-2009, housing prices had fallen an average of approximately 30 percent from their mid-2006 peak.[40]
- Stock market prices, as measured by the S&P 500 Index, plummeted 57 percent from a peak of 1,565 in October 2007 to a trough of 676 in March 2009.[41]
- The net worth of US households and nonprofit organizations sunk from approximately $67 trillion in 2007 to a trough of $55 trillion in 2009, a decline of $12 trillion or 28 percent.[42]
- The inflation-adjusted median household income dropped from a peak of $57,357 in 2007 to a trough of $52,695 in 2012—the lowest it had been since 1995.[43]
- Between 2000 and 2010, the number of urban and suburban households below the poverty line went from 23 to 53 percent.[44]
- By the end of the recession, the median male worker was making just $32,000 (in inflation-adjusted dollars), a level not seen since 2005.[45]
- The official unemployment rate spiked from 5 percent in 2008 to 10 percent by late 2009.[46]
- The number of unemployed Americans ballooned from approximately seven million in 2008 to fifteen million by 2009.[47]

Poor economic conditions and meager employment prospects compelled many individuals to think creatively about how to get back to work and provide for themselves and their families. Like generations of economically disadvantaged but entrepreneurially minded people before them, some saw street vending as just the ticket. Michael Wells, codirector of New York City's Street Vendor Project, reported a surge of calls from people who were trying to find a way to make a living after being laid off.[48] Asociación de Vendedores Ambulantes, a vendor association in Chicago, also worked with aspiring vendors who wished to start new businesses after struggling to find other work.[49]

Consequently, by the end of the first decade of the twenty-first century, street vending was again a burgeoning industry. In the 2012 Economic Census, food vendors alone reported revenues of approximately $660 million, with nonfood vendors reporting an additional $21 billion.[50] *New York Times* food columnist John T. Edge declared, "Street food is hip,"[51] and a *Washington Post* story on food trucks observed, "Street carts are the year's hottest food trend. Good, cheap food sates appetites in a recession. And low start-up costs are a magnet for entrepreneurs."[52]

Indeed, since the Great Recession, a new wave of vendors have joined the ranks of traditional "peddlers," making for a diverse group comprising immigrants, minorities, ex-professionals, retirees, and young entrepreneurs building new businesses.[53] In some cities, immigrants man many of the trucks, carts, and stands that line sidewalks and streets.[54] In Los Angeles, for example, Hispanic immigrants make up the great majority of vendors, but people from Asia and the Middle East are also well represented.[55] A survey of the city's vendors working in the popular downtown area found that most had lived in Los Angeles for less than six years and more than a quarter had only worked downtown for less than a year.[56]

This is not the case in every city, however. In the Eastern Market of Washington, DC, for example, only about 20 percent of vendors are immigrants, hailing from Asia, South America, or Africa.[57] Instead, the ranks of vendors in this as well as many other cities include young entrepreneurs building businesses outside traditional structures. Claudine Gumbel and her husband, Brian, for instance, developed Caravan, a boutique-on-wheels that brings new clothing fashions to people all over New York City.[58] Stephan Boillon, former executive chef at a downtown eatery in Washington, DC, began operating the El Floridano food truck in 2010. Three years later, he parlayed the street business into a brick-and-mortar restaurant called Mothership. As Boillon noted, "Without the truck, I don't think [Mothership] would have been possible."[59]

Boillon's story—just like Laura Pekarik's—demonstrates how in tough economic times and for individuals of less means the vending business model, with its low start-up and overhead costs, offers the potential of an accessible avenue into entrepreneurship, self-sufficiency, and success. Boillon's and Laura's stories also show how vending businesses can benefit cities through job creation and tax revenue—that is, if cities, like Chicago, aren't determined to shut them down.

That's what happened to Greg and Kristin Burke. Trained as an engineer, Greg built a flourishing career in the construction industry. And then came the Great Recession. Like millions of others across the country, he found himself unemployed in 2010. As the recession lingered, he struggled to find work in an industry hard hit and slow to see any measurable recovery. With few prospects on the horizon, Greg took matters into his own hands.

For years, Greg had been frying schnitzel (a hand-breaded fried pork or chicken cutlet) at Chicago Bears games, putting it between two pieces of bread, topping it with grilled onions and peppers, and handing it out for free to family and friends. People loved Greg's sandwiches and told him he should sell them for a living. In 2011, he started to do just that. He used his life savings to buy a vintage 1970s Jeep, converted it into a food truck, and became the Chicago Schnitzel King. Greg and his wife, Kristin, built a popular business, but the city's draconian rules eventually drove them out. "We had a strong, loyal following," Kristin said. "Unfortunately, because of the restrictive food truck laws we couldn't make enough money to survive and support our growing family."[60] Thanks to bottleneckers, the Chicago Schnitzel King could not stay in business, and in 2014 the Burkes moved to North Dakota.

Chicago's loss of the Burkes' business followed alleged reforms instituted by the city council. When Mayor Rahm Emanuel was elected in 2011, the popularity of food trucks was at an all-time high, as was demand to allow more of them on the city's streets. The mayor publicly supported trucks during his campaign, and in June 2012 he joined seven aldermen to propose changes to the city's vending ordinance.[61] But the proposal hardly made good on the mayor's campaign promises to challenge restaurant owners, who had blocked previous attempts to ease restrictions on mobile vendors.[62]

Cosponsored by Alderman Tom Tunney, the owner of four restaurants and the former chair of the Illinois Restaurant Association, the proposal reinforced the two-hundred-foot proximity restriction (by quadrupling fines for violations), banned vending from vacant lots even with the permission of the owners of the lots, and created the GPS requirement.[63] In interviews with reporters and committee hearings, officials made no secret of the ordinance's bottlenecking intent. "You want to not infringe on the brick-and-mortars," explained Alderman Proco "Joe" Moreno in the *Chicago Tribune*.[64] In a July 2012 debate on the proposal, Moreno later spoke of how the regulation's two-hundred-foot rule was meant to "dispel the competitive concerns of established businesses."[65]

During a July 19, 2012, hearing, Alderman Brendan Reilly similarly stated, "We want to make sure that we are guarding those folks who make substantial investments in the City of Chicago by buying restaurants."[66] At the same hearing, restaurant owners lined up in support of the proximity restriction as a way to reduce competition. One owner said that restaurants "deserve a little protection from other businesses and people parking in front of businesses and siphoning off our customers." Another testified, "We think it is essential to maintain with the ordinance, the 200-foot rule that is being promulgated to protect brick and mortar restaurants."[67] The president of the Illinois Restaurant Association supported the ordinance because it protects the "interests of brick-and-mortar restaurants."[68]

At a subsequent hearing, Alderman Walter Burnett Jr. agreed: "We don't want to hurt the brick-and-mortar restaurants."[69] Even a press release from the mayor's office acknowledged the protectionist elements in the bill.[70] The lone dissenting voice on the city council—Alderman John Arena—diagnosed the bottlenecking precisely: "A brick-and-mortar restaurant lobby got ahold of [the ordinance], and it was stuffed with protectionism and baked in the oven of paranoia."[71]

City leaders may have spoken openly about the ordinance's bottlenecking intent, but city attorneys were coyer. They primarily defended the regulation by stating that it prevents congestion on streets and sidewalks, controls litter, and encourages the availability of more retail food options in "food deserts."[72] Typical of bottleneckers everywhere, the city's attorneys introduced no evidence to substantiate their claims. But Laura Pekarik's attorneys did.

They first hired Dr. Renia Ehrenfeucht, a professor from the University of New Orleans and an expert on public spaces like sidewalks to research whether food trucks in Chicago actually contributed to greater congestion and litter. Ehrenfeucht's results were unequivocal—food trucks had no significant effects on either problem.[73] Food trucks do draw customers who stand in line on the sidewalk, she found, but pedestrians self-regulate, forming lines so as not to impede sidewalk traffic or create congestion. And rather than eat in the direct vicinity of a food truck, consumers customarily take their food purchases inside buildings or find nearby parks or seating areas in which to eat. Such areas are commonly equipped with trash receptacles, thus avoiding an increase in litter. Ehrenfeucht's results confirmed earlier research completed in Washington, DC, that found the presence of vendors on sidewalks did not drastically increase foot traffic or impede pedestrian flow.[74]

Laura's attorneys then asked Dr. Henry Butler, an economics professor from George Mason University, to study the extent to which the law increases food options in "food deserts." Food desserts, according to the US Department of Agriculture, exist in urban neighborhoods (and rural towns) without ready access to fresh, healthful, and affordable food. Such communities either lack any access to food or only have access to food from fast-food restaurants or convenience stores, not supermarkets or grocery stores. The USDA claims food deserts contribute to a poor diet, higher levels of obesity, and other diet-related diseases.[75] For city attorneys looking for a public health and safety rationale to justify their bottlenecking, food deserts seemed the perfect argument.

According to Chicago's logic, if, by way of the proximity restriction, food trucks were banned from operating in areas already heavily populated by other food establishments, the trucks would move into other neighborhoods with less representation by food retailers and restaurants—the food deserts.[76] Butler's research results indicated that this theory held no water. Using an innovative method of tracking the location of food trucks based on their social media communications, the GMU economist showed that food trucks did not, in fact, respond to the two-hundred-foot rule by taking their business to Chicago's food deserts.[77]

Nevertheless, the city persisted, pointing to the heavy presence of food trucks in the Hyde Park neighborhood—a lower-income area in

Chicago's South Side—as evidence that the two-hundred-foot rule was accomplishing its redistributive purpose. Again failing to present any data to support their assertions, city attorneys claimed that (a) Hyde Park was "underserved" by retail food establishments, and (b) the regulation was causing food trucks to operate there. As before, Butler used cutting-edge technology and data from the city's own Web site to undermine the notion that Hyde Park was underserved. Using GPS and mapping software to display the density of food establishments by neighborhood, the professor showed that among the city's seventy-seven named neighborhoods, Hyde Park ranked fifteenth on the number of retail food establishments available to residents, putting it in the top fifth of Chicago's communities.[78]

As for the reason food trucks gravitate to Hyde Park, Butler needed no advanced analytical tools. The answer was self-evident—Hyde Park is home to the University of Chicago and its almost six thousand students. Food trucks—like restaurants—hang their shingles in particular areas that customers frequently attend. Of course, food trucks aren't the only vending businesses that go where the customers lead them. Nor are they the only vending businesses that must contend with bottlenecking, as Silvio Membreno discovered in the South Florida city of Hialeah.

HOW TO PROHIBIT A LEGAL OCCUPATION

With its population of approximately 225,000, Hialeah is the sixth-largest city in Florida. Located a few miles northwest of Miami, it is home to the headquarters of Telemundo, the second-largest Spanish-language TV network in the country,[79] and is renowned for the Hialeah Park Race Track and the Audubon Bird Sanctuary, which teems with pink flamingos.[80] Hialeah also has one of the highest percentages of Spanish-speaking residents in the United States.[81] It was an ideal place in which to settle for an immigrant from Nicaragua looking for a better life in America.

When Silvio Membreno, then thirty-six, arrived in Hialeah in 1998, he found that it had a vibrant vendor community offering a wide range of goods, including churros (a fried dough pastry), fruits, vegetables, bottled water, guarapo (a sugarcane and lime drink), and fresh-cut flowers. Silvio would specialize in buying flowers in bulk, particularly roses of various colors, arranging them into bouquets, and selling them to customers from the back of his van while parked in a private parking lot near a Hialeah street corner. Silvio also went on to sell sunflowers, orchids, and other varieties upon request and availability.[82] Over the years, he has built up a steady clientele that values the quality flowers he provides at a reasonable price.

Like countless immigrants before him, Silvio came to America in the hope of providing better opportunities for his young family. While he was growing up, he never imagined he would abandon his native country, but years of war, corruption, and dictatorial regimes convinced him that he could not stay and raise his family there. During his lifetime, Silvio saw the fall of the corrupt and dictatorial Somoza family; the rise to power of the socialist Sandinistas led by Daniel Ortega; a ravaging war between the Contras and Sandinistas; and the rule of ineffective and corrupt anti-Sandinista leaders, which climaxed in a twenty-year prison sentence for President Arnoldo Alemán for embezzlement, money laundering, and corruption.[83] When he was in his twenties, Silvio watched as Nicaragua's economy collapsed; at its lowest point, it saw an astonishing inflation rate of 43,000 percent, one of the highest in world history.[84]

Although Silvio was fortunate to find work in his home country, he saw that his prospects for building a career and providing opportunities for his family were increasingly limited by the situation there, so he and his four children left their home and legally immigrated to Hialeah, where his brother already lived. Silvio began working in the construction industry, but he found it difficult to attend to his children's needs given the demands of the job. While driving around Hialeah, he noticed the active street vending scene and saw it as a way to provide for his family and still enjoy the flexibility he needed as a single father. Silvio also spotted a potential niche in the market for quick-service, fresh-cut flowers. Soon, be began street vending on the side, leaving construction altogether at the end of 1999 once his vending business was established.

Ever the entrepreneur, Silvio had ambitions beyond just selling flowers on street corners. Through hard work, networking, and investment in his business, Silvio expanded his enterprise in 2005 to include purchasing blooms in bulk from Ecuador and distributing them to local vendors throughout South Florida for resale.[85] At first, Silvio started sourcing his flowers from his home country only because it was a less expensive supplier for his vending business, but he soon realized that he could also provide stock to other vendors.

Today, the core revenue of Silvio's business remains the daily sales he makes from a street corner in Hialeah. Seven days a week, he begins his day at 5:00 a.m., removing the thorns from the flowers, arranging them in bundles of six or twelve to create bouquets, and wrapping them in plastic. A half-dozen bouquet goes for $5, and a dozen for $10. By 7:00 a.m., Silvio is on his corner selling flowers to drivers who wave him over while stopped at a red light or to customers who pull into the parking lot and buy from his van. He stays on the corner until 10:00 p.m., leaving during the day only to purchase more bulk flowers for the next day. To avoid losing sales, he has someone sell for him while he's away.[86]

Street vending has been the road to success for Silvio, but the city of Hialeah has erected road blocks to slow him and other entrepreneurs down. After Silvio began vending in the 1990s, he noticed and experienced firsthand how police harassed street vendors, even though no law specifically prohibited them from doing their jobs. He and other Hialeah vendors learned that bottleneckers' ends can be achieved through means other than traditional licensing.

Hialeah's city council designed a vending ordinance that used a litany of seemingly small restrictions to utterly hem in vendors in order to protect local brick-and-mortar businesses from competition. Indeed, a 2001 version of the ordinance stated in plain language: "[T]he purpose and intent of this ordinance is . . . that [brick-and-mortar] business owners may have the opportunity to realize the business expectations that would reasonably arise from operating a business out of a fixed location."[87]

As in Chicago, the centerpiece of Hialeah's regulations and the means of achieving its purpose was a proximity restriction. The one imposed in Hialeah made it illegal for a street vendor to vend within three hundred feet of any store that sold "the same or similar" merchandise.[88] In other words, Silvio and his fellow vendors had to be at least a football field away from any store with which they might compete—not to protect public health or safety, but rather to protect entrenched businesses from entrepreneurs who might offer consumers lower prices or better-quality goods.

The law also prohibited vendors from standing still. Unless in they were in the midst of a transaction with a customer, they had to remain in constant motion. Vendors were additionally banned from displaying their goods anywhere on public or private property. They were forbidden from placing their merchandise, supplies, or equipment on the ground—even when vending on private property with the permission of the property owner—only permitted to display what they could hold. For example, flower vendors like Silvio could not so much as set a bucket of flowers on the ground near their feet. Yet brick-and-mortar stores such as Home Depot were allowed to display flowers and other merchandise on the ground outside their buildings. Violations of the ordinance could draw fines of $500 per infraction per day.[89] As Silvio put it, "They are not treating me like a citizen who lives and works in Hialeah, but like a criminal."[90]

The ordinance's specificity demonstrates that the city council possessed an effective working knowledge of the vending business model—and suggests that it was using this knowledge to shield brick-and-mortar businesses from competition rather than to protect the public from health and safety risks. For merchandise vendors, just as for brick-and-mortar retail stores, product displays are an essential part of attracting customers and closing sales. Silvio and other flower vendors often create these by placing an assortment of flowers in buckets in a spot where potential customers driving or walking by can peruse the assortment before buying. Likewise, fruit and vegetable vendors often sell their goods from specially constructed racks on the backs of pickup trucks. Such vendors prefer to park in locations convenient to customers, typically where there is street-side parking.[91]

Displays of flowers and other merchandise spur impulse purchases, but vendors like Silvio also have regular customers who expect them to be present at their customary locations, rain or shine, seven days a week. Parking in lots next to street corners or with adjacent street parking allows vendors to sell to customers waiting at traffic lights or parked in nearby spots.[92]

With its specific restrictions and requirements—the prohibition on merchandise displays, the requirement that vendors remain in constant motion, the proximity restriction, and all the rest of the regulations—the city made the legal practice of vending prohibitively difficult, without actually going so far as to ban it outright. That many vendors continued to work successfully was a function not of some leniency of the ordinance but rather of uneven enforcement by police and code officers. In fact, the most predictable periods of vending ordinance enforcement tended to come around holidays such as Mother's Day or Valentine's Day, when vendors stood to make—or, in the case of enforcement, lose—the most money.[93]

Although Silvio believed firmly in the rule of law, he saw the city's ordinance as not only onerous but also unjust. He first attempted to pressure the city council to initiate change by engaging with the media. In October 2011, when that had proven futile, he sued the city in state court for violating his right to earn a living free from unnecessary government intrusion.

Eager to see the lawsuit go away, the city council approved changes to its statutes in January 2013,[94] but these alterations accomplished little. The new ordinance eliminated the proximity restriction—the most obvious of the bottlenecking provisions—but left everything else in place. It also *added* new regulations prohibiting food trucks and carts from remaining in one place while selling prepared foods, effectively limiting the purchase of such items by brick-and-mortar restaurants.

Silvio persisted with his lawsuit, and, in June 2014, Miami-Dade Civil Court judge Jorge Cueto upheld the city's regulations on summary judgment—that is, without a trial and without considering the evidence Silvio presented to show the ordinance makes vending *more* rather than less dangerous, as the city claimed.[95] Undeterred, Silvio appealed to Florida's Third District Court of Appeals. But in March 2016, a three-judge panel ruled that "reasonable people might believe" that the rules serve legitimate, nonprotectionist ends and that there was no need to examine evidence to the contrary.[96] The state's high court upheld the decision of the appeals court without comment several months later, thus putting an end to Silvio's suit.[97]

Rather than weighing Silvio's evidence and finding it unconvincing, Florida courts at each level simply refused to look. Equally troubling, the courts accepted Hialeah's assertion that the ordinance protects public safety without requiring the city to produce any evidence to that effect.[98] This is the essence of judicial abdication, and it gives bottleneckers free rein to shape policy to protect their interests at the public's expense.

The silver lining to this dark cloud is that Hialeah dropped its proximity restriction, the most blatantly protectionist provision in its ordinance, at the first sign of trouble. As other cities in Florida and elsewhere look to this ruling for guidance when crafting their own vending ordinances, they will not see any support for proximity restrictions. Indeed, Hialeah is not the only city to decline to defend such restrictions in court. In preemptivelty eliminating its proximity ban, Hialeah joined one of the country's largest cities—El Paso, Texas.

BOTTLENECKING ON THE BORDER

El Paso sits in the far reaches of West Texas—barely in Texas, in fact. Closer to Albuquerque and Tucson than to any comparably sized Texas city, the Sun City is sometimes overshadowed by Dallas, Houston, San Antonio, and Austin. It is, nevertheless, one of the fifty largest cities in America and one that boasts an active street vendor scene. Its 384 registered mobile food vendors[99] and 1,700 nonfood vending businesses—94 percent of which are run by self-employed individuals—make up an industry worth approximately $34 million in the local economy.[100]

One of El Paso's food vendors is Yvonne Castaneda. On a typical day, Yvonne awakens at 5 a.m. to begin preparing food for her business. She buys ingredients from a local supplier and then takes them to a commercial kitchen, where she prepares delicious, low-cost burritos greatly in demand by her regular customers. From there, she loads the burritos into her food truck and begins her route. Most days, Yvonne will stop at parks, construction sites, and a local plasma center to deliver food. Before the end of the day, she usually sells more than fifty burritos and an assortment of soda, candy, potato chips, and other prepackaged items.[101] Although Yvonne stops vending at around 4:00 p.m., her day doesn't end until about 6:00 p.m., after she has finished unloading and cleaning her truck and preparing for the next day. Each weekday, she follows the same schedule, serving a retinue of loyal customers who look forward to her burritos. On weekends, she orders food and supplies for her business, completes hours of paperwork and accounting tasks, and squeezes in time to support her high-school-aged daughter, Destiny, at sports and other school events.

Yvonne is proud of the business that she began in 1996, proud that on fifty burritos a day she can pay her business expenses—including replacing all of the components on her 1980s truck—and still support herself; her husband, Hector, who was put out of work by a severe on-the-job injury; and Destiny, after whom her food truck is named. As it has for countless other mobile vendors across the country, owning a food truck has offered Yvonne a gateway to self-sufficiency and entrepreneurship.[102] But El Pasoans haven't always had this option.

In 2009, city leaders effectively turned El Paso into a no-vending zone with the adoption of a new food truck ordinance.[103] The core of the ordinance was a proximity restriction that made those of Chicago and Hialeah look mild by comparison: El Paso's ordinance prohibited mobile food vendors from selling food within a thousand feet of a brick-and-mortar restaurant. Similar to Hialeah's rule, El Paso's also prohibited mobile vendors from parking and waiting for customers, meaning a vendor like Yvonne could not steadily park at her destinations for an hour to serve food to her lunch customers. Instead, she would have to keep driving until and unless a customer happened to see her and flag her down, and she would also have to be back on the move as soon as she completed the transaction.[104]

For any vendor, but especially for a food vendor, such "stop-and-wait restrictions" are utterly unrealistic. Even when the food is made in a kitchen prior to driving a route, serving food from a truck or cart requires setting up equipment, last-minute preparation, packaging, cleanup, and other related activities that make being in constant motion impossible. However, this logic was lost on city inspectors, who enforced the new law with hefty fines.[105] Some vendors, desperate to maintain their businesses, incurred thousands of dollars in fines.[106] In 2009 alone, Yvonne paid fifteen fines totaling more than $4,500, largely due to her uncertainty of the details of the new ordinance. "It's embarrassing," she said.[107] Fines came not only from local police but also from code compliance officers and health department officials.

The result was to push Yvonne out of locations where she had vended for years. "I feel like we're being run out of the city," she said.[108] She sought solutions, like paying to park in a private lot, but nothing she tried worked to attract customers.[109] Her sales, previously enough to support her family, deflated to half their normal volume. Before the new ordinance went into effect, Yvonne's daily sales typically came to approximately $450, giving her roughly $300 to work with after expenses. Slashing that in half left her struggling to make ends meet.[110]

In writing the 2009 ordinance, classic bottleneckers—the El Paso Restaurant Association and other industry representatives—had led the way. The committee that drafted the ordinance was chaired by individuals from the EPRA and the El Paso Bar Owner's Association and included representatives from the Chef's Association, convenience stores, and supermarkets. It also included one owner of a mobile food vending company, Daniel Morales. However, it seems Daniel participated on behalf of his own interests rather than those of food trucks at large.[111] A year after the ordinance's adoption, in a "special-privilege contract," the city sold his vending company the rights to twenty preapproved vending locations for five years, effectively giving Daniel a monopoly on sales of food on El Paso's downtown streets. "I think it's one of the greatest contracts they have created in El Paso," he boasted without irony or shame.[112]

One restaurant association member unabashedly described the 2009 ordinance's purpose as anticompetitive: "We just don't want the mobile units to get right on our doorstep and take our business away."[113] Even the city's director of public health admitted before the El Paso City Council that the ordinance was put in place "to address concerns of the fixed food establishment vendors.... [T]here's not a health reason or a Texas food rule that I can find that justifies that."[114]

For almost two years, she tried to work within the new law, but, faced with the very real prospect of losing the ability to provide for her family, Yvonne—a proud Texan and native of El Paso—took what was for her an unprecedented step. She sued her hometown in January 2011.

The decision was not an easy one for Yvonne. She had many ties to the community of her birth. After earning a nursing degree in college, she had worked as a licensed vocational nurse in a local hospital. When she and her husband decided to have a baby, she chose to pursue vending as a way to take advantage of the flexibility that came with being her own boss. Like most vendors, she had no formal training in the industry other than having taken a food-handling course required by the city and an optional business management course offered by the health department, but she learned quickly and her business grew steadily.

By the time she sued the city, she had built a clientele and established good working relationships with suppliers, others in the vending industry, and people she interacted with during her regular route. Her decision to sue angered and confused some people. "No one had ever challenged the city in this way, and when word got out, people were talking about it everywhere," Yvonne remembered. "Random people I did not know confronted me, telling me what I was doing was not right. Customers asked me about it, asked if I was trying to get money. I explained to them it was not about money but about the right to work."[115]

Unlike so many governments, the El Paso City Council reacted swiftly to correct its error—at least as swiftly as governments can move. On April 26, 2011, city officials voted unanimously to lift most of the 2009 restrictions placed on mobile food vendors.[116] For Yvonne, the decision was a business-saving event:

> I was suffering financially; my family was suffering. I lost a lot of customers, some of which I never got back. But it gave me a lot of comfort knowing I could park where I did before without breaking the law.[117]

As good as the decision worked out for vendors like Yvonne, it did not create a completely free market. Vending in the downtown area and most city parks continued to require a special permit that cost $200 to apply for and $2,000 a year to keep if approved by the city council.[118] For some, the permitting process and fees imposed a significant barrier. For businesses operating on already-thin margins, the time and cost of completing the application process was prohibitive.[119]

City officials seemed oblivious to the chilling effect of the permitting scheme. Veronica Soto, former executive director of the El Paso Downtown Management District, said city officials wanted to see some food trucks operating downtown, as they would add to the "uniqueness of the Downtown experience."[120] City representative Steve Ortega agreed, saying, "We need to get more dining options Downtown."[121]

BENEFITS OF VENDORS ABOUND

With these comments, El Paso leaders acknowledged—albeit somewhat tepidly—that street vendors can contribute value to their communities, though by referring to the benefits they provide only in terms of "uniqueness" and providing additional dining options, they significantly underestimated the scope of that value. By banning or severely limiting vending, cities forgo at least four types of contributions. The first is the availability of particular foods and goods that traditional retailers fail to provide in certain areas. For example, ethnic and immigrant populations often have particular tastes that existing retail options in their neighborhoods can't or don't accommodate.[122] Vendors can meet this demand by specializing in ethnic or international food or merchandise, and they can do so at prices more accessible to these communities.[123]

For example, many vendors offer African American shoppers ethnic products that they may be unable to find elsewhere.[124] Such products include fabrics, hats, jewelry, cosmetics, and clothes. Books written and published by and focusing on black people are another staple item sold by vendors serving African American communities. Karibu Books, for instance, began as a street vending business specializing in serving the African American market.[125] The owner, Simba Sana, left his accounting job at Ernst & Young to sell books as a vendor, eventually growing the business into a chain of brick-and-mortar stores popular with black patrons and authors alike.[126]

Simba's story is emblematic of a second type of economic contribution vendors can offer—upward mobility, and the entrepreneurship that comes with it. Vending's low start-up costs allow people who cannot afford to buy or rent brick-and-mortar storefronts to establish businesses with the potential to grow into larger enterprises.[127] Indeed, many vendors aspire to one day open a storefront business. Vending is a way for them to grab onto the first rungs of the economic ladder and gain the skills, experience, and capital necessary to pursue their dreams.[128] In Yvonne's home city of El Paso, for instance, Ian Atkins, one of the city's upscale mobile food pioneers, parlayed his food trailer—the Drifter—into the restaurant Tom's.[129]

An added benefit of such entrepreneurship is its potential to reduce the welfare rolls,[130] decrease unemployment and homelessness rates,[131] and increase economic self-sufficiency—indeed, to transform inner-city neighborhoods.[132] At least one nonprofit is using vending as a way to develop entrepreneurship among men transitioning out of an alcohol and drug addiction recovery program. Step 13, a recovery program based in Denver, Colorado—whose motto, "A Hand Up, Not a Handout," precisely describes its approach—recently launched a training program in which men operate a food truck at Colorado Rockies baseball games and other events. The hope is that participants will develop skills and experience they can apply to their own businesses or careers in the future.[133]

A third type of contribution vendors make is the increased economic activity they stimulate. Through their dealings—particularly their spending on the things they need to sustain their businesses—vendors offer direct and indirect economic input that ripples throughout their communities.[134] Where vending is prohibited or severely limited, businesses that sell or rent to vendors—such as wholesalers, grocery stores, and commercial property owners—lose out.[135] One study of Los Angeles *loncheras*, often called taco trucks, for example, found that food vendors spend in excess of $75 million a year in the city alone and more than $170 million in Los Angeles county.[136]

Loncheras are predominantly microenterprises owned and operated by Hispanic families in their own neighborhoods. The "taco truck" label is a misnomer, as the typical lonchera serves many dishes, from string-cheese tortas to spicy-shrimp cocktails. Although it is common for bottleneckers to say that vendors don't pay taxes, one such study estimated that owners of loncheras actually pay more than $15 million in taxes and regulatory fees to the city and more than $35 million to the county. And because vendors typically purchase locally, their spending is funneled directly into other city and county businesses, thus supporting thousands of jobs in the immediate area.

Another study completed a similar analysis of the economic impacts of street vendors in New York City in 2012, finding that the Big Apple's ten-thousand-some-odd vendors contribute more than $290 million in annual economic activity. This activity supports more than seventeen thousand jobs and generates more than $70 million in taxes at the local, state, and federal levels.[137] And this is in a city where vending is significantly constrained by bottlenecking regulations. Not one but two separate agencies regulate vendors in New York City. The Department of Consumer Affairs regulates and issues licenses required for vendors of general merchandise, while the Department of Health regulates and issues licenses and permits—both of which are required—for food vendors.[138]

A final type of contribution made by vendors is based on an effect quite the opposite of what bottleneckers fear: The business motivated by vendors can drive customers to brick-and-mortar businesses, rather than siphon them off. A few cities have already recognized this and acted accordingly. The East Liberty neighborhood of Pittsburgh, for example, has worked to *increase* the number of vendors on its streets—for the benefit of other businesses. According to Cherrie Russell, a spokesperson for the nonprofit East Liberty Development Inc. (ELDI), the idea of encouraging more vending came to her after she "noticed that there always seemed to be a lot of activity and life on the blocks where the vendors were set up."[139]

Tony Moquin, the district manager for a clothing store in the area similarly observed, "We've noticed that a lot of customers come into our store after they've stopped to look at what the street vendors are selling. We definitely like having them out here."[140] To produce similar effects, the ELDI encouraged vending by offering grants to offset licensing fees and teaching workshops on local codes, theft prevention, basic bookkeeping, and marketing. It also asked vendors to operate at least three days a week.[141]

When Harbor Springs, Michigan, invited food trucks into its town, city officials discovered something they hadn't quite expected: "Food trucks actually bring people downtown as opposed to just taking away from existing restaurants," said Tom Richards, the city manager of Harbor Springs. "They become an attraction and increase the number of people in your downtown."[142] And with more people comes increased business for brick-and-mortar establishments.

When Lakeland, Florida, began holding once-a-month food truck rallies in its downtown area, restaurant owners were initially displeased, fearing a significant loss of business. Instead, the opposite occurred: Every time a food truck rally kicked off, restaurants grew busier. One restaurant owner estimated the first rally produced a 30 percent increase in his business, an increase that remained even after the rally ended.[143] Like Harbor Springs' city officials, Lakeland restaurateurs discovered that food trucks can draw thousands of people into downtown areas. These people then discover shops and restaurants they've never seen before and bring friends and family back for return visits. One Lakeland restaurant owner—originally a food truck skeptic—was even inspired to build a truck of his own. "The concept is that it has a brick oven on the truck," explained the owner, Giovanni Moriello. "It was custom made by a friend of mine who put [it] in the truck. Lakeland doesn't have a brick oven pizza right now."[144]

Vending's positive effects on other businesses are not merely anecdotal. Systematic research also suggests that street vendors appear to represent little threat to brick-and-mortar businesses; in fact, not only do they coexist with them, they often actually benefit them. For example, 2013 survey research by the NPD Group, a global information company, indicated that food vendors do not, in fact, "steal" business from brick-and-mortar restaurants.[145] Instead, food truck meals and treats tend to be an impulse purchase for many buyers. While some food truck patrons are regulars, many are just occasional customers, thus leaving the regular businesses unthreatened for their customers

And, in 2015, the Economic Roundtable, a Los Angeles–based nonprofit public-policy research organization, mapped the locations of street vendors and stores and restaurants in Los Angeles and found that only a quarter of stores and restaurants were located in proximity to street vendors. This finding should assuage concerns that vendors are massing on the doorsteps of brick-and-mortar establishments. But perhaps the most telling finding in this study is that even when stores were located near vendors, the former were actually *more* likely to experience job growth, an important indicator of economic vitality. Conversely, stores and restaurants located further away from vendors lost more of their employees over the course of five years.[146]

The recognition of these benefits has, unfortunately, been slow in coming. Many cities continue to follow the bottlenecking pattern of Atlanta, though perhaps on a less grandly corrupt scale, in trying to keep good vendors down for the benefit of other private business interests. One of those vendors was Larry Miller, who, for four years, fought Mayor Kasim Reed and the city council to preserve his and other vendors' right to work. Larry eventually prevailed, but his victory came at a significant price—a price he began to pay on one warm, sunny day in April 2013.

ATLANTA'S BOTTLENECKING SHOWDOWN

For almost thirty years, Larry had been a fixture at Atlanta Braves games, not as a player or spectator but as a vendor selling shirts, hats, jerseys, and snacks to excited, loyal Braves fans.[147] On opening day in 2013, Larry and other vendors arrived at Turner Field only to be run off by police and threatened with fines or arrest.[148] As thousands of fans streamed through the turnstiles, Larry was relegated to a private lot away from the field, causing much of his $5,000 worth of merchandise to sit idle in his truck, all thanks to City Hall bottleneckers.

Larry's roots in Atlanta, indeed in the area around Turner Field, go back many years. He was born in the area around what started as Olympic Centennial Stadium and later became Turner Field. His grandfather laid train tracks around Atlanta, and his ancestors had lived in the area since the days when the city was known as Marthasville.[149] Larry finished high school and trade school in the late 1960s and, after a short time spent cooking in a restaurant, ended up at Southern Rural Action, an antipoverty program launched by Randolph Blackwell, a former aide to Martin Luther King Jr. At SRA, he acquired skills in project and business development and was soon leading efforts to build homes and promote light industry all over Georgia and in other regions of the Deep South.[150] In his fifteen years at SRA, Larry's efforts provided housing and jobs for thousands of poor rural citizens.

Although the work was rewarding, he eventually followed an urge to strike out on his own, an impulse nurtured by his father, who ran a successful shoe shine stand. Larry first began vending in 1985, selling merchandise and T-shirts out of the trunk of his car at the old Atlanta stadium. Longtime vendors at the stadium encouraged him to expand his efforts with a table and additional merchandise. By 1990, he had become a regular at Braves games, offering snacks, fully licensed Braves merchandise, parody shirts, and other goodies at steep discounts—all the while paying the required fees and taxes to city and state officials.[151]

"At that time, the vending ordinance was only one page long, but getting a permit was first-come, first-served at the police station," Larry remembered. "You had to line up days in advance to get a permit. I once paid a homeless man $300 to wait in line for me. He had to sleep out on the sidewalk with the others in line. At different times of the day I would drive over with food and stand in line while he went to the bathroom."[152]

Over the years, Larry built a successful business that allowed him to buy a home, raise children and grandchildren, and employ others.[153] In addition to vending at Turner Field, he expanded his business to serve Falcon Stadium, where he works Falcon football games. At both venues, his workdays are long—usually about fourteen hours. Larry arrives at the stadiums four hours before game time and stays until after everyone has left, usually three hours from the end of the game. Preparations before going to the park add another several hours in advance: The truck must be loaded with ice and water picked up from a wholesaler and peanuts cooked the night before. Postgame, Larry cleans and restocks.

When Atlanta's teams are on the road, Larry uses the time to search the Internet and local retail stores for licensed merchandise to sell. "It's hard to find," he said. "We buy a lot of our stuff from places like Ross or Marshalls when they are liquidating stock, and then we resell at the game, but those aren't predictable sources."[154]

For Larry, vending is more than a way to provide for his family—it is also an important part of giving back to his community and providing economic opportunities so that others can pursue independence and entrepreneurship. He demonstrated his commitment to the vending industry by serving on the city's Vending Review Board for ten years and as the president of the Atlanta Vendors Association, during which time he trained hundreds of vendors, financed their operations, and represented them in meetings with the city. As Larry explained, "For generations, street vending has been a way for people in Atlanta to work hard and climb the economic ladder"[155]—a climb bottleneckers seemed intent on cutting off.

The dustup leading to Larry's banishment from Turner Field began in 2009, when then mayor Shirley Franklin signed a twenty-year contract giving a street-vending monopoly to a multibillion-dollar Chicago-based mall management company, General Growth Properties. Although cities had previously awarded private groups exclusive vending rights to a particular street (such as Fremont Street in Las Vegas), a city had never before given a single company the "exclusive right to occupy and use all public property vending sites . . . including without limitation those vending sites currently occupied by public property vendors."[156] GGP's plan included building metal kiosks adorned with paid advertising throughout Atlanta, evicting the vendors who currently worked at those locations, and then renting the kiosks to the new vendors. Under its old permitting system, the city had only received the fees paid by vendors; under the deal with GGP, it would receive $125,000 annually plus 5 percent of advertising revenues.[157]

GGP planned to cover these costs by charging vendors between $6,000 and $20,000 a year in rent for the kiosks[158]—a steep increase from the $250 vendors previously had to pay each year for their permits.[159] When a city councilman expressed concern that many existing vendors could not afford these rents, city officials insisted the rents were reasonable and pointed to efforts to steer vendors toward small business loans.[160] The city's one "concession" to this concern was to reduce the rent for disabled veterans to $3,000 a year.[161]

But the exorbitant rents were not even the most blatant bottlenecking taking place. As part of its deal with GGP, Atlanta asked the management company to keep vendors from competing with nearby brick-and-mortar businesses. The contract with GGP stated that the company should control its lessees so that they only sell products that "complement and not compete with existing 'bricks & mortar' retailers in the areas of the vending units."[162] To accomplish this, city leaders granted GGP complete control over what vendors could sell in the kiosks.[163]

The motivation behind all of this bottlenecking was familiar: brick-and-mortar businesses wanted vendors cordoned off in order to protect their profits.[164] Business leaders also belittled vendors' contributions. "I'm not so sure that street vending is the way to rebuild downtown Atlanta," said Bill Howard, vice president of the Atlanta Convention and Visitors Bureau. "I would rather see shops full of merchants with a greater variety of goods and higher quality goods making long-term investments."[165]

Indeed, business owners and city leaders openly criticized vendors for creating a "tacky environment."[166] "Aesthetics is one of the most important features in developing and maintaining a city and civil society," wrote one bottlenecker in a newspaper editorial complaining that vendors conveyed a "bad image."[167] Mayor Reed caricatured vendors doing business as "swap meets."[168]

Criticisms like these and tensions between vendors and bottleneckers were nothing new. For decades, city leaders had sought to regulate this long-standing industry, which had grown to serve the needs and desires of Atlanta's urban dwellers. Vending, or "peddling," as it was then called, was first recognized in the city code in 1924 and restricted to disabled veterans, widows (who were originally only allowed to sell produce), and boys (but not girls) under sixteen selling flowers.[169] This regulation remained in place with some minor amendments up until 1985, when peddling was finally opened up to other citizens.

Of course, not all public peddlers before 1985 were disabled veterans, widows, or boys. Public vending flourished all over downtown Atlanta and in nearby areas. Beginning in the 1940s, the industry was mostly run by black men from Atlanta's neighborhoods. In the early 1980s, civil rights veterans Mayor Maynard Jackson and council member Carolyn Long Banks championed the flourishing trade as one of the few local businesses open to poor black people at that time.[170]

Much to the dismay of established businesses, these vendors sold more than produce and flowers to other lower-income people. They also supplied incense, clothes such as dashikis (colorful African shirts), jewelry, and handbags, among other things.[171] From the bottleneckers' perspective, these vendors served to "ghettoize" downtown, producing an "untidy" appearance[172] that needed to be controlled in order to protect brick-and-mortar businesses.[173]

What followed was a series of regulatory attempts, crackdowns, arrests, and grand plans to rein in a business that was perceived as an out-of-control nuisance.[174] Already-tense relations between vendors and city officials devolved into lawsuits after the 1996 Summer Olympics in Atlanta, challenging the decision by then mayor Bill Campbell to give a personal associate the right to sublease vending spots throughout the city. Thousands of vendors were pushed out, with many losing their businesses and life savings.[175] A few years later, Atlanta vendors made national news after scuffling with the National Football League over vending arrangements surrounding the Super Bowl in 2000.[176] And, in 2003, the city imposed a moratorium on issuing new vending permits.[177] So, by the time the GGP contract came along, vendors eyed city leaders with healthy suspicion.

The rollout of GGP's plan occurred in two phases. The first phase targeted downtown areas and the second phase took on Turner Field and a highly trafficked area known as Five Points.[178] As the first phase progressed, the bottleneckers were quick to pat themselves on the back. "I think [the kiosks] definitely have made a difference in the look and the feel of the park," said Cooper Holland, the Downtown Improvement District's project manager. "All and all the value is there," he added, but apparently his bottlenecking instincts were not fully satisfied: "We have to come up with a good mix [of products]."[179] The city's senior policy advisor David Bennett similarly enthused: "This program has many benefits. This is clearly better than it was before."[180]

Not everyone saw GGP's plans in such rosy terms, however. First was the cost. As one vendor explained, "Anyone with sense knows, if you're paying $1,500 a month in rent, you're not going to make any money."[181] This was particularly so given that the average vendor only made about $30,000 a year to start with.[182] As Larry Miller described, "We went from spending $150–$200 in permit fees to spending $6,000 a year. Tell me what business can do that."[183]

Street vendors typically work with quite small margins, making a 2,900 percent increase in operating costs utterly unaffordable. The vagaries of the vending market already involve substantial risks. Fluctuations in the weather, the economy, consumer demand, the labor supply, and even in traffic can all threaten the viability of a vending business. Thus a bottlenecker-imposed thirty-fold cost increase was virtually insurmountable for most.

Even without such artificial costs, vendors must move significant amounts of product in relation to their frequent status as microentrepreneurs to become and remain profitable. For example, one truck owner estimated that to be profitable, a food truck needs to generate around $200,000 in annual revenue; to generate a "good" salary for its owner, a truck needs to generate about $500,000 in annual revenue.[184]

On the expense side of the ledger, start-up costs for vendors are comparatively modest.[185] For food truck vendors, the greatest entry cost is the truck itself, which can cost $40,000 or more.[186] Fruit vendors and others who use carts rather than trucks incur substantially lower upfront costs. Lower-quality pushcarts without drainage systems can cost between $800 and $1,000. Pushcarts with drainage systems cost between $1,500 and $2,000 on average.[187]

Once in business, expenses come in the form of inventory, operational costs, labor, and taxes. Operational costs can include rental of storage space for the vending platform (truck, cart, or stand); insurance; fuel; maintenance; commissary fees for food vendors; advertising; and any number of smaller items.[188] One estimate put the weekly costs for an operational food truck at approximately $5,500.[189]

Although revenue minus expenses equals profits, vendors, like other types of small or microbusiness owners, typically take only a portion of that profit as income, putting the remainder back into their businesses. Based on survey data, an estimate of vendor incomes in downtown Los Angeles, for example, found that about a quarter of vendors took home less than $10,000 a year, while a third took home between $10,000 and $25,000. Another 14 percent had incomes of between $25,000 and $40,000 annually, with the rest enjoying higher incomes.[190]

Kim Simpson, a hotdog vendor in Denver, Colorado, exemplifies the economics of street vending.[191] Kim bought a cart on the Internet for $5,000. Each year, she pays $273 to guarantee her spot on the corner, $95 for a license to sell food, and a $75 vending fee. In 2002, she grossed $18,415—almost double her start-up costs—and, in 2003, she reported bringing in roughly $600 a week, netting about $400 after food costs, or approximately $20,000 for the year. Out of that, Kim pays herself a salary.[192]

Selling the amount of product necessary to turn a profit is challenging enough, but Atlanta made it even harder with the introduction of the kiosks. Just four by nine feet, the kiosks were markedly smaller than the tents and tables formerly used by vendors.[193] The tight confines severely limited the amount of merchandise vendors could maintain at the point of sale, thereby reducing the volume of sales so necessary for their profitability.

Even the alleged aesthetic improvements the kiosks were supposed to present failed to live up to the bottleneckers' self-congratulations. As Christine Gallant, a former chair of the Atlanta Vending Review Board, observed:

> I've watched the new vending kiosks go up.... The kiosks supposedly will make this heart of the downtown area more attractive to visitors.... The kiosks are big, ugly, closed-in metal boxes covered all over with advertising, with an opening in the front where the wares can be sold by the vendor. You can't tell from afar what's sold at the kiosk because there's no advertising for [what the vendor is selling] inside.[194]

The kiosks also limited vendors' ability to provide a particularly valuable benefit possible with open work areas—oversight of public safety. Such a function was utilized on May 1, 2010, when street vendors in New York's Times Square noticed that an SUV parked nearby was emitting smoke and alerted police officers.[195] The sharp-eyed vendors noticed the vehicle only minutes after it had been parked there. As Gallant noted, "Of course a street vendor noticed it. They're always looking around for customers. They are very sharp observers of their surroundings as well as human nature generally so they can make a sale."[196] Atlanta's new vendors, stuffed into a three-sided box, would be able to see very little of what was happening around them.

For Larry Miller, the insult of the scheme transcended aesthetics or public safety. "It's an advertising vehicle," he argued. "You put me inside a box, they sell the advertising on it and make money. And then I have to pay for it!"[197] Larry likened the relationship of a vendor in a kiosk to that of a sharecropper on rented land,[198] concluding, "Our concern is that the management company that has been given the contract is illegally taking away public streets to be rented back to us."[199]

So, on July 28, 2011, Larry sued Atlanta, arguing that the city lacked the power to grant an exclusive vending franchise and that its actions violated the Georgia constitution. After about eighteen months, the court agreed with Larry's arguments, in a decision issued December 21, 2012, by Fulton County Superior Court judge Shawn Ellen LaGrua.[200] The decision became final the following month, when the city chose not to appeal its loss. Larry's victory was short-lived, however. Several months later, Mayor Reed cracked down on most of the city's vendors, refusing to let them renew their vending licenses or operate.[201] The mayor justified his actions by asserting that the judge's decision had left the city with no vending law[202]—even though the court's opinion clearly stated that "the City may continue its other licensing and regulatory operations."[203]

Vendors attempted to negotiate with the mayor, but he dragged his feet in issuing a new ordinance that would allow vendors to resume work. To some, his actions appeared deliberate. As community activist Marcus Coleman said, "It reeks of retaliation for the amount of time it's taken to get a common-sense law to put people back to work."[204] For

Larry, the wait was crushing. And although he was able to find a private lot near Turner Field from which to vend, the location was terrible, with few customers walking by. "Where I normally saw thousands at my old location, I saw only a few hundred," he recalled. "I lost 90 percent of my business. I could not make my house payments, and my house went into foreclosure."[205]

Desperate to remedy the situation, Larry sued a second time to require the city to let people work under the original vending law, which the court's earlier decision had restored. Simultaneously, city councilman Michael Julian Bond introduced legislation during the summer of 2013 to allow vendors to work temporarily, but the city council rejected his proposed ordinance.[206] On October 8, 2013, as the baseball season—and Larry's prime earning season—drew to a close, Judge LaGrua ordered Mayor Reed to adopt a vending ordinance.[207] Astonishingly, despite the judge's clear command, Reed still refused to act.

Within minutes of the start of a contempt hearing on November 12, 2013, prompted by Larry's attorneys' requests, a city attorney presented Judge LaGrua with a certified copy of a new city vending law that had just been passed by the city council and signed by the mayor. The motivation for signing the new law was inescapably clear: At the council meeting that morning, Councilman C. T. Martin and others had urged the council to vote on the new ordinance, because the mayor's contempt hearing before LaGrua was about to take place,[208] and passing the ordinance would help the mayor avoid a contempt ruling.

The ordinance helped the mayor escape the charge, but its terms were of little consolation for vendors desperate to work. The new ordinance dictated the design of kiosks and carts, what merchandise could be sold, and where vendors could work. Overseen by the Atlanta Police Department, the plan unfolded in two phases. In the first phase, the law permitted thirty-one vendors—at nineteen kiosk locations and twelve cart locations—to operate in downtown Atlanta. The second phase allowed fifty-plus spots for carts citywide. Vendors were required to rent city-approved kiosks, at $2,500 per year, or purchase approved carts. Tents and folding tables of the kind used by Atlanta's vendors for years were no longer permitted. The popular downtown location of Five Points and public property near Turner Field remained off-limits, although vendors could sell on private property near the stadium.[209]

For Larry and other vendors at Turner Field, the new ordinance meant more waiting as the city deliberated over how to regulate vending at the ballpark. One year turned into two, and the city still failed to act, costing Turner Field vendors the entire 2014 season after they had already lost out on all of 2013. Larry and a few others were able to find vending locations on private property near the field, but, as Larry described, "It was meager."[210]

Finally, in early 2015, the city adopted an ordinance that allowed Turner Field vendors to return to work. On April 10, the opening day of the Atlanta Braves games that year, Larry and his fellow ballpark vendors returned to their traditional locations, surprised to discover that the city had purchased new tents for them—a source of contention in earlier negotiations. Moreover, as a result of filing claim letters after the ordinance's adoption, most of the vendors were supposed to receive compensation for damages incurred due to the city's inaction. Larry, unfortunately, was not among them. He had to go into arbitration with the city, which eventually produced a settlement agreement.

Although they are working now, Turner Field's vendors will again have their livelihoods disrupted. In 2017, the Braves will move to a new stadium being built in Cobb County, northwest of Atlanta.[211] The new stadium is fifteen miles away from Turner Field, and it remains unknown whether and under what conditions vending will be allowed. "They have their own vending ordinances up there, so who knows what will happen," commented Larry.[212]

Now aged sixty-five, Larry could retire, but he has other ideas. With the coming changes in the stadium, he is already planning ahead. A new professional soccer team will start playing at Falcon Stadium in 2017, so Larry may opt to spend summers there.[213] Ever the entrepreneur, he is pondering the opportunities. "I will have to get creative. I don't know anything about soccer," he laughed, "but I am learning. They are probably going to have one famous player that will mean good jersey sales."[214]

On the heels of the Great Recession, *Forbes* magazine contributor Brett Nelson wrote, "The U.S. economy needs all kinds of entrepreneurs.... [T]he relentless, seek-and-solve breed is our salvation. They are the ones forever craning their necks, addicted to 'looking around corners' and 'changing the world.'"[215] As the stories of Larry, Yvonne, Silvio, and Laura illustrate, successful entrepreneurship can be found in an occupation older than the Republic, and, as the next chapter demonstrates, it can also be in something as apparently simple as giving advice. But even that is sometimes too much for the bottleneckers.

CHAPTER 8

The Bottlenecking Vanguard

John "Bo" Rosemond had just walked into his hotel room when he received a call from his wife, Willie. "Bo, you received a strange letter from the Kentucky attorney general today."[1] After forty years of marriage, the sixty-five-year-old North Carolina psychologist recognized the alarm in his wife's voice immediately.

"Read it to me, honey," John responded.[2]

Willie started reading her husband the letter: "Dear Mr. Rosemond, The Office of Attorney General represents the Kentucky Board of Examiners of Psychology."[3] She continued reading, as the letter referred to the state's law for licensing psychologists and then to a column John had written in a local Kentucky newspaper a few months earlier.

For almost forty years, John has been writing a popular advice column on parenting—a column so popular, in fact, that it runs in more than two hundred newspapers across the country and has done so for longer than any other single-author column.[4] What makes the column so popular is that by the time John began writing it in 1976, his views on parenting had become unconventional and therefore entertaining. Unlike many others in his field, John does not subscribe to specific psychological theories related to raising children—particularly those that idealize or romanticize children[5]—but instead relies on "commonsense," developed, in part, by raising his own two children. As John described it,

> I believe many of the parenting problems we are having in America today, which are qualitatively and quantitatively much different than the kinds of parenting problems people had 50-plus years ago, are due to the fact that the parenting voices that have been coming out of the expert community for the last 40 years have led parents in the wrong direction in this country.[6]

In writing about "garden-variety" parenting problems, John espouses a no-nonsense approach to parenting and discipline. This approach includes such "tough love" notions as children "should be seen and not heard" and spankings should be administered as appropriate.[7] If children forget their homework or lunch, for example, John advises parents not to drop everything and deliver the forgotten item to their school. As a result, they will eventually start to remember to bring things with them. And he tells parents to stop giving their children repeated morning wake-up calls. Get them an alarm clock, he advises; if they oversleep and are late to school, they are less likely to do it again.[8] Not surprisingly, such views draw criticism from others. "Because I don't march to the beat of the party line, I am something of a lightning rod for controversy," John said.[9]

On May 7, 2013, lightning struck.

That was the day that his wife read to him the letter he had received from the Kentucky assistant attorney general, Brian Judy. The letter informed John that he was violating Kentucky law by operating as an unlicensed psychologist in the state—even though he lives and works three hundred miles away in North Carolina and has no clients in Kentucky. The method by which he had supposedly perpetrated his crime was his weekly column, which runs in the *Lexington Herald-Leader*.

According to the logic of Assistant Attorney General Judy and the Kentucky psychology board, John's column of February 12, 2013, violated state law because, as Willie continued reading over the phone, "Your response to a specific question from a parent about handling a teenager was a psychological service to the general public, which constituted the practice of psychology."[10] In other words, in the eyes of the Kentucky psychology board, answering individual questions from anonymous readers in an advice column is tantamount to one-on-one psychological counseling, an act that requires a state license.[11]

Willie continued reading: "Additionally, [state law] restricts the practice of psychology and the use of protected words, such as 'psychologist' only to those persons credentialed by this Board."[12] In other words, by calling himself a psychologist in the tagline of his column, John was committing a crime because he was not a Kentucky-licensed psychologist, despite the fact that his North Carolina license enabled him to use the title "psychologist."[13] For these alleged crimes, John faced statutory penalties of up to six months in jail or $500 in fines *per offense.*

To avoid such punishment, the assistant attorney general and psychology board demanded that John sign a "voluntary" agreement promising to no longer publish his advice column in Kentucky.

Willie finished reading the letter to John:

> I trust that you will agree to resolve this matter now without the time, expense, and delay of any further legal action. This correspondence has been sent to you by certified mail to ensure that you receive it.
>
> Sincerely yours,
> Jack Conway
>
> Attorney General
> Brian T. Judy
> Assistant Attorney General
> *Counsel, Kentucky Board of Examiners of Psychology*[14]

In other words, the Kentucky psychology board—composed almost entirely of licensed psychologists—was attempting to bottleneck John's speech.

To do so, the board was relying on a licensing law adopted in 1964. However, the state's bottlenecking in the field of psychology actually dates back to 1948, when Kentucky became one of the first states to adopt a certification titling law.[15] That law created the Board of Examiners in Psychology, which was made up of five PhD-level psychologists. In the 1980s and 1990s, the board was expanded to comprise nine members, including a few non-PhD psychologists and a member of the public,[16] but these modifications did little to change the profession's bottlenecking proclivities.

Such changes to the composition of licensing boards rarely do. In response to the "capture" of licensing boards by members of the licensed occupation, legislators in the 1960s and 1970s began requiring that boards include members of the public.[17] But studies in the years that followed found that such changes accomplished substantively little in the way of reining in bottlenecking.[18]

These findings are not entirely surprising, given that bottleneckers typically dominate licensing boards, with general ratios of six or eight bottleneckers for every member of the public. The Kentucky psychology board, for example, has eight licensed psychologists and just one public member. The public members' influence is therefore severely limited,[19] even when their views differ substantially from those of the bottleneckers making up the rest of the boards on which they sit.

Members of the public may also be less likely to oppose other board members due to their lack of technical expertise, which bottleneckers may take pains to emphasize. Bottleneckers have a clear interest in making the work they do seem as technically sophisticated, abstract, and specialized as possible in order to justify their own licensure. For decades, sociologists and other researchers have made note of how occupational practitioners use specialization or claims of abstract knowledge in order to set their work apart and justify being specially classified and recognized, as happens with licensure.[20] As the researchers claim,. by asserting that the nature of their work is extremely sophisticated, practitioners maintain an unfair and potentially harmful asymmetrical advantage in having exclusive knowledge about their field, such that laypeople cannot recognize when they are being bamboozled or even exposed to supposedly life-threatening risks.[21] In turn, practitioners reinforce the need to protect the public through licensing.

In the context of boards, this can manifest itself in bottleneckers' use of technical terms, jargon, abstract rhetoric, and other trappings of the occupation to intimidate a public member of the board into following other board members' lead. And, of course, in the spirit of getting along, a public member may simply feel uncomfortable criticizing the activities of an occupation when sitting next to representatives of that occupation.[22]

In Kentucky, even if the psychology board's single public member thought censoring John's speech was ill-advised, the bottleneckers' eight-to-one advantage would have rendered her position irrelevant. As it happened, board meeting minutes indicate that over the course of the months in which the board sought to censor John, the public member was either absent or appeared not to hold or express an opposing position.[23] The bottlenecking of John's speech moved forward without even marginal resistance.

For John's part, although he knew his parenting advice was sometimes controversial, he never thought he'd see a day when the government would censor him.[24] "I was incredulous," he said, describing his initial response to hearing Willie read the letter over the phone. "I could not possibly imagine such a blatant attempt to restrict my First Amendment rights."[25]

What John was experiencing was a new frontier in bottlenecking through unfettered license creep. For more than a century, legislators have heeded to bottleneckers' calls for regulation of the conduct of their respective occupations, determining who may or may not clean teeth, install and fix plumbing, style hair, sell caskets, or provide any number of different services. Licensing boards and regulators have expanded the licensing fences to encompass the practice of occupations at the margins of their own—as they have done with cosmetologists and hair braiders or dentists and teeth whiteners.

With the regulation of speech, licensing creep has taken a unique form—licensing speech as if it were conduct. Traditional licensing creep pushed the boundaries of what constitutes the practice of an occupation. This new manifestation of the old problem pushes the boundaries of the very definition of "practice" itself.

In John's case, for example, the Kentucky psychology board's position was that advice falls not under the category of *speech*, which is protected by the First Amendment, but rather under that of occupational *conduct*. Even more striking is the board's belief that advice given in a newspaper column—as opposed to advice given in person or by other means—constitutes conduct, not speech. It is true, of course, that giving advice is a large part of the practice of some occupations, including those of attorney, financial counselor, and even psychologist. The difference is that the act of giving advice in the practice of such occupations is part of a defined financial relationship and accompanies other occupational conduct, such as reviewing documents and case law, implementing psychological testing, and so forth.

In contrast to the other occupations, John does not know the identity of anyone who submits questions to him. Years ago, John took the questions he answered in his column from seminars he led around the country, but with the advent of the Internet the questions he now features come from anonymous submissions to his Web site.[26] This means that he does not enter into any formal financial relationship with letter writers around his clinical services; he does not know where the letter writers live; he does not know whether or not the parents who submit questions to him actually read his column or follow its advice; and he does not know whether the writers actually are even parents.[27] But because the Kentucky psychology board held to the idea that advice is conduct rather than speech, they moved to censor John's newspaper column.

Prior to writing his column, John had, in fact, practiced as a clinical psychologist for many years. After completing his master's degree in psychology from Western Illinois University in 1971—and doing a stint as the lead singer in a rock band that opened for REO Speedwagon—he worked as a psychologist in North Carolina, directing mental-health programs for children and leading a full-time practice in family psychology.[28] It was in 1976, during his directorship of an early intervention program at a mental health center, that John began writing a weekly column that quickly grew in popularity. Two years later, the *Charlotte Observer* purchased the column and subsequently put it into syndication.[29]

In 1989, John wrote his first parenting book. Like his columns, the book differed significantly from most other books on the market and consequently drew attention and controversy. It also exposed him to an even-wider audience and produced invitations to speak all over the United States, Europe, Canada, and Australia. As his renown grew, John eventually left his full-time practice in psychology and dedicated his time to writing and speaking—meeting with a few clients on occasion[30]—producing more than a dozen bestselling books and making appearances on national television programs such as *20/20*, *Good Morning America*, *The View*, *The Today Show*, *CNN*, and *CBS Later Today*.[31]

In all of John's years writing books and columns and appearing in the media—he is on the road about half of the year—no one had ever construed his advice as constituting the practice of psychology as commonly understood.[32] The US Department of Labor defined the practice of psychology as "diagnos[ing] or evaluat[ing] mental and emotional disorders of individuals through observation, interview, and psychological tests, and formulat[ing] and administer[ing] programs of treatment."[33] In his weekly newspaper column, John is not diagnosing and treating patients according to this definition. Instead, he is simply participating in a form of speech—an advice column—that goes back more than three hundred years.[34]

ADVICE COLUMNS—AS OLD AS NEWSPAPERS THEMSELVES

The first advice columns appeared in seventeenth- and eighteenth-century newspapers, which differed from their present-day progeny in that they contained little news. Instead, they offered readers commentary, speculation, and political satire. They served a partisan function and, above all, sought to entertain. It was in this context of rowdy, animated, and engaging journalism that the first advice column made its debut.[35]

In 1691, a clever bookseller, John Dunton, created a publication—the *Athenian Mercury*—dedicated solely to answering its readers' questions. Also establishing a society to answer questions posed by whoever wanted to submit them, Dunton offered to publish the questions and make the answers available to anyone who would buy and read the paper. From its earliest issues, the paper was a smashing success, providing fact, opinion, advice, and abuse in the answers to almost six thousand questions. Dunton expected questions of all types, so he enlisted others to help him answer questions in math, science, religion, and literature—bodies of knowledge in which he was ill equipped to respond. The authors of Dear Abby and Ask Ann Landers would do precisely the same centuries later.[36]

While questions of science and nature appeared often in the *Athenian Mercury*, morality and conduct were also popular subjects. One submission asked if it was a greater sin "to be a Nightwalker [prostitute] or to rebell against ones Parents." The answer noted that either option was damnable but said, "We refer you to the order of their setting down in the ten Commandments, where duty to Parents is press'd before Adultery is forbid." Another reader queried about the use of tobacco, wondering "whether it does not infect the genuine Purity of the Breath." The advice:

"Tis e'ne as you like it: Some think it a Notorious Stink...others that 'tis the best Smell in the World—And for the Querist, we'd advise him to be judg'd by his Mistress, and let her Nose rule his, if e're he expects his Lips should be acquainted with hers."[37]

The *Athenian* was the first of its kind, but it was soon followed by the *Little Review*, the *British Apollo*, and others.[38] The tradition continued in America, where, in 1800, the *Baltimore Herald* began printing and responding to readers' questions about their personal issues. In 1896, Elizabeth Meriwether Gilmer began writing the Dorothy Dix marriage column for the *New Orleans Times-Picayune*. The column's popularity was enormous. By 1940, it was syndicated in more than 270 newspapers worldwide with an estimated personal readership of sixty million, making Gilmer the most-read female writer of her era. By World War II, she was receiving one hundred thousand questions by mail each week. Pauline Phillips began writing her iconic Dear Abby column in 1956 under the pseudonym Abigail Van Buren. Following a similar path, Eppie Lederer, Phillips's twin sister, took over the Ask Ann Landers column in the *Chicago Sun-Times*, which began in 1943 with the name in the title a pseudonym for Ruth Crowley.[39] At one point, the combined daily readership of the sisters' columns was estimated at 130 million people. A popular competitor of the day, Dr. Joyce Brothers, who billed herself as "America's favorite psychologist," boasted a daily readership of twenty million.[40]

Although the content and approach of these columns varied,[41] the commonality was their enormous popularity—a phenomenon that continues to this day. What makes such columns so popular is that they deal with questions everyone has wondered about or worried about[42]—not to mention the entertainment value they provide and the basic human urge to be nosy that they satisfy.[43] No one reasonably expects that the authors are establishing a professional relationship with those whose questions they answer. Indeed, according to one study, advice columnists almost never advise their querists to seek professional help.[44]

And so it was for John Rosemond for almost forty years, until Dr. Thomas Neill, a retired licensed psychologist from Kentucky, took offense to John's column of February 12, 2013. In the article, John responded to a reader asking about a seventeen-year-old son, suggesting that he was a "highly spoiled underachiever." The advice given was classic John Rosemond: "As you now realize, your son is in dire need of a major wake-up call. Start by stripping his room to bare essentials, taking away any and all electronic devices, and suspending all of his privileges, including driving."[45]

The day after the column ran, Neill complained to his state's psychology board, calling John's advice "unprofessional and unethical." The doctor asserted that "while Mr. Rosemond's suggestions might work very well, they could also create serious problems for the youth and the family in question."[46] He also noted that John was better off instructing the family to seek professional help and asked the board to stop him from presenting himself as a psychologist in Kentucky. This amounted to forcing the columnist to omit the tagline in which he identified himself as a psychologist or else discontinue his column in Kentucky altogether.

Neill also sent a copy of the letter to John and to the *Lexington Herald-Leader*. "I was outraged by the letter," John remembered. "He appeared to be motivated by professional jealousy and a fundamental disagreement with my worldview, and I wrote him back and told him that. In his response, he admitted as much; he disagreed with my general point of view."[47] For the *Herald-Leader*'s part, Editor Peter Baniak countered that the newspaper had published John's column for at least three decades and would continue to do so. "This is a free-speech issue," Baniak said. "The state should not be attempting to dictate what kind of column can or can't be printed in a newspaper."[48]

If the psychology board was concerned that its bottlenecking might be violating John's First Amendment rights, it gave no appearance of it. Although Neill's letter was sent to the board in February 2013, John's case did not appear in the board's minutes until May 2013. Even then, the attention paid to it appears to have been perfunctory. Indeed, as then board chair Dr. Eva Markham later described, complaints of the type made against John received little scrutiny prior to enforcement by the board. As she described: "We generally don't conduct investigations. We simply look at the complaint and try to figure out how to contact the individual complained about and send a Cease and Desist Affidavit."[49]

John may have dismissed Neill's letter as professional carping, but receiving a cease-and-desist letter with threats of legal action by the state attorney general's office was another thing entirely. "I took the letter very, very seriously," John recalled. "I faxed a copy to my attorney, who helped me craft a response. I was in no financial position to fund a defense, especially against a state attorney general's office with pockets infinitely deeper than my own."[50]

Just a little more than a week after receiving the letter, John responded with a letter of his own in which he stated that he did not believe his advice column of February 12, 2013, constituted the unlicensed practice of psychology.[51] He pointed out that over the "past few decades there has been a proliferation of newspaper and magazine advice columns, radio advice programs, and television advice programs,"[52] featuring Dr. Phil, Dr. Laura, and many other national-level advice personalities[53] who educate and entertain by offering individualized advice in response to questions from readers, listeners, or viewers—all of them readily available to Kentuckians.

The response from Kentucky was . . . nothing. Neither the attorney general's office nor the psychology board replied in any way. On May 31, 2013, John tried again. He faxed a letter to Assistant Attorney General Judy, e-mailing a copy to the psychology board's administrator, asking for an additional forty-five days to respond to the board's demand that he complete the cease-and-desist affidavit or face punishment.[54] Again, he heard nothing back. The minutes of the psychology board's June meeting[55]—at which Assistant Attorney General Judy was present—show no sign that anyone was paying particular attention to John's case.

For John, the silence was disconcerting. "I did not know what to think," he recalled. The only communication he had received was the letter from the attorney general's office and the board, which he found "arrogant and threatening,"[56] accompanied by a cease-and-desist order. Together, the documents conveyed a clear message: the state of Kentucky considered John Rosemond a criminal.

John thought otherwise. As he first wrote to Assistant Attorney General Judy on May 16, 2013:

> Put simply, newspaper advice columns are protected speech under the First Amendment and do not constitute 'engaging in the practice of psychology,' particularly when the . . . American Psychological Association standard is followed. I have and will continue to adhere to

> that standard. Furthermore, my advice is limited to common parenting problems that are not the exclusive domain of psychologists.[57]

Not content to wait and see what action the state of Kentucky might take, on July 16, 2013, John filed a lawsuit against the psychology board and the attorney general—since the cease-and-desist letter originated from his office and was followed by his name—on First Amendment grounds. John also asked for a restraining order against the psychology board, which was, as far as he knew, preparing sanctions against him.

Suddenly, silence was replaced by action.

Two days after John filed his lawsuit, the psychology board met in closed session to discuss its response. It decided to agree to the restraining order and budget $10,000 to fight the lawsuit.[58] The board also began a swift backpedal. The original letter to John clearly stated that his column—based on its content—represented the practice of psychology. But after its July 18 meeting, according to the board, the primary problem was "Rosemond identifying himself as a psychologist despite not being licensed as one by Kentucky."[59] And, in its August 12 meeting, the board approved a settlement offer that would have required John to remove his professional title from the tagline of his column or identify the state in which he was licensed.[60]

Just as New Mexico sought to preserve its ability to regulate interior designers by reducing the restrictiveness of its law, the Kentucky psychology board sought to avoid litigation on First Amendment grounds by limiting its focus on John's use of a title. But for John, the modification still had no grounds.

In his May 16 letter, John had written: "The North Carolina Board, who is *my* licensing authority, has told me that I may call myself a psychologist without any restriction"[61] (emphasis in original). Thus, John's title in his column's tagline was earned and legally accurate. Kentucky's requirement that he remove or alter it in any way amounted to censorship by the board and a violation of his First Amendment rights.

The board was not alone in its backpedalling. The attorney general did a full-on reversal. A week after John filed his lawsuit, Attorney General Jack Conway issued a press release denying that the cease-and-desist order originated from his office. "I did not write that letter, I did not authorize that letter, and the letter was not sent on behalf of the Office of the Attorney General," Conway said.[62]

Although it defies credulity that a cease-and-desist order printed on an Office of the Attorney General letterhead, followed by the attorney general's name, and signed by an attorney in the office would be sent without the office's knowledge or approval, Kentucky does actually allow state boards and agencies to hire attorneys from the attorney general's office to serve on an hourly basis as board or agency attorneys.[63] Assistant Attorney General Brian Judy represented the psychology board according to just such an arrangement, and, according to a press release from the attorney general's office, his actions "had nothing to do with the Office of the Attorney General." The release further said that Judy's use of the office's letterhead was "not proper procedure."[64] Inside of a week, Conway's office successfully achieved its removal as the defendant in John's lawsuit.[65]

One might expect that the attorney general's office's reversal would have sent the psychology board a signal about the advisability of continuing to defend its actions, but the board pressed on, clinging to its position that it was protecting public health and safety for Kentucky citizens by censoring John's speech. Yet, as the lawsuit progressed, board members were compelled under oath to admit that they knew of no harm befalling Kentuckians as a result of John's columns,[66] including to the parents who submitted the question that John answered in the February 12 column, generating Neill's original complaint.[67]

In a deposition on August 28, 2014, then board chair Dr. Eva Markham dismissed as irrelevant any concern about the family who were the subject of the letter:

> Q. Did the Board attempt to determine whether the parents and the child who were the subject of Plaintiff Rosemond's column suffered any harm as a result of that column before it sent the letter to Mr. Rosemond?
>
> A. No.
>
> Q. Is that because the Board didn't believe that that was relevant?
>
> A. Correct.[68]

Moreover, when asked if John's column had ever harmed anyone, Markham's reply was: "Not to my knowledge."[69] And when asked if there was evidence that John's use of the title "psychologist" had misled anyone in Kentucky, the doctor acknowledged that there was no such evidence. She also indicated that she did not believe that people would necessarily assume from John's use of the title that he was licensed in Kentucky and admitted that the board bore no concern that someone might be misled. The use of the title in and of itself is what gave the board umbrage:

> Q. What is the Board's evidence that someone seeing the word psychologist in a newspaper column will assume that the author of that column is specifically licensed by the State of Kentucky?
> A. I'm not sure that people would assume that....
> Q. So, the Board is not aware of any evidence that anyone has actually been misled?
> A. No.
> Q. Is the Board's concern that it's hypothetically possible that people were misled?
> A. No.
> Q. Is the Board not concerned whether people were misled?
> A. That was not the basis of our action, that concern.
> Q. So, the Board ultimately doesn't care whether anyone was misled by that line in his column?
> A. We care that that line is in the column.
> Q. But whether anyone was misled is irrelevant to the Board?
> A. Basically, yes, in this matter.[70]

In other words, Kentucky's psychology bottleneckers produced no evidence of the need to regulate John's use of his legitimate title or any other element of his speech—the same type of speech that has dominated advice columns for hundreds of years. This lack of evidence played a key role in the outcome of his case.

On September 30, 2015—two years after John first filed his lawsuit—US District Judge Gregory F. Van Tatenhove found decidedly in John's favor. In point after point, Judge Van Tatenhove rejected the board's arguments and upheld John's right to speak. Van Tatenhove saw John's column not as a pecuniary relationship between client and professional but as "nothing more than a literary device."[71] Indeed, the judge noted that despite its protestations to the contrary, "the Board used [state statutes] to restrict Rosemond's speech because it took issue with the message he was conveying," rather than because it was sincerely attempting to protect the public from harm.[72]

In fact, Judge Van Tatenhove found that if anyone was causing harm it was the board itself:

> All [John Rosemond] did was write a column providing parenting advice to an audience of newspaper subscribers. To permit the state to halt this lawful expression would result in a harm far more concrete and damaging to society than the speculative harm which the State purportedly seeks to avoid.[73]

Concluding that the board had "unconstitutionally applied" state regulations to John's column, the judge permanently prohibited the board from "enforcing these laws in an unconstitutional manner against Rosemond or others similarly situated."[74] And he made clear whom he meant by "others similarly situated":

> If the State's interest is really in preventing persons unlicensed in the Commonwealth of Kentucky from holding themselves out as licensed professionals, it is difficult to understand how Dr. Phil, Dr. Oz, and countless other self-help gurus would not also be in the Government's crosshairs.[75]

In his decision, the judge rightly noted that John is among scores of paid authors who convey advice in columns, books, television, and other forms of traditional media. Were John guilty of an unlawful practice, so would be people like Suze Orman, Ruth Westheimer, and Dave Ramsey. But with the advent of the Internet, and social media in particular, the implications of license creep in regard to giving advice are no longer limited to authors paid to share their wisdom through traditional media. License creep can now also entangle something as simple as the unpaid, evangelistic bloggings of a man transformed—a man like Steve Cooksey.

THE CAVEMAN BLOGGER

On February 14, 2009, Steve Cooksey dragged himself off his couch, stumbling toward the kitchen in a stupor. Listless and fatigued in a way he had never experienced, Steve could barely stay awake. Overwhelmed with thirst, he gulped down Gatorade and juice in a vain attempt to satisfy a strange dehydration that had developed in his body and never seemed to be sated. He had felt increasingly sick for some weeks, even visiting the doctor a few times, but none of his suggestions seemed to help what seemed like a bad cold.

As he collapsed back onto the couch, Steve became increasingly short of breath. By the next morning, he felt like each new breath was going to be his last. He called to his wife and asked her to take him to an emergency clinic. After a few quick tests, the staff summoned an ambulance to rush him to a hospital. He was on the verge of a diabetic coma.[76]

That day, at the age of forty-seven, Steve learned he was among the twenty-nine million Americans who suffer from diabetes.[77] Americans spend hundreds of billions of dollars every year treating diabetes, and that amount will continue to rise dramatically as more and more prediabetics transition to the full disease.[78] Diabetes can be a devastating disease. On average, diabetics live ten fewer years than nondiabetics.[79] Diabetes is strongly associated with increased rates of heart and kidney disease, as well as high blood pressure.[80] Also, because excessively high blood sugar can destroy nerve endings in the eyes and extremities, diabetes is a leading cause of blindness and amputation.[81]

The rate of adult-onset diabetes—also called type 2 diabetes—has exploded in the last thirty years in lockstep with swelling obesity rates. In 1980, the national obesity rate among adults was approximately 15 percent.[82] By 2011, the rate had almost doubled to 27 percent. In Steve's home state of North Carolina, the rate was even greater—29 percent.[83] During this same period, the national rate of diagnosed diabetes more than doubled, from 2.8 percent of the population to 6.3.[84] In 2011, North Carolina's diabetes rate was even greater, at 10.2 percent.[85]

For Steve, the diagnosis was galvanizing. For years, he had known he needed to change his lifestyle. While growing up, he was very active, playing numerous sports through college and well into his twenties.

But as he took on more responsibility in his career in accounting and then in management, he worked increasingly long hours and exercised less. In the years leading up to his trip to the hospital, Steve commonly spent twelve hours a day working as a manager for a medical equipment company. The most exercise he ever saw was his six daily trips to and from his car,[86] and he struggled through cycles of significant weight gain and loss.

Steve's lack of exercise was exacerbated by poor eating habits. Growing up in North Carolina, he had eaten a diet full of Southern comfort foods: fried foods, biscuits, waffles, cereals, cinnamon rolls, creamy potatoes, corn bread, and sweet teas. As his career progressed, his long workdays were punctuated with breakfasts of biscuits, lunches of fast foods stuffed with bad fats and carbohydrates, and dinners composed of more fast food. He often would buy two complete takeout meals and finish them off on his fifteen-minute drive home.[87] To top that off, he usually ended his day with a few beers.[88]

The result was entirely predictable. Steve's weight grew to 235 pounds—75 pounds more than the ideal weight for his five-foot-ten-inch frame. He developed a litany of chronic ailments—hypertension, high cholesterol, bronchitis and asthma, plantar fasciitis, lower back pain, and acid reflux and indigestion.[89] His medicine chest was brimming with drugs: ibuprofen, Levaquin, lisinopril, Vytorin, amoxicillin, benzonatate, Xopenex, and, as a result of his trip to the hospital, insulin and Actos for diabetes.[90]

After being rushed to the hospital, Steve stayed for four days, during which time he spoke with an endocrinologist, who told him he would be on insulin the rest of his life, and a licensed nutritionist, who told him to eat a high-carbohydrate/low-fat diet. Determined to take charge of his life, he began reading extensively about the treatment of diabetes. The more he read, the more skeptical he became of following the high-carbohydrate/low-fat diet the nutritionist had advised to control his blood sugar. After all, carbohydrates directly *raise* blood sugar.

Steve decided to try something different. He drastically reduced his carbohydrate intake and increased his consumption of protein and fat. He also jogged and walked daily and began lifting weights. Within a month, his blood-sugar levels had normalized, and he was able to discontinue his insulin and other diabetes drugs. At a follow-up appointment, Steve's doctor acknowledged the results and told him to continue doing what he was doing.[91]

Steve eventually transitioned to the paleolithic, or "paleo," diet, meaning he eats only foods that were available to preagricultural humans—meats, fish, fats, nuts, vegetables, and fruit. He strictly minimizes agricultural grains and starches, sugar, and junk food. Coupled with running, jumping, and whole-body exercises, Steve became lean, fit, and energized and completely free of drugs and doctors, and he is now an advocate for paleolithic eating. Eager to use his experience to help others, he channeled his advocacy into a blog—*Diabetes Warrior*[92]—to spread the promising results of the "caveman diet."[93] However, proclaiming the good news got him into bad trouble with the bottleneckers, this time in the form of licensed dietetics.

Steve started his blog in 2010 as a way to share his view that a paleolithic diet and exercise are the best practices for diabetics. Throughout the site, Steve included disclaimers, making it clear that he was not a doctor, dietician, or any other licensed health professional. He was simply a passionate advocate sharing his beliefs with others in order to help them achieve the kind of personal transformation he had experienced.

Over time, Steve's readership grew into the thousands, and some of his readers sent him e-mails asking questions. These e-mailers often turned into friends, and he began mentoring others on their weight-loss journeys by drawing on his own experience. Steve received such good feedback from his mentees that he began offering a life-coaching service—for a nominal fee—similar to that offered by elite athletic trainers but aimed at people struggling to adopt a paleo lifestyle like his.

In 2011, Steve thought of a new way to share his knowledge and opinions. He began a Dear Abby–style advice column drawing on the paleolithic diet and exercise recommendations he gave on his blog. He posted anonymous questions from readers and gave advice based on his own experience and the numerous books and articles that he had read. That is where his trouble began.

Steve's activities came to the attention of the North Carolina Board of Dietetics/Nutrition after he attended a nutritional seminar for diabetics at a local church on January 12, 2012. The person running the seminar—the director of diabetic services at a local hospital—expressed the view that a high-carbohydrate/low-fat diet is best for diabetics. During a question-and-answer period of the seminar, various people, including Steve, expressed different views. Following the seminar, Steve discussed his opinions and experience with some fellow attendees, sharing his contact information with several of them. The following day, someone filed a complaint with the board against him for engaging in "nutritional counseling" without a license. The complaint prompted the head of the board to call Steve and inform him that he was under investigation.

On January 27, 2012, the state board e-mailed Steve a marked-up nineteen-page excerpt from his blog, including his Dear Abby–style advice column, on which the board had gone through his writings with a red pen, indicating on a line-by-line basis what he could and could not say. Examples of prohibited advice that Steve had given—that is, advice that only licensed dieticians could dispense—included:

- "Honestly, he needs to get off the 'carb up and shoot up' treatment plan."
- "Your friend must first and foremost obtain and maintain normal blood sugars."
- "Maintaining NORMAL blood sugars will allow his body to heal."
- "Cut the carbs to 30 g or less of TOTAL carbs per day and eating meats and veggies will help."
- "I do suggest that your friend eat as I do and exercise as best they can."[94]

Not only did the board seek to silence Steve's advice column but it also asserted that he could not act as an uncompensated mentor to friends and readers. It identified statements made by Steve's friends and readers—which he had posted on his Web site—thanking him for his mentorship and support as evidence that Steve had engaged in unlicensed "nutritional counseling."[95] The board also banned Steve from running his life-coaching service.

In so doing, the board was policing the Internet, looking for and shutting down what it viewed as unlicensed nutritional counseling. By extension, it was also making it illegal, according to the board's logic, for ordinary people to share personal diet advice on Facebook, Twitter, Internet forums, or other popular social media. In a world awash in diet and weight-loss advice disseminated on the Internet and TV and in books, magazines, and weight-loss meetings, the dieticians—like Kentucky's psychologists—were attempting to bottleneck speech.

According to the North Carolina Board of Dietetics/Nutrition, giving free dietary advice was a crime. Because Steve answered specific questions from readers and friends, rather than simply providing general information, the government contended he was practicing unlicensed, and thus criminal, "nutritional counseling." The bottlenecking of Steve's speech was the next step in a decadelong march by the sixty-five thousand-member Academy of Nutrition and Dietetics and its state chapters to cartelize their industry.

THE AND'S HISTORY OF BOTTLENECKING

Although the concept of dietetics—the science concerned with nutritional planning and preparation of foods—first appeared in Ancient Greece in the writings of Hippocrates and Plato,[96] it did not develop in the United States in a systematic fashion until the late nineteenth century, with a focus on preparing diets for patients with physician-ordered diet prescriptions.[97] The American Dietetic Association—as the Academy of Nutrition and Dietetics was originally known—formed in 1917 and worked closely with government officials to conserve food and improve public health and nutrition during World War I.[98] The new organization also immediately laid its bottlenecking foundation,[99] at first requiring aspiring dieticians to get a two-year and later a four-year degree followed by a six-month apprenticeship to receive the association's stamp of approval[100] and to work in government jobs.[101]

From its earliest years, the affiliation of the American Dietetic Association, or ADA, with the federal government played an important role in its ability to bottleneck the industry. Dieticians were formally admitted into government service in 1920, working most frequently in military and institutional settings.[102] From the 1920s through the 1940s, the ADA successfully pushed for legislation to increase the minimum requirements for these practitioners to work in government jobs.[103] Such government specification of barriers to entry for hiring gave the bottleneckers something to point to in subsequent years when they lobbied for state licensing laws.

The call for licensing laws came at the ADA's 1944 annual meeting, when the organization's president proclaimed: "For the protection of the profession, there is a need for improving the status of dietitians.... For the protection of the profession, the term dietitian should be legally defined and state registration of dietitians required."[104] The process for achieving licensing actually predated that call, with attempts in the 1930s in California and Minnesota to require legal status, and the effort intensified on the part of the ADA's state affiliates from the 1940s through the 1960s.[105]

With little to show for its efforts in those decades, the association started a process to create a formal registration system through its organization in 1967. The decision to do so came after a legal consultant recommended registration "as a first step toward licensure."[106] To protect the nomenclature of the registration, the ADA trademarked the acronym RD, which stands for registered dietician, so as to own the designation and take legal action against infringers. The registration went into effect in 1969.[107]

In 1973, the bottlenecking efforts were helped along considerably when the ADA was granted exclusive recognition as the accrediting agency for dietetic education,[108] allowing it to set educational standards for dietetic degrees and force colleges to comply with its mandates. This power came in especially handy once state licenses were created. The licenses required the completion of a four-year degree, over which the association now had exclusive control, allowing it to consolidate its control over the industry.

The mid-1970s saw the first coordinated national effort on the part of the ADA to push for state licensing. The organization created a model licensing law for state affiliates to follow in their lobbying efforts.[109] By the late 1970s, at least ten state affiliates were pushing for licensure. Although none of them were successful, the efforts would pay off in the decade to follow.

In 1981, the ADA created a political action committee, or PAC, to assist in its legislative and political efforts.[110] A year later, California adopted a titling law and became the first state to regulate dieticians. This bottlenecking milestone was achieved as a direct result of the lobbying efforts of the California Dietetics Association.[111] The titling laws of Louisiana and Alabama came shortly thereafter, followed by the adoption of the first full licensing bill in Texas in 1984.[112]

The year 1984 also saw about 60 percent of state associations becoming involved in the pursuit of licensure. This was, of course, encouraged by the ADA, which provided state associations with resources like the publication *Licensure/Entitlement for Dietitians*, outlining title definitions, a scope of practice, and sample bills for licensure, as well as offering workshops on licensure at which presenters discussed successful licensure strategies.[113] By 1985, eleven states required legal recognition for dieticians. In the two years that followed, ADA annual meetings included more licensure workshops to assist members from thirty-six states who were working toward licensure.[114]

The bottlenecking continued into the 1990s, led by an ADA strategic plan titled "Achieving Competitive Advantage."[115] Efforts to secure state regulations were complemented by a successful push by the association to create medical nutrition therapy; to gain federal recognition for nutritional therapy and other dietetic services, so that these practices could be reimbursed by the Centers for Medicare and Medicaid Services; and to limit the practice of medical nutrition therapy, or MNT, exclusively to RDs.[116] MNT is used to help treat medical conditions through tailored diets and counseling based on a patient's medical, psychosocial, and dietary history and a physical examination.[117] By successfully designating MNT as a specialized treatment and securing for themselves exclusive authority over it, the dieticians enjoyed further legal and economic protection.[118] But even as the bottleneckers were erecting a higher-and-higher fence around their occupation, alternative nutritionists were making progress on mounting challenges against them.

During the first decade of the twenty-first century, while the ADA and its fifty state affiliates were enjoying significant success in their bottlenecking activities, other nutrition associations began agitating for access to the occupational market. The National Association of Nutrition Professionals (NANP), Certification Board for Nutrition Specialists (CBNS), Clinical Nutrition Certification Board (CNBS), International & American Association of Clinical Nutritionists (IAACN), Nutrition Consultants (NC), Certified Nutrition Consultants (CNC), Certified Nutritionists (CN), School Nutrition Specialists (SNS), Certified Dietary Managers (CDM), and Certified Health Education Specialists (CHES), as well as naturopaths and homeopaths, and even practitioners of Chinese medicine all began muscling in on the ADA's territory.[119]

Feeling the threat from these competing organizations, the association increased its already-zealous bottlenecking to shut out the interlopers. It launched an aggressive campaign to train state dietetic boards to lobby on its behalf.[120] In 2011, the ADA also began a multiyear effort to target fourteen states simultaneously to introduce laws where none had existed previously, to increase restrictions in existing laws, and to extend licenses scheduled to expire.[121] In New York[122] and New Jersey,[123] for example, it introduced titling laws to cordon off the titles "'dietitian/nutritionist,' 'nutritionist,' 'dietitian,' 'dietician,' 'nutrition counselor,' 'nutrition consultant,' 'nutrition specialist,' 'LDN,' 'LD,' 'LN,' or any other title, designation, words, letters, abbreviations or insignia indicating the practice of dietetics/nutrition" and to establish state boards to oversee the scheme.[124] The ADA also fought off efforts to change existing regulation in ways that would have broken open its fence and allowed others to enter the occupation. In Ohio, for example, the association's state affiliate and the state dietetics board engaged in a coordinated effort to defeat legislation that would have allowed "alternative practitioners" to enter the field.[125]

Such efforts were supported by the association's revenues of $34 million[126] and helped along considerably by its fifty state affiliates and the government affairs office based in Washington, DC, which lobbies state and federal legislators, departments, and agencies.[127] In 2012, the ADA adopted its current name, the Academy of Nutrition and Dietetics. Although it seemed little more than a semantic change, it actually represented a significant signal of the body's attempt to tighten its control over the dietetics-and-nutrition industry.[128]

Since its founding in 1917, the organization had operated as the American Dietetic Association. As the National Association of Nutrition Professionals, Certification Board for Nutrition Specialists, and the rest of the alphabet soup of nutrition associations stormed the bottleneckers' gates, the ADA sought to shore up its fence by laying unequivocal claim to nutritional knowledge by taking on a new name. The year after it changed its name, the AND announced that a new title would be added to its trademarked position of RD: registered dietetic nutritionist, or RDN. In the press release announcing the change of the title, the academy proclaimed, "All registered dietitians are nutritionists–but not all nutritionists are registered dietitians."[129] As one observer noted,

> The Academy is striving to give RDs the exclusive right to provide dietetic advice and services—at the expense of nutritionists' claims. By attempting to limit nutritionists' influence, the Academy seeks to create professional and economic benefits for its members.[130]

Of course, all the regulations in the world are useless without enforcement, so the AND matched its legislative efforts with an organization-wide call for its members to file complaints of unlicensed practice with state dietetics boards. As the academy's director of regulatory affairs, Pepin Tuma, instructed members, "We must recognize the importance of licensure's role as a protective bulwark preventing unqualified competitors from performing nutrition care services, and increase our vigilance in reporting unlicensed competition."[131] Noting that board investigations are generally triggered by complaints, Tuma noted:

> The complaint process is integral to aggressive enforcement of dietitian licensing acts.... Given state budgetary constraints and states' expressed willingness to cite the paucity of complaints as a reason to abolish dietitian licensure, it is imperative for dietitians to recognize both our ethical obligation and our professional incentive in aggressively identifying and reporting violations.[132]

Such was the environment Steve Cooksey had unwittingly entered into with his blog on going paleo.

Under its twenty-year-old law,[133] the North Carolina Board of Dietetics/Nutrition had already been actively patrolling its licensing fence for years, investigating almost fifty people and organizations between 2007 and 2012 for practicing nutrition without a license, including athletic trainers, a nurse, a pharmacist, a spa, and even the medical department at Duke University.[134] One recipient of a cease-and-desist letter from the board—Dr. Liz Lipski, director of academic development for the Nutrition and Integrative Health programs at Maryland University of Integrative Health—held a PhD and master's degree in nutrition, but her credentials were not enough for the bottleneckers. As she wrote in testimony to the Federal Trade Commission:

> So even though I'd been in clinical practice for over 30 years and hold

> a doctorate in the field, I was unable to continue earning my livelihood as a nutritionist in North Carolina. My business employed 5 people, provided benefits to full time employees, and paid taxes.... As the attorney for the board in North Carolina said to let me know that what they did wasn't personal, "We do this all the time."[135]

Whereas Lipski was barred from practicing her lifelong profession despite having advanced credentials, the board threatened to take Steve Cooksey's blog away, even though he was not practicing nutrition, dietetics, or anything else. He was not paid for his paleo diet advice, did not see "patients" or "clients," did not complete physical examinations or consult people's dietary or medical history when answering anonymous questions sent to his blog, did not engage in the various practices defined by the dietetics licensing law,[136] and did not represent himself as a health professional in any way. In fact, Steve made his informal status abundantly clear. Every page on his blog posted the disclaimer: "I am not a doctor, dietitian nor nutritionist... in fact I have no medical training of any kind."[137]

But that was not enough for the bottleneckers, who presented him with a choice that was really no choice at all: continue writing and invite prosecution with 120 days in jail to follow,[138] earn a medical degree or a bachelor's degree in nutrition and then pass an examination after completing a nine-hundred-hour clinical internship,[139] or censor his blog. Steve reluctantly complied with the board's directives and altered the content of his blog in line with its directives.

In the weeks that followed, the censorship gnawed at him, however. "I was scared and worried, but at the same time I was angry," he recalled. "I could not tell people things that I thought would help them. It pissed me off."[140]

So in May 2012, Steve filed a free-speech lawsuit in Federal District Court in Charlotte, North Carolina.[141] He did not have to wait long for the first decision: Five months later, US district court judge Max Cogburn dismissed his case for lack of standing, meaning the judge rejected the case without even considering whether Steve's First Amendment rights were violated. Remarkably, Judge Cogburn concluded that since Steve had been able to edit his blog—as demanded by the bottleneckers—he was not punished and therefore suffered no injury.[142] It was an argument advanced by the state board,[143] and Judge Cogburn swallowed it whole.

The decision was absurd on its face. As Steve's attorney, Paul Sherman, noted, "If you self-censor to avoid the government arresting you, that is called having your speech chilled. That is a classic First Amendment injury."[144] Steve pressed on with an appeal before the US Fourth Circuit Court of Appeals in May 2013, and in a decision a month later the circuit court saw things the same way as Steve's attorney.

The federal appeals court ruled that due to the board's phone call to Steve, its red-penned instructions on how to censor his blog, and its letter telling him he would remain under its watchful eye, "a person of ordinary firmness would surely feel a chilling effect," as Cooksey did. "In fact, this case presents more persuasive evidence of chilling than another case from this court in which standing was achieved." In a refreshingly commonsense finding, the court concluded, "Therefore, we have no trouble deciding that Cooksey's speech was sufficiently chilled by the actions of the State Board to show a First Amendment injury-in-fact."[145] It returned the case to the lower court to rule on Steve's free-speech arguments.

Judge Cogburn never got the chance to do so, however. Unlike Kentucky's tone-deaf psychology board, the North Carolina dietetic board read the obvious tea leaves in the Fourth Circuit's ruling and adopted new guidelines that permit people to give ordinary diet advice without a government-issued license. Declaring victory, Steve dropped his lawsuit.[146] But North Carolina was not the only place where the dietetics bottleneckers have been forced to cede ground.

In December 2013, the ten-year-old dietetic licensing law in Illinois was amended to allow certified nutrition specialists and several other groups to practice their occupation. The Illinois Dietetics Association initially opposed the law, but it went along with the changes when they turned out to be fairly small.[147] The bigger threat to the bottleneckers' power came next door in Michigan.

In 2012, as part of a larger effort to reform licensing in the Wolverine State, Governor Rick Snyder created the Office of Regulatory Reinvention, which, among other things, released a report identifying dozens of licenses and boards ripe for reform or complete elimination.[148] The third recommendation in the report stated: "The occupations of dieticians and nutritionists should be de-regulated." The ORR's examination questioned "whether true public harm is prevented by licensing the occupations." Noting the "multiple national credentialing bodies for nutritionists that offer credentialing in lieu of state licensing," the report called for the elimination of the regulation and concluded, "Professional credentialing could be achieved through national credentialing bodies."[149]

This was not the first such report to recommend against regulating dieticians and nutritionists. In 1986, Virginia's Council on Health Regulatory Boards had released the results of a study of the dietetics occupation and recommended against licensure.[150] Not unlike the states that used sunrise reports to examine the need for interior design regulation, the council held hearings and gathered numerous kinds of data to draw its conclusions about dietetics. In classic bottlenecker fashion, the hearings were stacked with dieticians and nutritionists seeking to convince council members of the need for regulation through the use of "largely anecdotal evidence" and "isolated cases of harm or potential harm to consumers."[151]

With no systematic evidence of damage provided by the dietetics bottleneckers, the council went looking for some itself. It asked for complaint data from the state's Office of Consumer Affairs, a request that yielded only five complaints—four of them against the same weight-loss center.[152] The council proceeded to request insurance claim data from one of the largest insurance companies in the state. The company came back with no claims involving dieticians over an eight-year period.[153] The council then reviewed recommendations by a congressional committee, the Food and Drug Administration, the Federal Trade Commission, the Department of Justice, and other states: "In no case was state occupational regulation of dietitians and/or nutritionists recommended."[154]

The council's conclusion was unequivocal:

> In the final analysis, state health occupational regulation is defensible only when it is demonstrated that the lack of regulation presents a substantial risk to the public health, safety, and welfare, and that members of the public cannot adequately protect themselves by making informed choices in the marketplace and by other means. Occupational regulation, when it is appropriate, comes at increased cost to the consumer, and it should be implemented only when other

> mechanisms such as strengthened enforcement of existing laws and rules, public disclosure, and consumer redress for documented abuse are not feasible. The Council respectfully submits that these conditions are not met in the present case. It is therefore recommended that no state regulation of dietitians or nutritionists be implemented in the Commonwealth at this time.[155]

Despite this finding, less than ten years later, in 1995, Virginia adopted a titling law to restrict the use of the titles "dietician" and "nutritionist."[156]

Michigan's 2012 ORR report differed from the Virginia Council's report in that the ORR report recommended the elimination of a license that had already been in place since 2006, a license adopted after years of lobbying and multiple legislative attempts by the bottleneckers.[157] When House Bill 4688 was introduced in 2013 in the Michigan legislature to repeal the dietetic licensing law, the efforts to oppose it were textbook bottlenecking. The list of those testifying against the bill was long and included the AND,[158] dieticians from Wayne State University,[159] the Michigan Dietetic Association,[160] a practicing dietician,[161] the Michigan State Medical Society,[162] a member of the state dietetics board,[163] the president of the Southeastern Michigan Dietetic Association,[164] and numerous individuals who wrote letters.[165] As usual, their testimony referred to the need to protect public health and safety and made references to harm caused by unlicensed practitioners, although the most specific example of harm anyone could conjure up was that of a fitness instructor at a local gym advocating for the paleo diet.[166]

The ORR's report won the day, helped along by a longtime dietician and former member of the state Board of Dietetics and Nutrition, who testified that during her six years on the board it had never received any independent reports of harm resulting from unlicensed practitioners. Instead, all the complaints came from the dieticians themselves, some stemming from a Michigan State dietetic association contest that encouraged members to send reports to the board.[167] Added to this was testimony by the executive director of the Michigan Nutrition Association, who had looked across multiple states and state agencies for evidence of harm from unlicensed practice and found none.[168]

The lack of complaints was not unique to Michigan or even to the dietetic occupation in general. Just as in John Rosemond's profession of psychology, where complaints are rarely filed,[169] the same is true in related occupations.[170] In fact, as one observer noted, as far back as 1979,

> available statistics and preliminary inquiry show few disciplinary proceedings before occupational licensing boards and fewer disciplinary sanctions invoked by particular boards. Moreover, often complaints are by competitors, not consumers. Of course, the whole manner in which occupational licensing schemes [operate]—regulation by those who simultaneously practice the occupation—invites complaints by competitors.[171]

Even with Pepin Tuma's call for dieticians to "increase our vigilance in reporting unlicensed competition,"[172] it appears little has changed in almost forty years.

The lack of evidence of harm to the public by unlicensed dieticians, however, has not slowed the bottleneckers down. With licenses being required in thirty-six states and Washington, DC, and titling protection in four others,[173] the AND and its state affiliates continue to push for tighter restrictions.[174] Despite attempts to wrap their activities in the cloak of health and safety, the real reason for their regulatory fervor was made clear more than three decades ago by none other than Mary Haschke, the president of the AND:

> Like other professionals, dietitians can justify the enactment of licensure laws because licensing affords the opportunity to protect dietitians from interference in their field by other practitioners. Licensure also can protect dietitians by limiting the number of practitioners through restrictions imposed by academic, experience, and examination requirements. This protection provides a competitive advantage and therefore is economically beneficial for dietitians.[175]

Although the dietetic bottleneckers' motivation has not changed since the time Haschke made this statement, their idea of what constitutes "interference" has. As Steve Cooksey found, in the minds of today's bottleneckers, giving unpaid advice is more than just talk.

Conclusion

From the time of the founding of the United States, the American birthright of economic liberty—the right to earn an honest living free from onerous and unnecessary government intrusion—has been a cherished one.[1] This view was long upheld by the US Supreme Court. As Justice Stephen Johnson Field explained:

> And when the Colonies separated from the mother country no privilege was more fully recognized or more completely incorporated into the fundamental law of the country than that every free subject in the British empire was entitled to pursue his happiness by following any of the known established trades and occupations of the country, subject only to such restraints as equally affected all others.[2]

Likewise, according to Justice William O. Douglas, "The right to work . . . [is] the most precious liberty that man possesses."[3]

As the chapters of this book illustrate, state legislatures adopted increasing numbers of licensing regimes during the twentieth century[4] for reasons that seldom went beyond naked economic protectionism, and the courts approved of many of them.[5] But despite judicial deference to all this bottlenecking, such cases as those of Pastor Craigmiles and the monks of Saint Joseph Abbey demonstrate that contemporary courts will still scrutinize licensing systems to determine whether they achieve the necessary balance between protecting the public and respecting economic liberty, and strike down any that get the balance wrong.[6]

Elected officials' speeches also evidence a shift in how occupational licensing has been viewed. In 1992, while chairing the Senate Judiciary Committee hearings on Clarence Thomas, then senator Joseph Biden denounced advocates of judicial engagement on behalf of economic liberty.[7] More than twenty years later, in a 2015 speech at the Brookings Institution, he struck a much different note, praising efforts to beat back licensing: "The occupational licensing proposal recognizes that we want an economy that makes it easier for workers to start businesses and begin careers."[8]

That same year, in what is likely the first time a president of the United States has ever discussed occupational licensing in a public speech, President Obama spoke about "unnecessary licensing requirements" before the National Governors' Association: "States are leading the way in removing unnecessary licensing requirements so workers can start filling up some of the jobs that they already have the skills for."[9]

A few months later, the Obama administration released an almost-eighty-page report on occupational licensing that, among other things, cast a critical eye on the costs associated with licensing and the vast inconsistencies in licensing schemes across states and also made recommendations for state policy makers on how to reform licensing. The recommendations included reducing regulatory burdens, instituting rigorous review processes before the adoption or continuation of licensing systems can take place, and more effectively aligning licensing requirements with demonstrable threats to public health and safety to avoid creating unnecessarily onerous burdens.[10]

While such recommendations are laudable, they fall short of the most fundamental consideration that should be applied to licensing—the "presumption of liberty"—as proposed by noted Georgetown University professor of law Randy Barnett.

This presumption supposes that when considering new occupational regulations or the perpetuation of existing ones, the starting point should be a recognition of the freedom of practice, not a rush to licensure. Legislators should presume that individuals have the right to practice their chosen occupation free from government regulation unless and until those seeking licensure show otherwise with systematic evidence.

According to Professor Barnett, the presumption of liberty "requires the government to justify its restriction on liberty, instead of requiring the citizen to establish that the liberty being exercised is somehow 'fundamental,'" and not a gift he or she enjoys at the government's allowance.[11] Or, as statutes of one state—Virginia—put it:

> The right of every person to engage in any lawful profession, trade or occupation of his choice is clearly protected by both the Constitution of the United States and the Constitution of the Commonwealth of Virginia. The Commonwealth cannot abridge such rights except as a reasonable exercise of its police powers when it is clearly found that such abridgement is necessary for the preservation of the health, safety and welfare of the public.[12]

RESTORING THE "FIRST OBJECT OF GOVERNMENT"

Yet breaking open bottlenecks is about more than economic growth. It is also about creating a just society built, in part, on the right to earn an honest living free from arbitrary and unnecessary government encroachment. There is nothing just about the government telling people they may not work simply because the job they want to do and for which they are best suited creates too much competition for those more politically savvy.[13]

In 1787, James Madison wrote that the protection of property rights "is the first object of government."[14] To Madison, property rights extended to much more than real estate and personal belongings. He saw them as covering "everything to which a man may attach a value and have a right," including "opinions and the free communication of them" and "the free use of his faculties and free choice of the objects on which to employ them."[15] His disdain for the co-optation of government by one group at the expense of others was unequivocal, as was his inclusion of economic liberty and the right to earn an honest living under the rubric of property rights:

> That is not a just government, nor is property secure under it, where the property which a man has in his personal safety and personal liberty, is violated by arbitrary seizures of one class of citizens for the

> service of the rest . . . where arbitrary restrictions, exemptions, and monopolies deny to part of its citizens that free use of their faculties, and free choice of their occupations, which not only constitute their property in the general sense of the word; but are the means of acquiring property strictly so called.[16]

In condemning "*arbitrary* seizures of one class of citizens for the service of the rest" and "*arbitrary* restrictions, exemptions, and monopolies" (emphases added), Madison very well could have been describing the contemporary occupational licensing schemes that have resulted from decades of bottlenecking.

In fulfilling Madison's call for a just government and executing the "first object of government," elected officials today should protect the property rights of the citizens they serve, including the preservation of the freedom of practice. As this book clearly illustrates, the need to do so is more essential and urgent today than ever. Indeed, now is the time for citizens, judges, and legislators nationwide to call out those bad actors and their accomplices when they seek to use government power for their own ends—and to refer to them as what they are: "You're nothing but a bottlenecker!"

Acknowledgments

Few if any books are purely the work of the authors, and ours is no different. First, the concept for the book and the term "bottleneckers" came from John Kramer, who also provided sage editorial advice throughout the process. As the more than 1,600 endnotes illustrate, the research required for this book was immense, and John Ross provided invaluable research assistance throughout, even while maintaining the increasingly popular *Short Circuit* newsletter (http://ij.org/about-us/shortcircuit/). Mindy Menjou provided detailed, sharp-eyed editorial review and clever chapter titles. Finally, Dick Carpenter's wife, Mary, endured many early mornings and long, silent car rides to accommodate the writing required for this book. To all of you, we say, thank you.

Endnotes

INTRODUCTION

1 Sergio Bichao, "Police Stop Teens Seeking Snow Shoveling Work," *USA Today*, January 29, 2015, http://www.usatoday.com/story/news/nation/2015/01/28/teens-seeking-snow-shoveling-cash-run-afoul-law/22454761/.

2 Matt Campbell, "Hot Dog Selling Teen Shut Down by City Rules," WZZM13.com My Town, July 18, 2012, http://hollandzeeland.wzzm13.com/news/news/71716-hot-dog-selling-teen-shut-down-city-rules; "City Shuts Down Teen's Hot Dog Vendor Cart!," YouTube video, 4:02, produced by Makinac Media, posted by Mackinac Center for Public Policy, July 25, 2012, https://www.youtube.com/watch?v=5MK9Hwtzu8U.

3 Stuart Tomlinson, "Mistletoe Sale Gets 11-Year-Old Girl Booted from Portland Saturday Market," *Oregonian*, December 2, 2013, http://www.oregonlive.com/portland/index.ssf/2013/12/mistletoe_sale_gets_11-year-ol.html.

4 Madison Root, quoted in Mark Martin, "Girl Banned from Selling Mistletoe, Told to Beg," CBN News US, December 4, 2013, http://www.cbn.com/cbnnews/us/2013/December/Girl-Banned-from-Selling-Mistletoe-Told-to-Beg/.

5 Madison Root, quoted in Dan Cassuto, "Hundreds of Orders Pour in for Girl Banned from Selling Mistletoe," KATU 2, December 2, 2013, http://www.katu.com/news/local/Update-Hundreds-of-orders-pour-in-for-girl-banned-from-selling-mistletoe-234158611.html.

6 Madison Root, quoted in Tomlinson, "11-Year-Old Girl Booted."

7 Jaime Zahl, "No Lemonade for You; Seinfeld Lemonade Stand Shut Down in East Hampton Village,"*East Hampton Press*, August 25, 2015, http://www.27east.com/news/article.cfm/Amagansett/119742/No-Lemonade-For-You-Seinfeld-Lemonade-Stand-Shut-Down-in-East-Hampton-Village. It is not just the businesses of enterprising youth that are being shut down by authorities. On August 18, 2015, Jerry Seinfeld and his family set up a lemonade stand to raise money for his wife's charity. Neighbors complained to police, who closed the

stand because they said "street peddling" violates local ordinances. Joel Currier, "Lemonade Stand Wins Fight with City," *St. Louis Post-Dispatch*, August 12, 2004; Eddie Jimenez, "Officer Puts Squeeze on Lemonade Stand," *Contra Costa Times*, August 6, 2009. Chapter 7 of this book gets further into street vendors.

8 Dick M. Carpenter II, Lisa Knepper, Angela Erickson, and John K. Ross, *License to Work: A National Study of Burdens from Occupational Licensing* (Arlington: Instititute for Justice, 2012); William Ruger and Jason Sorens, *Freedom in the 50 States: An Index of Personal and Economic Freedom* (Arlington: Mercatus Center, George Mason University, 2009); Adam B. Summers, *Occupational Licensing: Ranking the States and Exploring Alternatives* (Los Angeles: Reason Foundation, 2007).

9 Carpenter et al., *License to Work*.

10 Ibid., 4–5.

11 Adam Smith, *The Wealth of Nations* (1776; repr., New York: Modern Library, 1937).

12 Heather Swanson, "The Illusion of Economic Structure: Craft Guilds in Late Medieval English Towns," *Past and Present Society* 121 (1988).

13 Ibid.

14 J. A. C. Grant, "The Guild Returns to America," *Journal of Politics* 4, no. 3 (1942).

15 Morris M. Kleiner and Alan B. Krueger, "The Prevalence and Effects of Occupational Licensing," *British Journal of Industrial Relations* 48, no. 4 (2010).

16 "State Recognition," Certification Board for Music Therapists, accessed June 3, 2016, http://www.cbmt.org/advocacy/state-recognition/.

17 "CODE: 076.127-01; TITLE(s): MUSIC THERAPIST (Medical Ser.)," *Directory of Occupational Titles*, accessed June 3, 2016, http://www.occupationalinfo.org/07/076127014.html.

18 Dena Register and Kimberley Sena Moore, *Advocate for Your Profession* (Downingtown, PA: Certification Board for Music Therapists, 2012).

19 Georgia General Assembly, "Minutes of the Senate Health & Human Services Committee" (Atlanta: Georgia General Assembly, 2012).

20 "Examination and SAE Prices," Certification Board for Music Therapists, accessed June 3, 2016, http://www.cbmt.org/examination.

21 S.B. 414, 2012 Georgia Legislative Session (2012).

22 Kleiner and Krueger, "Prevalence and Effects of Occupational Licensing."

23 *Merriam-Webster*, 11th ed., s.v. "bottleneck," http://www.merriam-webster.com/dictionary/bottleneck.

24 Our use of the word *bottleneck* is similar to Yuval Levin's treatment of the term in his discussion of what he calls "bottlenecks to prosperity." As he wrote, "A bottleneck narrows people's options. In some important respects, the path into and through the middle class has become narrower in America in recent decades; the goal must be to broaden it. . . . The path to rewarding work and economic independence, like the path to higher education, is often bottlenecked today. The oppressive array of licensing and professional-certification requirements in many states and regions obstructs the upward path of many lower-income Americans. Barbers, manicurists, interior designers, and countless other professional groups have successfully lobbied for stringent barriers to entry into their professions in order to minimize

competition. Such rules essentially install incumbents as gatekeepers. They are holdovers from a more consolidated American labor market and now generally serve merely as tools for well-established interests to keep out new competitors. Lifting and loosening the requirements would create new avenues of mobility for millions of people interested in those fields." Yuval Levin, *The Fractured Republic* (New York: Basic Books, 2016), 127–29.

CHAPTER 1 ▪ HOW BOTTLENECKERS GOT THEIR NAME

1 Stephen Miller, "Passionate Winemaker Won Fight to Sell Product across State Lines," *Wall Street Journal*, June 16, 2007, http://online.wsj.com/news/articles/SB118196054671037463.

2 Ellen Crosby, "She Vinified, Testified and Changed the Law," *Washington Post*, June 20, 2007, http://www.washingtonpost.com/wp-dyn/content/article/2007/06/19/AR2007061900379.html; Miller, "Passionate Winemaker Won Fight."

3 Matthew Barakat, "Virginia Vintner Takes Wine Fight to U.S. Supreme Court," *Southeast Missourian*, December 6, 2004, http://www.semissourian.com/story/151732.html.

4 Juanita Swedenburg, quoted in Patricia Sullivan, "Juanita Swedenburg; Fought Ban on Interstate Wine Sales," *Washington Post*, June 12, 2007, http://www.washingtonpost.com/wp-dyn/content/article/2007/06/11/AR2007061102194.html.

5 Ibid.

6 Miller, "Passionate Winemaker Won Fight."

7 Barakat, "Wine Fight to U.S. Supreme Court"; Peter Dujardin, "Seeing Red: Uncorking Interstate Sales; States' Wine Laws Considered Undue Burden," *Daily Press*, March 5, 2000, http://articles.dailypress.com/2000-03-05/business/0003040005_1_out-of-state-wineries-in-state-distributors-alcohol-control-laws; Sullivan, "Juanita Swedenburg."

8 Jennifer Fiedler, "Direct-Shipping Champion Juanita Swedenburg Dies at 82," *Wine Spectator*, June 14, 2007, http://www.winespectator.com/webfeature/show/id/Direct-Shipping-Champion-Juanita-Swedenburg-Dies-at-82_3618; Miller, "Passionate Winemaker Won Fight."

9 Miller, "Passionate Winemaker Won Fight."

10 Jan Crawford Greenburg, "A Spirited Debate over Wine Case: Vintner Takes Fight to Supreme Court," *Chicago Tribune*, December 8, 2004, http://articles.chicagotribune.com/2004-12-08/news/0412080330_1_direct-shipment-juanita-swedenburg-wineries.

11 Dujardin, "Uncorking Interstate Sales."

12 Harry Gene Levine, "The Alcohol Problem in America: From Temperance to Alcoholism," *British Journal of Addiction* 79, no. 4 (December 1984), 110.

13 Harry G. Levine and Craig Reinarman, "From Prohibition to Regulation: Lessons from Alcohol Policy for Drug Policy," *Milbank Quarterly* 69, no. 3 (1991).

14 Levine, "Alcohol Problem in America."

15 Clark Byse, "Alcoholic Beverage Control before Repeal," *Law and Contemporary Problems* 7, no. 4 (1940); Levine, "Alcohol Problem in America."
16 Levine, "Alcohol Problem in America"; Levine and Reinarman, "From Prohibition to Regulation."
17 Byse, "Alcoholic Beverage Control."
18 Levine and Reinarman, "From Prohibition to Regulation."
19 Garrett Peck, *Prohibition Hangover: Alcohol in America from Demon Rum to Cult Cabernet* (New Brunswick, NJ: Rutgers University Press, 2009).
20 Levine, "Alcohol Problem in America."
21 Pamela E. Pennock and K. Austin Kerr, "In the Shadow of Prohibition: Domestic American Alcohol Policy since 1933," *Business History* 46, no. 3 (2005).
22 Levine, "Alcohol Problem in America."
23 John D. Rockefeller Jr., quoted in Raymond B. Fosdick and Albert L. Scott, *Toward Liquor Control* (New York: Harper and Brothers, 1933), vii–viii.
24 John E. O'Neill, "Federal Activity in Alcoholic Beverage Control," *Law and Contemporary Problems* 7, no. 4 (1940).
25 John D. Rockefeller Jr., quoted in Fosdick and Scott, *Toward Liquor Control*, vii.
26 Levine and Reinarman, "From Prohibition to Regulation."
27 Fosdick and Scott, *Toward Liquor Control.*
28 Ronald A. Sarasin, "A Look at the Three-Tier System in America," *Beverage Industry* 89, no. 8 (1998).
29 Byse, "Alcoholic Beverage Control before Repeal"; Sarasin, "Three-Tier System in America"; Fosdick and Scott, *Toward Liquor Control.*
30 Levine and Reinarman, "From Prohibition to Regulation."
31 "The Control Systems," NABCA, accessed June 3, 2016, http://www.nabca.org/States/States.aspx; "Alcohol Control Systems: Wholesale Distribution Systems for Spirits," Alcohol Policy Information System, accessed June 3, 2016, http://alcoholpolicy.niaaa.nih.gov/Alcohol_Control_Systems_Wholesale_Distribution_Systems_for_Spirits.html?tab=maps&date=1/1/1998&dateStart=1/1/1998&dateEnd=1/1/2014&onlyChanges=True.
32 Washington State Liquor Control Board, *Beer and Wine Three-Tier System Review Task Force Report* (Olympia: Washington State Liquor Control Board, 2006).
33 Angela Logomasini, *A CARE-Less Rush to Regulate Alcohol: Wholesalers Attempt to Secure Regulatory Fiefdoms* (Washington, DC: Competitive Enterprise Institute, 2011).
34 Fosdick and Scott, *Toward Liquor Control*, 59. The authors further noted: "For the establishment of a licensed liquor trade means the deep intrenchment of a far-flung proprietary interest. This interest would have a large capital investment to be protected at all costs.... Moreover, such a vested interest is bound to employ aggressive tactics in its own defense. Liquor trade associations, open and disguised, would continuously oppose every restriction of opportunities to sell. Manufacturers, wholesalers and retailers, through their respective associations, would unite in resisting disestablishment of retail selling outlets whenever attempts were made to eliminate a portion of them either by local option votes or by reduction of the total number of licensed places." Ibid., 59.

35 O'Neill, "Federal Activity in Alcoholic Beverage Control."
36 Pennock and Kerr, "Shadow of Prohibition."
37 Ibid.
38 Logomasini, *Rush to Regulate Alcohol.*
39 Ibid.
40 Anat Baron, *Beer Wars*, directed by Anat Baron (Los Angeles: Ducks in a Row Entertainment Corporation, 2009), online video documentary, 89:00, http://beerwarsmovie.com/now-available/.
41 Ibid.
42 National Beer Wholesalers Association, *Celebrating America's Beer Distribution System: NBWA 2013–2014 Report* (Washington, DC: National Beer Wholesalers Association, 2014), Internet Archive Wayback Machine, posted by National Beer Wholesalers Association, accessed June 29, 2016, https://web.archive.org/web/20150306003055/http://www.nbwa.org/sites/default/files/NBWA_2013-2014_Annual%20Report.pdf.
43 National Beer Wholesalers Association, *NBWA 2014–2015 Report* (Washington, DC: National Beer Wholesalers Association, 2015).
44 "Top Organization Contributors" (based on data published by the FEC on March 9, 2015), OpenSecrets.org, https://www.opensecrets.org/orgs/list.php.
45 "National Beer Wholesalers Assn," OpenSecrets.org, accessed June 6, 2016, https://www.opensecrets.org/orgs/summary.php?id=D000000101&cycle=A.
46 National Beer Wholesalers Association, *NBWA 2012–2013 Report* (Washington, DC: National Beer Wholesalers Association, 2013).
47 National Beer Wholesalers Association, *2014 NBWA Legislative Conference Brochure* (Washington, DC: National Beer Wholesalers Association, 2014), https://www.nbwa.org/sites/default/files/2014-NBWA-Legislative-Conference-Brochure.pdf.
48 "Wines & Spirits Wholesalers of America," OpenSecrets.org, accessed June 6, 2016, https://www.opensecrets.org/orgs/summary.php?id=D000000356&cycle=A.
49 Craig Wolf, quoted in "Wines & Spirits Wholesalers of America PAC Achieves 95% Success Rate in Election," Wines & Spirits Wholesalers of America, accessed June 6, 2016, http://www.wswa.org/news/articles/2012/11/15/wine-spirits-wholesalers-of-america-pac-achieves-95-success-rate-in-election.
50 "Government Affairs," Wines & Spirits Wholesalers of America, accessed June 6, 2016, http://www.wswa.org/government-affairs.
51 "State Issues," Wines & Spirits Wholesalers of America, accessed June 6, 2016, http://www.wswa.org/government-affairs/state-issues/state-assocations-advisory-council.
52 "State Economics," Wines & Spirits Wholesalers of America, accessed June 6, 2016, http://www.wswa.org/facts-data/state-economics.
53 "America's Beer Distributors: Economic Impact by State," America's Beer Distributors, accessed June 6, 2016, http://www.nbwa.org/beer-report-map.
54 Data to calculate this total were drawn from vpap.org. Virginia Public Access Project, accessed June 6, 2016, http://www.vpap.org/.
55 Bart Watson, "U.S. Passes 4,000 Breweries," Brewers Association, September 28, 2015, https://www.brewersassociation.org/insights/4000-breweries/;

"Economic Impact: Beer Serves America," Beer Institute, accessed June 6, 2016, http://www.beerinstitute.org/economic-impact; Beer Institute, *Brewers Almanac* (Washington, DC: Beer Institute, 2012).

56 "By the Numbers: The Wine and Spirits Industry," Wines & Spirits Wholesalers of America, accessed June 6, 2016, http://www.wswa.org/facts-data.

57 "Beer, Wine & Distilled Spirits Wholesalers Industry Profile," First Research, last updated May 23, 2016, http://www.firstresearch.com/Industry-Research/Beer-Wine-and-Distilled-Spirits-Wholesalers.html.

58 Clint Bolick, *David's Hammer: The Case for an Activist Judiciary* (Washington, DC: Cato Institute, 2007); Frank J. Prial, "Juanita Swedenburg, 82, Dies; Won Suit on Wine Shipping," *New York Times*, June 16, 2007, http://www.nytimes.com/2007/06/16/us/16swedenburg.html?_r=0.

59 Bolick, *David's Hammer.*

60 Barbara C. Beliveau and M. Elizabeth Rouse, "Prohibition and Repeal: A Short History of the Wine Industry's Regulation in the United States," *Journal of Wine Economics* 5, no. 1 (February 2010).

61 Bolick, *David's Hammer.*

62 Ibid.

63 Ibid.; Greenburg, "Spirited Debate over Wine Case."

64 Bolick, *David's Hammer.*

65 Ibid.

66 Ibid.

67 Levine and Reinarman, "From Prohibition to Regulation."

68 Bob Archer, quoted in Peck, *Prohibition Hangover*, 153.

69 Juanita Duggan, quoted in Michael W. Lynch, "The Battle of the Grapes Goes to Court," *South Florida Sun-Sentinel*, February 17, 2000, http://articles.sun-sentinel.com/2000-02-17/news/0002160938_1_out-of-state-wineries-small-vintners-alcohol-sales.

70 Miller, "Passionate Winemaker Won Fight."

71 Heather Morton, "Three-Tier Cheers!," *State Legislatures Magazine*, June 1, 2015, National Conference of State Legislatures, http://www.ncsl.org/research/financial-services-and-commerce/three-tier-cheers-635689375.aspx; Beliveau and Rouse, "Prohibition and Repeal"; Warren Richey, "Can States Ban Certain Wine Parcels?," *Christian Science Monitor*, December 7, 2004, http://www.csmonitor.com/2004/1207/p02s01-usju.html.

72 Swedenburg v. Kelly, 232 F. Supp. 2d 135, 148 (S.D. NY 2002).

73 *Id.* at 150.

74 Swedenburg v. Kelly, 358 F.3d 223, 237 (2d Cir. 2004).

75 Bolick, *David's Hammer.*

76 John Fitzpatrick, quoted in Barakat, "Wine Fight to U.S. Supreme Court."

77 Lynch, "Battle of the Grapes."

78 Bolick, *David's Hammer.*

79 Granholm v. Heald, 544 U.S. 460, 466 (U.S. 2005).

80 *Id.* at 473.

81 Larry Peterson, "You Can Raise Your Glass: Although Georgia Does Not Have an Outright Ban on Such Shipments, It Has Restrictions That Make Them More Difficult," *Savannah Morning News*, May 16, 2005, http://savannahnow.com/stories/051605/3035574.shtml.

82 Transcript of oral argument can be found at: *Granholm*, 544 U.S. 460 at 56: 13–16 (nos. 03-1116, 03-1120, 03-1274).
83 Fiedler, "Juanita Swedenburg Dies at 82."
84 Peck, *Prohibition Hangover*, 6.
85 Fiedler, "Juanita Swedenburg Dies at 82."
86 Logomasini, *Rush to Regulate Alcohol.*
87 Dennis Grimes, "Direct to Consumer Wine Shipping—Toasting Juanita Swedenburg," Wine Tasting San Diego, July 12, 2009, Internet Archive Wayback Machine, https://web.archive.org/web/20090719101727/http://www.winetastingsandiego.com/2009/07/direct-to-consumer-wine-shipping-toasting-juanita-swedenburg; Andrew Staub, "In Pennsylvania, Shipping Wine a Complicated Affair," *PA Independent*, June 15, 2015, http://paindependent.com/2015/06/in-pennsylvania-shipping-wine-a-complicated-affair/; Paul Franson, "90% of U.S. Consumers Can Buy Wine Direct: With Massacusetts Now Open, Pennsylvania Is the Next Big Target," *Wines & Vines*, January 16, 2015, http://www.winesandvines.com/template.cfm?section=news&content=144717.
88 Logomasini, *Rush to Regulate Alcohol.*
89 "WSWA Applauds Introduction of Legislation Affirming States' Rights," Wine & Spirits Wholesalers of America, accessed June 6, 2016, http://www.wswa.org/news/articles/2011/03/17/wswa-applauds-introduction-of-legislation-affirming-states-rights; Chris Frates, "Liquid Gold: Donations Questioned," *Politico*, December 21, 2010, http://www.politico.com/story/2010/12/liquid-gold-donations-questioned-046653?o=0.
90 OpenSecrets.org, www.opensecrets.org, accessed June 6, 2016.
91 Specialty Wine Retailers Association, *Toward Liquor Domination: How Alcohol Wholesalers, Time and Money Have Corrupted the American Alcohol Industry; A Study of Political Money and the Alcohol Industry from 2005 to 2010*, National Association of Wine Retailers, July 2011, http://nawr.org/wp-content/uploads/2013/02/TowardLiquorDomination.pdf.
92 Allan E. Wiseman and Jerry Ellig, "The Politics of Wine: Trade Barriers, Interest Groups, and the Commerce Clause," *Journal of Politics* 69, no. 3 (2007).
93 Robert Taylor and Harris Meyer, "The Battle of Washington State," *Wine Spectator*, September 27, 2010, http://www.winespectator.com/webfeature/show/id/43651; Logomasini, *Rush to Regulate Alcohol.*
94 Taylor and Meyer, "Battle of Washington State"; Logomasini, *Rush to Regulate Alcohol.*
95 Melissa Allison, "Voters Kick State Out of Liquor Business," *Seattle Times*, November 8, 2011, http://www.seattletimes.com/seattle-news/voters-kick-state-out-of-liquor-business/.
96 Sue Stock, "Gallo Seeks a Favor of ABC," *Raleigh News & Observer*, March 1, 2011; Logomasini, *Rush to Regulate Alcohol.*
97 Bill Rufty, "Beer Proposals Dismay Florida Craft Brewers," *Lakeland Ledger*, April 14, 2014, http://www.theledger.com/article/20140414/NEWS/140419604/1410.
98 Malt Beverages, S.B. 1714, 2014 Florida Legislative Session (2014).
99 "The Growler: Beer to Go!," Beeradvocate, July 31, 2002, http://www.beeradvocate.com/articles/384/.

100 "Micro Brews and Craft Beers Taking Hold," *ABC News* video, 4:06, August 14, 2013, http://abcnews.go.com/WNN/video/micro-brews-craft-beers-taking-hold-19954506.

101 Alex Hobson, "Local Microbreweries Fight Senate Bill 1714," *ABC Action News*, last updated April 2, 2014, Internet Archive Wayback Machine, https://web.archive.org/web/20140528024540/http://www.abcactionnews.com/news/region-tampa/local-microbreweries-fight-senate-bill-1714?; Lloyd Dunkelberger, "Bill Craft Brewers Oppose Advancing in the Senate," *Gainesville Sun*, April 21, 2014, Gainesville.com, http://www.gainesville.com/article/20140421/ARTICLES/140429909?p=1&tc=pg; Alan Shaw, "Audio: Brewers and Distributor Lobbyist Talk about Florida's Craft Beer Battles," *Sarasota Herald-Tribune*, April 23, 2014, http://www.ticketsarasota.com/2014/04/23/audio-brewers-distributor-lobbyist-talk-floridas-craft-beer-battles/.

102 Malt Beverages, H.B. 1329, 2014 Florida Legislative Session (2014).

103 Holly Gregory, "Senator Jack Latvala: It's Time to Lift the Growler Ban," Bay News 9, December 20, 2014, http://www.baynews9.com/content/news/baynews9/news/article.html/content/news/articles/bn9/2014/12/17/growler_ban_latvala.html.

104 Quoted in Rufty, "Proposals Dismay Florida Craft Brewers."

105 Senate Bill 639 provides that "no manufacturer shall . . . accept payment in exchange for an agreement setting forth territorial rights." *Codified at* Texas Alcoholic Beverage Code § 102.75(7).

106 Edward Brown, "Beer and Sausage . . . Craft Brewers Are Suing to Stop What They Say Is a Money Grab by Big Distributors," *Fort Worth Weekly*, December 22, 2014, http://www.fwweekly.com/2014/12/22/beer-and-sausage/.

107 Ibid.

108 "Big Beer Drowns Small Competitors: Politicians Work under the Influence of $7 Million from Beer Distributors," Lobby Watch, March 7, 2013, Internet Archive Wayback Machine, https://web.archive.org/web/20130323012326/http://info.tpj.org/Lobby_Watch/pdf/AlcoholContribs.pdf.

109 A. 5125, 2013 New York Legislative Session (2013).

110 S. 3849, 2013 New York Legislative Session (2013).

111 Robert Taylor, "New York Faces New Wine Sale Restrictions: Consumers Could Have Fewer Choices If Legislation Squeezes Small Wholesalers, While State Liquor Authority Forbids Some Third-Party Wine Sales," *Wine Spectator*, April 25, 2013, http://www.winespectator.com/webfeature/show/id/48346.

112 Ibid.

113 Ibid.

114 Chris Churchill, "Baffling Wine Bill Leaves a Sour Taste," *Times Union*, February 8, 2014, http://www.timesunion.com/local/article/Churchill-Baffling-wine-bill-leaves-a-sour-taste-5217452.php.

115 Nida Samona, quoted in Peterson, "You Can Raise Your Glass."

116 "Statement of Craig A. Purser, President and CEO of National Beer Wholesalers Association," in *Legal Issues concerning State Alcohol Regulation* (Washington, DC: U.S. Government Printing Office, 2010), http://judiciary.house.gov/_files/hearings/printers/111th/111-125_55481.pdf; National Beer Wholesalers Association, "America's Beer Distributors Recognize National

Alcohol Awareness Month," March 31, 2015, https://www.nbwa.org/news/america%E2%80%99s-beer-distributors-recognize-national-alcohol-awareness-month-2.

117 John Peirce, quoted in State Governmental Organization Committee, *The "Tied House" Puzzle—Why the Three-Tier System Was Established and How Well Has It Worked?* (Sacramento: California Senate Committee on Government Organization, 2005), 18.

118 Beliveau and Rouse, "Prohibition and Repeal"; Bolick, *David's Hammer*; *Granholm*, 544 U.S. 460.

119 Federal Trade Commission, *Possible Anticompetitive Barriers to E-Commerce: Wine* (Washington, DC: Federal Trade Commission, 2003); Wiseman and Ellig, "Politics of Wine."

120 Alix M. Freedman and John R. Emschwiller, "Vintage System: Big Liquor Wholesaler Finds Change Stalking Its Very Private World," *Wall Street Journal*, October 4, 1999; Lynch, "Battle of the Grapes."

121 Peck, *Prohibition Hangover*.

122 Deb Carey, quoted in Jessica Vanegeren, "Craft Brewers Vent Anger over Budget Provision," *Capital Times*, June 7, 2011, Madison.com, http://host.madison.com/news/local/govt-and-politics/capitol-report/craft-brewers-vent-anger-over-budget-provision/article_1f004302-90ab-11e0-bd83-001cc4c002e0.html.

123 Quoted in Federal Trade Commission, *Possible Anticompetitive Barriers*, 22; see also Freedman and Emschwiller, "Vintage System."

124 Beliveau and Rouse, "Prohibition and Repeal"; *Granholm*, 544 U.S. 460.

125 Greenburg, "Spirited Debate over Wine Case."

126 In 1943, New York University economics professor Paul Studenski wrote of alcohol regulation: "We have succeeded in disassociating the liquor business from the worst types of political corruption with which it was connected in the old days. No longer do the brewers run the legislatures and municipal administrations by maintaining politicians on their payrolls." Paul Studenski, "Liquor Regulation: Success or Failure?," *National Municipal Review*, 32, no. 4 (1943), 183. More than seventy years later, it appears that distributors have succeeded brewers in terms of political influence.

127 Fosdick and Scott, *Toward Liquor Control*, 61. Eighty years later, economists made the same observation: "Economic rents create incentives to organize—in particular, to extract and/or take advantage of those rents or to protect them. The existence of organizations has potentially powerful political consequences." Daron Acemoglu and James A. Robinson, "Economics versus Politics: Pitfalls of Policy Advice," *Journal of Economic Perspectives* 27, no. 2 (2013), 177.

CHAPTER 2 ■ CASKET CARTELS: ROBBERY WITHOUT A PISTOL

1 "Economics of the Funeral Industry," PBS Thirteen *Homegoings*, accessed June 6, 2016, http://www.pbs.org/pov/homegoings/economics-of-the-funeral-industry.php#.VgvvV_lViko.

2 "Funeral Services Industry Profile," First Research, last updated March 28,

2016, http://www.firstresearch.com/industry-research/Funeral-Services.html; "Trends in Funeral Service," National Funeral Directors Association, accessed June 6, 2016, http://nfda.org/about-funeral-service-/trends-and-statistics.html.

3 Perianne Boring, "Death of the Death Care Industry and Eternal Life Online," *Forbes*, April 25, 2014, http://www.forbes.com/sites/perianneboring/2014/04/25/the-death-of-the-death-care-industry-and-eternal-life-online/; "Economics of the Funeral Industry," PBS Thirteen.

4 Daniel Sutter, "State Regulations and E-Commerce: The Case for Internet Casket Sales in Oklahoma," *Journal of Private Enterprise* 20, no. 2 (2005); "Consumer Information: Funeral Costs and Pricing Checklist," Federal Trade Commission Consumer Information, July 2012, http://www.consumer.ftc.gov/articles/0301-funeral-costs-and-pricing-checklist.

5 Darryl J. Roberts, *Profits of Death: An Insider Exposes the Death Care Industries* (Chandler, AZ: Five Star, 1997); Sutter, "State Regulations"; Daniel Sutter, "Casket Sales Restrictions and the Funeral Market," *Journal of Law, Economics and Policy* 3, no. 2 (2006); "Funeral Costs and Pricing Checklist," Federal Trade Commission.

6 Craigmiles v. Giles, 110 F. Supp. 2d. 658, 664 (E.D. Tenn. 2000).

7 Susan Adams, "Boxed Out," *Forbes*, October 18, 1999, 56; "Dying beyond Our Means," *Wall Street Journal*, October 26, 1999; Steven France, "Dusty Doctrines," *ABA Journal* 87, no. 5 (May 2001); Walter E. Williams, "Economic Liberty Vital to Civil Rights," *Deseret News*, November 14, 2001.

8 Jessica Mitford, *The American Way of Death Revisited* (New York: Vintage, 2000).

9 Maria Dickerson, "Culture of Death Takes on a New Life," *Detroit News*, May 14, 1995.

10 Roberts, *Profits of Death*.

11 Robert Wesley Habenstein and William M. Lamers, *The History of American Funeral Directing*, 7th ed. (Brookfield, WI: National Funeral Directors Association, 2010).

12 Ibid.

13 National Funeral Directors Association, quoted in Rebecca A. von Cohen, "The FTC Assault on the Cost of Dying," *Business and Society Review* 27 (Fall 1978), 49–50.

14 Habenstein and Lamers, *American Funeral Directing*.

15 Ibid.

16 Ibid.

17 Ibid.

18 Michigan Funeral Directors Association, quoted in ibid., 300.

19 Ibid.; Steven W. Kopp and Elyria Kemp, "The Death Care Industry: A Review of Regulatory and Consumer Issues," *Journal of Consumer Affairs* 41, no. 1 (2007).

20 National Funeral Directors Association, quoted in Habenstein and Lamers, *American Funeral Directing*, 314.

21 Spencer E. Cahill, "Some Rhetorical Directions of Funeral Direction: Historical Entanglements and Contemporary Dilemmas," *Work and Occupations* 22, no. 2 (1995).

22 Congressional Quarterly, *Funeral Business under Fire* (Washington, DC: Congressional Quarterly, 1982), http://library.cqpress.com/cqresearcher/document.php?id=cqresrre1982110500&type=hitlist&num=0; Habenstein and Lamers, *American Funeral Directing*.
23 Ruth Darmstadter, "Blocking the Death Blow to Funeral Regulation," *Business and Society Review* 42 (1983).
24 Congressional Quarterly, *Funeral Business under Fire*.
25 Cohen, "FTC Assault on the Cost of Dying."
26 Congressional Quarterly, *Funeral Business under Fire*.
27 Ibid. As late as 2012, funeral directors were still instructed in such sales tactics. A November 2012 issue of *Money* magazine reported, "'Upselling without Upsetting the Client' is one of the continuing-education courses approved by 27 state boards for funeral directors to maintain their licenses. The online class, which a MONEY writer signed up for, advises funeral directors about techniques to persuade customers to buy more than they need. The sweet spot for going above a client's budget: 20%. The course instructor encourages funeral directors to ask about the family's budget, then say, 'We are going to stay as close to that number as possible'—conditioning customers to think prices will stay within reason. Then directors are urged to use phrases like, 'We might go a little over your budget, but this particular add-on will go perfectly.'" Lisa Gibbs and Ismat Mangla, "The High Cost of Saying Goodbye," *Money* 41 (November 2012), 113.
28 Elizabeth Howell Boldt, "Nail in the Coffin: Can Elderly Americans Afford to Die?," *Elder Law Journal* 21, no. 1 (2013); Congressional Quarterly, *Funeral Business under Fire*; Kopp and Kemp, "Death Care Industry."
29 Darmstadter, "Blocking the Death Blow"; Kopp and Kemp, "Death Care Industry"; Fred S. McChesney, "Consumer Ignorance and Consumer Protection Law: Empirical Evidence from the FTC's Funeral Rule," *Journal of Law and Policy* 7, no. 1 (1990).
30 McChesney, "Consumer Ignorance."
31 Harry & Bryant Co. v. F.T.C., 726 F.2d 993 (4th Cir. 1984); Kopp and Kemp, "Death Care Industry."
32 Congressional Quarterly, *Funeral Business under Fire*.
33 Darmstadter, "Blocking the Death Blow"; "Funeral Parlors Win House Vote," *Chicago Tribune*, November 15, 1979; Congressional Quarterly, *Funeral Business under Fire*.
34 Pub. L. No. 96-252, Stat. § 19 (1980).
35 Kopp and Kemp, "Death Care Industry."
36 Ibid.
37 Ibid.
38 Quoted in Michael Kubasak, "Education Choices," *Director* 56 (February 1990), 22.
39 Pennsylvania Funeral Directors Ass'n, Inc. v. F.T.C., 41 F.3d 81 (3d Cir. 1994); Kopp and Kemp, "Death Care Industry."
40 Shelley Emling, "Turf War over Caskets: Cemetery Owner Challenges Funeral Homes' Monopoly," *Atlanta Journal-Constitution*, July 28, 1993.

41 Jim Wooten, "Creating a Casket Monopoly," *Atlanta Journal-Constitution*, May 3, 1992.
42 Ibid.
43 The law remained in place for six years. Then, in 1998, the owner of Peachtree Caskets Direct, a casket store, sued the state over the law. The following year, a federal district court found in favor of Peachtree and struck down Georgia's law, ruling that it was "not rationally related to any legitimate state interest." Gere B. Fulton, "Retail Casket Sales: A 'White Paper' on the Status of Litigation to Overturn State Restrictions on Retail Casket Sales" (white paper, Funeral Consumers Alliance, 2005), 5, Funeral Consumers Alliance, accessed June 7, 2016, http://www.funerals.org/forconsumersmenu/pdf-pamphlets/doc_download/4-retail-casket-sales-whitepaper; see also Wooten, "Creating a Casket Monopoly."
44 Public Chapter 553, 1972, tape transcript, Senate Floor, March 7, S.B. 1425, tape S-44.
45 Public Chapter 553, 1972, tape transcript, House Floor, March 14, S.B. 1452, tapes H-91, H-92, and H-93.
46 Sutter, "Casket Sales Restrictions."
47 Sutter, "State Regulations."
48 Nathaniel Craigmiles, quoted in Adams, "Boxed Out," 56; see also Duncan Mansfield, "State Closes Discount Casket Stores over Licensing," Associated Press Newswire, July 27, 1999.
49 France, "Dusty Doctrines"; Walter E. Williams, "Government and the Little Guy," *Commercial Appeal*, October 20, 2000.
50 Nathaniel Craigmiles, quoted in France, "Dusty Doctrines," 47.
51 Adams, "Boxed Out," 56; "Casket Dealers Win Fight with Funeral Homes," *Commercial Appeal*, December 8, 2002; Mansfield, "State Closes Discount Casket Stores"; Williams, "Economic Liberty."
52 "Dying beyond our Means," *Wall Street Journal*.
53 "Ruling Rejects Tenn. Ban on Casket Sale by Retailers," *Commercial Appeal*, August 22, 2000; "Casket Dealers Win Fight," *Commercial Appeal*; "Dying beyond Our Means," *Wall Street Journal*.
54 Nathaniel Craigmiles, quoted in "Dying beyond our Means," *Wall Street Journal*.
55 Ibid.; Mansfield, "State Closes Discount Casket Stores."
56 Nathaniel Craigmiles, telephone conversation with Dick Carpenter, December 30, 2014.
57 France, "Dusty Doctrines."
58 Bill Brewer, "State Closes Down Unlicensed Casket Firm; Chattanooga Company May Join Planned Lawsuit," *Knoxville News Sentinel*, July 24, 1999.
59 Arthur Giles, quoted in Bill Brewer, "Lawsuit to Challenge State Law on Casket Sales," *Knoxville News Sentinel*, September 16, 1999.
60 Ibid.; France, "Dusty Doctrines."
61 George F. Will, "Of Death and Rent Seeking: If Only Licensed Morticians Can Sell Caskets, Perhaps Only Podiatrists Should Sell Shoes," *Newsweek* 135, May 15, 2000.
62 Brewer, "Unlicensed Casket Firm."

63 Nathaniel Craigmiles, quoted in ibid.

64 Williams, "Economic Liberty."

65 "Former Tenn. Lawmaker John Ford Convicted of Taking Bribes," *Washington Post,* April 28, 2007, http://www.washingtonpost.com/wp-dyn/content/article/2007/04/27/AR2007042702110.html.

66 H.B. 835, 1999–2000 Tennessee Legislative Session (1999).

67 Rebecca Ferrar, "Burchett Offers Senate Proposal to Repeal 24-Hour Waiting Period for Cremations," *Knoxville News Sentinel,* February 15, 2000.

68 "Ford's Family May Benefit from Senator's Bill," *Commercial Appeal,* November 15, 1999.

69 Tom Humphrey, "Cremation Bill Clears State Senate Panel; Amended Legislation Still on Hold in House," *Knoxville News Sentinel,* March 1, 2000.

70 "Reversing a Mistake: Burchett's Bill Would Make Cremation Law More Consumer Friendly," *Knoxville News Sentinel,* February 4, 2000.

71 Howard Kerr, Bill Dunn, Gary Odom, Tre Hargett, Diane Black, William Baird, Tim Garrett et al., "CHAPTER NO. 779: HOUSE BILL NO. 2600," Tennessee General Assembly, accessed June 7, 2016, http://www.capitol.tn.gov/Bills/101/Chapter/PC0779.pdf.

72 *Craigmiles,* 110 F. Supp. 2d at 665.

73 Tennessee Board of Funeral Directors and Embalmers, teleconference meeting, 2000.

74 "Casket Dealers Win Fight," *Commercial Appeal.*

75 Craigmiles v. Giles, 312 F.3d 220, 224–25 (6th Cir. 2002).

76 *Id.* at 226.

77 *Id.* at 229.

78 Maria LaGanga, "Casket Controversy: A Cut-Rate Retailer Is Disliked by Funeral Directors and Shunned by Some Suppliers," *Los Angeles Times,* August 16, 1989. In 2010, Pastor Craigmiles closed his casket business due to health reasons. By that time, he was the last independent casket seller in Tennessee. According to him, manufacturers, caving to threats from funeral homes, refused to sell to other casket dealers. This is a strategy long employed by funeral directors. In 1989, for example, when a casket retailer, Hillmark Casket Gallery, opened in Santa Ana, California, competing funeral directors boycotted a local manufacturer who supplied the casket retailer, compelling the manufacturer and other businesses to stop selling to or otherwise deal with Hillmark. Susan Christian, "Casket Competition; Retailing: A Cypress Discount Store Hopes to Break the Domination of Big Funeral Homes Such as Forest Lawn, Its Neighbor across the Street," *Los Angeles Times,* October 17, 1991, http://articles.latimes.com/1991-10-17/business/fi-1015_1_funeral-home.

Two years later, the store (and another location owned by the same proprietors) went out of business. The practice intensified when the FTC changed its funeral rule in 1994 to force funeral homes to accept caskets purchased from third-party casket retailers. As Kevin Gray, the owner of discount casket stores in New York and California recalled, "[The funeral directors] closed ranks and blackballed any manufacturer who sold to us." The country's top three casket companies—Batesville, York, and Aurora—all refused to sell to casket retailers. Kevin Gray, quoted in Joanne Kimberlin,

"Monopolistic Funeral Homes Have the Law on Their Side, Critics Say," *Virginian-Pilot*, August 21, 2001.

79 Eliot Freidson, *Professional Powers: A Study of the Instituionalozation of Formal Knowledge* (Chicago: University of Chicago Press, 1986); Jason Potts, "Open Occupations—Why Work Should Be Free," *Economic Affairs* 29, no. 1 (2009); Robert A. Rothman, "Occupational Roles: Power and Negotiation in the Division of Labor," *Sociological Quarterly* 20, no. 4 (1979); Saundra K. Schneider, "Influences on State Professional Licensure Policy," *Public Administration Review* 47, no. 6 (1987); Howard G. Schutz, "Effects of Increased Citizen Membership on Occupational Licensing Boards in California," *Policy Studies Journal* 11, no. 3 (1983).

80 Robert Barnes, "A Legal Case That's Not So Open and Shut," *Washington Post*, May 30, 2012.

81 Ibid.; George F. Will, "The Monks' Appeal for Freedom," *Washington Post*, November 15, 2012.

82 David Muller, "Judge Sides with Monks in Coffin-Crafting Case in Covington," *New Orleans City Business*, July 21, 2011.

83 Robert Barnes, "A Victory for Monks in Fight over Caskets," *Washington Post*, October 25, 2012; Muller, "Judge Sides with Monks."

84 David Muller, "Monks Only a Minor Matter to Louisiana Coffin Crafters," *New Orleans City Business*, August 18, 2010.

85 Barnes, "A Legal Case."

86 Will, "Monks' Appeal for Freedom."

87 Jennifer Levitz, "Coffins Made with Brotherly Love Have Undertakers Throwing Dirt," *Wall Street Journal*, August 25, 2010.

88 Barnes, "A Legal Case."

89 Abbott Brown, quoted in ibid.

90 Scott Simon, quoted in ibid.

91 Muller, "Monks Only a Minor Matter."

92 Abbott Brown, quoted in Peter Finney Jr., "High Court Gives OK to Louisiana Monks to Make, Sell Simple Caskets," *Catholic News Service*, October 21, 2013, http://ncronline.org/news/faith-parish/high-court-gives-ok-louisiana-monks-make-sell-simple-caskets.

93 "Meeting of the Louisiana State Board of Embalmers and Funeral Directors . . ." (meeting minutes, February 16, 2011), Louisiana State Board of Embalmers & Funeral Directors, http://www.lsbefd.state.la.us/wp-content/uploads/2014/08/MFeb.16.2011.pdf.

94 "Meeting of the Louisiana State Board of Embalmers and Funeral Directors . . ." (meeting minutes, June 9, 2011), Louisiana State Board of Embalmers & Funeral Directors, http://www.lsbefd.state.la.us/wp-content/uploads/2014/08/MJun92011.pdf.

95 Barnes, "A Legal Case."

96 St. Joseph Abbey v. Castille, 835 F. Supp. 2d 149, 1 (E.D. La. 2011).

97 St. Joseph Abbey v. Castille, 712 F.3d 215, 11, 18 (5th Cir. 2013).

98 Throughout the lawsuit, the Louisiana Funeral Directors Association (LFDA) remained active in attempting to convince the public that its casket cartel was important. LFDA members received regular updates on the lawsuit, prepared

materials, talking points, and even media training from a political consultant and public relations expert. "Louisiana Funeral Directors Association Newsletter 2010 Third Quarter," on file with the authors. Based on comments by funeral directors to major media outlets, the media training was necessary. Funeral director Leonard Dunn told the *Wall Street Journal*: "I don't think the monks are actually making the caskets—I think it's a marketing gimmick." Boyd Mothe Jr., a fifth-generation funeral director, said transactions involving caskets are "complicated" and "a quarter of America is oversized. I don't even know if the monks know how to make an oversize casket." Levitz, "Coffins Made with Brotherly Love." The LFDA also pushed for its own attorney to be included on the team representing the board and increased members' dues in order to fund its continuing efforts to influence public opinion. "Louisiana Funeral Directors Association Newsletter 2010 Fourth Quarter," on file with the authors. After the board lost in court, the LFDA began an effort to burden non–funeral home casket sellers with the same regulations that apply to funeral homes, meeting with seven members of Congress to push for applying the FTC Funeral Rule to casket sellers. Ibid.; Finney, "Court Gives OK to Louisiana Monks."

99 Fred S. McChesney, "Rent Extraction and Interest-Group Organization in a Coasean Model of Regulation," *Journal of Legal Studies* 20, no. 1 (1991).

100 Clark Neily, "No Such Thing: Litigating under the Rational Basis Test," *N.Y.U. Journal of Law & Liberty* 1, no. 2 (2005); Clark M. Neily, *Terms of Engagement: How Our Courts Should Enforce the Constitution's Promise of Limited Government* (New York: Encounter Books, 2013).

101 Michael Burgin, *The Power of One Entrepreneur: Kim Powers Bridges, Funeral Home & Cemetery Owner* (Arlington: Institute for Justice, 2010).

102 Ibid.

103 Ibid.

104 Kim Powers Bridges, quoted in ibid., 14.

105 Ibid.; Will Kooi, "Oklahoma State Rep. Paul Wesselhoft: Tribes Should Be Allowed to Sell Caskets," *Journal Record*, July 29, 2010.

106 Kim Powers Bridges, quoted in Ray Carter, "Casket Seller Sues Okla. in Federal Court over Licensing Act," *Journal Record*, March 15, 2001.

107 Burgin, *Kim Powers Bridges*; *Craigmiles*, 110 F. Supp. 658 at 664.

108 Bob Tedeschi, "E-Commerce Report: Some Web Merchants Fill a Void, and Make a Profit, by Selling Coffins and Other Funeral Supplies Online," *New York Times*, February 3, 2003.

109 Robert M. Fells, quoted in ibid.

110 Jay Kravetz, quoted in ibid.

111 Those states include: Alabama (Ala. Code Ann. § 34-13-1[a][15]); Delaware (24 Del. Code Ann. §§ 31-3101, 31-3106); Idaho (Idaho Code § 54-1102); Louisiana (La. Rev. Stat. Ann. §§ 37:831[23], 37:848); Maine (32 Me. Rev. Stat. Ann. §§ 1400[5], 1501); Minnesota (Minn. Stat. §§ 149A.02[19],[20], and [21], 149A.50[1]); South Carolina (S.C. Code Ann. §§ 40-19-20[19], 40-19-30); Vermont (26 Vt. Stat. Ann. §§ 1211[2], 1251); and Virginia (Va. Code Ann. § 54.1-2800).

112 Burgin, *Kim Powers Bridges*, 14; see also Ray Carter, "Casket Sales Bill Dies in Oklahoma House Committee," *Journal Record*, February 20, 2003.

113 Robert E. Boczkiewicz, "Court Calls Oklahoma Casket Law Wasteful, But Only Legislation Can Change It," *Daily Oklahoman*, August 24, 2004; Carter, "Casket Seller Sues Okla."; Ray Carter, "Okla. Lawmaker Continues Fight to Lift Casket Sale Restrictions," *Oklahoma Business News*, January 27, 2003.
114 Kim Powers Bridges, quoted in Burgin, *Kim Powers Bridges*, 18.
115 Kim Powers Bridges, quoted in ibid., 18.
116 Ibid.
117 Carter, "Casket Seller Sues Okla."
118 Ibid.
119 Carter, "Casket Sales Bill Dies."
120 Carter, "Casket Seller Sues Okla."; Carter, "Casket Sales Bill Dies."
121 Quoted in Carter, "Casket Seller Sues Okla."
122 Carter, "Casket Sales Bill Dies"; Ray Carter, "Casket Sales Proposal Attracts New Allies," *Journal Record*, February 19, 2002.
123 Carter, "Casket Seller Sues Okla."
124 Edwin Kessler, quoted in Carter, "Casket Sales Bill Dies."
125 Ray Carter, "District Court Denies Dismissal of Casket Lawsuit," *Journal Record*, February 14, 2002; Ray Carter, "Federal Court Upholds Oklahoma Casket Sales Law," *Journal Record*, December 13, 2002.
126 State v. Stone Casket Co. of Oklahoma City, 976 P.2d 1074 (Okla. Ct. App. 1998); Carter, "Casket Seller Sues Okla."
127 Kim Powers Bridges, telephone conversation with Dick Carpenter, January 2, 2015. Ironically, years later, after Kim had built up her successful business, she received a résumé from the man who had previously written to her asking for a job.
128 Scott Smith and Joseph McCormick IV, speaking in "Profile: Enterprising Oklahoma Woman in Hot Water with Federal Judge for Selling Funeral Items at Low Price Online," *NBC Nightly News*, television broadcast, December 12, 2002.
129 Memorandum of Law of Amicus Curiae Federal Trade Commission, Powers v. Harris, No. CIV-01-445-F, 2002 WL 32036155 (W.D. Okla. Dec. 12, 2002), http://www.ftc.gov/sites/default/files/documents/amicus_briefs/powers-v.harris/okamicus.pdf.
130 Stephen P. Friot, quoted in Carter, "Court Upholds Oklahoma Casket Sales Law."
131 Stephen P. Friot, quoted in ibid.
132 Powers v. Harris, 379 F.3d 1208, 1221, 1227 (10th Cir. 2004).
133 *Id.* at 1221.
134 Kim Powers Bridges, quoted in Carter, "Oklahoma Casket Sales Law."
135 Kim Powers Bridges, quoted in Boczkiewicz, "Oklahoma Casket Law Wasteful."
136 Kooi, "Oklahoma State Rep. Paul Wesselhoft."
137 Ibid.
138 Paul Wesselhoft, quoted in ibid.
139 Ibid.

CHAPTER 3 ■ WHEN LICENSES CREEP

1 Jestina Clayton, telephone conversation with Dick Carpenter, November 4, 2014.

2 Jestina Clayton, speaking in "Episode 381: Why It's Illegal to Braid Hair Without A License," NPR: *Planet Money*, podcast audio, June 2012, http://www.npr.org/blogs/money/2014/10/15/356428708/episode-381-why-its-illegal-to-braid-hair-without-a-license.

3 Jestina Clayton, speaking in ibid.

4 Ibrahim Abdullah, *Between Democracy and Terror: The Sierra Leone Civil War* (Dakar: Council for the Development of Social Science Research in Africa, 2004); Alfred B. Zack-Williams, "Sierra Leone: The Political Economy of Civil War, 1991–98," *Third World Quarterly* 20, no. 1 (1999). When Sierra Leone gained independence from the United Kingdom in 1961, Sir Milton Margai, who had led the effort for independence, became the country's first prime minister and retained the title in the country's first general election in 1962. Sir Milton, a physician by training, was revered for his statesmanship, honesty, and humility. He led a period of stability following independence, but it proved short-lived. When he died unexpectedly in 1964, he was succeeded by his brother, a corrupt politician who was ousted a few years later. David Dalby, "The Military Take-Over in Sierra Leone," *World Today* 23, no. 8 (1967).

From 1967 onward, a series of leaders, parties, groups, and rivals battled over control of the country and its rich deposits of diamonds, gold, and other resources. Civilian governments gave way to military rule, followed by the re-emergence of civilian governments, most of them characterized by authoritarianism and consolidated power achieved through force and executions. Ibid.

5 Zack-Williams, "Sierra Leone."

6 Tom Harvey, "Woman Sues over Need for License to Braid Hair," *Salt Lake Tribune*, April 26, 2011.

7 Jestina Clayton, telephone conversation with Dick Carpenter, November 4, 2014.

8 Dennis Romboy, "Court Ruling: Centerville Woman Has a Right to Braid Hair without a Cosmetology License," *Deseret News*, August 9, 2012.

9 "The Braid: A Photo History," *Swide*, June 4, 2013, https://web.archive.org/web/20150107225134/http://www.swide.com/beauty/hair-styling-tips/the-history-of-the-braid-from-ancient-egypt-to-modern-braided-hairstyles/2013/06/04; Dick M. Carpenter II and John K. Ross, *The Power of One Entrepreneur: Melony Armstrong, African Hairbraider* (Arlington: Institute for Justice).

10 Shane White and Graham White, "Slave Hair and African American Culture in the Eighteenth and Nineteenth Centuries," *Journal of Southern History* 61, no. 1 (1995).

11 Anthony Synnott, "Shame and Glory: A Sociology Of Hair," *British Journal of Sociology* 38, no. 3 (1987).

12 White and White, "Slave Hair and African American Culture."

13 Ibid.

14 Noliwe M. Rooks, *Hair Raising: Beauty, Culture, and African American Women* (New Brunswick, NJ: Rutgers University Press, 1996).
15 White and White, "Slave Hair and African American Culture."
16 Roberta Matthews, quoted in Carpenter and Ross, *Melony Armstrong*, 28.
17 Ibid.; Denise Crittendon and Tonya Jeter, "Black Hair: A Crown of Glory and Versatility," *Crisis* 10, no. 2 (February/March 1994); Dia N. R. Sekayi, "Positive Self-Concept and Expressions of Blackness among African American Intellectual-Activists," *Urban Education* 32, no. 4 (1997).
18 Romboy, "Court Ruling."
19 Harvey, "Woman Sues over Need for License"; Romboy, "Court Ruling."
20 Harvey, "Woman Sues over Need for License"; Romboy, "Court Ruling."
21 Jestina Clayton, quoted in Jacob Goldstein, "So You Think You Can Be a Hair Braider . . . ," *New York Times Magazine,* June 17, 2012, 20.
22 Ibid.
23 Jestina Clayton, telephone conversation with Dick Carpenter, November 4, 2014.
24 Brooke Adams, "African Hair Braider Gets Win in Federal Court," *Salt Lake Tribune*, August 11, 2012; Romboy, "Court Ruling."
25 Jestina Clayton, quoted in Goldstein, "Hair Braider," 20; see also Romboy, "Court Ruling."
26 Adams, "African Hair Braider Gets Win."
27 Jestina Clayton, quoted in Romboy, "Court Ruling."
28 Adams, "African Hair Braider Gets Win."
29 Jestina Clayton, speaking in "John Stossel—The Licensing Racket," YouTube video, 7:01, from a broadcast televised in 2011, posted by LibertyPen, https://www.youtube.com/watch?v=3Kij_TtBXU8.
30 Adams, "African Hair Braider Gets Win."
31 Carpenter et al., *License to Work*; Angela C. Erikson, *White Out: How Dental Industry Insiders Thwart Competition from Teeth-Whitening Entrepreneurs* (Arlington: Institute for Justice, 2013).
32 Aaron S. Edlin and Rebecca Haw,"Cartels by Another Name: Should Licensed Occupations Face Antitrust Scrutiny?," *University of Pennsylvania Law Review* 162 (2014).
33 Erickson, *White Out.*
34 Goldstein, "Hair Braider"; Romboy, "Court Ruling."
35 Goldstein, "Hair Braider"; Romboy, "Court Ruling."
36 "Minutes of the Business and Labor Interim Committee" (meeting minutes, October 19, 2011), Utah State Legislature, http://utahlegislature.granicus.com/MediaPlayer.php?view_id=2&clip_id=14823&meta_id=470807.
37 Jestina Clayton, telephone conversation with Dick Carpenter, November 4, 2014.
38 Brad Masterson, quoted in Goldstein, "Hair Braider," 20.
39 "Advancing Our Industry," Professional Beauty Association, accessed June 7, 2016, https://probeauty.org/docs/membership/pba_fact_sheet.pdf.
40 "PBA Staff," Professional Beauty Association, accessed June 7, 2016, https://probeauty.org/staff.
41 "PBA Committees," Professional Beauty Association, accessed June 7, 2016, https://probeauty.org/committees/.

42 In 2013, Missouri state representative Andrew Koenig sponsored House Bill 590, which would have deregulated cosmetology. H.B. 590, 97th General Assembly (2013), Missouri House of Representatives, accessed August 2, 2016, http://house.mo.gov/billtracking/bills131/biltxt/intro/HB0590I.htm. The PBA mobilized its resources to defeat the bill. "Alert: Connecticut and Missouri Introduce Deregulation Legislation," Professional Beauty Association, February 19, 2013, Internet Archive Wayback Machine, https://web.archive.org/web/20130614205333/http://probeauty.org/blog/alert-connecticut-and-missouri-introduce-deregulation-legislation/. A year later, representatives Nick Marshall and Ronald Schieber sponsored House Bill 1891 to scrap licensing for a variety of professions, including cosmetology and barbering. Once again, the PBA rallied (PBA, "PBA Government Affairs Update," Professional Beauty Association, April 3, 2014, http://probeauty.org/progress/pba-government-affairs-update-legislative-progress/), and the bill never received a hearing.

43 "Form 990; Return of Organization Exempt from Income Tax: Professional Beauty Association, 2012," Foundation Center, accessed July 25, 2016, http://990s.foundationcenter.org/990_pdf_archive/201/201585064/201585064_201212_990O.pdf?_ga=1.28821044.964246206.1467211658.

44 Russell Berman, "GOP Leader Takes on Beauty Salon Licenses," *Hill*, May 22, 2014, http://thehill.com/regulation/business/206935-gop-leader-takes-on-beauty-salon-licenses.

45 "Deregulation Receives National Attention; An Open Letter to the Industry," Professional Beauty Association, July 10, 2014, Internet Archive Wayback Machine, https://web.archive.org/web/20140912125631/http://probeauty.org/blog/deregulation-receives-national-attention-an-open-letter-to-the-industry/.

46 "State Captains Directory," Professional Beauty Association, accessed June 7, 2016, https://probeauty.org/captains/.

47 Lynn Glaze, quoted in Bridget Sharpe, "PBA's State Captains Program Continues Growth, Bridges Communication Gap between Industry Professionals and State Legislators," Professional Beauty Association, August 28, 2014, https://probeauty.org/progress/pbas-state-captain-program-continues-growth/.

48 "PBA State Captain Works to Stop Deregulation in Indiana," Professional Beauty Association, March 28, 2013, http://probeauty.org/progress/pba-state-captain-john-halal-works-to-stop-deregulation-in-indiana/.

49 Dave Wolkins, quoted in Lesley Weidenbener, "Rep. Wolkins Withdraws Bill to Deregulate Cosmetologists," *Evansville Courier & Press*, January 25, 2012, http://www.courierpress.com/news/no-headline-ev_cosmetics.

50 Andrea Nagel, "PBA, NCA to Merge," *Women's Wear Daily*, November 30, 2009), 11.

51 Gordon Miller, quoted in Minerva Canto, "Braiders Seek Right to Practice Their Craft," *Topeka Capital-Journal*, September 16, 1999.

52 Myra Irizarry, "Beware the 'D' Word: Cosmetology Licensing under Attack," Professional Beauty Association, accessed May 19, 2016, 1, https://probeauty.org/docs/advocacy/beware_the_d_word.pdf.

53 Brenda Scharman, speaking in "Minutes of the Business and Labor Interim Committee"; see also "State Captains Directory," Professional Beauty Association.

54 Tamu Smith, speaking in "Business and Labor Interim Committee."
55 Brandy Pierson, speaking in ibid.
56 Romboy, "Court Ruling."
57 Adams, "African Hair Braider Gets Win."
58 Clayton v. Steinagel, 885 F. Supp. 2d 1212, 1215–16 (D. Utah 2012).
59 *Id.* at 1215.
60 *Id.* at 1215.
61 *Id.* at 1215.
62 Raymond Mayo, "Letter: Public Safety Mixup," *Deseret News*, August 14, 2012.
63 In the fall of 2012, cosmetologists pushed back, introducing a proposal explicitly writing braiders into cosmetology law. Cosmetology and Hair Braiding, 2013FL-0197/011, 2013 General Session, State of Utah (2012), Utah State Legislature, accessed August 2, 2016, http://le.utah.gov/interim/2012/pdf/00002345.pdf. The bill's drafters were clever. They advertised it as a deregulation bill, on the basis that it would have required fewer hours of training for braiders than for cosmetologists—six hundred instead of two thousand. Kraig Powell, "Keeping House," *Blog of Kraig Powell,* Utah House of Representatives, November 26, 2012, http://www.housepowell.com/2012-keeping-house-november-26/2012-keeping-house-november-26. The catch was, of course, that given the August 2012 ruling in Jestina's case the number of hours required for braiders was zero at the time of the bill's introduction.

When the bill made it to an October committee hearing, cosmetologists packed the room and lined up to testify about burns, skin diseases, and other conditions possible from cosmetology done wrong, all of which was entirely irrelevant, since hair braiders don't practice cosmetology. "Minutes of the Business and Labor Interim Committee" (meeting minutes, October 17, 2012), Utah State Legislature, http://www.le.utah.gov/Interim/2012/pdf/00002602.pdf; Robert Gehrke, "Legislature Again Tangling over Braiding," *Salt Lake Tribune*, October 18, 2012, http://www.sltrib.com/sltrib/news/55102447-78/2000-argued-braiders-braiding.html.csp; Lisa Riley Roche, "Licensing Exemptions, Changes for Hair Braiders Endorsed by Legislative Interim Committee," *Deseret News*, October 17, 2012, http://www.deseretnews.com/article/865564714/Licensing-exemptions-changes-for-hair-braiders-endorsed-by-legislative-interim-committee.html?pg=all; Connor Boyack, "New Bill Proposes Licensure and Regulation for Hair Braiders," Libertas Institute, October 17, 2012, http://libertasutah.org/center-for-free-enterprise/new-bill-proposes-licensure-and-regulation-for-hair-braiders/.

The move backfired when the bill was significantly modified in committee such that it actually *reduced* training requirements for cosmetologists from 2,000 to 1,600 hours and exempted braiders. In March 2013, the governor signed the bill (House Bill 238) into law. Cosmetology and Hair Braiding, H.B. 238, Utah State Legislature (2013), http://le.utah.gov/~2013/bills/static/HB0238.html.
64 Monica C. Bell, "The Braiding Cases, Cultural Deference, and the Inadequate Protection of Black Women Consumers," *Yale Journal of Law and Feminism* 19, no. 1 (2007); William H. Mellor, "City Hall's License to Kill Civil Society," *Policy Review*, July 1, 1996, Internet Archive Wayback Machine, https://web.

archive.org/web/20151224141450/http://www.hoover.org/research/city-halls-license-kill-civil-society.

65 "Hair Braiders Square Off with State over Licensing of Cosmetology Business: African-Styled Designs Are Growing in Popularity," *St. Louis Post-Dispatch*, November 9, 1997; Doug Bandow, "Economic Liberty and the 'Classic Cartel,'" *Las Vegas Review-Journal*, April 30, 1992.

66 John Stossel, "Trimming the Bureaucrats," *New York Sun*, April 6, 2005.

67 United States House of Representatives, *Hearing of the Committee of the District of Columbia on HR 3891* (Washington, DC: United States Congress, 1937), 41.

68 Quoted in ibid., 41.

69 Quoted in ibid., 8.

70 82 Cong. Rec. 5682 (1937) (transcript, Martin Dies, representative, Texas).

71 Bandow, "Economic Liberty."

72 "Review & Outlook (Editorial)—Asides: Barring Entry," *Wall Street Journal*, December 23, 1992; Bandow, "Economic Liberty."

73 John R. Emshwiller, "Regulation and Small Business: Entrepreneurs Employ Rules against Rivals," *Wall Street Journal*, June 16, 1992.

74 Bandow, "Economic Liberty."

75 Ibid.; Bell, "Braiding Cases."

76 William Raspberry, "Those 'Hidebound and Ridiculous" Regulators Are Only Doing Their Jobs," *Atlanta Journal-Constitution*, August 21, 1992.

77 Bandow, "Economic Liberty."

78 "Judge Upbraids Council," *Washington Post*, February 7, 1992.

79 Stanley Sporkin, quoted in Emshwiller, "Regulation and Small Business."

80 Uqdah v. District of Columbia, 785 F. Supp. 1015, 1020 n.4 (D.D.C. 1992).

81 Bell, "Braiding Cases"; Paul Avelar and Nick Sibilla, *Untangling Regulations: Natural Hair Braiders Fight against Irrational Licensing* (Arlington: Institute for Justice, 2014).

82 Taalib din Uqdah, quoted in Mellor, "License to Kill Civil Society."

83 Bhaskar Nair, "Black Hair Braiders Sue the State," Associated Press Newswire, October 2, 1997.

84 Cheryll Hosey, quoted in ibid.

85 Ibid.

86 "Ohio Hair Braiders Sue over State Licensing Requirements," *New York Times*, November 29, 1998.

87 Eric Fingerhut, quoted in Andrew Welsh-Huggins, "Hair Braiding Debate Creates Unusual Political Alliances," Associated Press Newswire, June 13, 1999.

88 Avelar and Sibilla, *Untangling Regulations.*

89 While authorities' actions on behalf of bottleneckers could be severe, they also sank to the level of absurd. In 1993, fifteen-year-old Monique Landers, of Wichita, Kansas, learned a hard lesson in how bottleneckers view entrepreneurs. Landers had been braiding her friends' and family members' hair at home and was earning $100 a month. For this, she was named one of five "Outstanding High School Entrepreneurs " by the National Foundation for Teaching Entrepreneurship, an honor that earned her a trip to New York City to receive the award. When local media featured her story, complaints flooded in to the Kansas Cosmetology Board, all of them initiated by cosmetology

school owners and salon owners demanding action under the state's then-sixty-six-year-old cosmetology law. "This is an issue of morals," said Fredrick Laurino, owner of Vernon's Kansas School of Cosmetology. "I feel sorry for the young lady. But I feel sorrier that a young lady in an entrepreneur program at school has been taught to break the law." In addition to sending Landers a letter threatening up to ninety days in jail, a fine, or both, the board notified her principal, the teacher who sponsored her entrepreneurship project, the governor, the district attorney, and the attorney general. As a result, Landers stopped braiding. Matthew Schofield, "Teen's Success Suffers Harsh Twist: She Stops Braiding Hair for Cash," *Kansas City Star,* June 26, 1993. See also "Monique in Tangles," *Wall Street Journal,* June 18, 1993.

90 Lisa Jones, "Hair Police State," *Village Voice,* September 22, 1998; Lisa Jones, "Hair Braider Gets in Legal Tangle over Licensing," *Austin American-Statesman,* December 4, 1997.

91 Stephen Humphries, "The State vs. Hair Braiders," *Christian Science Monitor,* March 15, 2000, 17; Jones, "Hair Police State"; Yolanda M. Adams, "Oak Cliff Braider Tangles with State's Cosmetology Board over Requirements," *Dallas Weekly,* November 4, 1997.

92 Dana Brantley, quoted in Adams, "Oak Cliff Braider"; see also Jones, "Legal Tangle over Licensing."

93 Reece overcame tremendous odds to become a successful businesswoman. Her parents succumbed to addiction, and at age seventeen she witnessed the murder of her grandmother, who had raised her. In 2011, at a celebration for her fifteenth year in business, Reece accepted awards from US congresswoman Karen Bass as well as state and local leaders. Jason Lewis, "Straight Outta Compton': Braids by SaBrina," *Los Angeles Sentinel,* April 22, 2011, http://lasentinel.net/straight-outta-compton-braids-by-sabrina.html. Today, Reece's salon runs a brisk business, accepting walk-ins seven days a week—though appointments with Reece herself must be made a month in advance. Braids by Sabrina, accessed June 8, 2016, http://www.braidsbysabrina.net/services.html; Jones, "Hair Police State"; Lee Hubbard, "Hair-Brained Politics: Braiding Is an Age-Old Tradition in the African-American Community, but California Regulators Are Cracking Down," *Salon,* September 13, 1999, http://www.salon.com/1999/09/13/hair/.

94 Quoted in Tony Perry, "Bias Suit Targets Hair Care Rules; Cosmetology: Group Says State Licensing of Stylists Discriminates against African Americans Who Specialize in Braiding. Officials Defend the Law," *Los Angeles Times,* http://articles.latimes.com/1997-01-29/news/mn-23264_1_american-hair; see also "License Sting," *Asian Wall Street Journal,* September 14, 1999.

95 Sabrina Reece, quoted in Jones, "Hair Police State."

96 "License Sting," *Asian Wall Street Journal.* In 2011, at a celebration for her fifteenth year in business, Reece accepted awards from Congresswoman Karen Bass, as well as from Los Angeles City Council members and the City of Compton. Lewis, "Straight Outta Compton."

97 Jones, "Hair Police State."

98 Cornwell v. Hamilton, 80 F. Supp. 2d 1101, 1106 (S.D. Cal. 1999).

99 *Id.* at 1111, 1118.

100 Cornwell v. Cal. Bd. of Barbering & Cosmetology, 962 F. Supp. 1260, 1275–77 (S.D. Cal. 1997).
101 Howard Fischer, "Hair Braiders Likely to Get a Break from Lawmakers," *Arizona Daily Star*, April 12, 2004.
102 Essence Farmer, telephone conversation with Dick Carpenter, January 26, 2015.
103 Fischer, "Hair Braiders Get a Break."
104 Essence Farmer, telephone conversation with Dick Carpenter, January 26, 2015.
105 S.B. 1159, 2004 Arizona Legislative Session (2004).
106 Deb Gullett, telephone conversation with Dick Carpenter, February 2, 2015.
107 Carpenter and Ross, *Melony Armstrong*, 6; Carpenter, "Effects of Entrepreneurship," 22.
108 Melony Armstrong, quoted in Carpenter and Ross, *Melony Armstrong*, 6.
109 Kevin Armstrong, telephone conversation with Dick Carpenter, April 7, 2007; Carpenter and Ross, *Melony Armstrong*.
110 Melony Armstrong, quoted in Carpenter and Ross, *Melony Armstrong*, 6.
111 Carpenter and Ross, *Melony Armstrong*, 7; Carpenter, "Effects of Entrepreneurship," 22.
112 Carpenter and Ross, *Melony Armstrong*, 11–12; Carpenter, "Effects of Entrepreneurship," 25.
113 Carpenter and Ross, *Melony Armstrong*, 9.
114 Carpenter and Ross, *Melony Armstrong*, 9; Carpenter, "Effects of Entrepreneurship," 25–26.
115 Carpenter and Ross, *Melony Armstrong*, 12; Carpenter, "Effects of Entrepreneurship," 25.
116 Carpenter and Ross, *Melony Armstrong*, 12; Carpenter, "Effects of Entrepreneurship," 25.
117 Hillman Frazier, speaking in *Locked Out: A Mississippi Success Story*, directed by Sean W. Malone (United States: Honest Enterprise, 2014), documentary motion picture.
118 Steve Holland, speaking in ibid.
119 Melony Armstrong, speaking in ibid.
120 Steve Holland, speaking in ibid.
121 Steve Holland, speaking in ibid.
122 Emily Wagster Pettus, "Mississippi Lawmakers Asked to Deregulate Hair Braiding," Associated Press Newswire, March 6, 2005.
123 Carpenter and Ross, *Melony Armstrong, African Hairbraider*; Carpenter, "Effects of Entrepreneurship."
124 Raspberry, "'Hidebound and Ridiculous' Regulators."
125 Taalib din Uqdah, quoted in Michelle Malkin, "Cornrows and Capitalism," *Seattle Times*, June 6, 1997.
126 Dana Calvo, "African Hairbraiders Challenge State Cosmetology Licensing Laws," Associated Press Newswire, January 28, 1997.
127 Lena Williams, "The Battle of the Braid Brigade," *New York Times*, January 26, 1997.
128 Bob von Sternberg, "Hair Braiders Celebrate Victory," *Star Tribune*, May 17, 2006.

129 David Hawley, "Hair Braiding Rules Fall; State Will No Longer Require License," *St. Paul Pioneer Press*, May 17, 2006.
130 Craig Westover, "Minnesota License Requirements Often Don't Line Up with Reality," *St. Paul Pioneer Press*, April 27, 2005.
131 Lillian Anderson, quoted in Sternberg, "Hair Braiders Celebrate Victory."
132 Anderson v. Minnesota Board of Barber and Cosmetologist Examiners, No. 05-5467 (Minn. Dist. Ct., Fourth Judicial Dist., June 10, 2005) (order granting permanent injunction).
133 "Your License, Please?," *Las Vegas Review-Journal*, October 20, 1997.
134 Bell, "Braiding Cases."
135 Quoted in Williams, "The Battle of the Braid Brigade."
136 Elaine Rucker, quoted in Harold Fischer, "Specialist in Braids Opposes Licensing, *Arizona Daily Star*, December 9, 2003.
137 Gloria Lau, "A Hair-Brained Scheme: Don't Like Competition? How about Getting Laws Passed to Keep It Out?," *Forbes*, October 20, 1997, 220.
138 Bell, "Braiding Cases"; Lau, "Hair-Brained Scheme."
139 Jones, "Hair Police State."
140 C. Barnes & Co., *Barnes Reports: U.S. Beauty Salons Industry* (NAICS 812112) (Woolwich, ME, 2012); First Research, *Industry Profile: Hair Care Services* (New York: Dun & Bradstreet, 2014); "Barbers, Hairdressers, and Cosmetologists: Job Outlook," Bureau of Labor Statistics, December 17, 2015, http://www.bls.gov/ooh/personal-care-and-service/barbers-hairdressers-and-cosmetologists.htm#tab-6; *Economic Snapshot of the Salon and Spa Industry*, Professional Beauty Association, August 2013, https://probeauty.org/docs/advocacy/2013_Economic_Snapshot_of_the_Salon_Industry.pdf.
141 "A Case of Regulatory Abuse," *Orange County Register*, August 23, 1999.

CHAPTER 4 ■ DESIGNED TO EXCLUDE: THE INTERIOR DESIGN CARTEL'S HOUSE OF LIES

1 "Local Interior Designer Sherry Franzoy Wins Award in National Competition," *Las Cruces Sun-News*, June 12, 2009.
2 Decorating Den Interiors formerly operated under the name Interiors by Decorating Den.
3 "Sherry Franzoy Recognized for Interior Design Business," *Las Cruces Sun-News*, May 26, 2014.
4 Ibid.
5 Todd J. Gillman, "Architects Fight D.C. Law Licensing Interior Designers," *Washington Post*, April 24, 1987; Stephen MacDonald, "The Infighting over Interiors between Architects and Designers," *St. Petersburg Times*, May 31, 1987; "Move to License Interior Designers," *New York Times*, January 23, 1986.
6 Rita Reif, "Post-World War II Building Boom Sparked Rapid Rise of Interior Design," *New York Times*, October 3, 1959.
7 Jane H. Guice, "The Propensity of State Legislatures to License Interior Designers," *Journal of Interior Design* 19, no. 2 (1993).
8 Reif, "Post-World War II Building Boom."
9 Allan Schulte, "Interior Designers May Soon Be Licensed," *Boston Globe*,

June 27, 1968; American Society of Interior Designers, *The History of ASID* (Washington, DC: American Society of Interior Designers, 2005); Marilyn Corson Whitney, "A History of the Professionalization of Interior Design Viewed through Three Case Studies of the Process of Licensure" (doctoral dissertation, Virginia Polytechnic Institute and State University, 2008).

10 Schulte, "Interior Designers"; American Society of Interior Designers, *History of ASID*; Whitney, "Professionalization of Interior Design."

11 Schulte, "Interior Designers"; American Society of Interior Designers, *History of ASID*; Sharon Marie Mariscal Bootman, "The Licensing and Certification of Interior Designers in the United States" (master's thesis, University of Arizona, 1992).

12 Quoted in Schulte, "Interior Designers."

13 Ibid.

14 Terence M. Green, "Interior Designers Seek Professional Recognition," *Los Angeles Times*, February 23, 1975.

15 James May, "LETTERS; To License or Not," *New York Times*, February 12, 1987.

16 "Two Design Groups Vote to Consolidate," *Los Angeles Times*, July 14, 1974.

17 Quoted in Linda Gillan, "Red Tape Increasing: Decorators Face Need for Business Know-How," *Los Angeles Times*, August 7, 1977.

18 American Society of Interior Designers, *History of ASID*; Buie Harwood, "NCIDQ's Early History: Important Developments from 1970 to 1990," *Journal of Interior Design* 38, no. 2 (2013).

19 National Council for Interior Design Qualification, *Guidelines for the Statutory Licensing of Interior Design Professionals* (New York: National Council for Interior Design Qualification, 1974).

20 Ibid., 11.

21 Ibid.

22 American Society of Interior Designers, *History of ASID*.

23 Ibid.

24 Gail Hayes Adams, quoted in ibid., 35.

25 MacDonald, "Infighting over Interiors"; "Move to License Interior Designers," *New York Times*.

26 Stephen MacDonald, "Building Battle: Interior Designers Pitted against Architects in Licensing Dispute," *Wall Street Journal*, May 6, 1987.

27 American Society of Interior Designers, *History of ASID*.

28 Ibid.

29 Ibid.

30 Ibid.

31 Patricia Leigh Brown, "Certified: Interior Designers to Be Licensed," *St. Louis Post-Dispatch*, August 9, 1990.

32 Ibid.; Patricia Leigh Brown, "A Legal Leg for Designers," *New York Times*, August 2, 1990; "Capital Adopts Law on Interior Design," *New York Times*, January 29, 1987; "Move to License Interior Designers," *New York Times*.

33 "Law on Interior Design," *New York Times*; Jura Koncius, "License to Design," *Washington Post*, February 19, 1987.

34 Whitney, "Professionalization of Interior Design."

35 Koncius, "License to Design."

36 Whitney, "Professionalization of Interior Design."
37 Ibid.
38 Ibid.
39 Quoted in ibid., 157.
40 Gillman, "Architects Fight D.C. Law"; Whitney, "Professionalization of Interior Design."
41 Carol Thompson, quoted in Gillman, "Architects Fight D.C. Law."
42 Valerie Barry, quoted in ibid.
43 Whitney, "Professionalization of Interior Design."
44 Koncius, "License to Design."
45 Gillman, "Architects Fight D.C. Law."
46 Ibid.
47 Quoted in "Law on Interior Design," *New York Times.*
48 Quoted in Denise A. Guerin, "Issues Facing Interior Design Education in the Twenty-First Century," *Journal of Inferior Design Education and Research* 17, no. 2 (1992), 11.
49 Quoted in American Society of Interior Designers, *History of ASID*, 49.
50 Quoted in ibid., 51.
51 Ibid.
52 Whitney, "Professionalization of Interior Design."
53 Ibid.
54 Ibid.
55 Ibid.
56 Ibid., 180.
57 Ibid.
58 Quoted in ibid., 181.
59 Ibid.
60 "In order for the profession to grow and advance, you must make an effort to educate legislators and the public about the scope and benefits of interior design," says an ASID Web page for students. "Student Legislative: Legislation, Politics and the Interior Designer," American Society of Interior Designers, accessed June 8, 2016, http://asidcanv.org/students/student-legislative-resources/. See also Marilyn Roberts, "President's Message," *Inside* 10, no. 2 (2008); Indiana Professional Licensing Agency, "Written Testimony: Connie Jung—Former President of the Interior Design Coalition of Indiana," in *SEA 421 Report: Establishing a Process for Self-Certification Registration, A Playbook for Future Occupational Regulation in Indiana* (September 2014), IN.gov, http://www.in.gov/pla/files/IPLALegislative_Report_-_Self-Certification_Registration.pdf; "How a Bill Becomes a Law," Interior Design Legislative Coalition of Pennsylvania, accessed June 30, 2016, http://www.idlcpa.org/index.php/11-legislative-info; Whitney, "Professionalization of Interior Design."
61 Adrienne Alexander, Chris Henjum, Jeremy Jones, Meg Luger-Nikolai, Aaron Rosenberger, and Caro Smith, *Regulating Interior Designers: Overview and Analysis of Public Policy and Law* (Minneapolis: University of Minnesota, 2009).
62 David E. Harrington and Jared Treber, *Designed to Exclude: How Interior Design Insiders Use Government Power to Exclude Minorities and Burden Consumers* (Arlington: Institute for Justice, 2009).

63 Dick M. Carpenter, "Regulation through Titling Laws: A Case Study of Occupational Regulation," *Regulation and Governance* 2, no. 3 (2008).

64 These reports include: In Colorado: M. Michael Cooke, *Interior Designers* (Denver: Colorado Department of Regulatory Agencies, Office of Policy and Research, 2000); Colorado Department of Regulatory Agencies, *Optical and Contact Lens Dispensers: 1995 Sunrise Review* (Denver: Colorado Department of Regulatory Agencies, 1995); Colorado Department of Regulatory Agencies, *2008 Sunrise Review: Interior Designers* (Denver: Colorado Department of Regulatory Agencies, 2008); in Georgia: William H. Roper, *Review of Senate Bill 305 Which Proposes to License Interior Designers in Georgia* (Atlanta: Georgia Occupational Regulation Review Council, 1989); in South Carolina: State Reorganization Commission, *Review of Occupational Registration and Licensing for Interior Designers* (Columbia, SC: State Reorganization Commission, 1991); in Virginia: Michael W. Cannady, *The Study of the Need for Certifying Interior Designers* (Richmond: Virginia Board of Commerce, 1988); in Washington: Washington State Department of Licensing, *Sunrise Review of Interior Designers* (Olympia: Washington State Department of Licensing, 2005).

65 Roper, "Review of Senate Bill 305"; South Carolina State Reorganization Commission, *Occupational Registration and Licensing*; Cooke, *Interior Designers*.

66 Washington State Department of Licensing, *Sunrise Review*.

67 In California: California Department of Consumer Affairs, *Joint Legislative Sunset Review Committee Findings and Recommendations: Review and Evaluation of the Interior Design Certification Program* (Sacramento: California Department of Consumer Affairs, 1996); in Maryland: Shannon McMahon and Cheryl Matricciana, *Sunset Review: Evaluation of the State Board of Certified Interior Designers* (Annapolis, MD: Department of Legislative Services Office of Policy Analysis, 2002); in Texas: Carrie Holley-Hurt, Steven Ogle, Michelle Downie, Faye Rencher, Janet Wood, and Joe Walraven, *Sunset Staff Review of the Texas Board of Architectural Examiners, Texas Board of Professional Engineers, Self-Directed Semi-Independent Agency Project Act* (Austin: Sunset Advisory Commission, 2012).

68 George Voinovich, quoted in Whitney, "Professionalization of Interior Design," 83–84.

69 Bill Teets, quoted in Tom Ford, "Lack of Regulation Seals Fate of Interior Designer," *Crain's Cleveland Business*, April 20, 1998, 4.

70 Scott Olson, "Interior Designers Want Certification Option, Architects Oppose Bill That Also Gives Them Authority to Approve Drawings," *Indianapolis Business Journal* 26, no. 7 (April 25, 2005); Scott Olson, "Interior Designers Push for Certification," *Indianapolis Business Journal* 25, no. 1 (March 15, 2005).

71 *Veto Message, SEA 490* (State of Indiana) (2007) (Mitch Daniels, governor), https://static.votesmart.org/static/vetotext/14776.pdf.

72 *Veto Message of Senate Bill 84* (State of Colorado) (2007) (Bill Ritter, governor), https://static.votesmart.org/static/vetotext/14651.pdf.

73 Melanie Spencer, "The Inside Scoop on Legislation to Regulate Interior Design," *Austin American-Statesman*, May 3, 2007.

74 Brown, "Legal Leg for Designers."

75 Bootman, "Licensing and Certification of Interior Designers"; Sarah Ashley Chaney, "Interior Design Identity: A Proposal to Shift Public Perception with Public Relations Strategies" (master's thesis, Florida State University, 2007).
76 Quoted in Brown, "Interior Designers To Be Licensed."
77 Quoted in Brown, "Legal Leg for Designers."
78 Quoted in Whitney, "Professionalization of Interior Design."
79 Beverly Bryant, "New Law Defines Role of Interior Decorator," *Oklahoman*, June 25, 2006; "Interior Designers Elect Officers, Set Legislative Goals," *Oklahoman*, November 27, 2004; Julie Wyatt, "Designers, Decorators Fulfill Distinct Roles," *Oklahoman*, July 27, 2006.
80 Richard Mize, "Questions and Answers with Laura Tribble: State Interior Designers Act Regulates, Certifies Title of 'Interior Designer,'" *Oklahoman*, June 29, 2006.
81 Kim Paddleford, quoted in Bryant, "New Law Defines Role."
82 Melanie Spencer, "Texas Decorators Sue to Use Title 'Interior Designer,'" *Austin American-Statesman*, January 24, 2008; Chaney, "Interior Design Identity."
83 Ibid.
84 Ibid.
85 Whitney, "Professionalization of Interior Design."
86 Chaney, "Interior Design Identity."
87 Dollar amounts and uses were taken from ASID's 990 forms.
88 Harrington and Treber, *Designed to Exclude.*
89 Catherine H. Lovell and Hanria R. Egan, "Fiscal Notes and Mandate Reimbursement in the Fifty States," *Public Budgeting & Finance* 3, no. 3 (1983).
90 *Interior Design and Licensure Board* (fiscal impact report, last updated March 5, 2007), 1–2, New Mexico Legislature, http://www.nmlegis.gov/Sessions/07%20Regular/firs/SB0535.pdf.
91 Amanda L. Husson, "Make Your Visitors Feel Right at Home," *Las Cruces Sun-News*, September 28, 2007.
92 S. Derrickson Moore, "What's Cooking at the Las Cruces Home and Garden Show?," *Las Cruces Sun-News*, March 7, 2009.
93 "Local Interior Designer Sherry Franzoy," *Las Cruces Sun-News.*
94 "Sherry Franzoy Recognized," *Las Cruces Sun-News.*
95 Ibid.
96 Madeleine McDermott Hamm, "Design Line," *Houston Chronicle*, January 24, 1993.
97 Melanie Spencer, "Interior Decorators Sue State over 'Designer' Designation," *Austin American-Statesman*, May 10, 2007.
98 Spencer, "Inside Scoop on Legislation."
99 Ibid.
100 Ibid.
101 Ibid.
102 Donna Stockton-Hicks, quoted in ibid.
103 Ibid.
104 Vickee Byrum, quoted in Dick M. Carpenter, *Designing Cartels: How Industry Insiders Cut Out Competition* (Arlington: Institute for Justice), 1.

105 Vickee Byrum, quoted in ibid., 1.
106 Vickee Byrum, quoted in ibid., 1.
107 Spencer, "Interior Decorators Sue."
108 Donna Vining, quoted in ibid.
109 Dick M. Carpenter, "Who's Misleading Whom? Defining Titles in Occupations 'On the Make,'" *National Social Science Journal* 35, no. 2 (2011).
110 Taken from e-mail on file with the authors. In addition to sending the e-mail, Roberts reissued her plea the following year in TAID's newsletter, asking for members to find "examples of how people who have not been educated on how to protect the health and safety of the public have actually endangered or potentially endangered the users of code regulated public spaces.... We MUST have this information to give to legislators this session." Roberts, "President's Message," 1.
111 Marilyn Roberts, speaking in "No Harm from Unregulated Interior Designers in Texas Says Marilyn Roberts," YouTube video, 0:43, originally broadcast on *Austin News*, KXAN-NBC, February 18, 2009, posted by Institute of Justice, March 13, 2009, https://www.youtube.com/watch?v=zTzVfpoFL9A.
112 Helen Anders, "Designers Lobby to Limit Where Decorators Work," *Austin American-Statesman*, February 18, 2009.
113 Texas Ethics Commission, *GPAC: General Purpose Committee Campaign Finance Report* (January 19, 2008), Texas Association of Interior Design PAC, http://204.65.203.5/public/361888.pdf; Texas Ethics Commission, *General Purpose Committee Campaign Finance Report* (April 28, 2009), Texas Association of Interior Designers PAC; Texas Ethics Commission, *Correction Affidavit for Political Committee* (August 1, 2008), Texas Association of Interior Design PAC, http://204.65.203.5/public/411527.pdf; Texas Ethics Commission, *GPAC: General-Purpose Committee Campaign Finance Report* (October 11, 2008), Texas Association of Interior Design PAC, http://204.65.203.5/public/388337.pdf; Texas Ethics Commission, *GPAC: General-Purpose Committee Campaign Finance Report* (January 12, 2009), Texas Association of Interior Design PAC, http://204.65.203.5/public/399183.pdf.
114 "House Research Organization Bill Analysis" (document, April 6, 2009), Legislative Reference Library of Texas, http://www.lrl.state.tx.us/scanned/hroBillAnalyses/81-0/HB1484.PDF.
115 "House Journal: Eighty-First Legislature, Regular Session; Proceedings" (summary of proceedings, April 7, 2009), Texas House of Representatives, http://www.journals.house.state.tx.us/hjrnl/81r/pdf/81RDAY45FINAL.PDF#page=8.
116 "Senate Journal: Eighty-First Legislature, Regular Session; Proceedings" (summary of proceedings, April 27, 2009), Texas House of Representatives, http://www.journals.senate.state.tx.us/sjrnl/81r/pdf/81RSJ04-27-F.PDF#page=8.
117 H.B. 1484, Legislative Session 81(R) (2009), http://www.capitol.state.tx.us/BillLookup/Actions.aspx?LegSess=81R&Bill=HB1484; Byrum v. Landreth, 566 F.3d 442 (5th Cir. 2009).
118 Lee Howard, "Professionals Fight Law to Restrict Use of 'Interior Designer,'" the *Day*, October 12, 2008.
119 Ibid.

120 Ibid.
121 Roberts v. Farrell, 630 F. Supp. 2d 242, 252 (D. Conn. 2009).
122 Alexander et al., *Regulating Interior Designers.*
123 Ibid.
124 Jeffrey J. Selingo, "How Job Licensing Increases the Cost of College," *Washington Post*, January 29, 2015, http://www.washingtonpost.com/news/grade-point/wp/2015/01/29/how-job-licensing-increases-the-cost-of-college/.
125 Quoted in "Pushback Felt in Effort to License Interior Designers," *Hutchinson Leader*, October 31, 2013.
126 Jeanne Malmgren, "Changes in Laws Should Help Consumers," *St. Petersburg Times*, July 28, 1991.
127 "Disciplinary Cases," Smith, Thompson, Shaw, Minacci & Colón, P.A., accessed June 8, 2016, http://www.stslaw.com/practice-areas/board-of-architecture/disciplinary-cases.
128 Arian Campo-Flores, "In Florida, Interior Decorators Have Designs on Deregulation," *Wall Street Journal*, April 15, 2011, http://www.wsj.com/articles/SB10001424052748703551304576260742209315376.
129 Eva Locke, telephone conversation with Dick Carpenter, February 13, 2015.
130 Ibid.
131 Federal Reserve, cited in Associated Press, "Florida among States Hardest Hit by Great Recession as Wealth of U.S. Families Shrinks to 1992 Levels," *Palm Beach Post*, June 11, 2012, http://www.palmbeachpost.com/news/business/florida-among-states-hardest-hit-by-drop-in-net-wo/nPRBr/.
132 Eva Locke, telephone conversation with Dick Carpenter, February 13, 2015.
133 Eva Locke, quoted in Lloyd Dunkelberger, "Interior Design Law Is Disputed," *Sarasota Herald-Tribune*, September 16, 2011.
134 Katie Sanders, "Business Group Says Florida Is One of Three States That Regulates Commercial Interior Designers," *St. Petersburg Times*, March 18, 2011; Locke v. Shore, 682 F. Supp. 2d 1283 (N.D. Fla. 2010), *aff'd*, 634 F.3d 1185 (11th Cir. 2011).
135 ASID filed an amicus curiae brief with the court in support of the law. "Circuit Court Upholds Florida's Interior Design Licensure" (news release, 2011), American Society for Interior Designers, accessed June 8, 2016, https://www.asid.org/content/circuit-court-upholds-florida%E2%80%99s-interior-design-licensure#.VhU7nvlViko.
136 Locke v. Shore, 634 F.3d 1185, 1195 (11th Cir. 2011).
137 Zac Anderson, "Legislative Session Reviews Debate on Jobs," *Herald-Tribune* Politics, January 14, 2012, http://politics.heraldtribune.com/2012/01/14/legislative-session-renews-debate-on-jobs/; Tami Luhby, "States Look to Repeal 'Job-Killing' Regulations," CNN Money, March 4, 2011, http://money.cnn.com/2011/03/04/news/economy/state_regulation_repeal_governor/.
138 Janet Zink, "Fewer Professions on List for Deregulation Proposal," *St. Petersburg Times*, May 3, 2011; Luhby, "'Job-Killing' Regulations."
139 Campo-Flores, "Designs on Deregulation."
140 Ibid.
141 Ibid.
142 Eva Locke, telephone conversation with Dick Carpenter, February 13, 2015.

143 Michelle Earley, quoted in Campo-Flores, "Designs on Deregulation."
144 Sanders, "Florida Is One of Three States"; Zink, "Deregulation Proposal."
145 Dunkelberger, "Interior Design Law Is Disputed."
146 *Locke*, 682 F. Supp.
147 Steven M. Simpson, "Judicial Abdication and the Rise of Special Interests," *Chapman Law Review* 6 (2003).
148 James Madison, quoted in Robert S. Alley, ed., *James Madison on Religious Liberty* (Amherst, NY: Prometheus Books, 1985), 73.
149 James Madison, "The Federalist No. 48: These Departments Should Not Be So Far Separated As To Have No Constitutional Control over Each Other" (essay, February 1, 1788), Congress.gov, https://www.congress.gov/resources/display/content/The+Federalist+Papers.
150 Chaddock v. Day, 42 N.W. 977, 978 (Mich. 1889).
151 Jonathan Rauch, *Government's End: Why Washington Stopped Working* (New York: Public Affairs, 1999).
152 Simpson, "Judicial Abdication."

CHAPTER 5 ■ TO SPEAK FREELY, PEE IN THIS CUP

1 William T. Sherman, quoted in Carl Sandburg, *Abraham Lincoln: The Prarie Years and the War Years* (Pleasantville, NY: Reader's Digest Association, 1954), 626.
2 William T. Sherman, quoted in Jean V. Berlin and Brooks D. Simpson, ed., *Sherman's Civil War: Selected Correspondence of William T. Sherman, 1860–1865* (Chapel Hill: University of North Carolina Press, 1999), 731.
3 Bruce Catton, *The American Heritage Short History of the Civil War* (New York: Laurel, 1960).
4 William Tecumsah Sherman, *General Sherman's Official Account of His Great March through Georgia and the Carolinas…* (New York: Bunce & Huntington, 1865).
5 John P. Dyer, "Northern Relief For Savannah during Sherman's Occupation," *Journal of Southern History* 19, no. 4 (1953); Sherman, *General Sherman's Official Account.*
6 Reed W. Smith, "How Two Veteran Journalists in Opposing Media Encouraged a Sense of Community in a Georgia Town," *Journalism History* 34, no. 2 (2008).
7 Ibid.
8 "General Characteristics of the Population: 1970," in *1970 Census of Population and Housing: Census Tracts, Savannah, Ga., Standard Metropolitan Statistical Area* (Washington, DC: US Government Printing Office, 1971–72), 1–6, Hathi Trust Digital Library, accessed June 8, 2016, http://babel.hathitrust.org/cgi/pt?id=umn.31951d02969204n;view=1up;seq=11;size=175.
9 "Quick Facts: United States," United States Census Bureau, accessed June 9, 2016, http://quickfacts.census.gov/qfd/states/13/1369000.html.
10 Smith, "Two Veteran Journalists in Opposing Media."
11 Glenn W. Gentry, "Walking with the Dead: The Place of Ghost Walk Tourism in Savannah, Georgia," *Southeastern Geographer* 47, no. 2 (2007).

12 John Berendt, *Midnight in the Garden of Good and Evil* (Random House: New York, 1994), 28, 34.

13 Ibid., 36.

14 Paula Anca Farca, "White, Straight Lady Savannah of John Berendt's Midnight in the Garden of Good and Evil," *Notes on Contemporary Literature* 37, no. 3 (2007).

15 Clara Juncker, "Simulacrum Savannah: Midnight in the Garden of Good and Evil," *Literature Film Quarterly* 33, no. 3 (2005).

16 Glenn W. Gentry and Derek H. Alderman, "'A City Built upon Its Dead': The Intersection of Past and Present through Ghost Walk Tourism in Savannah, Georgia," *South Carolina Review* 47, no. 2 (2015).

17 Carl Solana Weeks, "Midnight in the Garden of Good and Evil," in *NEW GEORGIA Encyclopedia*, last modified September 16, 2014, http://www.georgiaencyclopedia.org/articles/arts-culture/midnight-garden-good-and-evil.

18 Lee Thomas, *The Qualitative and Quantitative Benefits of Film-Induced Tourism in Georgia* (Atlanta: Georgia Film, Music & Digital Entertainment Office, 2008).

19 Ibid.

20 Gentry and Alderman, "City Built upon Its Dead."

21 Alan Blinder, "Lawsuit May Reshape Tourist Industry in History-Rich Savannah," *New York Times*, December 20, 2014, http://www.nytimes.com/2014/12/21/us/lawsuit-may-reshape-tourist-industry-in-history-rich-savannah.html?_r=1. According to City Council meeting minutes from 1978, the licensing ordinance was first considered on January 12, with W. D. Salter, operator of Savannah Scenic Tour Service, being the only person present to speak on behalf of the regulation. It is not unusual for a proponent to be the only person in attendance to testify in favor of a licensing ordinance. When the proposed regulation was considered again the following month, Salter was joined by Joan Summer, of the Historic Savannah Foundation, who objected to a section prohibiting tours between the hours of 4:30 p.m. and 6:00 p.m. She suggested the section would create a decided economic hardship, since many of her organization's tours could take place at any hour of the day. The section was later removed. The meetings provide no indication that City Council members discussed evidence of the need for regulation or that anyone appeared to oppose the license.

22 "Occupational Employment Statistics: OES Data," Bureau of Labor Statistics, last modified April 14, 2016, http://www.bls.gov/oes/2000/oes_7520.htm.

23 "Occupational Employment Statistics: May 2015 Metropolitan and Nonmetropolitan Area Occupational Employment and Wage Estimates; Savannah, GA," Bureau of Labor Statistics, last modified March 30, 2016, http://www.bls.gov/oes/current/oes_42340.htm.

24 "Tour Guide Study Manual & Permitting Process," City of Savannah, June 9, 2016, http://www.savannahga.gov/index.aspx?NID=149; Eric Curl, "Washington Court Ruling Won't Impact Savannah Tours," *Savannah Morning News*, July 16, 2014, http://savannahnow.com/news/2014-07-15/city-washington-court-ruling-wont-impact-savannah-tours.

25 David Cogswell, "Tour Guide Licensing Issue Heads to Supreme Court," *Travel Pulse*, November 19, 2014, http://www.travelpulse.com/news/tour-operators/tour-guide-licensing-issue-heads-to-supreme-court.html.

26 "Sample Test Questions," 1, City of Savannah, accessed May 23, 2016, http://www.savannahga.gov/DocumentCenter/View/4363.
27 Ibid., 2.
28 G. G. Rigsby, "Savannah Tour Guide Manual Is Detailed; Test Is Hard," *Savannah Morning News*, August 14, 2011, http://m.savannahnow.com/exchange/2011-08-14/savannah-tour-guide-manual-detailed-test-hard#gsc.tab=0.
29 Curl, "Washington Court Ruling."
30 James Caskey, quoted in ibid.
31 Victoria Bekiempis, "Should Tour Guides Be Licensed?," *Newsweek*, November 27, 2014. http://www.newsweek.com/should-tour-guides-be-licensed-286723.
32 Dan Leger, telephone conversation with Dick Carpenter, May 27, 2015.
33 MJTX15,"'History Teacher Loves the Tour': Review of Savannah Dan Walking Tours," *TripAdvisor* (blog), May 22, 2015, https://www.tripadvisor.com/ShowUserReviews-g60814-d1463308-r273813307-Savannah_Dan_Walking_Tours-Savannah_Georgia.html.
34 Cali4nia Dreamer, "'Don't Miss Savannah Dan…': Review of Savannah Dan Walking Tours," *TripAdvisor* (blog), May 20, 2015, https://www.tripadvisor.com/ShowUserReviews-g60814-d1463308-r273388342-Savannah_Dan_Walking_Tours-Savannah_Georgia.html.
35 Ibid.
36 Dan Leger, telephone conversation with Dick Carpenter, May 27, 2015.
37 Ibid.
38 Ibid.
39 Kathleen Lingle Pond, *The Professional Guide: Dynamics of Tour Guiding* (New York: Van Nostrand Reinhold, 1993).
40 Jeroen Bryon, "Tour Guides as Storytellers—from Selling to Sharing," *Scandinavian Journal of Hospitality and Tourism* 12, no. 1 (2012).
41 According to the US Bureau of Labor and Statistics, tour guides make an average hourly wage of $12.56, or $26,120 annually. "Occupational Employment and Wages, May 2015," Bureau of Labor Statistics, last modified March 30, 2016, http://www.bls.gov/oes/current/oes397011.htm. See also Jonathan R. Wynn, "City Tour Guides: Urban Alchemists at Work," *City & Community* 9, no. 2 (2010).
42 Pond, *Professional Guide.*
43 Ibid.
44 Athinodoros Chronis, "Coconstructing Heritage at the Gettysburg Storyscape," *Annals of Tourism Research* 32, no. 2 (2005).
45 Pond, *Professional Guide.*
46 Suzanne B. Schell, "On Interpretation and Historic Sites," *Journal of Museum Education* 10, no. 3 (1985).
47 "Occupational Employment and Wages, May 2015," Bureau of Labor Statistics, last modified March 30, 2016, http://www.bls.gov/oes/current/oes397011.htm.
48 Beth A. Wielde Heidelberg, "Managing Ghosts: Exploring Local Government Involvement in Dark Tourism," *Journal of Heritage Tourism* 10, no. 1 (2015).
49 Bryon, "Tour Guides as Storytellers"; Rosemary Black and Betty Weiler, "Quality Assurance and Regulatory Mechanisms in the Tour Guiding Industry: A Systematic Review," *Journal of Tourism Studies* 16, no. 1 (2005).

50 Bridget Lidy, quoted in Blinder, "Lawsuit May Reshape Tourist Industry."
51 Doreen Carvajal, "Now! Read the True (More or Less) Story!; Publishers and Authors Debate the Boundaries of Nonfiction," *New York Times*, February 24, 1998, http://www.nytimes.com/1998/02/24/books/now-read-true-more-less-story-publishers-authors-debate-boundaries-nonfiction.html?pagewanted=all.
52 Penny Colman, "A New Way to Look at Literature: A Visual Model for Analyzing Fiction and Nonfiction Texts,"*Language Arts* 84, no. 3 (2007).
53 Ralph Keyes, *The Post-Truth Era: Dishonesty and Deception in Contemporary Life* (New York: St. Martin's Press, 2004), 151.
54 Phil Sellers, quoted in Julia Ritchey, "Tour Guides File Lawsuit over Savannah's Licensing Requirements," *Savannah Morning News*, November 18, 2014.
55 At the time of this writing, those individuals include Adam Wilkins, the owner of Oglethorpe Tours; Vaughnette Goode-Walker, the owner of Footprints of Savannah Walking Tours; Charles Brazil, the general manager of Old Town Trolley Tours; and Jamie Caskey, the owner of Cobblestone Tours. The fifth member, Eric Meyerhoff, is married to Harriet Meyerhoff, the owner of Personalized Tours of Savannah.
56 Phil Sellers, quoted in Julia Ritchey, "Amid Tour Industry Growth, a New Resource for Would-Be Guides," *Savannah Morning News*, November 5, 2014, http://savannahnow.com/exchange/2014-11-04/amid-tour-industry-growth-new-resource-would-be-guides/.
57 Sidney L. Carroll and Robert J. Gaston, "Occupational Restrictions and the Quality of Service Received: Some Evidence," *Southern Economic Journal* 47, no. 4 (1981); Stanley J. Gross, *Professional Licensure and Quality: The Evidence* (Washington, DC: Cato Institute, 1984); Morris M. Kleiner, "Occupational Licensing," *Journal of Economic Perspectives* 14, no. 4 (2000); Morris M. Kleiner, *Licensing Occupations: Ensuring Quality or Restricting Competition* (Kalamazoo, MI: Upjohn Institute, 2006).
58 Milton Friedman, *Capitalism and Freedom* (Chicago: University of Chicago Press, 1962).
59 Gross, *Professional Licensure and Quality.*
60 Carroll and Gaston, "Occupational Restrictions and Quality of Service."
61 Kathryn Healey, "The Effect of Licensure on Clinical Laboratory Effectiveness: With Special Reference to Its Effect on Quality of Output" (PhD doctoral diss., University of California, Los Angeles, 1973).
62 John J. Phelan, *Economic Report on the Regulation of the Television Repair Industry in Louisiana and California* (Washington, DC: U.S. Government Printing Office, 1974).
63 Carroll and Gaston, "Occupational Restrictions and Quality of Service."
64 Ibid.
65 Ibid.
66 Ibid.
67 Carroll and Gaston, "Occupational Restrictions and Quality of Service."
68 William D. White and Theodore R. Marmor, "New Occupations, Old Demands: The Public Regulation of Paraprofessionals," *Journal of Policy Analysis and Management* 1, no. 2 (1982).
69 Sidney L. Carroll and Robert J. Gaston, "Barriers to Occupational Licensing

of Veterinarians and the Incidence of Animal Disease," *Agricultural Economic Review* 30 (1978); ibid.

70 Chris Paul, "Physician Licensure Legislation and the Quality of Medical Care," *Atlantic Economic Journal* 12, no. 4 (1984).

71 Morris M. Kleiner and Daniel L. Petree, "Unionizing and Licensing of Public School Teachers: Impact on Wages and Educational Output," in *When Public Sector Workers Unionize*, ed. Richard B. Freeman and Casey Ichniowski (Chicago: University of Chicago Press, 1988).

72 Ibid.

73 Joshua D. Angrist and Jonathan Guryan, "Does Teacher Testing Raise Teacher Quality? Evidence from State Certification Requirements," *Economics of Education Review* 27 (2008).

74 Morris M. Kleiner and Robert T. Kudrle, "Does Regulation Affect Economic Outcomes? The Case of Dentistry," *Journal of Law and Economics* 43, no. 2 (2000).

75 Morris M. Kleiner and Richard M. Todd, *Mortgage Broker Regulations That Matter: Analyzing Earnings, Employment, and Outcomes for Consumers* (Cambridge, MA: National Bureau of Economic Research, 2007).

76 David Skarbek, "Occupational Licensing and Asymmetric Information: Post-Hurricane Evidence from Florida," *Cato Journal* 28, no. 1 (2008).

77 Ibid., 73.

78 Michelle Freenor, telephone conversation with Dick Carpenter, May 28, 2015.

79 Ibid.

80 Ibid.

81 Lupus Foundation of America, accessed June 9, 2016, http://www.lupus.org/.

82 Michelle Freenor, telephone conversation with Dick Carpenter, May 28, 2015.

83 Ibid.

84 Ibid.

85 Dan Leger, telephone conversation with Dick Carpenter, May 27, 2015.

86 "Savannah's *Original* Ghost Tour," Ghost Talk Ghost Walk, accessed May 23, 2016, http://ghosttalkghostwalk.com/.

87 The city imposes a preservation fee of $1 per person, per tour that must be collected by every guide.

88 Jean Soderlind, telephone conversation with Dick Carpenter, May 28, 2015.

89 Ibid.

90 Conceived in 1966, the Model Cities Program was an element of Johnson's Great Society and War on Poverty. It created 150 five-year experiments to develop new antipoverty programs and alternative forms of municipal government. The program ended in 1974. As a scholarly review described the program, "Model Cities programs were meant to be five-year experiments in new forms of municipal government and to provide greater understanding of the lives of the impoverished, improved methods for dealing with their problems, replication on a larger scale, and ultimately the elimination of urban poverty. On a more practical level, Model Cities served as a safety valve to vent the strident demands of racial minorities, especially urban Latinos and African Americans. This was largely accomplished through the provision of jobs and what amounted to civics training in the mechanics of local politics

and, ultimately, the creation of a new tier of political leadership." Bret A.Weber and Amanda Wallace, "Revealing the Empowerment Revolution: A Literature Review of the Model Cities Program," *Journal of Urban History* 38, no. 1 (201), 174.

91 Jean Soderlind, telephone conversation with Dick Carpenter, May 28, 2015.

92 Ibid.

93 Ibid.

94 Jean Soderlind, telephone conversation with Dick Carpenter, May 28, 2015.

95 Julie Stoiber, "About That History Test... Should City Tour Guides Be Licensed?," *Philadelphia Inquirer*, March 30, 2007, http://articles.philly.com/2007-03-30/news/25237235_1_tour-guides-philadelphia-city-council-meryl-levitz; Tait v. City of Philadelphia, 639 F. Supp. 2d 582 (E.D. Pa. 2009). For some years prior, Avery had gathered anecdotes for the letter by taking tours and noting inaccuracies conveyed by tour guides. "And I didn't reveal that I have been lobbying City Council to educate, test and license Philadelphia tour guides before they are turned loose on the tourists," he said. Ron Avery, "Nuggets of Nonsense: Philadelphia Tour Guides Should Be Educated, Tested and Licensed," *Philadelphia Inquirer*, April 23, 2007, http://articles.philly.com/2007-04-23/news/25241590_1_guides-spruce-street-philadelphia.

96 Stoiber, "Should City Tour Guides Be Licensed?"

97 Blondell Reynolds-Brown, quoted in ibid.

98 Avery, "Nuggets of Nonsense."

99 Stoiber, "Should City Tour Guides Be Licensed?"

100 Ibid.; Avery, "Nuggets of Nonsense."

101 Committee on Parks, Recreation, and Cultural Affairs, "Bill 070229" (Philadelphia: Council of the City of Philadelphia, 2008). Bill 080024 is an ordinance amending chapter 9-200 of the Philadelphia Code, "Commercial Activities on Streets," by adding a new section providing for the certification of tour guides.

102 For a discussion of such regimes, some of which are multiple years in length, see Black and Weiler, "Quality Assurance and Regulatory Mechanisms."

103 "§ 9-214 Tours on the Public Right-of-Way in the Center City Tourist Area...," Philadelphia Decoded, accessed June 9, 2016, http://phillycode.org/9-214/.

104 Committee on Parks, Recreation, and Cultural Affairs, "Bill 070229."

105 Quoted in ibid., 43.

106 Mark Beyerle, quoted in ibid., 71–72. Beyerle also noted how the bill burdened out-of-town tour guides who brought groups from other cities into Philadelphia and how retired guides who still do the occasional tour would be forced out of the market because they likely would not wish to take an exam. Committee on Parks, Recreation, and Cultural Affairs, "Bill 070229."

107 Ron Avery, quoted in ibid., 37.

108 Mike Tait, telephone conversation with Dick Carpenter, May 28, 2015.

109 Mike was joined in the lawsuit by Ann Boulais and Josh Silver.

110 *Tait*, 639 F. Supp. 2d at 596–597.

111 Mike Tait, telephone conversation with Dick Carpenter, May 28, 2015.

112 Ibid.

113 Avery, "Nuggets of Nonsense."

114 Amy Needle, quoted in Stoiber, "Should City Tour Guides Be Licensed?"

115 Pond, *Professional Guide.*

116 Before the 1990s, the phrase "heritage tourism" was virtually unknown. People have always visited historic sites, but the decades since the 1990s have brought explosive growth in heritage tourism. Anne Farrisee, "Heritage Tourism: Telling the Rest of the Story," *Georgia Historical Quarterly* 83, no. 1 (1999); Arline Magnoni and Monica Cable, "Whose Culture Is It Anyway? Anthropological Perspectives on Identity and Representation in the Context of Ethnic and Heritage Tourism," *Journal of Heritage Tourism* 3, no. 4 (2008); Tiya Miles, "Goat Bones in the Basement: A Case of Race, Gender and Haunting in Old Savannah," *South Carolina Review*, 47, no. 2 (2015).

Heritage tourism is a type of tourism focused on the "notion of cultural inheritance preserved in and passed on through historic places." Miles, "Goat Bones in the Basement," 28. Although it is sometimes defined by the nature of the site and its history, or the "personal intention and subjective experience of the tourist who encounters the site in question, 'heritage tourism' generally connotes an activity in which visitors connect with sites (cultural, natural, or built locations) through the hook of 'heritage'—'that which is inherited from the past.'" Miles, "Goat Bones in the Basement," 28.

Although "heritage tourism tends to focus on positive, warmly remembered history" (Heidelberg, "Managing Ghosts," 3), not everyone agrees that it is an accurate presentation of history. As one historian wrote, "Heritage should not be confused with history, although it often is. History convinces by truth; heritage 'exaggerates and omits, candidly invents... and thrives on ignorance and error.' Heritage uses historical tales, but stitches them into unverifiable forms; heritage is not a testable version of the past, but a credulous allegiance, a declaration of faith, an uncritical endorsement. It frequently sets myth above truth—magnificent myth perhaps, but myth nonetheless." Vaughan B. Baker, "Mad, Bad, and Dangerous: Conceptions and Misconceptions of Louisiana's History and Heritage," *Louisiana History* 42, no. 3 (2001), 267–68. For cities that rely on tourism economies, the definition of heritage tourism is largely academic. "Heritage tourists spend more money, stay longer and in more hotels, and are more likely to shop and fly than other tourists. Farrisee, "Heritage Tourism," 102. Consequently, many sites actively compete to meet the demand."

117 Gentry and Alderman, "City Built upon Its Dead."

118 Robert C. Thompson, "'Am I Going to See a Ghost Tonight?': Gettysburg Ghost Tours and the Performance of Belief," *Journal of American Culture* 33, no. 2 (2010).

119 Gentry and Alderman, "City Built upon Its Dead"; Miles, "Goat Bones in the Basement."

120 Gentry and Alderman, "City Built upon Its Dead."

121 Kevin Fox Gotham, "Marketing Mardi Gras: Commodification, Spectacle, and the Political Economy of Tourism in New Orleans," *Urban Studies* 1, no. 7 (2002).

122 Gentry, "Walking with the Dead."

123 Miles, "Goat Bones in the Basement."

124 Thompson, "'Am I Going to See a Ghost Tonight?'"; Original Ghost Tour, accessed June 9, 2016, http://www.ghosttour.com/philadelphia.html.

125 Heidelberg, "Managing Ghosts"; Miles, "Goat Bones in the Basement"; Devon Robbie, "Touring Katrina: Authentic Identities and Disaster Tourism in New Orleans," *Journal of Heritage Tourism* 3, no. 4 (2008).
126 Gentry and Alderman, "City Built upon Its Dead."
127 Heidelberg, "Managing Ghosts."
128 On Wednesday, November 13, 1974, twenty-three-year-old Ronald DeFeo Jr. entered Henry's Bar in Amityville and declared, "You got to help me! I think my mother and father are shot!" Indeed they were; DeFeo himself had shot and killed them and his four siblings. He was convicted and sent to prison for life. The subsequent owners of the house, the Lutzes, lived in it for only twenty-eight days, leaving after claiming to have been terrorized by paranormal phenomena.
129 Peter Imbert, quoted in Lisa Munoz, "Amityville Latest Ghouls: Tourists! Crowds Expected for Remake of Flick," *New York Daily News*, April 10, 2005, http://www.nydailynews.com/archives/boroughs/amityville-s-latest-ghouls-tourists-crowds-expected-remake-flick-article-1.618967.
130 Heidelberg, "Managing Ghosts."
131 Robbie, "Touring Katrina."
132 Phaedra C. Pezzullo, "'This Is the Only Tour That Sells': Tourism, Disaster, and National Identity in New Orleans," *Journal of Tourism and Cultural Change* 7, no. 2 (2009).
133 Ibid.
134 Bryon, "Tour Guides as Storytellers."
135 Stoiber, "Should City Tour Guides Be Licensed?"; see also Bryon, "Tour Guides as Storytellers."
136 Bryon, "Tour Guides as Storytellers."
137 Ibid.
138 Frank Rizzo, quoted in Committee on Parks, Recreation, and Cultural Affairs, "Bill 070229," 13.
139 Emily M. Drew, "Strategies for Antiracist Representation: Ethnic Tourism Guides in Chicago," *Journal of Tourism and Cultural Change* 9, no. 2 (2011).
140 Ibid.
141 Lynnell L. Thomas, "'Roots Run Deep Here': The Construction of Black New Orleans in Post-Katrina Tourism Narratives," *American Quarterly* 61, no. 3 (2009).
142 Mary LaCoste, quoted in Christopher Tidmore, "First Amendment Lawsuit Filed by Local Tour Guides," *Louisiana Weekly*, December 19, 2011, http://www.louisianaweekly.com/first-amendment-lawsuit-filed-by-local-tour-guides/.
143 David Redmon, "Playful Deviance as an Urban Leisure Activity: Secret Selves, Self-Validation, and Entertaining Performances," *Deviant Behavior: An Interdisciplinary Journal* 24 (2003); Catherine Vesey and Frédéric Dimanche, "From Storyville to Bourbon Street: Vice, Nostalgia and Tourism," *Journal of Tourism and Cultural Change* 1, no.1 (2003).
144 Tidmore, "First Amendment Lawsuit."
145 Ibid.
146 Martha Carr, "New Orleans Taxicab Bureau's New Leader Was Taxi Director for Atlanta Police," *Times-Picayune*, June 7, 2011, http://www.nola.com/politics/index.ssf/2011/06/mitch_landrieu_names_new_taxic.html.

147 Tidmore, "First Amendment Lawsuit."
148 Ibid.
149 Ryan Berni, quoted in ibid.
150 Robert Freeland, quoted in "High Court Asked to Rule on Tour-Guide Licensing," Associated Press, November 17, 2014, New Orleans City Business, http://neworleanscitybusiness.com/blog/2014/11/17/high-court-asked-to-rule-on-tour-guide-licensing/.
151 Jonathan R. Wynn, *Walking Tours as Narrative: Recovering the Spatial and Experiential Dynamics in Theories of Culture* (New York: CUNY Graduate Center, 2004).
152 Chronis, "Coconstructing Heritage"; Gentry and Alderman, "City Built upon Its Dead"; Magnoni and Cable, "Whose Culture Is It Anyway?"; Ian McDonnell, *The Role of the Tour Guide in Transferring Cultural Understanding* (Sydney: University of Technology, 2001).
153 Richard D. Knabb, Jamie R. Rhome, and Daniel P. Brown, *Tropical Cyclone Report Hurricane Katrina, 23–30 August 2005* (Washington, DC: National Oceanic and Atmospheric Administration, 2006).
154 Ibid.
155 Pezzullo, "Tourism, Disaster, and National Identity"; Phaedra C. Pezzullo, "Tourists and/as Disasters: Rebuilding, Remembering, and Responsibility in New Orleans," *Tourist Studies* 9, no. 1 (2010); Robbie, "Touring Katrina."
156 Robbie, "Touring Katrina."
157 Pezzullo, "Tourism, Disaster, and National Identity."
158 Ibid.; Pezzullo, "Tourists and/as Disasters."
159 Thomas, "Roots Run Deep Here."
160 Robbie, "Touring Katrina."
161 Ibid.
162 Ibid.
163 Quoted in ibid., 261.
164 Chronis, "Coconstructing Heritage."
165 Bryon, "Tour Guides as Storytellers."
166 Still others embellish stories with exaggeration and myth. As one New York City guide, a history PhD student at Columbia University, described, folklore and stories with questionable facts are common elements in tour guide narratives. That's, in fact, what University of Massachusetts professor Jonathan Wynn found in his study of tour guides in New York City, a city that requires a license to work as a guide. Wynn, "City Tour Guides."

Wynn took tours all over the city, noting what stories guides told and interviewing them afterward to discern the motivation for the various tales. Often, he found the stories were what one guide described as "good natured schmaltz." For example, outside the White Horse Tavern, a guide for a "Literary Pub Crawl and Walking Tour" told the group that in the bar, "Professional psychics still feel the presence of [Welsh poet] Dylan Thomas." Later, at another bar, the guide declared, "It is said that [actor and director] Orson Welles, while working on [the movie] Citizen Kane, left a $1,500 bar tab—and that was at a time when beer was a nickel." On another tour, entitled "The Immigrant Labor Experience," the guide ended the presentation by telling a story that an assassination plot against Leon Trotsky, a Russian Marxist revolutionary, was first hatched at a local cafeteria. After one tour guide told an apocryphal story about how a building in northern Manhattan received its name, Wynn asked the guide about his use of the story: "Well that story has been told and told and told and retold. It may well be true, it may just be a story. You can imagine it getting its name for some reason like that, which is kind of wonderful." Wynn, "City Tour Guides," 153.

Then there is the problem of the uncertainty of history itself. Knowledge of the past is often limited and based on incomplete records and conflicting and biased recollections. Schell, "On Interpretation." For example, an historic home in Augusta, Georgia, popular among tourists, that was for years identified as the prerevolutionary Robert Mackay House was years later discovered to be the 1795 Ezekiel Harris House, requiring tour guides to change their stories significantly. Farrisee, "Heritage Tourism." In another example, much of the present history of Gettysburg can be traced back to highly fragmented and divergent "early accounts of participants in the battle, their diaries and letters. Later, some of the veterans recorded the events in written texts based on their reconstructed memories. Much of the present history developed from these early accounts," meaning the foundation of these stories lies in various soldiers' recollections of the events and thus is contingent on the belief in their truthfulness and accuracy. Chronis, "Coconstructing Heritage." The idea that the history of "Gettysburg is not a fixed entity embedded within an uncontested narrative" suggests that tour guides must choose from a plethora of narratives and conflicting texts and often draw several possible interpretations out of sheer necessity. Ibid., 394.

The same is arguably true of the history of New Orleans, and it will only become more true with the passing of time. Hurricane Katrina is a fairly recent event at the time of this writing, but its history is already being refracted through numerous individual lenses. In the future, the storm will be remembered differently by tour guides, who, without direct experience of it, will rely on disparate sources. Robbie, "Touring Katrina." Eventually, Katrina will be woven into a history of New Orleans already rich in myth, legend, exaggeration, and caricature. Baker, "Mad, Bad, and Dangerous." "That's history," a tour guide explained to Jonathan Wynn, "it's not all true. And the untruths tell a story too—about the context, about what stories get told, and what stories are ignored." Wynn, "City Tour Guides," 153.

167 Tom Nagelin, quoted in Jaquetta White, "History Test Gets N.O. Tour Guides Riled Up," *Times-Picayune*, January 1, 2012, http://www.nola.com/business/index.ssf/2012/01/history_test_gets_no_tour_guid.html.

168 John Reed Swanton, *Indian Tribes of the Lower Mississippi Valley and Adjacent Coast of the Gulf of Mexico* (Washington, DC: Government Printing Office, 1911).

169 White, "N.O. Tour Guides Riled Up."

170 Americana Music Triangle, accessed June 9, 2016, http://americanamusictriangle.com/.

171 Herman Fuselier, "Music Triangle Makes Room for Lafayette," *Lafayette Advertiser*, May 6, 2015, http://www.theadvertiser.com/story/entertainment/music/2015/05/06/music-triangle-makes-room-lafayette/70916182.

172 Candy Kagan, telephone conversation with Dick Carpenter, May 25, 2015.

173 Candace Kagan, quoted in Tania Dall, "Local Tour Guides File Lawsuit against City of New Orleans," WWL-TV, December 31, 2011.
174 Candy Kagan, telephone conversation with Dick Carpenter, May 25, 2015.
175 Ibid.
176 Ibid.
177 Tidmore, "First Amendment Lawsuit."
178 Ibid.
179 Susie Morgan, quoted in Jim Mustian, "N.O. Tour Guide Licensing Constitutional, Appeals Court Says," *New Orleans Advocate*, June 3, 2014, http://www.theneworleansadvocate.com/home/9351541-172/no-tour-guide-licensing-constitutional; see also Kagan v. City of New Orleans, 957 F. Supp. 2d 774 (E.D. La. 2013), *aff'd*, 753 F.3d 560 (5th Cir. 2014).
180 Mark Waller, "Arguments in the Tour Guide Free Speech Lawsuit against New Orleans Unfolded in Appeals Court on Wednesday," *Times-Picayune*, April 30, 2014, http://www.nola.com/business/index.ssf/2014/04/arguments_in_the_tour_guide_fr.html.
181 Fifth U.S. Circuit Court of Appeals, quoted in Mustian, "N.O. Tour Guide Licensing Constitutional"; see also *Kagan*, 753 F.3d.
182 Mustian, "N.O. Tour Guide Licensing Constitutional."
183 White, "N.O. Tour Guides Riled Up"; Mustian, "N.O. Tour Guide Licensing Constitutional."
184 Candy Kagan, telephone conversation with Dick Carpenter, May 25, 2015.
185 Richard A. Webster, "Taxicab Inspector in Custody As Protesters Demand the Removal of Director Malachi Hull," *Times-Picayune*, November 22, 2013, http://www.nola.com/politics/index.ssf/2013/11/taxicab_inspector_in_custody_a.html.
186 Richard A. Webster, "New Orleans Taxicab Bureau Investigator Found Guilty in Assault on Tour Guide," *Times-Picayune*, March 3, 2015, http://www.nola.com/crime/index.ssf/2015/03/new_orleans_taxicab_bureau_inv_2.html.
187 Steve Hendrix, "Segway Tour Pioneers Have New Reason to Celebrate: Overturning D.C. Licensing Rules," *Washington Post*, July 3, 2014, https://www.washingtonpost.com/local/washingtons-segway-tour-king-takes-a-victory-lap-after-winning-court-battle/2014/07/03/38a97d2e-02c6-11e4-8fd0-3a663dfa68ac_story.html.
188 Ibid.
189 Stuart Millar, "This Is Ginger, and It's the Future. Not At All like the Sinclair C5: Eagerly Awaited Revolutionary Urban Transport Device Turns Out to Be a Scooter," *Guardian*, December 4, 2001.
190 Dean Kamen, quoted in John Heilemann, "Reinventing the Wheel," *Time*, December 2, 2001, http://content.time.com/time/business/article/0,8599,186660,00.html.
191 Tom Vanderbilt, "Why Haven't We Segued into the Segway: What Happened to the Revolution in Personal Transportation Promised by the Segway?," *Toronto Star*, May 9, 2013.
192 Peter Leo, "A Weak Segway," *Pittsburgh Post-Gazette*, August 25, 2006.
193 Bill and Tonia think that Segs in the City would have been the first Segway tours in the world if a Paris shop hadn't beat them by three months. Hendrix, "Overturning D.C. Licensing Rules."

194 Ibid.

195 "Tourists Beware: A Report from the Seamy Underworld of Unlicensed Tour Guides," *Economist*, May 10, 2014, http://www.economist.com/news/united-states/21601832-report-seamy-underworld-unlicensed-tour-guides-tourists-beware; Hendrix, "Overturning D.C. Licensing Rules."

196 Janice Rogers Brown, quoted in "A Test for City Tour Guide Regulations: What Does the First Amendment Protect?," *Washington Post*, July 3, 2014, http://www.washingtonpost.com/...st-for-city-tour-guide-regulations-what-does-the-first-amendment-protect/2014/07/03/31b9057e-0227-11e4-8fd0-3a663dfa68ac_story.html.

197 Hendrix, "Overturning D.C. Licensing Rules."

198 Bill Main, quoted in ibid.

199 Gil Sandler, "Where Did City Get Its Charming Nickname? Baltimore Glimpses," *Baltimore Sun*, August 18, 1998, http://articles.baltimoresun.com/1998-08-18/news/1998230119_1_charm-city-mencken-bill-evans.

200 Rachel Weiner and Wesley Robinson,"D.C. Tour Guides Win Court Battle with City," *Washington Post*, June 27, 2014, http://www.washingtonpost.com/local/crime/dc-tour-guides-win-challenge-of-licensing-test/2014/06/27/a5e7fd82-fe13-11e3-8176-f2c941cf35f1_story.html.

201 Michelle Hackman, "A Good Day to Be a Washington Tour Guide, Thanks to the D.C. Circuit," *Wall Street Journal* law blog, June 27, 2014, http://blogs.wsj.com/law/2014/06/27/a-good-day-to-be-a-washington-tour-guide-thanks-to-the-d-c-circuit/.

202 District of Columbia Department of Consumer and Regulatory Affairs, "District of Columbia Sightseeing Tour Guide: Professional Licensing Examination Study Reference," Pearson, accessed June 9, 2016, https://www.asisvcs.com/publications/pdf/690906.pdf.

203 Hackman, "Washington Tour Guide."

204 Weiner and Robinson, "D.C. Tour Guides Win Court Battle."

205 Rhonda Briel, speaking in "DC Guide License Experience—Part I," YouTube video, 4:33, posted by USA Tour Pros, February 22, 2009, https://www.youtube.com/watch?v=a-YE3FvoWxE.

206 Rhonda Briel, speaking in "DC Guide License Experience—Part II," YouTube video, 5:30, posted by USA Tour Pros, February 22, 2009, https://www.youtube.com/watch?v=za2WocldfSQ.

207 Rhonda Briel, speaking in "DC Guide License Experience—Part III," YouTube video, posted by USA Tour Pros, February 23, 2009, https://www.youtube.com/watch?v=9JIZc-7rfKk. Rhonda's experience is not unique. Others have described similar things being asked of them. As Faye Brenner recalled: "I already knew that the application for the license was mired in red tape. In fact, I took a class in 'Cutting through the Red Tape in Getting a DC Tour License' with First Class a couple of months ago, and after downloading the application and being totally overwhelmed, I thought perhaps I could dodge it.... There are two types of tour guide licenses: A and B. I even learned that a question on one of the 7 different tour guide tests is what is the difference [between the different types of licenses]! The tour guide A license allows you to start a tour in DC; tour guide B requires you to start the tour outside of DC.... The

requirements for either license include a long list of paperwork and a 100-question test: physician's statement, 'clean-hands' document (not affirming your hygiene, but the fact that you don't owe DC any more than $100), 6 letters of recommendation, a business license, DC tax certificate, fingerprints, and a criminal report. After successfully submitting all of those, you can sit for the test comprised of 100 questions: multiple choice, true and false, fill-in-the-blank, and picture identification. Legend has it that the pictures have been copied so many times that it is sometimes difficult to make out the photo let alone identify, locate, and state its purpose." "D.C. Tour Guide License," Faye Brenner, *Touring with Faye* (blog), last modified March 2, 2010, http://touringwithfaye.blogspot.com/2010/03/dc-tour-guide-license.html.

208 Bill and Tonia also complied with a temporary moratorium on Segways on the National Mall itself. The moratorium, lifted in 2010, was in place while the National Park Service investigated whether Segways cause any harm to the turf—they don't.

209 Paul L. Friedman, quoted in Weiner and Robinson, "D.C. Tour Guides Win Court Battle"; see also Edwards v. District of Columbia, 943 F. Supp. 2d 109 (D.D.C. 2013).

210 Quoted in Hackman, "Washington Tour Guide"; see also *Edwards*, 943 F. Supp. 2d.

211 John Gonzalez and Kris van Cleave, "D.C. Tour Guide License Regulation Draws Scrutiny in Appeals Hearing," WJLA, Washington, DC: abc 7, May 5, 2014, http://www.wjla.com/articles/2014/05/d-c-tour-guide-license-regulation-draws-scrutiny-in-appeals-hearing-102802.html.

212 Edwards v. District of Columbia, 755 F.3d 996 (D.C. Cir. 2014); Pete Yost, "Washington Tour Guides Win Appeals Court Ruling," Associated Press, June 27, 2014, http://www.sandiegouniontribune.com/news/2014/jun/27/washington-tour-guides-win-appeals-court-ruling/.

213 Janice Rogers Brown, quoted in Hackman, "Washington Tour Guide"; see also *Edwards*, 755 F.3d.

214 Nick Gass, "Court: D.C. Guide Rules Unconstitutional," *Politico* blog, June 27, 2014, http://www.politico.com/blogs/under-the-radar/2014/06/court-dc-guide-rules-unconstitutional-191245.html; *Edwards*, 755 F.3d.

215 Quoted in Yost, "Washington Tour Guides"; see also *Edwards*, 755 F.3d.

216 Janice Rogers Brown, quoted in "A Test for City Tour Guide Regulations," *Washington Post*; see also *Edwards*, 755 F.3d.

217 Weiner and Robinson, "D.C. Tour Guides Win Court Battle."

218 Janice Rogers Brown, quoted in Gass, "D.C. Guide Rules Unconstitutional"; see also *Edwards*, 755 F.3d.

219 Quoted in Hackman, "Washington Tour Guide"; see also *Edwards*, 755 F.3d.

220 Quoted in Hackman, "Washington Tour Guide"; see also *Edwards*, 755 F.3d.

221 Sarah McCammon, "Does the First Amendment Apply to Tour Guides?," *Marketplace*, December 3, 2014, http://www.marketplace.org/topics/economy/does-first-amendment-apply-tour-guides.

222 "Savannah," GeorgiaGov, accessed June 10, 2016, http://georgia.gov/cities-counties/savannah.

223 Michelle Freenor, telephone conversation with Dick Carpenter, May 28, 2015.

224 Michelle's husband, Steve, was also a plaintiff in the lawsuit. Although he is a history professor at a local college and therefore can be assumed to know a thing or two about history, Steve has been unable to work as a tour guide because he lacks a license.
225 Quoted in Blinder, "Lawsuit May Reshape Tourist Industry."
226 McCammon, "First Amendment."
227 Russ Bynum, "Tour Guides Press Ahead with Speech Lawsuit against Savannah," *Savannah Morning News*, March 22, 2015, http://savannahnow.com/news/2015-03-22/tour-guides-press-ahead-speech-lawsuit-against-savannah.
228 Dan Leger, telephone conversation with Dick Carpenter, May 27, 2015.
229 Freenor v. Mayor of Savannah, No. 4:14-cv-00248-WTM-GRS, Joint Status Report 7, March 12, 2015, ECF No. 23.
230 Jean Soderlind, telephone conversation with Dick Carpenter, May 28, 2015.
231 Bill Durrence, quoted in Blinder, "Lawsuit May Reshape Tourist Industry."
232 Ibid.
233 "A Test for City Tour Guide Regulations," *Washington Post*.
234 Weiner and Robinson, "D.C. Tour Guides Win Court Battle."
235 Black and Weiler, "Quality Assurance and Regulatory Mechanisms."
236 Ibid.
237 Pond, *Professional Guide*.
238 Ibid.
239 Black and Weiler, "Quality Assurance and Regulatory Mechanisms."
240 Ibid., 31.
241 The Professional Tour Guide Association of Florida endorses a $300 course for tour guide certification through a community college in Miami. Miami Dade College, School of Continuing Education & Professional Development, "Tour Guide Certification," accessed June 10, 2016, https://sisvsr.mdc.edu/ce/showclass.aspx?ref=838760.
242 "Welcome to the CPTA Website," Chicago Tour-Guide Professionals Association, accessed June 10, 2016, http://www.tourguidesofchicago.com/.
243 "Trained Guides," Professional Tour Guide Association of San Antonio, accessed June 10, 2016, http://www.sanantoniotourguide.org/training.php.
244 "Certification," San Diego Professional Tour Guide Association, accessed June 10, 2016, http://www.sdtourguides.com/certification.
245 "Becoming a Member," San Francisco Tour Guide Guild, accessed June 10, 2016, http://www.sftgg.org/become-a-member.php.
246 "Membership Benefits & Application," Professional Tour Guide Association: St. Louis, MO, accessed June 10, 2016, http://www.ptgastl.org/membership-benefits-application/.
247 "Certification," Dallas/Fort Worth Area Tour Guide Association, accessed June 10, 2016, http://www.dfwtourguides.com/certification.htm.
248 "PTGAH: A Resource for Houston Tour Guides," Professional Tour Guide Association of Houston, accessed June 10, 2016, http://ptgah.org/web/.
249 "Certified Professional Las Vegas Tour Guide Program and Training," Las Vegas Tourist Guides Guild, accessed June 10, 2016, http://www.lvtgg.com/cptg/.

250 "RMGA Certification Program," Rocky Mountain Guides Association, accessed June 10, 2016, http://rockymountaintourguides.com/rmga-certification-.html.
251 "APT Tour Guide Certification Programs," APT: Association of Philadelphia Tour Guides, accessed June 10, 2016, http://www.phillyguides.org/training-certification.aspx.
252 Associated Press, "Savannah to Stop Testing Tour Guides after Legal Battle," YAHOO! News, October 15, 2015, https://www.yahoo.com/news/savannah-stop-testing-tour-guides-legal-battle-211512078.html?ref=gs.
253 W. Brooks Stillwell, quoted in Russ Bynum, "Savannah Prepares Retreat in Speech Fight with Tour Guides," Associated Press, October 14, 2015, http://bigstory.ap.org/article/285b921fbbfa42748670f6eb1940a134/savannah-prepares-retreat-speech-fight-tour-guides.
254 W. Brooks Stillwell, quoted in ibid.
255 Speaking in "Savannah City Council 10/15/15," Savannah Government Television video, 2:41, October 15, 2015, http://savannahgovtv.pegcentral.com/player.php?video=43032deca10dc761add72fdf8936d164.
256 Eric Curl, "Savannah to Drop Tour Guide Test, Restrict Hours," *Savannah Morning News*, September 29, 2015, http://savannahnow.com/news/2015-09-29/savannah-drop-tour-guide-test-restrict-tour-hours#.
257 W. Brooks Stillwell, quoted in Bynum, "Savannah Prepares Retreat."
258 Van Johnson, quoted in ibid.

CHAPTER 6 ■ THE REGULATORY STONE AGE

1 Martin Luther King Jr., *Stride toward Freedom: The Montgomery Story* (New York: Harper & Row, 1958).
2 Randall Kennedy, "Martin Luther King's Constitution: A Legal History of the Montgomery Bus Boycott," *Yale Law Journal* 98, no. 6 (1989).
3 King, *Stride toward Freedom.*
4 Ibid.
5 Ibid.
6 Kennedy, "Martin Luther King's Constitution"; King, *Stride toward Freedom.* Some volunteer drivers came from an unanticipated source. As King explained, "Many white housewives, whatever their commitment to segregation, had no intention of being without their maids. And so every day they drove to the Negro sections to pick up their servants and returned them at night." King, *Stride toward Freedom*, 78–79.
7 King, *Stride toward Freedom*, 77.
8 Taylor Branch, *Parting the Waters: America in the King Years 1954–63* (New York: Simon & Schuster, 1988); David J. Garrow, *Bearing the Cross: Martin Luther King, Jr., and the Southern Christian Leadership Conference* (New York: William Morrow, 1986); King, *Stride toward Freedom.*
9 Branch, *Parting the Waters.*
10 Kennedy, "Martin Luther King's Constitution."
11 King, *Stride toward Freedom.*

12 Ibid.
13 Branch, *Parting the Waters.*
14 Ibid.
15 King, *Stride toward Freedom*, 158.
16 Lamont H. Yeakey, "The Montgomery, Alabama Bus Boycott, 1955–1956" (PhD diss., Columbia University, 1979).
17 Branch, *Parting the Waters*; King, *Stride toward Freedom.* One prominent segregation supporter later called the delay "another blunder" on the part of the city. Branch, *Parting the Waters*, 193.
18 King, *Stride toward Freedom.*
19 Branch, *Parting the Waters*; Garrow, *Bearing the Cross*; King, *Stride toward Freedom.*
20 Branch, *Parting the Waters*; Garrow, *Bearing the Cross*; King, *Stride toward Freedom.* Because the Supreme Court's orders would not take effect until they reached Montgomery, and due to a delay in the orders, the boycott went on for another month without having access to the carpool, requiring protestors to walk to and from work. Branch, *Parting the Waters*; King, *Stride toward Freedom.*
21 Branch, *Parting the Waters.*
22 Ibid.; Garrow, *Bearing the Cross*; King, *Stride toward Freedom.*
23 Branch, *Parting the Waters*; Garrow, *Bearing the Cross*; King, *Stride toward Freedom.*
24 Stephen K. McNees, "The 1990–91 Recession in Historical Perspective," *New England Economic Review* (January/February 1992).
25 Olivier Blanchard, "Consumption and the Recession of 1990–1991," *American Economic Review* 83, no. 2 (1993); Robert E. Hall, "Macro Theory and the Recession of 1990–1991," *American Economic Review* 83, no. 2 (1993); McNees, "1990–91 Recession."
26 Jennifer M. Gardner, "The 1990–91 Recession: How Bad Was the Labor Market?," *Monthly Labor Review* 117, no. 6 (1994).
27 Steven Greenhouse, "The 1992 CAMPAIGN: The Economy; Despite Recession's End, Bush May Face Unusually Harsh Public Judgment," *New York Times*, May 11, 1992.
28 Gardner, "1990–91 Recession."
29 Alison Mitchell, "Vans Vie Illegally for New York Bus Riders," *New York Times*, January 24, 1992; Aaron Reiss, "New York's Shadow Transit," *New Yorker*, June 14, 2014, http://projects.newyorker.com/story/nyc-dollar-vans/; Howard Husock, "Enterprising Van Drivers Collide with Regulation: Commuters in Queens and Brooklyn Love Their Private Van Services, Better than the Public-Sector Alternative. Guess Who Hates Them," *City Journal* 6, no. 1 (1996).
30 Reiss, "New York's Shadow Transit"; Lisa Margonelli, "The (Illegal) Private Bus System That Works," *Atlantic*, October 5, 2011, http://www.theatlantic.com/national/archive/2011/10/the-illegal-private-bus-system-that-works/246166/; Mitchell, "Vans Vie Illegally"; Jim Zarroli and Renee Montagne, "Commuter Van Wars," National Public Radio: *Morning Edition*, radio broadcast, June 2, 1998; John Tierney, "Man with a Van," *New York Times*, August 10, 1997.
31 Robert Heisler, *The Power of One Entrepreneur: Hector Ricketts, Transportation Entrepreneur* (Arlington: Institute for Justice, 2010).

32 Sumathi Reddy, "Illegal, but Very Popular," *Wall Street Journal*, September 13, 2012.
33 Reiss, "New York's Shadow Transit."
34 Hector Ricketts, telephone conversation with John K. Ross, June 23, 2015.
35 Ross D. Eckert and George W. Hilton, "The Jitneys," *Journal of Law & Economics* 15, no. 2 (1972).
36 F. W. Doolittle, "The Economics of the Jitney Bus Operation," *Journal of Political Economy* 23, no. 7 (1915); Eckert and Hilton, "Jitneys"; Julian C. Chambliss, "A Question of Progress and Welfare: The Jitney Bus Phenomenon in Atlanta, 1915–1925," *Georgia Historical Quarterly* 92, no. 4 (2008).
37 Eckert and Hilton, "Jitneys."
38 Santos v. City of Houston, 852 F. Supp. 601, 603 (S.D. Tex. 1994).
39 Even while they were outlawed, jitneys thrived for decades in Chicago—tolerated as long as operators bribed city officials to keep them running. In 1978, a jitney-fleet owner testified that he'd paid the taxi commissioner $93,000 "because [the commissioner] could put him out of business." Ron Grossman, "Before Uber There Was Jitney: Earlier Quasi-Regulated Service Enjoyed a Long Ride in Chicago," *Chicago Tribune*, March 9, 2014, http://articles.chicagotribune.com/2014-03-09/site/ct-jitney-cab-flashback-0309-20140309_1_jitney-cabs-taxi.

Since then, city leaders have sporadically attempted to legalize jitneys out of concern that public transit and taxicabs fail to service large pockets of the city. Jeff Borden, "Chicago Mulls Return of Jitneys to Streets; Private Vehicles Would Help Shortage of Cabs," *Crain's Chicago Business*, December 3, 1994, http://www.chicagobusiness.com/article/19941203/ISSUE01/100010660/chicago-mulls-return-of-jitneys-to-streets-private-vehicles-would-help-ease-shortage-of-cabs.
40 August Wilson, *Jitney* (New York: Penguin USA, 2002).
41 Timothy McNulty, "Pittsburgh Jitney Service Illegal, but Thriving," *Pittsburgh Post-Gazette*, September 7, 2013, http://www.post-gazette.com/news/transportation/2013/09/07/Pittsburgh-jitney-service-illegal-but-thriving/stories/201309070167.
42 Lisette Corsa, "A Life in Transit," *Miami New Times*, June 8, 2000, http://www.miaminewtimes.com/news/a-life-in-transit-6355846. Other reasons customers prefer jitney service include their low cost—a dollar per trip—and familiar milieu, with some Miami jitney services boasting drivers conversant in Spanish and Creole. Adam Beasley, "Minibus Jitneys a Transit Alternative," *Miami Herald*, May 19, 2008; William Booth, "Miami's Jitney War: Entrepreneurs Drive Bus Riders Away," *Washington Post*, July 29, 1992.
43 McNulty, "Pittsburgh Jitney Service Illegal."
44 Husock, "Van Drivers Collide with Regulation"; Willie James, "Commuter Vans 'Steal' Riders" (letter to the editor), *Wall Street Journal*, July 23, 1997.
45 Randall Fitzgerald, *Mugged by the State: Outrageous Government Assaults on Ordinary People and Their Property* (Washington, DC: Regnery, 2003); Suzanne Rostler, "Blow Out: New City Rules on Van Services Could Drive Firms off the Road," *Crain's New York Business* 10, no. 37.
46 William T. Jones, "Origins of the Certificate of Public Convenience and

Necessity: Developments in the States, 1870–1920," *Columbia Law Review* 79, no. 3 (1979).

47 Ibid.

48 Ibid.; Timothy Sandefur, "A Public Convenience and Necessity and Other Conspiracies against Trade: A Case Study from the Missouri Moving Industry," *Civil Rights Law Journal* 24, no. 2 (2014).

49 Jones, "Certificate of Public Convenience and Necessity"; Sandefur, "Case Study from Missouri Moving Industry."

50 Sandefur, "Case Study from Missouri Moving Industry."

51 Ibid.

52 Ibid.

53 Jones, "Certificate of Public Convenience and Necessity."

54 Timothy Sandefur, "CON Job: State 'Certificate of Necessity' Laws Protect Firms, Not Consumers," *Regulation* 34, no. 2 (2011).

55 Jones, "Certificate of Public Convenience and Necessity."

56 Ibid.

57 Ibid.

58 Richard R. B. Powell, "Jitney Regulation in New York," *Cornell Law Review* 2, no. 2 (1917).

59 James C. Nelson, *The Effects of Entry Control in Surface Transport* (Cambridge, MA: National Bureau Committee for Economic Research, 1965).

60 Ibid.

61 Yong Li, "The Economic Effects of Surface Transport Deregulation" (master's thesis, Massachusetts Institute of Technology, 2002); James Sloss, "Regulation of Motor Freight Transportation: A Quantitative Evaluation of Policy," *Bell Journal of Economics and Management Science* 1, no. 2 (1970).

62 Andrew R. Goetz and Timothy M. Vowles, "The Good, the Bad, and the Ugly: 30 Years of US Airline Deregulation," *Journal of Transport Geography* 17, no. 4 (2009); Steven A. Morrison, "The Effects of Airline Deregulation in the United States" (discussion paper, Economic Research Institute, Economic Planning Agency, 1995).

63 Sandefur, "CON Job."

64 Thomas A. Aloia, Vivian Ho, and Mara N. Short, "Certificate of Need Regulations and the Availability and Use of Cancer Resections," *Annals of Surgical Oncology* 15, no. 7 (2008); Traci L. Eichmann and Rexford Santerre, "Do Hospital Chief Executive Officers Extract Rents from Certificate of Need Laws?," *Journal of Health Care Finance* 37, no. 4 (2011); Jon M. Ford and David L. Kaserman, "Certificate-of-Need Regulation and Entry: Evidence from the Dialysis Industry," *Southern Economic Journal*, 59, no. 4 (1993); Charlene Harrington, James H. Swan, John A. Nyman, and Helen Carrillo, "The Effect of Certificate of Need and Moratoria Policy on Change in Nursing Home Beds in the United States," *Medical Care* 35, no. 6 (1997); Salvatore J. Pacella, Matthew Comstock, and William M. Kuzon Jr., "Certificate-of-Need Regulation in Outpatient Surgery and Specialty Care: Implications for Plastic Surgeons," *Plastic and Reconstructive Surgery* 116, no. 4 (2005); Ioana Popescu, Mary S. Vaughan-Sarrazin, and G. E. Rosenthal, "Certificate of Need Regulations and Use of Coronary Revascularization after Acute Myocardial Infarction," *Journal*

of the American Medical Association 295, no. 18 (2006); Short et al., "Certificate of Need Regulations"; Pamela C. Smith and Dana A. Forgione, "The Development of Certificate of Need Legislation," *Journal of Health Care Finance* 36, no. 2 (2009).

65 Keith B. Anderson, "Regulation, Market Structure, and Hospital Costs: Comment," *Southern Economic Journal* 58, no. 2 (1991); John J. Antel, Robert L. Ohsfeldt, and Edmund R. Becker, "State Regulation and Hospital Costs," *Review of Economics and Statistics* 77, no. 3 (1995); Eichmann and Santerre, "Chief Executive Officers Extract Rents"; Ford and Kaserman, "Certificate-of-Need Regulation and Entry"; Myron D. Fottler, Patrick A. Rivers, and Mustafa Zeedan Younis, "Does Certificate of Need Really Contain Hospital Costs in the United States?," *Health Education Journal* 66, no. 3 (2007); John A. Nyman, "The Effects of Market Concentration and Excess Demand on the Price of Nursing Home Care," *Journal of Industrial Economics* 42, no. 2 (1994); Patrick A. Rivers, Myron D. Fottler, and Jemima A. Frimpong, "The Effects of Certificate of Need Regulation on Hospital Costs," *Journal of Health Care Finance* 36, no. 4 (2010); Smith and Forgione, "Development of Certificate of Need Legislation."

66 Steven B. Caudill, Jon M. Ford, and David L. Kaserman, "Certificate of Need Regulation and the Diffusion of Innovations: A Random Coefficient Model," *Journal of Applied Econometrics* 10, no. 1 (1995).

67 Charles Millard, quoted in Joseph P. Fried, "A New Law Escalates the War against Unlicensed Vans," *New York Times*, February 13, 1994.

68 Hector Ricketts, quoted in Heisler, *Hector Ricketts*, 5.

69 "Van Drivers Win Round," *New York Daily News*, March 25, 1999.

70 Fitzgerald, *Mugged by the State*; "Thwarting a Van Driver," *New York Times*, June 26, 1997; Tierney, "Man with a Van."

71 Archie Spigner, quoted in Fitzgerald, *Mugged by the State*, 117; see also "Driving the Poor Out of Business," *Wall Street Journal*, March 3, 1997.

72 Taxi and Limousine Commission, quoted in "Driving the Poor Out of Business," *Wall Street Journal*.

73 Archie Spigner, quoted in "Dream On," *Wall Street Journal*.

74 "The Vans Roll," *Wall Street Journal*, August 13, 1997.

75 Fried, "War against Unlicensed Vans"; Hector Ricketts, "Roadblocks Made Just for Vans," *New York Times*, November 22, 1997.

76 Hector Ricketts, telephone conversation with John K. Ross, June 23, 2015.

77 Lateef Ajala, quoted in Heisler, *Hector Ricketts*, 19.

78 Zarroli and Montagne, "Commuter Van Wars"; "Let the Poor Walk," *Wall Street Journal*, September 10, 1997; Megan Riesz, "Van-Demonium! Cops Crack Down Dollar Vans, Activist Group Calls It Racist, *Brooklyn Paper*, April 14, 2014, http://www.brooklynpaper.com/stories/37/16/dtg-78-dollar-van-crackdown-2014-04-18-bk_37_16.html; "Dream On," *Wall Street Journal*.

79 Hector Ricketts, telephone conversation with John K. Ross, June 23, 2015.

80 "Let the Poor Walk," *Wall Street Journal*.

81 Andy Newman, "Council Votes to Continue Curb on Vans," *New York Times*, October 30, 1997.

82 "Hooray for the Vans!," *New York Post*, March 25, 1999.

83 Ewa Kern-Jedrychowska, "1,000 'Dollar Vans' Seized since Last Year, but Most

Return to Street," DNAInfo.com, September 23, 2014, http://www.dnainfo.com/new-york/20140923/jamaica/1000-dollar-vans-seized-since-last-year-but-most-return-street.

84 Heisler, *Hector Ricketts.*

85 Reiss, "New York's Shadow Transit"; Riesz, "Van-Demonium!"

86 Margonelli, "(Illegal) Private Bus System."

87 Quoted in Kern-Jedrychowska, "1,000 'Dollar Vans' Seized."

88 Glenn Garvin, "America's Economic Refugees: In an Overregulated Economy, the Best Preparation for Survival May Be a Third World Education," *Reason* 25, no. 6 (November 1, 1993).

89 Ani Ebong, quoted in ibid., 22.

90 Ani Ebong, quoted in ibid., 22.

91 Gorman Gilbert and Robert E. Samuels, *The Taxicab: An Urban Transportation Survivor* (Chapel Hill: University of North Carolina Press, 1982).

92 Ibid.

93 Edward O. Welles, "It's Not the Same America: Barriers to Succeeding in Business Include Regulation, Special Interests, Protectionism, Access to Capital and Welfare," *Inc.* 16, no. 5 (1994).

94 *Regulatory Barriers to Minority Entrepreneurs: Hearing Before the Subcommittee on Regulation and Paperwork of the Committee on Small Business*, House of Representatives, 104th Cong. 30 (1995) (testimony of Leroy Jones, owner/driver, Quick Pick Cabs).

95 *Affidavit of Girma Molalegne*, Jones v. Temmer, D. Colo. (1993) (testimony of Girma Molalegne, cofounder, Quick Pick Cabs).

96 Henry S. Farber, "Is Tomorrow Another Day? The Labor Supply of New York City Cabdrivers," *Journal of Political Economy* 113, no. 1 (2005); Jill Esbenshade, Muna Aden, Andy Anderson, Amy Ash, Linzi Berkowitz, Roberto Danipour, Lea Marzo et al., "Driven to Despair: A Survey of San Diego Taxi Drivers" (unpublished manuscript, San Diego State University, 2013); Robert Bruno, *Driven into Poverty: A Comprehensive Study of the Chicago Taxicab Industry; Report I: Income* (unpublished manuscript, University of Illinois, Chicago, 2009); Bob Hohler, Marcella Bombardieri, and Jonathan Salzman, "For Cab Drivers, Risk and Reward Are a Mismatch: A Reporter Returns to the Wheel after Many Years and Finds Much Has Changed. Cabbies Are Often Cheated, and Danger Lurks at Every Turn," ed. Thomas Farragher, *Boston Globe*, April 2, 2013, https://www.bostonglobe.com/metro/2013/04/01/spotlight/IkU7kjxSy2d1N8eYhDTBaL/story.html.

97 Masabumi Miyamoto, Shunsuke Konno, Yoshikazu Gembun, Xinyu Liu, Kazufumi Minami, and Hiromoto Ito, "Epidemiological Study of Low Back Pain and Occupational Risk Factors among Taxi Drivers," *Industrial Health* 46 (2008).

98 Carolina Bigert, Per Gustavsson, Johan Hallqvist, Christer Hogstedt, Marie Lewné, Nils Plato, Christina Reuterwall, and Patrick Schéele, "Myocardial Infarction among Professional Drivers," *Epidemiology* 14, no. 3 (2003).

99 Fumio Kobayashi, Takemasa Watanabe, Misuzu Watanabe, Yasuhiro Akamatsu, Teruyuki Tomita, Taisuke Nakane, Hikari Furui et al., "Blood Pressure and Heart Rate Variability in Taxi Drivers on Long Duty Schedules," *Journal of Occupational Health* 44, no. 4 (2002).

100 Irene Figà-Talamanca, Chiara Cini, G. C. Varricchio, Franco Dondero, Loredana Gandini, Andrea Lenzi, Francesco Lombardo, Luciano Angelucci, Francesca R. Patacchioli, and Renato Di Grezia, "Effects of Prolonged Autovehicle Driving on Male Reproductive Function: A Study among Taxi Drivers," *American Journal of Industrial Medicine* 30, no. 6 (1996).

101 Sara Abraham, Aparna Sundar, and Dale Whitmore, *Toronto Taxi Drivers: Ambassadors of the City; A Report on Working Conditions* (Toronto: Ryerson University, 2008); Esbenshade et al., "Driven to Despair"; Bruno and Schneidman, "Driven into Poverty"; Legal Assistance to Microenterprises Project, *Driving Austin, Driving Injustice: A Report on the Working Conditions of Taxi Drivers in Austin* (Austin: Legal Assistance to Microenterprises Project, 2010).

102 Gary Blasi and Jacqueline Leavitt, *Driving Poor: Taxi Drivers and the Regulation of the Taxi Industry in Los Angeles* (Los Angeles: UCLA, 2006).

103 Walter E. Williams, *Race & Economics: How Much Can Be Blamed on Discrimination?* (Stanford, CA: Hoover Institution Press, 2011).

104 "The Early Years: 1907–1935," Official Website of the City of New York, accessed June 10, 2016, http://www.nyc.gov/html/media/totweb/taxioftomorrow_history_earlyyears.html.

105 Edmund W. Kitch, Marc Isaacson, and Daniel Kasper, "The Regulation of Taxicabs in Chicago," *Journal of Law and Economics* 14, no. 2 (1971).

106 Joshua M. Lupkin, s.v. "Taxis, Liveries, and Limousines," in *Encyclopedia of Chicago*, accessed June 14, 2016, http://www.encyclopedia.chicagohistory.org/pages/1232.html.

107 Mark W. Frankenna and Paul A. Pautler, *An Economic Analysis of Taxicab Regulation* (Washington, DC: Federal Trade Commission, 1984).

108 Kitch et al., "Regulation of Taxicabs."

109 Ibid.

110 Gilbert and Samuels, *Urban Transportation Survivor*; Ron Grossman, "Flashback: Chicago's Violent Taxi Wars of the 1920s; Gunfire, Brawls Proliferated as Cab Companies Waged a Turf Battle in Jazz Age," *Chicago Tribune*, May 18, 2014, http://articles.chicagotribune.com/2014-05-18/site/ct-cab-wars-flashback-per-0518-20140518_1_taxi-checker-yellow-cab-co; Kate Eaton, "Checkered Past: Hertz, Markin Create Colorful, Stormy Cab Industry," *Chicago Tribune*, October 26, 1997, http://articles.chicagotribune.com/1997-10-26/travel/9710260127_1_checker-cab-cab-company-owner-dealership.

111 Graham Russell Hodges, *Taxi! A Social History of the New York City Cabdriver* (Baltimore: Johns Hopkins University Press, 2007).

112 Frankenna and Pautler, *Taxicab Regulation*; Gilbert and Samuels, *Urban Transportation Survivor*; Kitch et al., "Regulation of Taxicabs."

113 Frankenna and Pautler, *Taxicab Regulation*; Gilbert and Samuels, *Urban Transportation Survivor*. In 1932, for example, the United States had 150,000 taxis; prior to the start of the Depression in 1929, only 84,000 existed (Gilbert and Samuels, *Urban Transportation Survivor*), representing a 79 percent increase in only four years. Exacerbating this addition was the practice of car manufacturers, who tried to shore up sagging sales by unloading cars on taxi owners. The owners in turn leased the cars to a surging number of drivers for

three to four dollars a day, and the drivers then had to recoup these costs by hustling for business. Ibid.

114 Kitch et al., "Regulation of Taxicabs."

115 Frankenna and Pautler, *Taxicab Regulation*; Kitch et al., "Regulation of Taxicabs."

116 Frankenna and Pautler, *Taxicab Regulation.*

117 Gilbert and Samuels, *Urban Transportation Survivor.*

118 Ibid.

119 Ibid.

120 A second association representing smaller owners, the American Taxicab Association, formed in 1943. In 1966, it merged with NATO to form the International Taxicab Association (ibid.), eventually adding "Livery" to its name in 1990. In 2000, the International Taxicab & Livery Association became the Taxicab, Limousine & Paratransit Association. Today, the TLPA represents airport shuttles, executive sedans, limousines, nonemergency medical transportation, paratransits, and taxicabs. The association is the industry's largest trade organization, representing 1,100 members and more than a hundred thousand vehicles. "History," Taxicab, Limousine, & Paratransit Association, accessed June 10, 2016, http://www.tlpa.org/History.

121 Gilbert and Samuels, *Urban Transportation Survivor*; Kitch et al., "Regulation of Taxicabs."

122 Frankenna and Pautler, *Taxicab Regulation*; Kitch et al., "Regulation of Taxicabs."

123 Gilbert and Samuels, *Urban Transportation Survivor.*

124 Lawrence Van Gelder, "Medallion Limits Stem from the 30's," *New York Times*, May 11, 1996.

125 Gilbert and Samuels, *Urban Transportation Survivor.*

126 Ibid.; Frankenna and Pautler, *Taxicab Regulation.*

127 Kitch et al., "Regulation of Taxicabs."

128 Ibid.

129 United States v. Yellow Cab Co., 332 U.S. 218, 221, n. 1 (U.S. 1947), overruled by Copperweld Corp. v. Independence Tube Corp., 467 U.S. 752 (U.S. 1984).

130 Van Gelder, "Medallion Limits"; Leonard Silk, "How Monopolies Work: Taxicab Market in Chicago Affords a Case Study for Other Endeavors," *New York Times*, February 9, 1972.

131 Gilbert and Samuels, *Urban Transportation Survivor.*

132 Kitch et al., "Regulation of Taxicabs."

133 L. Carol Shaw, Gorman Gilbert, Christine Bishop, and Evelyn Pruitt, *Taxicab Regulation in U.S. Cities* (Washington, DC: U.S. Department of Transportation, 1983); Paul R. Verkuil, "The Economic Regulation of Taxicabs," *Rutgers Law Review* 24 (1969).

134 "Taxicab Mess," *New York Times*, July 25, 1969.

135 Frankenna and Pautler, *Taxicab Regulation.*

136 Ibid.; Verkuil, "Economic Regulation of Taxicabs."

137 Department of Transportation, cited in Phoebe D. Morse to Margaret Lynch (FTC staff comment letter, April 20, 1989), Federal Trade Commission, https://www.ftc.gov/sites/default/files/documents/advocacy_documents/ftc-staff-

comment-massachusetts-department-public-utilities-transportation-division-concerning/v890038.pdf.

138 Verkuil, "Economic Regulation of Taxicabs."

139 Thomas C. Palmer, "Taxi Turmoil: Limousines' Increase Worries Cabbies," *Boston Globe*, January 17, 1995.

140 Alan Finder, "Dinkins Plan Would Alter Taxi Industry," *New York Times*, January 27, 1992.

141 Jack Newsham, "What to Do about Taxi Medallions," *Boston Globe*, August 5, 2015, https://www.bostonglobe.com/ideas/2015/08/05/what-about-taxi-medallions/hhKyQX9eYPTX7dpfoiJeiK/story.html.

142 Josh Barro, "Under Pressure from Uber, Taxi Medallion Prices Are Plummeting," *New York Times*, November 27, 2014, http://www.nytimes.com/2014/11/28/upshot/under-pressure-from-uber-taxi-medallion-prices-are-plummeting.html; Andrew J. Hawkins, "Meet the Taxi Industry's Last, Best Hope to Survive the Uber Age," *Crain's New York Business*, August 27, 2015, http://www.crainsnewyork.com/article/20150827/BLOGS04/150829899/meet-the-taxi-industrys-last-best-hope-to-survive-uber-age?CSDropAuthCookieSpecified=1&CSDropAuthCookie=1&userLogin.password=OJZ60153.

143 Christopher Moraff, "The Medallion Financial Story," *Monitor Daily* (May/June 2008), http://www.monitordaily.com/article-posts/medallion-financial-stor/.

144 Andrew Murstein, quoted in ibid.

145 Ilan Kolet, "Fear Inflation? Buy a Cab," *Bloomberg Businessweek*, September 22, 2011, http://www.bloomberg.com/bw/magazine/fear-inflation-buy-a-cab-09222011-gfx.html; Derek Thompson, "Better than Stocks, Better than Gold: The Taxi Medallion as Inflation Hedge," *Atlantic*, September 24, 2011, http://www.theatlantic.com/business/archive/2011/09/better-than-stocks-better-than-gold-the-taxi-medallion-as-inflation-hedge/245602/.

146 Gilbert and Samuels, *Urban Transportation Survivor*.

147 Ibid.

148 Paul Stephen Dempsey, "Taxi Industry Regulation, Deregulation, & Reregulation: The Paradox of Market Failure," *Transportation Law Journal* 24 (1996).

149 Ibid.

150 Ibid.

151 John E. Kramer and William H. Mellor, *Opening Boston's Taxicab Market* (Washington, DC: Institute for Justice, 1995).

152 Adrian T. Moore, "Indianapolis's Road to Regulatory Reform; A New Path in Licensing and Permits," *Regulation* 21, no. 1 (1998).

153 Stephen Goldsmith, "Regulation and Urban Marketplace," *Regulation* 17, no. 4 (1994), 79.

154 Quoted in Welles, "Not the Same America," 87.

155 *Regulatory Barriers to Minority Entrepreneurs: Hearing Before the Subcommittee on Regulation and Paperwork of the Committee on Small Business*, House of Representatives, 104th Cong. 30 (1995) (testimony of Leroy Jones, owner/driver, Quick Pick Cabs).

156 Williams, *Race & Economics*.

157 Ani Ebong, quoted in Garvin, "America's Economic Refugees," 22.

158 Freda Poundstone, quoted in Welles, "Not the Same America," 87; see also Carson Reed, "Odd Partnership Defeated Taxicab Bill," *Rocky Mountain Business Journal*, May 13, 1985.
159 Welles, "Not the Same America"; Colorado Public Utilities Commission, *The Taxi Industry in the Denver Metropolitan Area* (Denver: Colorado Public Utilities Commission, 2008).
160 Colorado Public Utilities Commission, *Taxi Industry*.
161 Welles, "Not the Same America."
162 Ani Ebong, quoted in Garvin, "America's Economic Refugees," 23.
163 Jones v. Temmer, 829 F. Supp. 1226 (D. Colo. 1993), *vacated*, 57 F.3d 921 (10th Cir. 1995).
164 Fitzgerald, *Mugged by the State*.
165 Ani Ebong, quoted in Garvin, "America's Economic Refugees," 23.
166 Ani Ebong, quoted in ibid., 23.
167 Williams, *Race & Economics*.
168 *Jones*, 829 F. Supp. at 1234–35.
169 Col. Stat. § 40-10-105 (1994).
170 Garvin, "America's Economic Refugees."
171 Under the old regime, new applicants had to prove to commissioners that (1) existing companies were unable or unwilling to provide service to a given area, and, *if* that could be accomplished, that (2) their new company would do no harm to existing companies. Under the 1994 rules, if a company satisfied the PUC as to the first proposition, the burden of proof shifted to the intervening incumbents to prove that they would be harmed.
172 Colorado Public Utilities Commission, *Taxi Industry*.
173 Joel Warner, "Mean Streets," *Westword*, November 30, 2010, http://www.westword.com/news/mean-streets-5110813; D. Giles Clasen, "Union Taxi-Fare Is Fair," *Denver Voice* 13, no. 6 (2009), http://www.denvervoice.org/ourvoice/2009/7/1/feature-union-taxi-fare-is-fair.html; Beth Potter, "State Rules Derailing a Taxi Dream," *Denver Post*, October 9, 2006; Kelly Pate Dwyer, "Ex-Freedom Cab Drivers Fail to Win OK for New Taxi Firm," *Denver Post*, July 11, 2004.
174 Warner, "Mean Streets"; Dwyer, "Drivers Fail to Win OK"; Potter, "Derailing a Taxi Dream"; Kelly Pate Dwyer, "Denver Cabbies Seek to Start Own Company," *Denver Post*, July 4, 2004.
175 Colorado Public Utilities Commission, *Taxi Industry*.
176 Joel Warner, "Are Denver Cab Companies Ready for an Uber-Bumpy Ride?," *Westword*, March 20, 2014, http://www.westword.com/news/are-denver-cab-companies-ready-for-an-uber-bumpy-ride-5123724.
177 Quoted in Kristi Arellano and Tom McGhee, "'Fed-Up' Taxi Drivers Strike over Fees," *Denver Post*, June 19, 2001.
178 Warner, "Uber-Bumpy Ride."
179 Warner, "Mean Streets"; Felisa Cardona, "Immigrants Win Arbitration Awards after Alleging Racism at Denver Taxi Company," *Denver Post*, March 11, 2012, http://www.denverpost.com/news/ci_20148549/immigrants-win-arbitration-awards-after-alleging-racism-at.
180 Ray Gifford, quoted in Warner, "Uber-Bumpy Ride."
181 Allison Sherry, "Cabbies Back Bill for Indy Taxi Services," *Denver Post*, March

11, 2007; Warner, "Mean Streets"; "Green Light for Cabbies: Bill Would End Outdated Policy of 'Regulated Competition,'" *Rocky Mountain News*, January 29, 2007.

182 Col. Stat. § 40-2-101. (2008).

183 Brandon Johansson, "After Years-Long Battle with State Commission, Aurora-Based Cab Service Starting the Meter This Spring," *Aurora Sentinel*, December 20, 2013, http://www.aurorasentinel.com/news/years-long-battle-state-commission-aurora-based-cab-service-starting-meter-spring/.

184 *In the Matter of the Application of Mile High Cab*, docket No. 08A-407CP, decision No. R10-0745, slip op. at 67 (Colorado Public Utilities Commission 2010) (recommended decision of administrative law judge).

185 Quoted in Warner, "Uber-Bumpy Ride."

186 *Application of Mile High Cab* at 77.

187 Mekonnen Gizaw, telephone conversation with John K. Ross, June 23, 2015.

188 Vincent Carroll, "We Were Taken for a Ride," *Denver Post*, March 16, 2011; Joel Warner, "Taxicab Controversy: PUC Allows 300 New Cabs after Rejecting Mile High Cabs' Request for 150," *Westword*, March 7, 2011, http://www.westword.com/news/taxicab-controversy-puc-allows-300-new-cabs-after-rejecting-mile-high-cabs-request-for-150-5847423.

189 Warner, "Mean Streets."

190 Brandon Johansson, "Cab Service Starting the Meter."

191 Mile High Cab, Inc. v. Colorado Pub. Utils. Comm'n, 302 P.3d 241 (Colo. 2013).

192 *In the Matter of the Application of Mile High Cab*, docket No. 08A-407CP, decision No. R13-1518 (Colorado Public Utilities Commission 2013) (recommended decision of administrative law judge).

193 Mark Harden, "Mile High Cab Rolls into Metro Denver after Multiyear Fight," *Denver Business Journal*, July 28, 2014, http://www.bizjournals.com/denver/blog/earth_to_power/2014/07/mile-high-cab-begins-operations-in-metro-denver.html.

194 Mekonnen Gizaw, telephone conversation with John K. Ross, June 23, 2015.

195 "Colorado Lawmakers Have Right Idea on Taxis," *Denver Post*, April 6, 2015.

196 Col. Stat. § 40-10.1-203 (2015).

197 George F. Will, "Cabs and Cupidity," *Washington Post*, May 27, 2007.

198 Nick Dranias, *The Land of 10,000 Lakes Drowns Entrepreneurs in Regulations* (Arlington: Institute for Justice, 2006).

199 This number does not include the seasonal licenses the city grants in the winter or the forty special licenses it issues for handicapped services.

200 Katherine Kersten, "Newcomer Fights City's Taxi Cartel and May Triumph," *Star Tribune*, June 29, 2006.

201 Minneapolis Department of Regulatory Services, Division of Licenses & Consumer Services, *Taxicab Vehicle Licenses Convenience and Necessity* (document, June 21, 2006), Minneapolismn.gov, http://www.minneapolismn.gov/www/groups/public/@council/documents/webcontent/convert_265885.pdf.

202 Quoted in Kevin Diaz, "70 More Taxicabs to Grab; Minneapolis OKs Hard-Fought Boost," *Star Tribune*, August 26, 1995.

203 Michael Isikoff, "FTC to Sue Two Cities over Taxi Regulations," *Washington Post*, May 10, 1984; "Hacking Away at the FTC," June 15, 1984, *Wall Street Journal.*

204 Michael Isikoff, "FTC's Authority over Cities Hit; Panel Trying to Shield Cities from FTC Suits," *Washington Post*, May 31, 1984.
205 Dennis Farney and David Rogers, "Senate Turns Back Attempt to Stop FTC from Filing Antitrust Suits against Cities," *Wall Street Journal*, June 29, 1984.
206 Irvin Molotosky, "U.S. Drops Charges on Taxicab Limits: Trade Commission Challenged Minneapolis Regulations," *New York Times*, May 14, 1985.
207 Dennis J. McGrath, "New Minneapolis Cabdrivers Face Classes, Homework," *Star Tribune*, July 29, 1989.
208 Ilga Eglitis, "Big Taxi Customer Felt Ill-Served, So He Started Cab Firm," *Star Tribune*, September 7, 1989.
209 Rob Hotakainen, "City Hopes Required Training Will Help 'Refine' Cabdrivers, Cut Complaints," *Star Tribune*, December 10, 1989.
210 Quoted in Eglitis, "Customer Felt Ill-Served." The company went out of business in 1994, and all its permits were sold to an existing company. Kevin Diaz, "$150 Special Cab Licenses Sell for $25,000," *Star Tribune*, January 29, 1994.
211 Diaz, "$150 Special Cab Licenses."
212 Kevin Diaz, "Plan to Reshape Taxi Industry Is Fought by Drivers," *Star Tribune*, April 10, 1994.
213 Kevin Diaz, "Mayor Vetoes Effort for More Minneapolis Taxis," *Star Tribune*, February 3, 1995.
214 Steve Minn, quoted in Kevin Diaz, "More Competition Is Worst Threat, Say Embattled Cabbies," *Star Tribune*, January, 28, 1995.
215 Steve Brandt, "More Taxis OK'd over Mayor's Veto," *Star Tribune*, September 16, 1995.
216 Kevin Diaz, "New Taxi Licenses on Hold for Now," *Star Tribune*, October 6, 1995.
217 Larry Williams, quoted in Kevin Diaz, "Drivers Fret over Call for More Minneapolis Cabs," *Star Tribune*, January 23, 1995.
218 Mark Connor, "Case Study: Building a Reputation; Fairer Fares: Rainbow Taxis Owners Keep Driver and Passenger Top of Mind," Upsizemag.com, accessed June 11, 2016, http://www.upsizemag.com/primer/case-study-building-a-reputation.
219 Kevin Diaz, "70 New Taxi Licenses for Minneapolis: Cab Drivers Fought Plan, Said It Would Cut Profits," *Star Tribune*, February 22, 1996.
220 Former Mpls code § 341.270(a), (b) (2005).
221 Diaz, "70 New Taxi Licenses for Minneapolis"; Diaz, "70 More Taxicabs to Grab"; Steve Brandt, "Mayor Vetoes Changes in Taxi Ordinance," *Star Tribune*, September 1, 1995.
222 Dranias, *Land of 10,000 Lakes.*
223 Kersten, "Newcomer Fights City's Taxi Cartel."
224 Ibid.; Kevin Giles, "Hailing, Howling Follow New Cab Rules: Everyone Agrees That Minneapolis' New Taxi Ordinance Will Mean Changes; The Real Debate: Will They Make Things Better or Worse?," *Star Tribune*, October 10, 2006.
225 Gary Schiff, quoted in ibid.
226 Paul Ostrow, quoted in ibid.
227 Minneapolis Department of Regulatory Services, *Minneapolis Taxicab Vehicle License.*

228 Abdisalam Hashim, quoted in Abdirahman Aynte, “Minneapolis Lifts Cap on Taxi Cab Licenses,” *Twin Cities Daily Planet*, October 7, 2006, http://www.tcdailyplanet.net/minneapolis-lifts-cap-taxi-cab-licenses/; see also Minneapolis Department of Regulatory Services, *Minneapolis Taxicab Vehicle License.*

229 Quoted in Jeremiah E. Fruin, *Statement to the Minneapolis City Council for Repeal of the Archaic Concept of Public Convenience and Necessity*, written statement, 2006, on file with the authors.

230 Minneapolis Taxi Owners Coalition, Inc. v. City of Minneapolis, 572 F.3d 502 (8th Cir. 2009).

231 “Taxis Don’t Match Minneapolis Market: City Council Should Lift Cap on Taxi Licenses, Reform System,” *Star Tribune*, October 5, 2006; see also Kevin Diaz, “Minneapolis Maps Out Downtown’s Future,” *Star Tribune*, December 22, 1996.

232 Luis Paucar, quoted in Terry Collins, “Catching a Cab in Minneapolis May Get Easier: A Federal Judge’s Decision Clears the Way for More Taxis to Operate in Minneapolis,” *Star Tribune*, December 19, 2007.

233 Ibid.; Eric Roper, “A Bumper-to-Bumper Crop of Cabs; Some Minneapolis Taxi Drivers Say Lifting Limit on Licenses Has Swamped the Market,” *Star-Tribune*, May 9, 2012.

234 Zack Williams, quoted in Aynte, “Minneapolis Lifts Cap.”

235 R. & R., Minneapolis Taxi Owners Coal., Inc. v. City of Minneapolis, 2007 WL 4531332, 6 (D. Minn. Oct. 29, 2007) (No. 07-1789).

236 *Id.*

237 *Minneapolis Taxi Owners Coalition, Inc.*, 572 F.3d at 508.

238 Luis Paucar, quoted in J. Justin Wilson, “U.S. Supreme Court Rejects Challenge to Minneapolis Taxi Entrepreneur’s Right to Compete” (Arlington: Institute for Justice, February 22, 2010), http://ij.org/press-release/us-supreme-court-rejects-challenge-to-minneapolis-taxi-entrepreneuracanacs-right-to-compete/.

239 “Minneapolis Taxicabs: The Licenses and Consumer Services Division Regulates Approximately 950 Taxi Vehicles and 1300 Taxi Drivers in Minneapolis,” Minneapolismn.gov, last modified March 22, 2016, http://www.ci.minneapolis.mn.us/licensing/taxi/index.htm; “Taxicabs Licensed in Minneapolis,” Minneapolismn.gov, accessed June 14, 2016, http://www.ci.minneapolis.mn.us/www/groups/public/@regservices/documents/webcontent/convert_255574.pdf.

240 Zack Williams, quoted in Roper, “Bumper-to-Bumper Crop of Cabs.”

241 Failure to issue new licenses was nothing new in Milwaukee. In 1958, city officials discovered that every single cab in the city was operating illegally. The city’s code stipulated that “no permit shall be granted to operate any vehicle that was not lawfully operating on Oct. 1, 1929.” “Taxi Law Turns Back the Clock,” *New York Times*, March 22, 1958.

242 Jatinder Cheema, quoted in Jason Adkins, *Unhappy Days for Milwaukee Entrepreneurs: Brew City Regulations Make It Hard for Businesses to Achieve the High Life* (Arlington: Institute for Justice, 2010), 26.

243 In 1990, the bottleneckers’ lobbyist called the hearings an “antagonistic, chaotic and time consuming debate which occurs each October as cab drivers make a frenzied scramble for available permits.” *Complaint*, Sanfelippo v. City of Milwaukee, E.D. Wis. (2014) (Joe Sanfelippo Cabs, G.C.C., Roy WMS, Frenchy’s Cab Company, and 2 Sweets, plaintiffs).

244 Ibid.

245 Ibid.

246 R. & R., *Minneapolis Taxi Owners Coal.*, 2007 WL 4531332.

247 *Id.*

248 *Complaint for Declaratory and Injunctive Relief*, Ibrahim v. City of Milwaukee, Cir. Ct. Wis. (2011) (Ghaleb Ibrahim, Jatinder Cheema, and Amitpal Sing, plantiffs).

249 Quoted in Marie Rohde, "Taxi Tycoon: County Supervisor Joe Sanfelippo Is Co-Owner of a Near-Monopoly Cab Conglomerate That Squeezes the Pay of Drivers and Starves the Town of Taxis. And He Refuses to Talk to Reporters about It," *Milwaukee Magazine* (February 2012).

250 R. & R., *Minneapolis Taxi Owners Coal.*, 2007 WL 4531332.

251 Ibid. According to transportation expert Sam Staley's estimation, using conservative assumptions cabdrivers would have to dedicate nearly half of their income to service loan payments if they took out a commercial loan to finance the purchase of a permit. Sam Staley, *Economic Effects of Taxi Vehicle Caps in Milwaukee*, (report, August 14, 2012), on file with the authors.

252 Adkins, *Unhappy Days for Milwaukee Entrepreneurs.*

253 Ghaleb Ibrahim, quoted in Rohde, "Taxi Tycoon," 40.

254 John Weishan, quoted in Bruce Murphy, "Can County Board Solve Taxicab Problem: The Board's Resolution Got Media Play but Will Probably Accomplish Nothing," *Urban Milwaukee*, November 21, 2013, http://urbanmilwaukee.com/2013/11/21/murphys-law-can-county-board-solve-taxicab-problem/.

255 Jatinder Cheema, quoted in Adkins, *Unhappy Days for Milwaukee Entrepreneurs*, 26.

256 Mike De Sisti, "Get In. Shut Up. Hang On!," *Milwaukee Journal Sentinel*, March 28, 2010, http://www.jsonline.com/news/milwaukee/89370867.html.

257 Bruce Murphy, "Terrible Town for Taxis: How a City Permit System Enabled a Cartel to Dominate the Taxicab Business, Stifling Competition and Providing Poor Service," *Urban Milwaukee*, April 23, 2013, http://urbanmilwaukee.com/2013/04/23/murphys-law-terrible-town-for-taxis/.

258 "Calling 'Taxi!' at the Airport," *Milwaukee Business Journal*, June 9, 2002, http://www.bizjournals.com/milwaukee/stories/2002/06/10/editorial1.html?page=all.

259 Rekha R., comment on American United, "Taxi-American United Taxi Company," *Yelp* (blog), January 3, 2014, http://www.yelp.com/biz/taxi-american-united-taxi-company-milwaukee.

260 Michael R., comment on Yellow Cab, "Yellow Cab," *Yelp* (blog), October 10, 2011, http://www.yelp.com/biz/yellow-cab-milwaukee.

261 Rohde, "Taxi Tycoon."

262 Bruce Murphy, "The Mystery of Sanfelippo's Taxicab Empire: Why Is Rep. Joe Sanfelippo the Registered Agent for All of His Brother's Many Companies?," *Urban Milwaukee*, April 30, 2013, http://urbanmilwaukee.com/2013/04/30/murphys-law-the-mystery-of-sanfelippos-taxicab-empire/; Rohde, "Taxi Tycoon."

263 Joe Sanfelippo's platform: "Continue improving the business climate by eliminating outdated, costly regulations so that Wisconsin can compete

for businesses that will provide reliable, good paying jobs for our citizens." "Issues," Joe Sanfelippo: State Assembly, Internet Archive Wayback Machine, posted October 9, 2012, https://web.archive.org/web/20121009024719/http://joesanfelippo.com/issues/.

264 Steve Schultze, "Proposal Offered for County to Take over City's Taxi Regulation," *Milwaukee Journal Sentinel*, August 9, 2013, http://www.jsonline.com/news/milwaukee/proposal-offered-for-county-to-take-over-citys-taxi-regulation-b99723131z1-219034201.html.

265 "About Joe," Joe Sanfelippo: State Assembly, accessed June 11, 2016, http://joesanfelippo.com/bio/; Rohde, "Taxi Tycoon"; Murphy, "Mystery of Sanfelippo's Taxicab Empire."

266 "Airport Directory," AOPA, accessed June 11, 2016, http://www.aopa.org/airports/WI03.

267 Sanfelippo denied the inflated gas price. Rohde, "Taxi Tycoon"; Murphy, "Mystery of Sanfelippo's Taxicab Empire."

268 Michael Sanfelippo, quoted in Bruce Vielmetti, "Cab Drivers to Sue Milwaukee over Limit on Permits," *Milwaukee Journal Sentinel*, September 26, 2011, http://www.jsonline.com/news/milwaukee/130609278.html.

269 Rohde, "Taxi Tycoon"; Ryan Ekvall, "Milwaukee Taxicab War Test of Free Market," WisconsinWatchdog.org, February 24, 2012, http://watchdog.org/4921/wirep-milwaukee-taxicab-battle-test-of-free-market/. The bill applied only to "first-class" cities—those with populations over 150,000. While one other city, Madison, has a population of over 150,000, city officials there have opted not to seek the first-class designation, which entails greater financial responsibility for services. League of Wisconsin Municipalities, *The Reporter's Guide to Wisconsin City & Village Government* (Madison: League of Wisconsin Municipalities, 2003).

270 Jason Stein and Bill Vielmetti, "Assembly Backs New City Taxi Licensing System: 'Medallion' System Similar to Those in New York, Chicago," *Milwaukee Journal Sentinel*, February 22, 2012, http://www.jsonline.com/news/milwaukee/assembly-backs-new-city-taxi-licensing-system-8c4a2bb-140077583.html; Ekvall, "Milwaukee Taxicab War."

271 Wisconsin Assembly, Committee on Transportation, "Record of Committee Proceedings: Committee on Transportation; Assembly Bill 529," Wisconsin State Legislature, February 7, 2012, http://docs.legis.wisconsin.gov/2011/related/records/ab529/atra_02142012.pdf; Collin Roth, "Assembly Candidate Joe Sanfelippo 'Protects' Milwaukee Taxi Cartel," Media Trackers, July 31, 2012, http://mediatrackers.org/wisconsin/2012/07/31/assembly-candidate-joe-sanfelippo-protects-milwaukee-taxi-cartel.

272 A.B. 529, 2011–2012 Wisconsin Legislature (2011), http://docs.legis.wisconsin.gov/2011/proposals/ab529.

273 Wisconsin Senate, Committee on Transportation and Elections, "Record of Committee Proceedings: Committee on Transportation and Elections; Assembly Bill 529," Wisconsin State Legislature, March 8, 2012, http://docs.legis.wisconsin.gov/2011/related/records/ab529/stra_03302012.pdf.

274 Tr. Mot. Hearing, Ibrahim v. City of Milwaukee (Cir. Ct. Wis. Apr. 16, 2013) (No. 11-cv-15178) (unpublished transcript), 60.

275 Joe Sanfelippo Cabs Inc. v. City of Milwaukee, 46 F. Supp. 3d 888 (E.D. Wis. 2014).
276 Don Walker and Jason Silverstein, "Milwaukee Common Council Unanimously Lifts Cap on Taxi Permits," *Milwaukee Journal Sentinel*, July 22, 2014, http://www.jsonline.com/news/milwaukee/council-lifts-cap-on-taxi-permits-b99315839z1-268118062.html.
277 Don Walker, "Ald. Bauman Says City Will Fight Cab Lawsuit," *Milwaukee Journal Sentinel* blog, February 20, 2014, http://www.jsonline.com/blogs/news/246366311.html.
278 *Joe Sanfelippo Cabs*, 46 F. Supp. 3d.
279 Alison Bauter, "Hearing on Taxi Lawsuit Set as Independent Drivers Line Up for City Licenses," *Milwaukee Business Journal*, September 2, 2014, http://www.bizjournals.com/milwaukee/news/2014/09/02/hearing-on-taxi-lawsuit-set-as-independent-drivers.html.
280 Compl., *Joe Sanfelippo Cabs*, 46 F. Supp. 3d.
281 Bob Bauman, quoted in Walker, "Bauman Says City Will Fight."
282 *Joe Sanfelippo Cabs*, 46 F. Supp. 3d.
283 Jason Silverstein, "Flurry of Drivers Apply for Milwaukee Cab Permits under New Ordinance," *Milwaukee Journal Sentinel*, September 2, 2014, http://www.jsonline.com/news/milwaukee/dozens-of-drivers-apply-for-cab-permits-in-city-hall-under-new-taxi-ordinance-b99343007z1-273605211.html.
284 (List of active City of Milwaukee public passenger vehicle permits), Milwaukee, August 13, 2015, on file with the authors.
285 *Joe Sanfelippo Cabs*, No. 14-cv-1036, 2015 WL 8161306, 3 (E.D. Wis.) (December 7, 2015).
286 Even as he was actively litigating, Michael Sanfelippo chose to develop the downtown lot at which he kept his cabs into an apartment building. "The city killed the cab business and I don't have too many cabs anymore," he said in April 2015. "We're only occupying half of that parking lot, so now it's time to move forward." Sean Ryan, "Updated: Walker's Point Will See 120 New Apartments in Three Buildings, Starting in May," *Milwaukee Business Journal*, April 19, 2015, http://www.bizjournals.com/milwaukee/blog/real_estate/2015/04/walkers-point-will-see-120-new-apartments-in-three.html.
287 Saad Malik, e-mail conversation with John K. Ross, September 10, 2015.
288 James Cooper, Ray Mundy, and John Nelson, *Taxi! Urban Economies and the Social and Transport Impacts of the Taxicab* (Farnham, UK: Ashgate Gower, 2010).
289 Robert Hardaway, "Taxi and Limousines: The Last Bastion of Economic Regulation," *Hamline Journal of Law & Public Policy* 21, no. 319 (2000).
290 Connecticut retains its decades-old PCN laws, though the state's Supreme Court recently ruled that the Department of Transportation has long erred by presuming competition is harmful. Martorelli v. Dep't of Transp., 114 A.3d 912 (Conn. April 28, 2015). Other jurisdictions with PCN standards on the books include Delaware; Montana; Nebraska; Memphis, Tennessee; New Orleans; Palm Beach County, Florida; Charleston, South Carolina; Mobile, Alabama; Birmingham, Alabama; and Winston-Salem, North Carolina.
291 Rhode Island implemented a minimum fare in 2015. Other jurisdictions

with minimum fares on the books include Houston; Austin, Texas; Miami-Dade County, Florida; Atlanta; Little Rock, Arkansas; Hillsborough County (including Tampa), Florida; and Portland, Oregon.

292 Martin Romjue and Myla Diaz, "2014–2015 LCT Fact Book & Industry Guide," *Limousine, Charter, & Tour*, 2014, http://files.lctmag.com/PDFs/2014-LCT-Magazine-Fact-Book-Statistics.pdf.

293 Ibid.

294 "Industry Snapshot: Limousine Service (NAICS 485320)," United States Census Bureau, June 11, 2016, http://thedataweb.rm.census.gov/TheDataWeb_HotReport2/econsnapshot/2012/snapshot.hrml?NAICS=485320.

295 "100 Largest Fleets," *Limousine, Charter, & Tour*, June 13, 2012, http://www.lctmag.com/page/40041/top-100-largest-fleets-2012; John L. Smith, "Bell Owner Fights to Keep His Big Share of Limousine Market," *Las Vegas Review-Journal*, July 19, 1996.

296 Edward Wheeler, telephone conversation with John K. Ross, August 5, 2015.

297 John L. Smith, "Laws Give Limo Company Luxury Ride over Competition," *Las Vegas Review-Journal*, May 1, 1996; Smith, "Bell Owner Fights."

298 Edward Wheeler, telephone conversation with John K. Ross, August 5, 2015.

299 John L. Smith, "Bell Trans Always Gives Rough Rides to Limousine Applicants," *Las Vegas Review-Journal*, July 17, 1996.

300 Quoted in Julie Penn, "Las Vegas Limousine Rivalry in High Gear," *Las Vegas Review-Journal*, October 20, 1986.

301 Louis Nimmo, quoted in John L. Smith, "Entrepreneur Being Taken for a Ride by Limo Companies," *Las Vegas Review-Journal*, May 26, 1996.

302 Quoted in ibid.

303 Louis Nimmo, quoted in ibid.

304 Scott Gulbransen, "Airport Shuttle Provides Convenience to the Area," *Las Vegas Review-Journal*, October 14, 1998; David Hare, "Airport Shuttle Delivers Locals Only," *Las Vegas Business Press*, January 1, 2001.

305 "Renegade LV Limo Owner Loses Bid for Licensing,"*Las Vegas Sun*, September 30, 1998, http://lasvegassun.com/news/1998/sep/30/renegade-lv-limo-owner-loses-bid-for-licensing/; Mike O'Callaghan, "First-Class Transportation for People in Wheelchairs," *Las Vegas Sun*, September 19, 1998, http://lasvegassun.com/news/1998/sep/19/where-i-stand---mike-ocallaghan-first-class-transp/.

306 Quoted in Smith, "Bell Trans Gives Rough Rides"; see also Smith, "Bell Owner Fights."

307 Quoted in Sharon Gerrie, "New Limo Firms Face Bumpy Regulatory Ride: Applicants Charge State Helps Big Firms Stifle Competition," *Las Vegas Business Press*, December 6, 1999.

308 *Historical Las Vegas Visitor Statistics* (Las Vegas: Las Vegas Convention and Visitors Authority, 2015).

309 Hardaway, "Taxi and Limousines."

310 "Lawmakers Hear PSC Overhaul Ideas," *Las Vegas Review-Journal*, May 17, 1997; Fitzgerald, *Mugged by the State.*

311 Edward Wheeler, telephone conversation with John K. Ross, August 5, 2015.

312 Whittemore is currently in federal prison, having been convicted of campaign-finance violations. To get around contribution limits, he had funneled money

to family, friends, and employees, who then donated $150,000 to Nevada senator Harry Reid. United States v. Whittemore, 776 F.3d 1074 (9th Cir. 2015).

313 Ed Vogel, "Nevada Power Broker Whittemore Now a Pariah," *Las Vegas Review-Journal*, February 26, 2012.

314 "PSC Overhaul Ideas," *Las Vegas Review-Journal.*

315 Steven Miller, "Limousine Lumps," *Nevada Journal* 7, no. 2 (1999), http://archive.nevadajournal.com/nj99/02/limousine.htm; "Independent Limousine Operators Challenge State Regulation," *Las Vegas Sun*, May 4, 1998, http://lasvegassun.com/news/1998/may/04/independent-limousine-operators-challenge-state-re/.

316 A.B. 366, 1997 Nevada Legislative Session § 128 (1997).

317 Ibid.; Miller, "Limousine Lumps."

318 Associated Press, "Las Vegan Says He Has Lost $100,000 on Struggling Business," May 5, 1998.

319 Dennis Colling, quoted in Michael W. Lynch, "Flat Tire for Free Enterprise in Las Vegas," *Investor's Business Daily*, December 3, 1998, https://reason.com/archives/1998/12/03/flat-tire-for-free-enterprise.

320 Ibid.

321 William Clutter, quoted in Fitzgerald, *Mugged by the State*, 125.

322 Bill Gang, "Maverick Limousine Operator Takes a Hit in Court," *Las Vegas Sun*, January 21, 1999, http://lasvegassun.com/news/1999/jan/21/maverick-limousine-operator-takes-hit-in-court/; Fitzgerald, *Mugged by the State.*

323 "Operators Challenge State Regulation," *Las Vegas Sun.*

324 Federally licensed independent driver Gary Lunquist spent seventeen hours in jail stuffed into a cell built for twenty with sixty other detainees, including violent criminals. A single father, he was not allowed to call his daughter to tell her not to worry when he didn't come home—until 5:30 a.m. the following morning. Richard Lowre, "Driven to a Life of Crime," *Las Vegas Review-Journal*, July 19, 1998.

325 Edward Wheeler, "Limo Lawsuit: The Public Gets Cheated by Las Vegas Limo Cartel," *Las Vegas Review-Journal*, March 4, 2001.

326 Edward Wheeler, telephone conversation with John K. Ross, August 5, 2015.

327 William A. Clutter d/b/a BC Transportation Consultants vs. Transportation Services Authority of Nevada, No. A386841, slip op. (D. Nev. May 16, 2001).

328 Lynch, "Flat Tire for Free Enterprise."

329 John West, quoted in Fitzgerald, *Mugged by the State*, 124.

330 "Nevada Limousine Trial Pits Operators against Regulators," *Las Vegas Sun*, February 14, 2001, http://lasvegassun.com/news/2001/feb/14/nevada-limousine-trial-pits-operators-against-regu/; "Busting the Protection Racket," *Las Vegas Review-Journal*, February 16, 2001.

331 "Judge Weighs Argument That Nevada Law Protects Limousine Monopolies," *Las Vegas Sun*, August 29, 2000, http://lasvegassun.com/news/2000/aug/29/judge-weighs-argument-that-nevada-law-protects-lim/.

332 Rich Lowre, quoted in Steven Miller, "His Master's Voice," *Nevada Journal* 7, no. 6 (1999), http://archive.nevadajournal.com/nj99/06/democracy.htm.

333 Edward Wheeler, quoted in ibid.

334 S.B. 491, Nevada Legislature 70th Session (1999), https://www.leg.state.nv.us/Session/70th1999/Reports/history.cfm?ID=3067.

335 Miller, "His Master's Voice."
336 *William A. Clutter d/b/a BC Transportation Consultants*, No. A386841, 11–12.
337 *Id.*
338 "Minutes of Senate Committee on Transportation" (meeting minutes, Carson City, NV, May 24, 2001), Nevada Legislature, http://www.leg.state.nv.us/71st/Minutes/Senate/TRN/Final/1485.html; "Minutes of the Meeting of the Assembly Committee on Transportation" (meeting minutes, Carson City, NV, May 31, 2001), Nevada Legislature, http://www.leg.state.nv.us/71st/Minutes/Assembly/TRN/Final/1595.html.
339 S.B. 576, Nevada Legislature 71st Session (2001), http://www.leg.state.nv.us/Session/71st2001/Reports/history.cfm?ID=4772
340 Simpson, "Judicial Abdication."
341 Sharon Gerrie, "TSA Unanimously Disapproves West's Limousine Certificate," *Las Vegas Business Press*, April 24, 2000; Fitzgerald, *Mugged by the State.*
342 "Trial Pits Operators against Regulators," *Las Vegas Sun.*
343 "Wheeler Obtains License from TSA," *Limousine, Charter & Tour*, November 13, 2001, http://www.lctmag.com/operations/news/11648/wheeler-obtains-license-from-tsa.
344 Edward Wheeler, telephone conversation with John K. Ross, August 5, 2015.
345 Ibid.
346 Quoted in Cy Ryan, "LV Limo Owners Move to Restrict Numbers," *Las Vegas Sun*, May 21, 2003.
347 Maggie Carlton, quoted in ibid.
348 Richard N. Velotta, "Limousines Back on Legislative Agenda," *Las Vegas Sun*, August 19, 2004; "AB518," Nevada Legislature, accessed June 11, 2016, https://www.leg.state.nv.us/Session/72nd2003/Reports/history.cfm?ID=1048.
349 Brent Bell, quoted in Richard N. Velotta and Cy Ryan, "Lawmakers Weigh Limits on Limousine Numbers," *Las Vegas Sun*, April 6, 2004; see also Cy Ryan, "Legislative Panel Ponders Limits on Limo Licenses," *Las Vegas Sun*, April 16, 2004.
350 Velotta, "Limousines Back on Legislative Agenda."
351 "Rigged Rides," *Wall Street Journal*, March 16, 1999.
352 The three companies are Bell Trans, Bell Limo, and Presidential Limousine. The last acquired its certificate over the Bells' objections in the 1980s—before itself being acquired by the Bells. Penn, "Las Vegas Limousine Rivalry"; "Nation's Largest Livery Operator Squeezes Optimum Efficiency from 264 Vehicles," *Limousine, Charter, & Tour*, January 1, 1994, http://www.lctmag.com/operations/article/42586/nations-largest-livery-operator-squeezes-optimum-efficiency-from-264-vehicles.
353 Jeff German, "Owner of Limo Service Indicted," *Las Vegas Review-Journal*, December 14, 2012; Richard N. Velotta, "State Revokes Licenses of Las Vegas Limo Company," *Las Vegas Review-Journal*, October 31, 2014, http://www.reviewjournal.com/news/las-vegas/state-revokes-licenses-las-vegas-limo-company; U.S. Attorney's Office, "Limousine Company Owner Pleads Guilty to Racketeering Charge," Federal Bureau of Investigation, December 19, 2014, https://www.fbi.gov/lasvegas/press-releases/2014/limousine-company-owner-pleads-guilty-to-racketeering-charge.

354 Omni Limousine, Ed's former company, now has a license to operate thirty-nine vehicles.
355 Ali Bokhari, telephone conversation with John K. Ross, August 11, 2015.
356 Ibid.
357 Ali Bokhari, telephone conversation with John K. Ross, August 3, 2015.
358 Ibid.
359 Metropolitan Government of Nashville and Davidson County, *Report of Taxicab and Other Passenger Vehicles for Hire in Nashville* (Nashville: RPM Transportation Consultants, 2012), http://www.taxi-library.org/nashville-2012.pdf.
360 Limousines and sedans were far from unregulated, however. State vehicle inspection and insurance requirements applied to Nashville sedans, and Ali would end up carrying $2.5 million in liability insurance for each vehicle—the minimum required by the National Limousine Association, of which Ali has been a member since 2005. By comparison, the city required $50,000 in insurance for cabs, while the state required $1.5 million in insurance for black cars. Mark W. Frankenna, "Nashville's Anti-Competitive 'Black Car' Regulations: A Local Jury Approves a Piece of Music City Corporate Welfare," *Regulation* 36, nos. 2–3 (2013).
361 Ali Bokhari, telephone conversation with John K. Ross, August 3, 2015; Frankenna, "'Black Car' Regulations."
362 Dennis Ferrier, "Metro Faces Allegations of Limiting Competitive Prices," WSMV.com, January 2, 2013, http://www.wsmv.com/story/20489478/metro-faces-allegations-of-limiting-competitive-prices.
363 *Deposition of William Faeth*, Bokhari v. Metropolitan Government of Nashville and Davidson Co., M.D. Tenn. (2012) (testimony of William Faeth, vice president, Tennessee Livery Association).
364 Frankenna, "'Black Car' Regulations."
365 Ibid.
366 Nevertheless, the consultant called for the city to protect cabs from livery services.
367 Metropolitan Government of Nashville, *Taxicab and Other Passenger Vehicles*, § 3, 23.
368 Andy Humbles, "Some Nashville Limo Company Owners to Fight New Regulations," *Tennessean*, January 4, 2011.
369 Joseph Pleasant, "Limousine Owners May Fight Changes to Ordinance in Federal Court," WKRN.com, January 3, 2011, http://wkrn.com/2011/01/03/limousine-owners-may-fight-changes-to-ordinance-in-federal-court/; "Tennessee Association Forms, Tackles New Ordinance That Defines Limousines," *Limousine Digest* 19, no. 10 (2009).
370 Quoted in "Tennessee Association Forms," *Limousine Digest*, 60
371 Ali Bokhari, telephone conversation with John K. Ross, August 3, 2015.
372 *Testimony of William Faeth*, Bokhari v. Metropolitan Government of Nashville and Davidson Co., M.D. Tenn. (2012) (William Faeth, vice president, Tennessee Livery Association).
373 The ordinance also required that vehicles be taken out of service at seven years or 350,000 miles.

374 J. L. Greene, "How Big Car Services Use Legislation to Drive over Competition," *Huffington Post*, December 7, 2011, http://www.huffingtonpost.com/2011/11/18/livery-services-use-legis_n_1101708.html.
375 Duane W. Gang, "Nashville Limo Owners Want to Stop Enforcement of $45-Per-Trip Minimum Fare," *Tennessean*, April 3, 2012; Frankenna, "'Black Car' Regulations."
376 Ali Bokhari, telephone conversation with John K. Ross, August 3, 2015.
377 Frankenna, "'Black Car' Regulations."
378 Bo Mitchell, quoted in Humbles, "Owners to Fight New Regulations."
379 Quoted in ibid.
380 Ali Bokhari, speaking in "Nashville's Sedan Drivers Fight City Effort to Run Them off the Road," YouTube video, 2:58, posted by Institute for Justice, April 19, 2011, https://www.youtube.com/watch?v=BMJbx--kWdA.
381 *Testimony of Brian McQuiston*, Bokhari v. Metropolitan Government of Nashville and Davidson Co., M.D. Tenn (2013) (statement of Brian McQuiston, director, Metropolitan Transportation Licensing Commission).
382 Gang, "$45-per-Trip Minimum Fare."
383 *Deposition of William Faeth*, Bokhari v. Metropolitan Government of Nashville and Davidson Co., M.D. Tenn. (2012) (testimony of William Faeth, vice president, Tennessee Livery Association).
384 J. L. Greene, "Nashville Transportation Licensing Commission Admits to Using Police Badges," *Huffington Post*, April 6, 2012, http://www.huffingtonpost.com/2012/04/06/nashville-police-badges-tlc_n_1408723.html.
385 Ali Bokhari, telephone conversation with John K. Ross, August 3, 2015.
386 "Commission Admits to Using Police Badges."
387 Michael Cass, "Police Chief Blasts Nashville Vehicle Inspectors," *Tennessean*, April 25, 2012.
388 Gail Kerr, "Taxi System Was a Wreck, and Dean Cleaned It Up," *Tennessean*, July 25, 2012.
389 Michael Cass, "Nashville Council Slashes Minimum Fee to Hire Limo, Sedan to $9.75," *Tennessean*, January 7, 2014. The city also agreed not to enforce the requirement that drivers return to a central location after each trip. The requirement that operators use newer vehicles remains on the books, however. As a result, Ali had to upgrade his fleet at significant expense.
390 Quoted in E. J. Boyer, "As Tourism Increases, Spyridon Looks at Taxis, Black-Car Services," *Nashville Business Journal*, November 27, 2013, http://www.bizjournals.com/nashville/blog/2013/11/as-tourism-increases-spyridon-talks.html; see also Greene, "Big Car Services."
391 Black-car services are not the only competitive innovations taxi companies face in Nashville and many other cities. Recent years have seen the rise of ride sharing and companies like Uber and Lyft. Boyd Cohen and Jan Kietzmann, "Ride On! Mobility Business Models for the Sharing Economy," *Organization & Environment* 27, no. 3 (2015).

Taking advantage of contemporary technology, ride-sharing companies are matching customers needing transportation to drivers in their areas. K. Casey Strong, "When Apps Pollute: Regulating Transportation Network Companies to Maximize Environmental Benefits," *University of Colorado Law Review* 86

(2015). Because ride-sharing drivers use new technologies to reduce overhead costs and do no operate under the same inefficient regulations as taxi drivers, they can charge significantly less and operate with greater efficiency. Scott Wallsten, *The Competitive Effects of the Sharing Economy: How Is Uber Changing Taxis?* (report, Washington, DC: Technology Policy Institute, June 2015), https://techpolicyinstitute.org/wp-content/uploads/2015/06/the-competitive-effects-of-the-2007713.pdf.

Although some have predicted the demise of the traditional taxi service due to ride sharing, bottlenecking by taxi owners has resulted in efforts by city officials to preserve the taxi industry and the licensing schemes that regulate it, as well as efforts to regulate ride sharing. Sarah Cannon and Lawrence H. Summers, "How Uber and the Sharing Economy Can Win Over Regulators," *Harvard Business Review*, October 13, 2014, https://hbr.org/2014/10/how-uber-and-the-sharing-economy-can-win-over-regulators; Hannah A. Posen, "Ridesharing in the Sharing Economy: Should Regulators Impose Über Regulations on Uber?," *Iowa Law Review* 101 (2015).

392 Ali Bokhari, telephone conversation with John K. Ross, August 3, 2015.
393 Hector Ricketts, telephone conversation with John K. Ross, June 23, 2015.
394 Ibid.
395 Ibid.
396 Ibid.

CHAPTER 7 ■ THE SCHNITZEL KING IS NO MORE

1 "Non-Hodgkin Lymphoma (NHL)," Lymphoma Research Foundation, accessed June 12, 2016, http://www.lymphoma.org/site/pp.asp?c=bkLTKaOQLmK8E&b=6300139.
2 Karen Chadra, "Cupcakes for Courage: New Elmhurst Store Is All about Cupcakes—and So Much More," *Elmhurst Patch*, August 20, 2012, http://elmhurst.patch.com/groups/business-news/p/cupcakes-for-courage-new-elmhurst-store-is-all-about-ffccf598d9.
3 Helen Tangires, *Public Markets and Civic Culture in Nineteenth-Century America* (Baltimore: Johns Hopkins University Press, 2003).
4 James M. Mayo, *The American Grocery Store: The Business Evolution of an Architectural Space* (Westport, CT: Greenwood, 1993).
5 Daniel M. Bluestone, "'The Pushcart Evil': Peddlers, Merchants, and New York City's Streets, 1890–1940," *Journal of Urban History* 18, no. 1 (1991).
6 Mayo, *American Grocery Store.*
7 Ibid.
8 Ibid.
9 Ibid.
10 David Ward, "Population Growth, Migration, and Urbanization, 1860–1920," in *North America: The Historical Geography of a Changing Continent*, 2nd ed., ed. Thomas F. McIlwraith and Edward K. Muller (Rowman & Littlefield, 2001).
11 Ward, "Population Growth."
12 Bluestone, "'Pushcart Evil'"; Alfonso Morales, "Peddling Policy: Street Vending

in Historical and Contemporary Context," *International Journal of Sociology and Social Policy* 20, nos. 3–4 (2000); Suzanne Wasserman, "Hawkers and Gawkers: Peddling and Markets in New York City," in *Gastropolis: Food & New York City*, ed. Annie Hauck Lawson and Jonathan Deutsch (New York: Columbia University Press, 2009).

13 Christine Gallant, "A Defense of City's Street Vendors," *Atlanta Journal-Constitution*, August 11, 2011; Morales, "Peddling Policy."

14 Bluestone, "'Pushcart Evil.'"

15 Alfonso Morales and Gregg W. Kettles, "Healthy Food Outside: Farmers' Markets, Taco Trucks, and Sidewalk Fruit Vendors," *Journal of Contemporary Health Law and Policy* 26 (2009).

16 U.S. Department of the Interior Census Office, "Progress of a Nation," in *Report on Population of the United States at the Eleventh Census: 1890* (Washington, DC: Government Printing Office, 1897); U.S. Department of Commerce; "Occupation," in *Sixteenth Census of the United States: 1940*, vol. 3 (Washington, DC: Government Printing Office, 1943).

17 Robert Frommer, Bert Gall, and Lisa Knepper, *Streets of Dreams* (Arlington: Institute for Justice, 2011).

18 Ibid.

19 Aaron Nicodemus, "Worcester to Host One-Day Food Truck Festival in July," *Worcester Telegram & Gazette*, March 11, 2012.

20 "Chapter 14. Business Licenses, Taxes and Regulations; Article 14: Licensed Street Vendors," in *Code of the City of Lawrence, Kansas*, 6-77–6-78, City of Lawrence Kansas, accessed August 2, 2016, https://lawrenceks.org/assets/city-code/chapter06.pdf.

21 Lauren Etter, "Moving Violations: In Chicago, Cooking and Driving Don't Mix," *Wall Street Journal*, last modified December 13, 2010, http://online.wsj.com/article/SB10001424052748704008704575638842201629742.html.

22 Frommer et al., *Streets of Dreams.*

23 Angela A. Erickson, "Food Safety Risk of Food Trucks Compared to Restaurants," *Food Protection Trends* 35, no. 5 (2015).

24 Jesús Alberto Hermosillo, "Loncheras: A Look at the Stationary Food Trucks of Los Angeles" (master's thesis, University of California, Los Angeles, 2012); Jennifer Lee, "Street Vending as a Way to Ease Joblessness," *City Room* (blog), *New York Times*, April 29, 2009, http://cityroom.blogs.nytimes.com/2009/04/29/street-vending-as-a-way-to-eae-joblessness.

25 Article I, Section 6, of the Illinois Constitution protects the right of individuals "to be secure in their persons, houses, papers and other possessions against unreasonable searches, seizures, invasions of privacy or interceptions of communications by eavesdropping devices or other means." Further, because GPS tracking devices can reveal so much, the government must show that the devices are necessary and that their use is circumscribed. But nothing in Chicago's law limits how, when, or for what reason city officials can access or use the information these devices transmit. This kind of discretion is incompatible with the decisions of the US and Illinois supreme courts, which have said that the "'time, place, and scope' of the inspection [must be] limited." New York v. Burger, 482 U.S. 691, 711 (U.S. 1987).

26 The district was then known as the Medical Center District.
27 Triple A Servs., Inc., v. Rice, 528 N.E. 2d 267 (Ill. App. Ct. 1988), *rev'd*, 545 N.E. 2d 706 (Ill. 1989).
28 *Triple A Servs.*, 528 N.E. 2d 267 at 270.
29 *Id.* at 270. Nor did the committee fail to analyze the ban because it regularly saw similar legislation. According to the staffer, committee members had never encountered a similar ordinance before.
30 From the ruling: "We reiterate that no evidence was presented at the hearing to establish that mobile food vendor vehicles in the District had any impact upon the District's performance of its purposes to provide care for the sick and injured and for the study of diseases. The substance of the testimony of the defense witnesses at the hearing simply was that the mobile food vendor vehicles' presence in the District was cosmetically offensive to them personally." *Id.* at 279.
31 Triple A Servs. Inc. v. Rice, 545 N.E. 2d 706 at 709, 710 (Ill. 1989).
32 Elan Schpigel, "Chicago's Overburdensome Regulation of Mobile Food Vending," *Northwestern Journal of Law & Social Policy* 10, no. 2 (2015).
33 *Amended Complaint for Declaratory Judgment and Injunctive Relief*, Burke v. City of Chicago, Cir. Ct. Ill. (2013) (Greg Burke, Kristin Casper, and LMP Services, plaintiffs).
34 Robert Davis, "City Council Puts Its Business on Back Burner and Goes Fishin'," *Chicago Tribune*, July 26, 1991.
35 Janet Ginsburg, "City Cracks Down on Mobile Food Vendors," *Chicago Tribune*, July 27, 1991.
36 Robert Davis, "City Dishes Out a Compromise to Food Vendors," *Chicago Tribune*, September 6, 1991.
37 Patrick Huels, quoted in Robert Davis and Janet Ginsburg, "Loop Food Vendors Try to Keep a Place in Sun," *Chicago Tribune*, September 1, 1991.
38 Ted Mazola, quoted in Davis, "City Dishes Out a Compromise."
39 Burke et al., "Amended Complaint."
40 "S&P/Case-Shiller 20-City Composite Home Price Index," Federal Reserve Bank of St. Louis Economic Research, last modified May 31, 2016, http://research.stlouisfed.org/fred2/series/SPCS20RSA.
41 "Graph: S&P 500," Federal Reserve Bank of St. Louis Economic Research, accessed June 12, 2016, http://research.stlouisfed.org/fred2/graph/?id=SP500.
42 "Graph: Households and Nonprofit Organizations; Net Worth, Level," Federal Reserve Bank of St. Louis Economic Research, accessed June 12, 2016, http://research.stlouisfed.org/fred2/graph/?id=TNWBSHNO.
43 Carmen DeNavas-Walt and Bernadette D. Proctor, *Income, Poverty, and Health Insurance Coverage in the United States: 2014* (Washington, DC: U.S. Census Bureau, 2015).
44 Alan Berube and Elizabeth Kneebone, "Parsing U.S. Poverty at the Metropolitan Level," *The Avenue* (blog), Brookings Institute, September 22, 2011, http://www.brookings.edu/blogs/the-avenue/posts/2011/09/22-metro-poverty-berube-kneebone.
45 "Income," United States Census Bureau, accessed June 12, 2016, http://www.census.gov/hhes/www/income/data/historical/people/2010/P05AR_2010.xls.

46 "Graph: Civilian Unemployment Rate," Federal Reserve Bank of St. Louis Economic Research, accessed June 12, 2016, http://research.stlouisfed.org/fred2/graph/?id=UNRATE.
47 "Graph: Unemployment Level," Federal Reserve Bank of St. Louis Economic Research, accessed June 12, 2016, http://research.stlouisfed.org/fred2/graph/?id=UNEMPLOY.
48 Lee, "Street Vending."
49 Claire Bushey, "Legalize It," *Chicago Reader*, May 28, 2009, http://www.chicagoreader.com/chicago/legalize-it/Content?oid=1141442.
50 "Industry Snapshot: Mobile Food Services (NAICS 722330); 2012 Sales per Capita," U.S. Census Bureau, accessed August 2, 2016, http://thedataweb.rm.census.gov/TheDataWeb_HotReport2/econsnapshot/2012/snapshot.hrml?NAICS=722330; United States Census Bureau, "Industry Snapshot: Other Direct Selling Establishments (NAICS 454390)," Institute of Justice, accessed August 9, 2016, http://ij.org/wp-content/uploads/2016/08/HR2-Econ-Report-Page.pdf.
51 John T. Edge, quoted in Rick Allen, "'Street Food' Sees Uptick in Local Popularity: Speaker at Food Series Says Outdoor Vendors Are Now 'Hip,'" Ocala.com, April 16, 2010, http://www.ocala.com/article/20100416/articles/4161007.
52 Jane Black, "Street-Food Truck Rolls into Red Tape," *Washington Post,* December 2, 2009, http://articles.washingtonpost.com/2009-12-02/news/36921704_1_food-truck-farmers-markets-fojol-bros.
53 Sarah Kaplan,"As the Upstart Food Truck Industry Matures, Where Is D.C.'s Mobile Lunch Scene Headed?," *Washington Post*, July 29, 2014, https://www.washingtonpost.com/lifestyle/food/as-the-upstart-food-truck-industry-matures-where-is-dcs-mobile-lunch-scene-headed/2014/07/28/0a2f1f42-0e99-11e4-8c9a-923ecc0c7d23_story.html; Baylen J. Linnekin, Jeffrey Dermer, and Matthew Geller, "The New Food Truck Advocacy: Social Media, Mobile Food Vending Associations, Truck Lots, & Litigation in California & Beyond," *Nexus* 17 (2011/2012); Elizabeth Kregor, "Food Trucks, Incremental Innovation, and Regulatory Ruts," *University of Chicago Law Review Dialogue* 82, no. 1 (2015); Hannah Kapell, Peter Katon, Amy Koski, Jingping Li, Colin Price, and Karen Thalhammer, *Food Cartology: Rethinking Urban Spaces as People Places* (Portland, OR: Portland Bureau of Planning and Urban Vitality Group, 2008); "Tweet to Eat: Find Your Food through Social Networking," *AARP the Magazine* (September/October 2010), Internet Archive Wayback Machine, posted August 15, 2010, https://web.archive.org/web/20100815163540/http://www.aarp.org/technology/innovations/info-07-2010/tweet-to-eat.html.
54 Alfonso Morales and Steve Balkin, "www.openair.org: Linking Street Vendors to the Internet," *International Journal of Sociology and Social Policy* 20, nos. 3–4; Ryan T. Devlin, "Illegibility, Uncertainty and the Management of Street Vending in New York City" (paper presented at the Breslauer graduate student symposium "The Right to the City and the Politics of Space," University of California, Berkeley, 2006); Gregg W. Kettles, "Regulating Vending in the Sidewalk Commons," *Temple Law Review* 77, no. 1 (2004); Morales, "Peddling Policy."

55 Anastasia Loukaitou-Sideris and Liette Gilbert, "Shades of Duality: Perceptions and Images of Downtown Workers in Los Angeles," *Journal of Architectural and Planning Research* 17, no. 1 (2000).

56 Ibid.

57 Robert Shepherd, "'I Bought This at Eastern Market': Vending, Value, and Social Relations in an Urban Street Market," in *Economic Development, Integration, and Morality in Asia and the Americas*, vol. 29, ed. Donald Wood (Bingley, UK: Emerald).

58 Karen Edwards, "Shop and Go," *Entrepreneurship* 34, no. 6 (2006), 97.

59 Stephan Boillon, quoted in Tim Carman, "The $20 Diner: Mothership Is Park View's New Refueling Zone," *Washington Post*, May 2, 2013, http://www.washingtonpost.com/goingoutguide/the-20-diner-mothership-is-park-views-new-refueling-zone/2013/05/01/482bffd2-adaf-11e2-a986-eec837b1888b_story.html?hpid=z5. In 2015, Mothership closed, and Boillon relaunched the El Floridano food truck. Jessica Sidman, "Mothership Will Close, El Floridano Food Truck Will Return," *Washington City Paper* blog, January 28, 2015, http://www.washingtoncitypaper.com/blogs/youngandhungry/2015/01/28/mothership-will-close-el-floridano-food-truck-will-return/.

60 Kristin Burke, quoted in Hilary Gowins, "City Rules Lure, Push Away Food Truck Flavors," *Huffington Post*, July 19, 2014, http://www.huffingtonpost.com/hilary-gowins/city-rules-lure-push-away-food-trucks_b_5600872.html.

61 Monica Eng, "Food Truck Ordinance Savory to Some, Sour to Others," *Chicago Tribune*, July 9, 2012, http://articles.chicagotribune.com/2012-07-09/news/ct-met-food-truck-followup-20120709_1_food-truck-truck-operators-fines; Kate MacArthur, "Chicago Moves At Least to Permit Full-Kitchen Food Trucks," *Crain's Chicago Business*, June 25, 2012, http://www.chicagobusiness.com/article/20120625/NEWS0702/120629886/chicago-moves-at-last-to-permit-full-kitchen-food-trucks#ixzz1yugvtJ6u.

62 Fran Spielman, "Rahm Would OK Mobile Food Trucks Restaurants Oppose," *Chicago Sun-Times*, February 2, 2011, Internet Archive Wayback Machine, https://web.archive.org/web/20110204172544/http://www.suntimes.com/news/politics/3605280-418/emanuel-chicago-plan-stores-restaurants.html; MacArthur, "Full-Kitchen Food Trucks."

63 "Putting the Brakes on Food Trucks," *Chicago Tribune*, July 25, 2012, http://articles.chicagotribune.com/2012-07-25/opinion/ct-edit-trucks-20120725_1_food-trucks-gps-spaces; John Byrne, "City Council Approves Food Truck Ordinance," *Chicago Tribune*, July 25, 2012, http://articles.chicagotribune.com/2012-07-25/news/chi-chicago-city-council-approves-food-truck-ordinance-20120725_1_food-truck-brick-and-mortar-restaurant-beth-kregor; Fran Spielman, "Restaurant-Owning Alderman Demands Limits on Mobile Food Truck Proposal," Mobile-Cuisine.com, accessed June 29, 2016, http://mobile-cuisine.com/off-the-wire/restaurant-owning-alderman-demands-limits-on-mobile-food-truck-proposal/. Burke et al., "Amended Complaint."

The 2012 ordinance did, however, allow food trucks to prepare food on board—something that had been illegal since the previous 1991 ordinance. "Putting the Brakes on Food Trucks," *Chicago Tribune*.

64 Proco Moreno, quoted in Monica Eng, "Food Truck Plan Gains Mobility: Chicago Proposal Would Create Zones for Trucks, Allow Operation in

Parking Spaces Away from Restaurants," *Chicago Tribune*, June 26, 2012, http://articles.chicagotribune.com/2012-06-26/news/ct-met-chicago-food-trucks--20120626_1_food-truck-mobile-food-ordinance.

65 Burke et al., "Amended Complaint."

66 Brendan Reilly, quoted in ibid., 14.

67 Quoted in ibid., 14.

68 Quoted in ibid., 14.

69 Walter Burnett Jr., quoted in ibid., 15.

70 Mayor of Chicago, "Mayor Emanuel to Legalize Cook-on-Site Food Truck Industry across Chicago" (press release, June 26, 2012), City of Chicago, http://www.cityofchicago.org/city/en/depts/mayor/press_room/press_releases/2012/june_2012/mayor_emanuel_tolegalizecook-on-sitefoodtruckindustryacrosschica.html.

71 John Arena, quoted in Byrne, "Food Truck Ordinance."

72 *Defendant's Responses and Objections to Plaintiffs' Interrogatories*, Burke v. City of Chicago, Cir. Ct. Ill. (2013).

73 Renia Ehrenfreucht, *Food Trucks in Chicago* (report, 2013), on file with the authors.

74 Frommer et al., *Streets of Dreams*.

75 Michele ver Ploeg, Vince Breneman, Tracey Farrigan, Karen Hamrick, David Hopkins, Phil Kaufman, Biing-Hwan Lin et al., *Access to Affordable and Nutritious Food: Measuring and Understanding Food Deserts and Their Consequences* (Washington, DC: US Department of Agriculture, 2009), http://www.ers.usda.gov/media/242675/ap036_1_.pdf.

76 *Defendant's Responses and Objections, Burke*.

77 *Plaintiff's Supplemental Response to Defendant's First Set of Interrogatories*, Cir. Ct. Ill. (2015) (Robert Frommer, plaintiff).

78 Ibid.

79 Rene Rodrigues, "Telemundo: Revitalized and Stronger than Ever," *Miami Herald*, October 25, 2015, http://www.miamiherald.com/news/business/biz-monday/article41256162.html.

80 Hialeah was also the site of two unrelated bits of aviation history. In 1937, Amelia Earhart said her final goodbyes to the continental United States from the city, where a park and school are named in her honor. In 1927, twelve-year-old Paul Tibbets dropped Baby Ruth candy bars from a biplane onto the Hialeah Race Track, before going on to drop an atom bomb on Hiroshima, Japan, out of his B-29 Superfortress *Enola Gay* eighteen years later. "37 Things You Probably Didn't Know about Hialeah, Florida," MOVOTO, accessed June 12, 2016, http//www.movoto.com/hialeah-fl/hialeah-facts/; Barry Schiff, "Test Pilot," *AOPA Pilot* (June 2015), 42, 46.

81 John Salvador Molloy, "Herald's Choices for Hialeah Council," *Miami Herald*, October 26, 2015, http://www.miamiherald.com/opinion/editorials/article41501550.html.

82 *Affidavit of Silvio Membreno*, Membreno v. City of Hialeah, Fla. Cir. Ct. (2014) (written statement of Silvio Membreno, flower vendor and vending activist).

83 Ed Brown and Jonathan Cloke, "Neoliberal Reform, Governance and Corruption in Central America: Exploring the Nicaraguan Case," *Political Geography* 24 (2005). The corruption leading up to Alemán's conviction

should not be underestimated: "After the overthrow of the Somoza regime in 1979, mass confiscations and expropriations occurred as the Sandinistas set up farm cooperatives and implemented a socialist economic structure." Upon losing power in the 1990 election, the Sandinistas sabotaged as much as possible for the incoming president. They attempted to retain power indirectly by adding more than twelve thousand new people to government payrolls. In an economic scheme so outrageous it earned the title "La Piñata," the outgoing party approved large and valuable property grants to its leaders and others devoted to the Sandinista cause to the tune of 1.55 million hectares (approximately one-fourth of all agricultural land in Nicaragua). These grants included more than six thousand homes in desirable locations and seventy-six hectares of rural land. Along the way, the party destroyed property records, making later reclamation impossible. And on the way out the door, it squandered most of the budget and oil reserves for 1990, leaving the new administration completely impoverished. Robert C. Harding, "Military Extrication and Democracy in Nicaragua, Guatemala, and Argentina in the 1990s: A Comparative Study" (paper presented at the Meeting of the Latin American Studies Association, Washington, DC, 2001).

84 Jose Antonio Ocampo, "Collapse and (Incomplete) Stabilization of the Nicaraguan Economy," in *The Macroeconomics of Populism in Latin America*, ed. Rudiger Dornbusch and Sebastian Edwards (Chicago: University of Chicago Press, 1991).

85 Arian Campo-Flores, "Street Vendors Battle Limits," *Wall Street Journal*, January 21, 2013, http://www.wsj.com/articles/SB10001424127887323783704578246211086583502.

86 *Deposition of Silvio Membreno*, Membreno v. City of Hialeah, Florida, Fla. Cir. Ct. (2014) (testimony of Silvio Membreno, flower vendor and vending activist).

87 Hialeah Code of Ordinances 2001-94, 1 [repealed].

88 Hialeah Code of Ordinances § 18-306 [repealed].

89 Hialeah Code of Ordinance 13-01, § 3.

90 Silvio Membreno, quoted in Brenda Medina and Janey Fugate, "Judge Rules against Hialeah Street Peddlers," *Miami Herald*, June 15, 2014, http://www.miamiherald.com/news/local/community/miami-dade/hialeah/article1966630.html.

91 *Appellants' Initial Brief*, Membreno v. City of Hialeah, Fla. 3d Dist. Ct. App. (2015) (Silvio Membreno and Florida Association of Vendors, plaintiffs).

92 Ibid.

93 Ibid.

94 Campo-Flores, "Street Vendors Battle Limits"; Medina and Fugate, "Judge Rules against Hialeah Street Peddlers."

95 Medina and Fugate, "Judge Rules against Hialeah Street Peddlers."

96 Membreno v. City of Hialeah, 188 So. 3d 13, 34-5 (Fla. 3d Dist. Ct. App. 2016).

97 *Membreno*, No. SC16-606 (Fla. Supreme Court June 27, 2016) [order denying petition for review].

98 From the appeals court ruling: "We decline the Street Vendors' argument that they are entitled to a trial on whether or not any of these considerations can be established or disproven by evidence admitted in a court of law." *Membreno*, 188 So. 3d at 35.

99 Pilar Arias, "Special Report: Food Truck Madness Hits El Paso: Nearly 400 Trucks Feeding Locals on the Streets," KVIA.com, November 20, 2014, http://www.kvia.com/news/special-report-food-truck-madness-hits-el-paso/29852750.
100 "2012 Nonemployer Statistics: El Paso, TX Metro Area, NAICS 45439, Other Direct Selling Establishments," U.S. Census Bureau, accessed August 2, 2016, http://censtats.census.gov/cgi-bin/nonemployer/nondetl.pl?MSA=21340&CSA=NO&Year=2012&areaname=El+Paso%2C+TX+Metro+Area&Noise=NO&x=13&y=9&State=00000&selBox=2&County=00000&Path=s&Sic=44-45.
101 Frommer et al., *Streets of Dreams.*
102 Ibid.
103 Ramon Bracamontes,"Mobile Food Vendors Get Voice," *El Paso Times*, January 27, 2011.
104 Ibid.
105 Patrick Manning, "El Paso Food Vendors Biting at City Laws," Fox Business, February 14, 2011, http://smallbusiness.foxbusiness.com/legal-hr/2011/02/14/el-paso-food-vendors-biting-city-laws/.
106 Bracamontes,"Mobile Food Vendors Get Voice."
107 Yvonne Castaneda, quoted in Manning, "Vendors Biting at City Laws"; also taken from Yvonne Castaneda, telephone conversation with Dick Carpenter, April 17, 2015.
108 Yvonne Castaneda, quoted in Gaby Loria, "Mobile Food Vendors File Federal Suit against City of El Paso," KVIA.com, July 15, 2012, http://www.kvia.com/news/Mobile-Food-Vendors-File-Federal-Suit-Against-City-of-El-Paso/541950.
109 Yvonne Castaneda, telephone conversation with Dick Carpenter, April 17, 2015; Manning, "Vendors Biting at City Laws."
110 Manning, "Vendors Biting at City Laws."
111 Hearing, El Paso City Council (August 11, 2009).
112 Daniel Morales, quoted in Matt Dougherty, "Exclusive Vending Contract Keeps Gourmet Food Trucks from Downtown," KVIA.com, May 18, 2012, http://www.kvia.com/news/Exclusive-Vending-Contract-Keeps-Gourmet-Food-Trucks-from-Downtown/15242230.
113 Susie Diaz, quoted in Loria, "Mobile Food Vendors."
114 Hearing, El Paso City Council, Regular Council Meeting (April 26, 2011) (testimony of Michael Hill, director of public health, City of El Paso).
115 Yvonne Castaneda, telephone conversation with Dick Carpenter, April 17, 2015.
116 Ramon Bracamontes, "Rules on Mobile Food Vendors Eased," *El Paso Times*, April 27, 2011; Marty Schladen, "New Rules to Ease Up on Mobile Food Sellers," *El Paso Times*, April 6, 2011.
117 Yvonne Castaneda, telephone conversation with Dick Carpenter, April 17, 2015.
118 Vic Kolenc, "Mean Streets for Mobile Vendors: Though Some El Paso Regulations Eased, Downtown Still Restricted," *Burlington Record*, March 19, 2012, http://www.burlington-record.com/ci_20198774/mean-streets-mobile-vendors-though-some-el-paso.
119 Ibid.
120 Veronica Soto, quoted in ibid.
121 Steve Ortega, quoted in ibid.
122 John Gaber, "Manhattan's 14th Street Vendor's Market: Informal Street

Peddlers' Complementary Relationship with New York City' Economy," *Urban Anthropology* 23, no. 4 (1994).

123 Hermosillo, "Loncheras"; Yvonne V. Jones, "Street Peddlers as Entrepreneurs: Economic Adaptation to an Urban Area," *Urban Anthropology* 17, nos. 2–3 (1988); Linnekin et al., "New Food Truck Advocacy"; Lenore Lauri Newman and Katherine Burnett, "Street Food and Vibrant Urban Spaces: Lessons from Portland, Oregon," *Local Environment* 18, no. 2 (2013).

124 Regina Austin, "'An Honest Living': Street Vendors, Municipal Regulation, and the Black Public Sphere," *Yale Law Journal* 103, no. 8 (1994).

125 Steven M. Zeitchik, "From Incense to Book Sense: Ex-Street Vendors' Black Bookstore Flourishes," *Publishers Weekly* 245, no. 41 (1998).

126 Karibu books closed in 2008. Andrea K. Walker, "Karibu Book Chain Is Closing: Stores Promoted African-American Writers Black-Themed Book Chain Closing," *Baltimore Sun*, January 24, 2008, http://articles.baltimoresun.com/2008-01-24/business/0801240202_1_karibu.

127 Ray Bromley, "Street Vending and Public Policy: A Global Review," *International Journal of Sociology and Social Policy*, 20, nos. 1–2 (2000); Stephen Clowney, "Invisible Businessman: Undermining Black Enterprise with Land Use Rules," *University of Illinois Law Review* (2009); Kettles, "Regulating Vending"; Gregg W. Kettles, "Legal Responses to Sidewalk Vending," in *Street Entrepreneurs: People, Place and Politics in Local and Global Perspective*, ed. John C. Cross and Alfonso Morales (London: Routledge, 2007).

128 Clowney, "Undermining Black Enterprise"; Alex Mayyasi, "Food Truck Economics," *Priceonomics*, March 14, 2013, http://priceonomics.com/post/45352687467/food-truck-economics.

129 Vic Kolenc, "Despite Road Blocks, El Paso Food Trucks Keep on Truckin'," *El Paso Times*, March 18, 2012.

130 Bromley, "Street Vending and Public Policy."

131 Austin, "'An Honest Living.'"

132 Clowney, "Undermining Black Enterprise."

133 Step 13, "Ice Cream Cart/Entrepreneurship Program" (newsletter, Denver, 2015).

134 Bromley, "Street Vending and Public Policy"; Clowney, "Undermining Black Enterprise."

135 Bromley, "Street Vending and Public Policy."

136 Hermosillo, "Loncheras."

137 Dick Carpenter, *Upwardly Mobile: Street Vending and the American Dream* (Arlington: Institute for Justice, 2015).

138 "Street Vending," Official Website of the City of New York, accessed June 12, 2016, http://www.nyc.gov/html/sbs/nycbiz/downloads/pdf/educational/sector_guides/street_vending.pdf.

139 Cherrie Russell, quoted in "Pittsburgh Neighborhood Promotes Street Vendors," Associated Press State & Local Wire, April 7, 2003.

140 Tony Moquin, quoted in ibid.

141 "Pittsburgh Neighborhood," Associated Press State & Local Wire, March 14, 2014.

142 Tom Richards, quoted in Nathan Edwards, "Communities Exploring Option to Welcome Food Truck Businesses," UpNorthLive.com, March 4, 2014, http://

upnorthlive.com/news/local/communities-exploring-option-to-welcome-food-truck-businesses.

143 Ryan Raiche, "Food Truck Rallies in Lakeland Continue to Draw Crowds, despite Skeptical Restaurant Owners," *ABC Action News*, December 12, 2013, http://www.abcactionnews.com/news/region-polk/lakeland/food-truck-rallies-in-lakeland-continue-to-draw-crowds-despite-the-skeptical-restaurant-owners.

144 Giovanni Moriello, quoted in ibid.

145 "Food Trucks Primarily Replace a Quick Service Restaurant Visit, Says NPD," NPD Group (press release, August 19, 2013), https://www.npd.com/wps/portal/npd/us/news/press-releases/food-trucks-primarily-replace-a-quick-service-restaurant-visit-says-npd/.

146 Yvonne Yen Liu, "Impact of Street Vendors on Brick and Mortars," *Economic Roundtable* blog, February 19, 2015, http://economicrt.org/blog/impact-of-street-vendors-on-brick-and-mortars/.

147 Ernie Suggs, "Atlanta Vendors: Vendors Shut Out on Opening Day; City's Crackdown Being Done Out of Spite, Says Attorney," *Atlanta Journal-Constitution,* April 2, 2013.

148 Ibid.

149 Bill Torpy, "You Have to Have Fortitude to Do This," *Atlanta Journal-Constitution*, September 4, 2011.

150 In his early days at SRA, Larry was assigned to drive Martin Luther King Jr.'s children to and from school after King was assassinated. Larry's later work took him to Plains, Georgia, where he met Jimmy Carter, then a rural peanut farmer who was already ascending through the halls of power, having finished two terms in the state Senate and working toward the governorship a few years later.

151 Bob Ewing, "The Battle to Save American Street Vending," *Freeman*, October 26, 2011, http://fee.org/freeman/the-battle-to-save-american-street-vending/.

152 Larry Miller, telephone conversation with Dick Carpenter, April 22, 2015.

153 Ewing, "American Street Vending."

154 Larry Miller, telephone conversation with Dick Carpenter, April 22, 2015.

155 Larry Miller, quoted in Mike Morris, "City Curbing Vendors: Atlanta Police Tell Them They Can't Sell on Public Property," *Atlanta Journal-Constitution*, March 29, 2013.

156 Miller v. City of Atlanta, No. 2011CV203707, 2 (Fulton Cty. Super. Ct.) (December 21, 2012) [order granting plaintiff's motion for summary judgment].

157 Christine Gallant, "Street Vendors Lose with New Pact," *Atlanta Journal-Constitution*, July 10, 2009; Eric Stirgus, "Not Everyone Sold on Plan to Manage Street Vendors," *Atlanta Journal-Constitution*, June 5, 2008; Ernie Suggs, "Vendors Critical of Kiosk Policy: Atlanta Plans to Expand Program to Five Points and Turner Field," *Atlanta Journal-Constitution*, June 9, 2010.

158 "Plan to Charge Atlanta Vendors Rent Opposed," Associated Press Newswire, June 16, 2009; Suggs, "Vendors Critical of Kiosk Policy."

159 Stirgus, "Not Everyone Sold on Plan."

160 "Atlanta Vendors Rent Opposed," Associated Press Newswire; Eric Stirgus, "Kiosk Plan Charges Vendors a $500 Fee; Mayor Hopes Monthly Tab Will Aid Downtown," *Atlanta Journal-Constitution*, June 15, 2009.

161 "Atlanta Vendors Rent Opposed," Associated Press Newswire; Stirgus, "Plan Charges Vendors a $500 Fee."

162 GGP and Atlanta Vending Contract, Scope of Services, § 2.1.3, on file with the authors.

163 Steve Visser, "Street Vendors Ask for Court Help," *Atlanta Journal-Constitution*, November 15, 2011.

164 Evens Charles, "Vendors Magnets for Trouble," *Atlanta Journal-Constitution*, April 24, 2013.

165 Bill Howard, quoted in Melissa Turner, "Vendors Leery of City Regulating Their Trade: Increased Competition for Downtown Merchants Feared,"*Atlanta Journal-Constitution*, August 13, 1997.

166 Steve Visser, "Street Vending Regulations: Atlanta Mayor Tries to Avoid Sanctions," *Atlanta Journal-Constitution,* November 5, 2013.

167 Charles, "Vendors Magnets for Trouble." Just such a reason was given in court to justify Chicago's ban on food vendors in the Illinois Medical District. Though overturned by the state supreme court, two appellate judges were unimpressed, noting, "The substance of the testimony of the defense witnesses at the hearing simply was that the mobile food vendor vehicles' presence in the District was cosmetically offensive to them personally." Triple A Services, Inc. v. Rice, 174 Ill. App.3d 654 (1988), 673, *rev'd*, 545 N.E. 2d 706 (Ill. 1989).

168 Kasim Reed, quoted in Katie Leslie, "New Public Vending Program Unveiled: Vendors Won't Be Allowed at Five Points, Officials Say," *Atlanta Journal-Constitution*, October 30, 2013.

169 Gallant, "Defense of City's Street Vendors."

170 Christine Gallant, "Council Should Lead on Vending Issue," *Atlanta Journal-Constitution,* July 26, 2013.

171 Gallant, "Defense of City's Street Vendors."

172 Alma E. Hill, "Upsetting the Apple Carts: Plan for Uniformity Draws Mixed Reviews," *Atlanta Journal-Constitution*, August 6, 1991; Gallant, "Defense of City's Street Vendors."

173 Turner, "Vendors Leery of City."

174 Christine Gallant, "Let Street Vendors Keep Their Space Downtown," *Atlanta Journal-Constitution*, June 30, 2006; Julie B. Hairston, "City, Street Vendors to Test Program," *Atlanta Journal-Constitution*, May 27, 1999; Alma E. Hill, "Upsetting the Apple Carts: Plan for Uniformity Draws Mixed Reviews," *Atlanta Journal-Constitution*, August 6, 1991; Jennifer Parker, "Applicants Line Up as City Gets Ready to License Street Vendors," *Atlanta Journal-Constitution*, July 15, 1993; Maria Saporta and Ernie Suggs, "NFL, Vendor Groups Fail to Resolve Differences; Super Friday: Super Bowl XXXIV: Titans vs. Rams, 6 p.m. Sunday, Georgia Dome. TV: ABC," *Atlanta Journal-Constitution*, January 28, 2000; Kathy Scruggs, "City Urged to Ease Law on Permits; Shoeshine Man Picks Up Vendor's Support," *Atlanta Journal-Constitution*, September 11, 1991; Eric Stirgus, "Plan Charges Vendors a $500 Fee"; "Mayor Hopes Monthly Tab Will Aid Downtown," *Atlanta Journal-Constitution*, June 15, 2009; Turner, "Vendors Leery of City"; Melissa Turner, "Crackdown on Atlanta Street Vendors Begins Today," *Atlanta Journal-Constitution*, July 30, 1998.

175 Ewing, "American Street Vending"; Lyle V. Harris, "City Adopts Games Plan

for Marketing, but Street Vendors Say They've Been Shut Out," *Atlanta Journal-Constitution*, March 21, 1995; Saporta and Suggs, "Groups Fail to Resolve Differences."

176 Saporta and Suggs, "Groups Fail to Resolve Differences."
177 Gallant, "Street Vendors Lose."
178 Ernie Suggs, "Kiosk Regulations: Turner Field Vendors File Suit," *Atlanta Journal-Constitution*, July 29, 2011.
179 Cooper Holland, quoted in Suggs, "Vendors Critical of Kiosk Policy."
180 David Bennett, quoted in ibid.
181 Quoted in Torpy, "You Have to Have Fortitude."
182 Stirgus, "Not Everyone Sold on Plan."
183 Larry Miller, quoted in Suggs, "Vendors Critical of Kiosk Policy."
184 Mayyasi, "Food Truck Economics."
185 Ibid.
186 Linnekin et al., "New Food Truck Advocacy"; Mayyasi, "Food Truck Economics."
187 Rocio Rosales, "Survival, Economic Mobility and Community among Los Angeles Fruit Vendors," *Journal of Ethnic and Migration Studies* 39, no. 5 (2011).
188 Hermosillo, "Loncheras"; Linnekin et al., "New Food Truck Advocacy"; Rosales, "Los Angeles Fruit Vendors."
189 Mayyasi, "Food Truck Economics."
190 Loukaitou-Sideris and Gilbert, "Shades of Duality."
191 Amy Wilson, "Trading an Office for the Sidewalk: Kim Simpson, Denver," *Money* 32, no. 9 (September 2003), 32, 37.
192 These numbers and examples represent legal vendors. On any given day, thousands of people vend illegally, not to get rich but simply to survive—they can find no other work. Kettles, "Regulating Vending." Some of these illegal vendors make $20 to $30 per day. Ibid. Summer months can be more profitable—yielding $50 to $200 a day—while winter months may see vendors losing money. Rosales, "Los Angeles Fruit Vendors." An illegal churros vendor in New York reported taking home $80 a day for twelve hours of work selling a quota of three hundred churros. Hannah Palmer Egan, "The Illegal Underground Economy behind Churros," *Village Voice*, August 8, 2013, http://www.villagevoice.com/2013-07-10/restaurants/black-market-churros/. Children in Los Angeles who vend illegally can take home to their parents $150 to $240 a day; others report making $200 to $700 per week. Emir Estrada and Pierrette Hondagneu-Sotelo, "Intersectional Dignities: Latino Immigrant Street Vendor Youth in Los Angeles," *Journal of Contemporary Ethnography* 40, no. 1 (2011).
193 Torpy, "You Have to Have Fortitude."
194 Christine Gallant, "Atlanta Street Vendors Can Deter Crime, Too," *Atlanta Journal-Constitution*, May 12, 2010.
195 "Police Examining Video from Times Square," CNN, May 3, 2010, http://www.cnn.com/2010/CRIME/05/02/times.square.closure/index.html.
196 Gallant, "Atlanta Vendors Can Deter Crime."
197 Larry Miller, quoted in Torpy, "You Have to Have Fortitude."
198 Visser, "Vendors Ask for Court Help."
199 Larry Miller, quoted in Suggs, "Vendors Critical of Kiosk Policy."

200 Jeremiah McWilliams, "Atlanta Vendors: Ruling Complicates City Vending Plans, Plan for Company to Manage Vendors Struck Down; 2013 Permits On Hold," *Atlanta Journal-Constitution*, January 4, 2013; Katie Leslie, "Street Merchants: Vendors Flood City Hall Seeking Permits; City Officials Contend Judge's Ruling Voided Street Food Program, Sellers Just Want Program in Place," *Atlanta Journal-Constitution*, July 2, 2013.

201 Kate Brumback, "Atlanta Sidewalk Vendors Gather at City Hall to Protest Recent Vending Crackdown," Associated Press Newswire, April 13, 2013; Morris, "City Curbing Vendors"; Rodney Carmichael, "Atlanta Vendors Kicked to the Curb; City Cracks Down after Judge Tosses Controversial Contract," *Creative Loafing*, April 11, 2013, http://clatl.com/atlanta/atlanta-vendors-kicked-to-the-curb/Content?oid=7987130.

202 Leslie, "Vendors Flood City Hall"; Katie Leslie, "Street Vendors Hoping for Return: New Ruling from Judge Might Make Operation Possible by Year's End," *Atlanta Journal-Constitution*, June 28, 2013; Katie Leslie and Ernie Suggs, "Street Merchants: Judge Clarifies Vendor Ruling: But Questions Remain about the Status of 2003 Program," *Atlanta Journal-Constitution*, July 3, 2013.

203 *Miller*, No. 2011CV203707 at 4.

204 Marcus Coleman, quoted in Leslie, "Vendors Flood City Hall."

205 Larry Miller, telephone conversation with Dick Carpenter, April 22, 2015. Larry kept his house only by applying for help at Home Safe Georgia, a mortgage-assistance program.

206 Michael Julian Bond, "Temporary Program Gets Vendors Working," *Atlanta Journal-Constitution*, July 26, 2013; Arlinda Smith Broady, "Metro Week in Review: Aug. 18–Aug. 24," *Atlanta Journal-Constitution*, August 25, 2013; Katie Leslie, "Street Merchants: Vending Program under Review: Vendors Could Operate While They Wait for New Program to Be Instituted," *Atlanta Journal-Constitution*, July 16, 2013; Katie Leslie, "Street Vendor Program Stalls: Bill Would Have Allowed Limited Return to Work," *Atlanta Journal-Constitution*, August 21, 2013.

207 Rhonda Cook, "Judge Rules in Favor of Vendors," *Atlanta Journal-Constitution*, October 10, 2013.

208 Steve Visser, "Mayor Wins 1 in Court in Turner Field Vending Case," *Atlanta Journal-Constitution*, November 14, 2013; Visser, "Street Vending Regulations."

209 Jonathan Shapiro and Michell Eloy, "Amid Legal Battle, Atlanta City Council OKs New Street Vending Program," WABE.org, November 4, 2013, http://news.wabe.org/post/amid-legal-battle-atlanta-city-council-oks-new-street-vending-program; Visser, "Street Vending Regulations."

210 Larry Miller, telephone conversation with Dick Carpenter, April 22, 2015.

211 Tim Tucker, "Braves Move to Cobb: Suntrust Buys Stadium Name," *Atlanta Journal-Constitution*, September 17, 2014.

212 Larry Miller, telephone conversation with Dick Carpenter, April 22, 2015.

213 Doug Roberson, "Festive Welcome for MLS," *Atlanta Journal-Constitution*, April 17, 2014.

214 Larry Miller, telephone conversation with Dick Carpenter, April 22, 2015.

215 Brett Nelson, "The Real Definition of Entrepreneur—and Why It Matters," *Forbes*, June 5, 2012, http://www.forbes.com/sites/brettnelson/2012/06/05/the-real-definition-of-entrepreneur-and-why-it-matters/.

CHAPTER 8 ■ THE BOTTLENECKING VANGUARD

1 Willie Rosemond, quoted by John Rosemond, telephone conversation with Dick Carpenter, June 29, 2015.
2 Ibid.
3 Willie Rosemond, quoted in ibid.
4 Longer-running columns, such as Dear Abby, have been written by multiple authors.
5 Rachel Aretakis, "Advice Columnist John Rosemond Sues Kentucky Agency, Claiming Censorship," *Lexington Herald-Leader*, July 16, 2013, http://www.kentucky.com/2013/07/16/2716394/kentucky-agency-attempts-to-block.html.
6 John Rosemond, quoted in Adeel Ahmed, "Parenting Columnist John Rosemond in Lexington, Citing Defense of First Amendment," *Ace Weekly*, July 17, 2013, http://www.aceweekly.com/2013/07/parenting-columnist-john-rosemond-in-lexington/.
7 Sara Burrows, "Kentucky Censors N.B.-Based Syndicated Columnist: Rosemond Sues after State Officials Tell Him to Stop Publishing Advice," *Carolina Journal*, July 16, 2013, http://www.carolinajournal.com/articles/display_story.html?id=10337.
8 Brian Cooper, "Free-Speech Fight Embroils Parenting Expert," *Telegraph Herald*, August 6, 2013.
9 John Rosemond, quoted in Aretakis, "Rosemond Sues Kentucky Agency."
10 Brian T. Judy, quoted in Rachel Aretakis, "Judge Rejects Restraining Order against Ky. Psychology Board in John Rosemond Case," *Lexington Herald-Leader*, July 18, 2013, http://www.kentucky.com/news/politics-government/article44434965.html. `
11 Burrows, "Kentucky Censors Columnist."
12 Brian T. Judy to John Rosemond, May 7, 2013, Frankfort, KY, 1, Institute for Justice, https://www.ij.org/images/pdf_folder/first_amendment/ky_psych/cease-and-desist-letter-rosemond.pdf.
13 John is a licensed "psychological associate" in North Carolina under N.C. Gen. Stat. sections 90-270.2(7) and 270.11(b). As a licensed psychological associate, he is authorized under North Carolina law to call himself a "psychologist." N.C. Gen. Stat. § 90-270.2(9).
14 Brian T. Judy to John Rosemond, May 7, 2013, 3.
15 According to Carlson's examination of the history of licensing for psychologists: "Certification, to control the use of the term *psychologist,* usually developed first. Licensing, which was aimed at regulating the practice of psychology, tended to come later. In most states, the examining boards were initially set up on a nonstatutory basis and later became established through frequently hard-won appropriate legislation. Connecticut, however, pioneered with its law, passed in 1945. Five years later, there were only three more state boards in existence (Virginia, Kentucky, and Ohio). By 1960 there were 32." Harold S. Carlson, "The AASPB Story: The Beginnings and First 16 Years of the American Association of State Psychology Boards, 1961–1977,"*American Psychologist* 33, no. 5 (1978). See also "Notes: Regulation of Psychological Counseling and Psychotherapy," *Columbia Law Review* 51, no. 4 (1951); Sheila A. Schuster, Brief History of KRS 319—Kentucky Psychology Licensing Law: 1948

– 2011" (unpublished manuscript, 2011), https://c.ymcdn.com/sites/kpa.site-ym.com/resource/resmgr/Advocacy/KRS_319_History_thru_2011.pdf.

16 Schuster, "Brief History of KRS 319."

17 Elizabeth Graddy and Michael B. Nichol, "Public Members on Occupational Licensing Boards: Effects on Legislative Regulatory Reforms," *Southern Economic Journal* 55, no. 3 (1989).

18 Ibid.; Elizabeth Graddy and Michael B. Nichol, "Structural Reforms and Licensing Board Performance," *American Politics Research* 18, no. 3 (1990); Marc T. Law and Zeynep K. Hansen, "Medical Licensing Board Characteristics and Physician Discipline: An Empirical Analysis," *Journal of Health Politics, Policy and Law* 35, no. 1 (2010); Schneider, "State Professional Licensure Policy"; Schutz, "Effects of Increased Citizen Membership"; Shirley Svorny, "State Medical Boards: Institutional Structure and Board Policies," *Federation Bulletin* 84, no. 2 (1997).

19 Svorny, "State Medical Boards."

20 Andrew Delano Abbott, *The System of Professions: An Essay about the Division of Expert Labor* (Chicago: University of Chicago Press, 1988); David Brain, "Practical Knowledge and Occupational Control: The Professionalization of Architecture in the United States," *Sociological Forum* 6 (1991); Magali Sarfatti Larson, *The Rise of Professionalism: A Sociological Analysis* (Berkeley: University of California Press, 1977); Brian P. West, "Exploring Professional Knowledge: The Case of Accounting," *Journal of Sociology* 34, no. 1 (1998).

21 George A. Akerlof, "The Market for Lemons: Qualitative Uncertainty and the Market Mechanism," *Quarterly Journal of Economics* 84, no. 3 (1970); Skarbek, "Occupational Licensing."

22 Schneider, "State Professional Licensure Policy."

23 "Board of Examiners of Psychology: Meeting Minutes," Ky.gov: Public Protection Cabinet, Office of Occupations and Professions, accessed June 13, 2016, http://psy.ky.gov/Pages/minutes.aspx.

24 Burrows, "Kentucky Censors Columnist."

25 John Rosemond, quoted in Brian Doherty, "Banning Advice Columnists in the Name of Occupational Licensing," reason.com, July 16, 2013, http://reason.com/archives/2013/07/16/banning-advice-columnists-in-the-name-of.

26 JohnRosemond.com, accessed June 13, 2016, www.rosemond.com.

27 *Complaint for Declaratory and Injunctive Relief*, Rosemond v. Conway, E.D. Ky. (2013) (John Rosemond, plaintiff).

28 "About John Rosemond," JohnRosemond.com, last modified June 13, 2016, http://www.rosemond.com/About-John-Rosemond.html.

29 Megan Charles, "Parenting Advice Columnist, John Rosemond, Ordered to Cease and Desist in Kentucky," *Inquisitr*, July 21, 2013, http://www.inquisitr.com/861600/parenting-advice-columnist-john-rosemond-ordered-to-cease-and-desist-in-kentucky/.

30 Aretakis, "Rosemond Sues Kentucky Agency."

31 "About John Rosemond," JohnRosemond.com.

32 This is, in fact, something to which John is particularly attuned. As he described in a letter to the Kentucky attorney general's office: "The American Psychological Association's 2008 position paper on newspaper columns that are

written by psychologists states that the ethical obligations of said psychologists '... consist primarily of performing in a competent fashion and taking care not to leave the impression that a psychologist-patient relationship is created.' I adhere to this standard in writing my column. There has been no dispute as to my competence, and I have always been sensitive to the psychologist-patient issue, which is why I voluntarily retain a PhD column supervisor.... I have voluntarily retained a PhD supervisor for my column for more than twenty years. That Licensed Practicing Psychologist, who has been approved by the North Carolina Psychology Board, alerts me when a specific column might come close to stepping over the line of 'engaging.' Where one of my columns comes close to that line, I err on the side of caution and refrain from publishing it. Tellingly, my licensed supervisor vetted the February 12, 2013 column giving rise to this complaint and found no problem." *Complaint for Declaratory and Injunctive Relief, Rosemond*, 40 (John Rosemond, plaintiff).

33 *Summary Report for: 19.3031.02—Clinical Psychologists*, O*NET OnLine, last modified 2016, http://www.onetonline.org/link/summary/19-3031.02.

34 W. Clark Hendley, "Dear Abby, Miss Lonelyhearts and the Eighteenth Century: The Origins of the Newspaper Advice Column," *Journal of Popular Culture* 11, no. 2 (Fall 1977).

35 Ibid.

36 Ibid.

37 Quoted in ibid., 347.

38 Ibid.

39 *Complaint for Declaratory and Injunctive Relief, Rosemond.*

40 Joseph J. Moran, "Newspaper Psychology: Advice and Therapy," *Journal of Popular Culture* 22, no. 4 (1989).

41 Ibid.

42 Hendley, "Dear Abby."

43 Ibid.; Moran, "Newspaper Psychology."

44 Moran, "Newspaper Psychology."

45 *Complaint for Declaratory and Injunctive Relief, Rosemond*, 34 (John Rosemond, plaintiff); see also Aretakis, "Rosemond Sues Kentucky Agency."

46 T. Kerby Neill, quoted in Aretakis, "Rosemond Sues Kentucky Agency."

47 John Rosemond, telephone conversation with Dick Carpenter, June 29, 2015.

48 Peter Baniak, quoted in Aretakis, "Rosemond Sues Kentucky Agency."

49 *Deposition of Eva Markham*, Rosemond v. Markham, E.D. Ky. (2014) (testimony of Eva Markham, chair, Kentucky Board of Examiners of Psychology).

50 John Rosemond, telephone conversation with Dick Carpenter, June 29, 2015.

51 *Complaint for Declaratory and Injunctive Relief, Rosemond* (John Rosemond, plaintiff).

52 *Id.* at 11.

53 The list includes: Jeanne Phillips (Dear Abby); Susan Orman (The Suze Show); Ruth Westheimer (Sexually Speaking); Dave Ramsey (The Dave Ramsey Show); John Gray (Mars and Venus); Dan Savage (Savage Love); Drew Pinsky (Loveline); Amy Dickinson (Advice for the Real World); Carolyn Hax (Advice from Carolyn Hax); Kathy Nickerson (RelationTips); Enid Traisman (Dear Enid); Carol Ross (Unsolicited Advice); Clara Garza (Clara's Free Online

Advice Column); J. Lynne (The ABC's of Life); Alison Blackman (Advice Sisters); Diana Kirschner (Love in 90 Days); Cheryl Strayed (Dear Sugar); Cary Tennis (Since You Asked); Emily Yoffe (Dear Prudence); Harriet Mosatche (Ask Dr. M); Anita McDaniel (Ask Dr. K); Diane von Furstenberg (Dear Diane von Furstenberg); Miriam Steinberg-Egeth (Miriam's Advice Well); Chuck Klosterman (The Ethicist); Judith Lee (Ask Judith); Sherry Blake (Ask Dr. Sherry); Paul Carrick Brunson (Modern Day Matchmaker); Elizabeth Carroll (Ask E. Jean); Jeffrey Seglin (The Right Thing); Amy Alkon (The Advice Goddess); Cherie Bennett (Hey, Cherie!); Robert Wallace (Tween 12 and 20); Amy Richards (Ask Amy); Helen Williams (The Dr. Helen Show); Romel Axibal (How to Bend Your Spoon); Carol Scott (Stress Relief Radio); Greg and Lisa Popcak (More 2 Life); Jenn Berman (The Love and Sex Show with Dr. Jenn); Roy Master (Advice Line); Erin Tillman (The Dating Advice Girl); Joy Browne (The Dr. Joy Browne Show); Jeanne Laskas (Ask Laskas); Margo Howard (Dear Margo); Judith Martin (Miss Manners); Marcy Sugar and Kathy Mitchell (Annie's Mailbox); Ellie Tesher (Ask Ellie); Cheryl Lavin (Tales from the Front and Relationship Advice by Cheryl Lavin); Marguerite Kelly (Family Almanac); Jessica Leigh (Questionable Advice); Harlan Cohen (Help Me, Harlan!); Josey Vogels (My Messy Bedroom and Dating Girl); Jan Denise (Naked Relationships); Steven Ward (Tough Love); Deborah Tillman (America's Supernanny); Joe Smith (Hey Joe!); Matt Moody (CallDrMatt.com); Jamie Turndorf (Ask Doctor Love); Wayne and Tamara Mitchell (Direct Answers from Wayne and Tamara); Sarah Brisden (Advice Diva); Judy Kuriansky (Love, Sex, and Relationship Advice); and Wendy Atterberry (Dear Wendy).

54 *Complaint for Declaratory and Injunctive Relief, Rosemond* (John Rosemond, plaintiff).

55 "The Kentucky Board of Examiners of Psychology Minutes" (meeting minutes, Frankfort, KY, June 3, 2013), Ky.gov: Public Protection Cabinet, Office of Occupations and Professions, http://psy.ky.gov/Minutes%20Library/Meeting%20Minutes,%20June%203,%202013.pdf.

56 John Rosemond, telephone conversation with Dick Carpenter, June 29, 2015.

57 *Complaint for Declaratory and Injunctive Relief, Rosemond*, 40.

58 "The Kentucky Board of Examiners of Psychology Minutes" (meeting minutes, Frankfort, KY, July 18–19, 2013), Ky.gov: Public Protection Cabinet, Office of Occupations and Professions, http://psy.ky.gov/Minutes%20Library/Meeting%20Minutes,%20July%2018%20and%2019,%202013.pdf.

59 Amy Zhang, "Kentucky to Delay Enforcing Law against Advice Columnist Pending First Amendment Lawsuit," Reporters Committee for Freedom of the Press, July 24, 2013, https://www.rcfp.org/browse-media-law-resources/news/kentucky-delay-enforcing-law-against-advice-columnist-pending-first-.

60 "The Kentucky Board of Examiners of Psychology Minutes" (meeting minutes, Frankfort, KY, August 12, 2013), Ky.gov: Public Protection Cabinet, Office of Occupations and Professions, http://psy.ky.gov/Minutes%20Library/Meeting%20Minutes,%20July%2018%20and%2019,%202013.pdf; Zhang, "Kentucky to Delay Enforcing Law."

61 *Complaint for Declaratory and Injunctive Relief, Rosemond*, 41 (John Rosemond, plaintiff).

62 John Conway, quoted in Kentucky Office of the Attorney General, "Attorney General Conway Corrects Misinformation in John Rosemond Stories" Kentucky Attorney General Andy Beshear, accessed June 13, 2016, http://ag.ky.gov/pdf_news/john_rosemond.pdf.

63 Kentucky Office of the Attorney General, "John Rosemond Agrees to Dismiss Attorney General Conway from Lawsuit" (press release, July 25, 2013), Kentucky.gov, http://migration.kentucky.gov/Newsroom/ag/rosemonddismiss.htm.

64 Kentucky Office of the Attorney General, "Attorney General Conway Corrects Misinformation."

65 Kentucky Office of the Attorney General, "Rosemond Agrees to Dismiss Attorney General Conway."

66 *Deposition of Sally Brenzel*, Rosemond v. Markham, No. 13-42, E.D. Ky. Sept. 30 (2015) (testimony of Sally Brenzel, board member, Kentucky Board of Examiners of Psychology).

67 *Deposition of Eva Markham*, *Rosemond*, No. 13-42.

68 *Id.* at 21.

69 *Id.* at 21.

70 *Id.* at 27.

71 *Rosemond*, No. 13-42 at 12.

72 *Id.* at 13.

73 *Id.* at 20–21.

74 *Id.* at 21.

75 *Id.* at 19.

76 "My Personal Diabetes Story," Steve Cooksey, *Diabetes Warrior* (blog), last modified January 24, 2010, http://www.diabetes-warrior.net/2010/01/24/mystory.

77 "Statistics about Diabetes: Overall Numbers, Diabetes and Prediabetes," American Diabetes Association, last modified April 1, 2016, http://www.diabetes.org/diabetes-basics/statistics/.

78 Ibid.

79 Shlomo Melmed, Kenneth S. Polonsky, P. Reed Larsen, and Henry M. Kronenberg, *Williams Textbook of Endocrinology*, 12th ed. (New York: Saunders, 2011).

80 Ibid.

81 Cynthia M. Ripsin, Helen Kang, and Randall J. Urban, "Management of Blood Glucose in Type II Diabetes Mellitus," *American Family Physician* 79, no. 1 (2009); "Statistics about Diabetes," American Diabetes Association.

82 Cynthia L. Ogden and Margaret D. Carroll, "Prevalence of Overweight, Obesity, and Extreme Obesity among Adults: United States, Trends 1960–1962 through 2008–2008" (Hyattsville, MD: Centers for Disease Control and Prevention, 2010), http://www.cdc.gov/nchs/data/hestat/obesity_adult_07_08/obesity_adult_07_08.pdf.

83 "Nutrition, Physical Activity and Obesity: Data, Trends and Maps," Centers for Disease Control, accessed June 13, 2016, http://nccd.cdc.gov/NPAO_DTM/IndicatorSummary.aspx?category=28&indicator=29&year=2011&yearId=14.

84 "Crude and Age-Adjusted Rates of Diagnosed Diabetes per 100 Civilian, Non-Institutionalized Population, United States, 1980–2014," Centers for Disease

Control, last modified December 1, 2015, http://www.cdc.gov/diabetes/statistics/prev/national/figage.htm.

85 "Diagnosed Diabetes: Age-Adjusted Percentage, Adults—Total, 2014," Centers for Disease Control, accessed June 13, 2016, http://gis.cdc.gov/grasp/diabetes/DiabetesAtlas.html.

86 Cooksey, "Personal Diabetes Story."

87 "My First Year... with Diabetes," Steve Cooksey, *Diabetes Warrior* (blog), February 22, 2010, http://www.diabetes-warrior.net/2010/02/22/my-first-year-with-diabetes/.

88 Ibid.

89 "About Me: My Diabetes Story," Steve Cooksey, *Diabetes Warrior* (blog), accessed June 13, 2016, http://www.diabetes-warrior.net/about-me-and-diabetes/.

90 "Labels of Drugs I Took Pre-Low Carb Primal," Steve Cooksey, *Diabetes Warrior* (blog), December 31, 2010, http://www.diabetes-warrior.net/2010/12/31/labels-of-drugs-i-took-pre-low-carb-primal/.

91 Cooksey, "Personal Diabetes Story."

92 *Diabetes Warrior* (blog), accessed June 13, 2016, http://www.diabetes-warrior.net/.

93 Matt McMillen, "The Paleo Diet," WebMD, December 1, 2013, http://www.webmd.com/diet/paleo-diet.

94 Steve Cooksey, quoted in "Vegetarian & Diabetes Question," *Diabetes Warrior* (blog), accessed June 13, 2016, http://www.diabetes-warrior.net/2011/12/02/vegetarian/.

95 North Carolina Board of Dietetics/Nutrition to Steve Cooksey, (e-mails, January 18, 2012, January 19, 2012, January 27, 2012, and April 9, 2012), on file with the authors.

96 Nahla Hwalla and Maria Koleilat, "Dietetic Practice: The Past, Present and Future," *La Revue de Santé de la Méditerranée orientale* 10, no. 6 (2004).

97 Romina L. Barritta Defranchi and Jennifer K. Nelson, "Evolution and Trends of the Dietetics Profession in the United States of America and in Argentina: North and South United by Similar Challenges," *ALAN* 59, no. 2 (2009), http://www.alanrevista.org/ediciones/2009/2/art-1/; Hwalla and Koleilat, "Dietetic Practice."

98 Defranchi and Nelson, "Evolution and Trends of Dietetics Profession."

99 Hwalla and Koleilat, "Dietetic Practice."

100 Defranchi and Nelson, "Evolution and Trends of Dietetics Profession."

101 Jo Anne Cassell, *Carry the Flame: The History of the American Dietetic Association* (Chicago: American Dietetic Association, 1990).

102 Ibid.

103 Ibid.

104 Quoted in ibid., 141.

105 Ibid.

106 Ibid., 289.

107 Ibid.; Defranchi and Nelson, "Evolution and Trends of Dietetics Profession"; Mary Lou South, "Reflections of a Diamond: 75 Years for ADA," *Journal of the American Dietetic Association* 93, no. 8 (1993).

108 Cassell, *Carry the Flame*; Defranchi and Nelson, "Evolution and Trends of Dietetics Profession"; South, "75 Years for ADA."
109 Cassell, *Carry the Flame.*
110 Ibid.
111 Ibid.
112 Ibid.; Virginia Council on Health Regulatory Boards, *The Need for the Regulation of Dietitians and Nutritionists* (Richmond: Commonwealth of Virginia, 1987).
113 Cassell, *Carry the Flame.*
114 Ibid.
115 Karen Stein, "The Academy's Governance and Practice: Restructuring for the Challenges of the Turn of the 21st Century," *Journal of the Academy of Nutrition and Dietetics* 112, no. 11 (2012).
116 Ibid.
117 Joyce Green Pastors, Hope Warshaw, Anne Daly, Marion Franz, and Karmeen Kulkarni, "The Evidence for the Effectiveness of Medical Nutrition Therapy in Diabetes Management," *Diabetes Care* 25, no. 3 (2002).
118 Stein, "Turn of the 21st Century."
119 Liz Lipski, "Health Care Workshop, Project No. p13-71207: Testimony Examining Health Care Competition" (Washington, DC: Federal Trade Commission, 2014); Kristen Schepker, "Dietitians vs. Nutritionists: Licensure Battles Underscore Growth of the Field," *Holistic Primary Care* 13, no. 2 (Summer 2012), http://holisticprimarycare.net/topics/topics-o-z/practice-development/1346-dietitians-vs-nutritionists-licensure-battles-underscore-growth-of-the-field-; Pepin A. Tuma, *Market Place Relevance: Regulatory and Competitive Environment of Dietetic Services: HOD Backgrounder* (Chicago: American Dietetic Association, 2011).
120 Lipski, "Health Care Competition."
121 Ibid.; Darrell Rogers, *Limiting Competition: Dietetic Licensure by the Academy of Nutrition and Dietetics* (Washington, DC: Federal Trade Commission, 2014).
122 A. 05666/S. 3556, 2011–12 New York Legislative Session (2012), http://nyassembly.gov/leg/?bn=S03556&term=2011.
123 Dietitian/Nutritionist Licensing Act, S. 833, 2012–13 New Jersey Legislative Session (2012), ftp://www.njleg.state.nj.us/20122013/S1000/833_I1.HTM.
124 Dietitian/Nutritionist Licensing Act, quoted in Schepker, "Dietitians vs. Nutritionists."
125 "Ohio Board of Dietetics: Minutes of the Board Meeting" (meeting minutes, Columbus, OH, July 20, 2012), Ohio Board of Dietetics, http://www.dietetics.ohio.gov/minutes/July2012min.pdf.
126 Academy of Nutrition and Dietetics/Foundation, *Fiscal Year 2014 Annual Report* (Chicago: Academy of Nutrition and Dietetics/Foundation, 2014), eatrightPRO, accessed July 13, 2016, http://www.eatrightpro.org/~/media/eatrightpro%20files/about%20us/annual%20reports/2014annualreport.ashx.
127 Hwalla and Koleilat, "Dietetic Practice."
128 Kristin K. Smith, "Turf Wars and Corporate Sponsorship: Challenges in the Food System and the Academy of Nutrition and Dietetics" (master's thesis, University of Vermont, 2014).

129 Academy of Nutrition and Dietetics, "Where Should You Get Your Nutrition Advice? Seek the Guidance of the Food and Nutrition Experts" (press release, March 13, 2013), PR Newswire, http://www.prnewswire.com/news-releases/where-should-you-get-your-nutrition-advice-seek-the-guidance-of-the-food-and-nutrition-experts-197836311.html.

130 Quoted in Smith, "Turf Wars and Corporate Sponsorship," 42.

131 Tuma, *Market Place Relevance*, 10–11.

132 Ibid., 10.

133 David Donovan, "Stone Age Diet Guru Sues State in U.S. District Court for the Western District of North Carolina over Licensing," *North Carolina Lawyers Weekly*, May 31, 2012, http://nclawyersweekly.com/2012/05/31/stone-age-diet-guru-sues-state-over-licensing/.

134 Sara Burrows, "Nutrition Board Casts Net Far beyond Paleo-Diet Blogger," *Carolina Journal*, October 17, 2012, http://www.carolinajournal.com/exclusives/display_exclusive.html?id=9589.

135 Lipski, "Health Care Competition," 5–6.

136 N.C. Gen. Stat. § 90-352 defines the practice of dietetics/nutrition as: "The integration and application of principles derived from the science of nutrition, biochemistry, physiology, food, and management and from behavioral and social sciences to achieve and maintain a healthy status." Moreover, "The primary function of dietetic/nutrition practice is the provision of nutrition care services," which involves: (1) assessing the nutritional needs of individuals and groups and determining resources and constraints in the practice setting; (2) establishing priorities, goals, and objectives that meet nutritional needs and are consistent with available resources and constraints; (3) providing nutrition counseling in health and disease; (d) developing, implementing, and managing nutrition care systems; and (5) evaluating, making changes in, and maintaining appropriate standards of quality in food and nutrition services." "Article 25: Dietetics/Nutrition," in NC General Statutes, § 90-352: Definitions, North Carolina General Assembly, accessed July 20, 2016, http://www.ncleg.net/EnactedLegislation/Statutes/PDF/ByArticle/Chapter_90/Article_25.pdf.

137 Steve Cooksey, quoted in Jennifer Abel, "Diabetes Warrior Blogger Facing Jail Time for Dietary Advice," *Daily Dot*, April 24, 2012, http://www.dailydot.com/news/diabetes-warrior-steve-cooksey-blog-jail/.

138 Sara Burrows, "State Threatens to Shut Down Nutrition Blogger: Nutrition Board Says He Needs a License to Advocate Dietary Approaches," *Carolina Journal*, April 23, 2012, http://www.carolinajournal.com/exclusives/display_exclusive.html?id=8992.

139 John Stossel, "Bad Rules Protect No One," *TribLIVE*, October 21, 2012, http://triblive.com/home/2787759-74/cooksey-speech-advice-carolina-licensing-north-protect-rules-sherman-state#axzz3vdoENhFR; George Will, "Free Speech and Free Advice under Siege," *Herald-Sun*, September 27, 2012.

140 Steve Cooksey, telephone conversation with Dick Carpenter, June 15, 2015.

141 Adam Liptak, "Blogger Giving Advice Resists State's: Get a License," *New York Times*, August 7, 2012, http://www.nytimes.com/2012/08/07/us/nutrition-blogger-fights-north-carolina-licensing-rebuke.html?_r=0.

142 Brian Doherty, "License to Blog," *Reason* 44, no. 9 (February 1, 2013).

143 Sara Burrows, "Paleo Diet Blogger Loses Round One of Free Speech Case," *Carolina Journal*, October 11, 2012, http://www.carolinajournal.com/exclusives/display_exclusive.html?id=9575.
144 Paul Sherman, quoted in Doherty, "License to Blog," 14.
145 Cooksey v. Futrell, 721 F.3d 226, 21 (4th Cir. 2013).
146 Mitch Weiss, "Blogger Says He's Feels Vindicated in Free Speech Fight," Associated Press, February 20, 2015.
147 Julie Deardorff, "Who Gives the Best Nutrition Advice?," *Chicago Tribune*, January 28, 2013, http://articles.chicagotribune.com/2013-01-28/health/ct-met-nutrition-advice-20130128_1_dietitians-nutrition-and-dietetics-health-coach.
148 Office of Regulatory Reinvention, *Recommendations of the Office of Regulatory Reinvention regarding Occupational Licensing* (2012), Michigan.gov, accessed June 14, 2016, http://www.michigan.gov/documents/lara/ORR_Occupational_Licensing_Recommendations_382437_7.pdf.
149 Ibid., 25, 86.
150 Virginia Council on Health Regulatory Boards, *Regulation of Dietitians and Nutritionists.*
151 Ibid., 10.
152 Ibid.
153 Ibid.
154 Ibid., 16.
155 Ibid., 5.
156 Va. Code Ann. § 54.1-2731 (1995).
157 CoCo Newton, "Michigan Ends Monopolistic Dietitians Licensure Law," *Crazy Wisdom Community Journal* blog, May/August 2016, http://www.crazywisdomjournal.com/blog/2015/6/4/michigan-ends-monopolistic-dietitians-licensure-law; House Fiscal Agency, "Repeal Licensure of Dieticians & Nutritionists" (legislative analysis, Lansing, MI, November 11, 2013), Michigan Legislature, https://www.legislature.mi.gov/documents/2013-2014/billanalysis/house/pdf/2013-HLA-4688-AC9131F3.PDF; Jessica Evans, "Local Health and Fitness Pros Working to Repeal Law That Would Restrict Who Could Give Nutritional Advice," *Harbor Light*, June 5, 2013, http://harborlightnews.com/main.asp?SectionID=3&SubSectionID=28&ArticleID=16079; *Statement of John M. Dempsey, Dickinson Wright PLLC, In Support of H.B. 4688 to Michigan Senate Committee on Regulatory Reform* (2014) (testimony, John M. Dempsey), Michigan Legislature, accessed June 14, 2016, http://legislature.mi.gov/documents/2013-2014/CommitteeDocuments/Senate/Regulatory%20Reform/Testimony/2014-SCT-REG_-06-05-1-08-John%20M.%20Dempsey.PDF; John Engler to Michigan House of Representatives, January 4, 1999 (veto message, H.B. 4274, 4296, 4789), Michigan Legislature http://www.legislature.mi.gov/publications/MPLA/1998/1998-mpla-vetomessages.pdf.
158 Academy of Nutrition and Dietetics, "The American Dietetic Association," *Journal of the Academy of Nutrition and Dietetics*, suppl. 2, 113, no. 6, Michigan House of Representatives, accessed June 14, 2016, http://house.mi.gov/sessiondocs/2013-2014/testimony/Committee238-10-29-2013.pdf.
159 *Testimony to the House Regulatory Reform Committee*, 97th Legislature (October 29, 2013) (testimony of Mary Width, registered dietitian; senior

lecturer, dietetics, Wayne State University; co-course director, clinical nutrition, Wayne State Medical School), Michigan House of Representatives, accessed June 14, 2016, http://house.mi.gov/sessiondocs/2013-2014/testimony/Committee238-10-29-2013-1.pdf.

160 "Michigan Dietetic Association," Michigan House of Representatives, accessed June 14, 2016, http://house.mi.gov/sessiondocs/2013-2014/testimony/Committee238-10-29-2013-4.pdf.

161 *Testimony to the House Regulatory Reform Committee*, 97th Legislature (October 15, 2013) (testimony of Lee McDonagh, registered dietitian nutritionist; lead nutrition specialist, Center for Eating Disorders, Huron Oaks Eating Disorder Recovery Program), Michigan House of Representatives, accessed June 14, 2016, http://house.mi.gov/sessiondocs/2013-2014/testimony/Committee238-10-22-2013-2.pdf.

162 Kenneth Elmassian to Ann Hoffman, August 6, 2013, Michigan House of Representatives, http://house.mi.gov/sessiondocs/2013-2014/testimony/Committee238-10-15-2013-2.pdf.

163 Eileen Mikus to Representative Crawford and Committee, October 14, 2013, Michigan House of Representatives, accessed June 14, 2016, http://house.mi.gov/sessiondocs/2013-2014/testimony/Committee238-10-15-2013-6.pdf.

164 Carroll Zinser to Senate Regulatory Reform Committee, June 5, 2014, Michigan House of Representatives, accessed June 14, 2016, http://legislature.mi.gov/documents/2013-2014/CommitteeDocuments/Senate/Regulatory%20Reform/Testimony/2014-SCT-REG_-06-05-1-11-Carol%20Zinser,%20Southeastern%20Michigan%20Dietetic%20.PDF.

165 Derek Webber to Chairman Crawford and Committee Members, October 14, 2013; *Testimony about House Bill 4688*, House Committee on Regulatory Reform (testimonies of Derek Webber, president, Standard Process; Craig Oster, cofounder and director, the HEALERS campaign; Mayssou N. Hamade, registered dietitian/nutritionist, clinical nutrition manager; Carla Wysko; Susanne Consiglio, registered dietitian/nutritionist, Nutrition Balance, LLC/executive director, Michigan Academy; Holly Guzman, registered dietitian/nutritionist, board certified specialist in pediatric nutrition, certified nutrition support clinician; Lester Kobylak, senior staff, Department of Internal Medicine, Henry Ford Hospital; Laura Freeland, assistant professor, director of nutrition and dietetics department, Madonna University, et al.) (October 15, 2013), Michigan House of Representatives, http://house.mi.gov/sessiondocs/2013-2014/testimony/Committee238-10-15-2013-8.pdf.

166 *Opposition to House Bill 4688*, 97th Legislature (June 5, 2014) (testimony of Patricia Willard, registered dietitian/nutritionist, Michigan Academy of Nutrition and Dietetics), Michigan House of Representatives http://legislature.mi.gov/documents/2013-2014/CommitteeDocuments/Senate/Regulatory%20Reform/Testimony/2014-SCT-REG_-06-05-1-19-Patricia%20Willard,%20Michigan%20Academy%20of%20Nutriti.PDF.

167 *Testimony Before the House Regulatory Reform Committee*, 97th Legislature (October 15, 2013) (testimony of Coco Newton), Michigan House of Representatives, http://house.mi.gov/sessiondocs/2013-2014/testimony/Committee238-10-15-2013-5.pdf.

168 "Michigan Nutrition Association Support for HB 4688," Michigan House

of Representatives, accessed June 14, 2016, http://legislature.mi.gov/documents/2013-2014/CommitteeDocuments/Senate/Regulatory%20Reform/Testimony/2014-SCT-REG_-06-05-1-07-Michigan%20Nutrition%20Association.PDF.

169 Barbara A. Van Horne, "Psychology Licensing Board Disciplinary Actions: The Realities," *Professional Psychology: Research and Practice* 35, no. 2 (2004).

170 Jacquelyn St. Germaine, "Ethical Practices of Certified Addiction Counselors: A National Survey of State Certification Boards," *Alcoholism Treatment Quarterly* 15, no. 2 (1997); Jodi L. Saunders, Mary Barros-Bailey, Rebecca Rudman, Donald W. Dew, and Jorge Garcia, "Ethical Complaints and Violations in Rehabilitation Counseling: An Analysis of Commission on Rehabilitation Counselor Certification Data," *Rehabilitation Counseling Bulletin* 51, no. 1 (2007).

171 Quoted in Jonathan Rose, "Occupational Licensing: A Framework for Analysis," *Arizona State Law Journal* (1979), 192.

172 Tuma, *Market Place Relevance*, 11.

173 Academy of Nutrition and Dietetics. "Summary of Licensure Statutes by State," eatrightPRO, last modified November 2013, http://www.eatrightpro.org/resource/advocacy/quality-health-care/consumer-protection-and-licensure/summary-of-licensure-statutes-by-state.

174 "American Dietetic Association Speeds Up Race for Monopoly—Updated," ANH-USA, February 10, 2012, http://www.anh-usa.org/american-dietetic-association-speeds-up-its-race-for-monopoly/.

175 Mary Haschke, "President's Page: Licensure for Dietitians: The Issue in Context," *Journal of the American Dietetic Association* 84, no. 4 (1984), 455. Haschke's refreshing honesty did not stop there: "Those in the professions who have examined honestly the true purpose served by licensure have acknowledged quickly that those professional groups which seek licensure are motivated primarily by the anticipated benefit to members of the profession. Yet, the purported purpose of licensing is to protect the public.... Examination of the societal pressures reveals that the primary push in favor of licensure has come from practitioners. Although the stated purpose of licensure is to benefit the public, few pleas for licensure have come from the public. Further, rarely has the public's need for licensure been definitively demonstrated. Campaigns for licensure have been orchestrated by practitioners as a way to identify and protect their areas of endeavor." Ibid., 455.

CONCLUSION

1 Neily, "Rational Basis Test"; Timothy Sandefur, "Right to Earn a Living," *Chapman Law Review* 6 (2003).

2 Slaughter-House Cases, 83 U.S. 36, 105 (U.S. 1872) (Justice Stephen Field, dissenting).

3 Barsky v. Bd. of Regents, 347 U.S. 442, 472 (U.S. 1954) (Justice William Douglas, dissenting).

4 Kleiner, *Licensing Occupations*.

5 Neily, "Rational Basis Test"; Timothy Sandefur, "Is Economic Exclusion a

Legitimate State Interest? Four Recent Cases Test the Boundaries," *William & Mary Bill of Rights Journal* 14, no. 3 (2006).

6 *Craigmiles*, 312 F.3d; *St. Joseph Abbey*, 712 F.3d.

7 Bandow, "Economic Liberty."

8 Joseph Biden, speaking in "Opening & Keynote Remarks: Robert E. Rubin; the Honorable Joe Biden," Hamilton Project video, 34:07, from a forum hosted in Washington, DC, by the Hamilton Project on March 11, 2015, http://www.hamiltonproject.org/multimedia/video/expanding_employment_opportunities_u.s._vice_president_biden_remarks_v/.

9 Barack Obama, "Remarks by the President to the National Governors Association," White House: President Barack Obama, February 23, 2015, https://www.whitehouse.gov/the-press-office/2015/02/23/remarks-president-national-governors-association-february-23-2015.

10 Department of the Treasury Office of Economic Policy, Council of Economic Advisers, & Department of Labor, *Occupational Licensing: A Framework for Policymakers* (Washington, DC: White House, 2015).

11 Randy E. Barnett, "Kennedy's Libertarian Revolution; Lawrence's Reach," *National Review Online*, July 10, 2003, http://www.nationalreview.com/article/207453/kennedys-libertarian-revolution-randy-barnett; see also George F. Will, "Testing the Waters of Economic Liberty," *Washington Post*, December 16, 2011, http://www.washingtonpost.com/opinions/testing-the-waters-of-economic-liberty/2011/12/15/gIQAP0NDzO_story.html.

12 "Code of Virginia: § 54.1–100. Regulations of Professions and Occupations," LIS Virginia Law, accessed June 14, 2014, https://leg1.state.va.us/cgi-bin/legp504.exe?000+cod+54.1-100.

13 Miles Kimball, "When the Government Says 'You May Not Have a Job,'" *Confessions of a Supply-Side Liberal* (blog), August 18, 2012, http://blog.supplysideliberal.com/post/29693166160/when-the-government-says-you-may-not-have-a-job.

14 James Madison, "The Federalist Papers: 'The Same Subject Continued: The Union as a Safeguard against Domestic Faction and Insurrection'" (essay, November 23, 1787), Congress.gov, http://thomas.loc.gov/home/histdox/fed_10.html.

15 James Madison, quoted in Jack N. Rakove, ed., *James Madison: Writings: 1772–1836* (New York: Library of America, 1999), 515.

16 James Madison, quoted in ibid., 516.

Index

Page numbers followed by *n* and *nn* indicate notes.